Radical Black Theatre in the New Deal

The John Hope Franklin Series in African American History and Culture

Waldo E. Martin Jr. and Patricia Sullivan, *editors*

Radical Black Theatre in the New Deal

· ·

KATE DOSSETT

University of North Carolina Press Chapel Hill

The University of North Carolina Press has been a member
of the Green Press Initiative since 2003.

Library of Congress Cataloging-in-Publication Data
Names: Dossett, Kate, author.
Title: Radical black theatre in the New Deal / Kate Dossett.
Other titles: John Hope Franklin series in African American history and
    culture.
Description: Chapel Hill : University of North Carolina Press, 2020. |
    Series: The John Hope Franklin series in African American history and
    culture | Includes bibliographical references and index.
Identifiers: LCCN 2019053418 | ISBN 9781469654416 (cloth) |
    ISBN 9781469654423 (paperback) | ISBN 9781469654430 (ebook)
Subjects: LCSH: Federal Theatre Project (U.S.)—History. | African American
    theater—United States—History—20th century.
Classification: LCC PN2270.A35 D67 2020 | DDC 792.089/96073—dc23
LC record available at https://lccn.loc.gov/2019053418

Cover illustration: "WPA Federal Theatre presents *The Case of Philip
Lawrence*, a new play based on Geo. McEntee's [sic] *11 PM*, A Negro Theatre
Production" (poster). Library of Congress Prints and Photographs Division,
Work Projects Administration Poster Collection, LC-USZC4-3640. *The Case
of Philip Lawrence* (1936) was adapted by the Harlem Negro Unit from
George MacEntee's *Eleven P.M.* It was the first play to be staged by the
Harlem Negro Unit after it came under the direction of black theatre
professionals Gus Smith, Carlton Moss, and Harry V. Edward.

Portions of chapter 4 were previously published in "Staging the Garveyite
Home: Black Masculinity, Failure, and Redemption in Theodore Ward's
Big White Fog," *African American Review*, 43:4 (2009): 557–76. Portions
of chapter 5 were previously published in "Commemorating Haiti on the
Harlem Stage," *Journal of American Drama and Theatre* 22: 1 (2010):
83–119. All material used here with permission.

In memory of Teresa Dossett and Katrina Honeyman

For Elizabeth

Contents

Illustrations

Acknowledgments

This project was first inspired by black theatre communities who created daring and exhilarating theatre as part of the Federal Theatre Project in the 1930s. Along the way, it has been inspired by contemporary theatre practitioners. In 2016, the National Theatre in London gave me the opportunity to run a two-day workshop on African American Playwriting in the Twentieth Century. The theatre professionals who participated over the course of the weekend echoed many of the same concerns of black theatre makers in the 1930s, but they also engaged with black Federal Theatre dramas in ways that created fresh meaning. We heard from the playwright Bonnie Greer and director Paulette Randall on the challenges and delights of writing and directing black dramas in Britain and the United States, while many of the workshop participants shared their frustration with the racial and gender politics of canon makers, who have long excluded a rich and diverse black theatre heritage. Most workshop participants—of which black British and African American women were in a majority—had never heard of the black dramas and dramatists who developed new works as part of the Federal Theatre Project. The National was then staging the most often revived African American dramatists of the twentieth century: August Wilson (*Ma Rainey's Black Bottom*) and Lorraine Hansberry (*Les Blancs*). Meanwhile, at the National's Clore Learning Centre, we were studying long neglected dramas written by black dramatists and paid for by the U.S. federal government between 1935 and 1939. The director Ola Ince and National Theatre actors Jermaine Dominique, Terri Ann Bobb-Baxter, Tamara Lawrance, and Kadeem Pearse brought these dramas to life in staged readings of Abram Hill and John Silvera's *Liberty Deferred* and Theodore Ward's *Big White Fog*. We were blown away by their performance, by how they spoke to the needs of the present: Hill and Silvera's biting satire—it includes a scene set in Lynchotopia, a land inhabited by victims of white lynch mobs—offers a way to reflect on the histories of resistance to the dehumanization of black bodies out of which the Movement for Black Lives arose; and Ward's family drama offers a feminist critique that is also a sympathetic portrait of black masculinity.

The difficulties of accessing black theatre's literary and production heritage is a key theme of this book and one that ties the history of black theatre to the politics of knowledge production today, for decisions about which black dramas are studied and staged in theatres in the English-speaking world are still shaped by what was considered worthy of preserving over the last century and even before. As a white woman working in a research-supportive university in Britain, being able to access this heritage has been both a privilege, and a problem. It raises questions about who gets to access and mediate these histories, to whom black theatre history belongs, and how my own privileged position within the academy shapes the particular choices I made in researching black Federal Theatre. For this book, I was concerned that histories of knowledge production were not hidden from view, that in fact they took center stage. Early on I recognized that these are histories that will continue to evolve, rather than offer neat resolution.

The opportunity to talk with and learn from black feminist scholars has helped me think about how to write histories of black theatre that center on the experiences and values of those who make it. It has been a privilege to read the work produced by, and discuss black women's history with, many fabulous scholars, and especially Kim Warren, Nicole King, Ayesha Hardison, Althea Legal-Miller and Imaobong Umoren. At American Studies, History and Literature conferences from Leeds to London, Ghent to Copenhagen, and Washington, D.C., to Lisbon, colleagues, students, and broader audiences have responded generously, critically, and thoughtfully to the project. I am particularly grateful to colleagues at the Universities of Birmingham, Cambridge, East Anglia, Glasgow, Manchester, Nottingham, Oxford, Sussex, Queen Mary London, and Sydney and at the Institute of Historical Research, who shared their ideas and critiqued my work at departmental research seminars. The 2018 Protest and Censorship Conference hosted by Cara Rodway at the British Library and Laura MacDonald for the American Theatre and Drama Society helped me think about the multiplicity of ways in which theatre engages and reinvigorates political debates and also introduced me to the playwright Naomi Wallace. I am grateful to Naomi for her thoughtful and generous engagement with chapter 2 of this book and for her extraordinary drama, *Things of Dry Hours*, which has helped historians to see the 1930s in new ways.

Many people have engaged directly with written forms of this project. I am especially thankful to James Hatch, Nathan Grant, and anonymous reviewers for the *African American Review* and *Journal of American Drama and Theatre*, who read my essays on black Federal Theatre dramas at an earlier stage of the project. Many colleagues and friends gave generously of their time by reading parts of the book manuscript. I am particularly grateful to Nick Grant, whose brilliant work on African Americans and South Africa has helped me think through the dynamic relationship between anticommunism and black activism; to Sue Currell, whose work on little magazines and the racial politics of the left has taught us so much; and to Bridget Bennett, for asking the big questions that remind us of the importance of the nineteenth century for historians of the twentieth. Ann Schofield has shown interest in this project from the get-go and has helped in so many ways: by reading my work, by always being willing to talk theatre, and by workshopping countless dramas as they emerge from the imagination of my young daughter. I owe a massive debt to Celeste-Marie Bernier, who read the manuscript in its entirety and whose scholarship and academic activism remind us that academic conventions can be changed. Robert Jones read much of the manuscript in its early stages and challenged me early on to think harder about black theatre manuscripts. I am grateful to the anonymous readers who read the manuscript for UNC Press and their generous and constructive criticism. Also at UNC Press, Dylan White and Chuck Grench have offered valuable guidance, helping to steer the manuscript from my computer to a place in the fine company of books published in the John Hope Franklin Series.

There are very many archivists and librarians who have engaged generously with this project over the years and offered expertise, wisdom, and much more besides. I am indebted to the staff of the Music Division of the Library of Congress, the National Archives at College Park, and the Schlesinger Library, as well as archivists in Special Collections at the Universities of Washington and Emory Universities. The Billy Rose Theatre Division of the Performing Arts Library, and Schomburg Research Center for Research in Black Culture in New York City have a wealth of treasures, and it was a privilege to be able to spend so much time consulting collections at these fabulous centers for cultural history. I am particularly indebted to Lena Donnelly, who helped me discover the gems of the GMU Federal Theatre Project collection, stayed late so I could finish looking at manuscripts, and gave me rides back to D.C. Leah also introduced me to the late Lorraine Brown, former director of the Center for Research at the Federal Theatre Project at George Mason University. By the time I met her, Lorraine was a much cited and widely respected scholar, whose years of work had helped restore the Federal Theatre Project archive. However, her early career, as a Professor of Women, Gender & Sexuality Studies and English Literature, had been rather different. In the 1970s the Federal Theatre was dismissed, as both unimportant and subversive, mediocre art and dangerous propaganda, and Lorraine was often asked why she was bothering with that old lefty rubbish. The important, sensitive, and pioneering work done by Lorraine Brown and a generation of Federal Theatre scholars has done much to rescue the FTP from near oblivion. In the early 1970s Lorraine discovered the unprocessed archives in a Library of Congress warehouse. Over the course of the decade the archive was recovered and catalogued at the newly established Center for Research on the Federal Theatre Project at George Mason University. Yet much of what we know—especially of black theatre—comes not directly from the official records, but from the pioneering oral history project it inspired and from the Federal Theatre actors, directors, playwrights, administrators and audience members who offered their stories and donated archival materials to the GMU archive. These efforts to center black knowledge production are critical in allowing future scholars to understand the ambition, scope, and influence of black creatives in 1930s American theatre as well as to model archives of black agency in the twenty-first century.

The recovery of the Federal Theatre archive took place at the same time black theatre manuscripts were beginning to be published in anthologies. The first anthologies showcased contemporary works and reflected the new dramas of the Black Arts Movement. However in 1974, James Hatch and Ted Shine published *Black Theater U.S.A.*—a landmark anthology that documented the history and evolution of black theatre since the middle of the nineteenth century. For many years Hatch and his partner, the late Camille Billops collected and preserved the work and papers of black cultural producers in New York City. The Camille Billops and James V. Hatch collection is now deposited in Special Collections at Emory University Library. Without this archive and without *Black Theater U.S.A.* our knowledge of and access to black theatre history would be much diminished.

Friendships—new and old—made the many U.S research trips for the project a delight. I am very grateful to Alyson and Tim Vert, who opened their home, their hearts, and their dogs to me in Washington, D.C.; while in New York, Tuomas Hiltunen, Angelika Ohl, Anneli McDowell, Cordelia Hagmann, and Sallie Sanders housed and fed me, and made New York City a home away from home. Numerous and prolonged research trips to the United States were made possible by funding from the British Academy and by generous and regular periods of research leave awarded by the School of History and Faculty of Arts at the University of Leeds.

While working on the project in the United Kingdom, I have been inspired by many wonderful women whom I have had the great fortune to work alongside at the University of Leeds. First and foremost was the late Katrina Honeyman, an inspiring scholar, generous mentor, and great friend. I also wish to mention Anyaa Anim-Addo, Sara Barker, Say Burgin, Gina Denton, Laura King, Elisabeth Leake, Andrea Major, Addi Manolopoulou, Claire Martin, Lauren McCarthy, Jessica Meyer, Sabina Peck, and Danielle Sprecher. For more than a decade I have had the privilege to teach a year-long course on the Harlem Renaissance to undergraduates. Their energy, passion, excitement, and concern for black cultural histories has inspired me each and every year, and I am grateful for this opportunity to engage afresh and in good company with the plays, poems, and many other literary works of black creatives.

Very many friends and family members have opened their homes, kitchens, and arms to me, and have known when to ask (and more importantly, when not to ask), "How's the book?" I am especially indebted to Sasha Handley, a great friend and brilliant historian, as well as to Zoe Hilton, James Campbell, Jane Wilkinson, and Nim Sheriff. My sister, Julie Dyer, and father, David Dossett, have been unfailing in their support and know how much I owe them. This book would not have been possible without the support and generosity of my partner, Robert. He has read and discussed much of this project over the last decade, often late into the night, offering reassurance and challenge in equal measure, and broadening my ambition for this book and much more besides. I cannot thank him enough.

This project has spanned the birth of my daughter Elizabeth and the death of my cherished friend Katrina and of my fiercely supportive mother, Teresa Dossett. In different ways, their energy, passion for living, and belief that things can be made better inspires me every day. I dedicate this book to them.

Abbreviations in the Text

ANT   American Negro Theatre

CPUSA   Communist Party of the USA

FTP   Federal Theatre Project

HCC   Harlem Cultural Committee

ILD   International Labor Defense

NAACP   National Association for the Advancement of Colored People

NNC   National Negro Congress

NPC   Negro Playwrights Company

NSB   National Service Bureau

NUL   National Urban League

UNIA   Universal Negro Improvement Association

WPA   Works Progress Administration

Radical Black Theatre in the New Deal

Introduction

Leaping for Freedom: Black Theatre Manuscripts and Black Performance Communities

· ·

Ah wont turn an' run ef Ah sees 'im—Ol' Massa say, Nigguh, put down that gun!— Know whut Ah makes 'im say? Put down dat gun—MISTUH NIGGUH!
—Theodore Browne, *Go Down Moses,* 1938

In the final scene of Theodore Browne's *Go Down Moses* (1938), new recruits to the Union army prepare to attack a Confederate fort. They spur each other on, rehearsing the direct confrontation with white power upon which their freedom depends and mocking the attempts of former slave-masters to control their identity as free men.[1] Whether as armed soldiers in the U.S. Civil War or as playwrights in the Federal Theatre, for black men to compel white men to address them as equals was a radical act. Cast and rehearsed by the Harlem Negro Unit in 1939, *Go Down Moses* challenged racial hierarchies that governed how black and white Americans faced each other, in the theatre, and also on the battlegrounds of America's past.[2] Browne was an actor and playwright for the Seattle Negro Unit, one of seventeen Negro Units set up by the Federal Theatre Project (FTP) in 1935, where African Americans worked as dramatists, actors, directors, designers, composers, and theatre technicians. During the four years of the project, black Americans were able to confront white power directly on the pages of Federal Theatre manuscripts. To make the leap from page to stage, however, often called for indirection. African Americans were sometimes required to perform racially subordinate roles, both on and off stage. Joe Staton, an actor and writer on the Seattle Negro Unit, remembered the difficulty of staging theatre that affirmed black Americans' conception of themselves but that "didn't look like anything rehearsed."[3] White spectators were accustomed to the idea that black Americans were "natural" performers rather than trained artists. These racially coded notions of black performance permeate the publicity and administrative records of the Works Progress Administration (WPA), the federal agency with responsibility for the FTP. In a press release to promote the dramas of the Hartford Negro Unit, the WPA took pains to present black creativity within frameworks acceptable to white Americans: "Negroes are not content with being the best natural actors in the world they persist in some of its best playwriting as well. They don't sit down at a typewriter to do this—it's a gift peculiar to the Negro actor which gets under way when he rehearses a play, which prompts him, in the emotional excitement of acting, to substitute his own lines and business when he forgets portions of his role."[4]

The idea that the federal government paid unemployed black cultural producers to create theatre during America's deepest recession may come as a surprise to many Americans. Arousing equally strong passions on the part of its supporters and opponents in the 1930s, the significance of this controversial theatre project was buried amid the ideological battles over the legacy of the New Deal in the early years of the Cold War. In public memory, the New Deal has long become associated with work relief programs that paid unemployed workers to construct public buildings and highways.[5] Indeed, the largest of all New Deal relief agencies, the WPA, spent over three-quarters of its total appropriation on construction projects.[6] However, the WPA supported a broad and diverse jobs program that recognized the scale of devastation wrought by the Depression, including on the creative economy. As FTP director Hallie Flanagan, explained: "painters, actors, and musicians, could get just as hungry as bridge builders and ditch diggers. . . . their various skills are as worthy of preservation."[7] Set up in 1935, the WPA absorbed and expanded the Federal Emergency Relief Agency (FERA). FERA had provided loans to states for emergency direct relief when it was established in 1933 as part of a suite of agencies created to address the immediate crisis of the Depression. Two years on, with millions of Americans still facing unemployment, the Emergency Relief Appropriation Act (1935) established the WPA with an initial purse of $5 billion, the largest federal appropriation to date. By the time the WPA was wound down in 1943, it had employed eight and a half million Americans with a total expenditure of $10.75 billion. Nearly a quarter of American families were supported by WPA wages during the eight years of its operation.[8]

Funding programs for unemployed artists had begun before the WPA. Under FERA, 13,000 actors, musicians, and technicians were employed to stage variety and vaudeville shows in schools, churches, and Civilization Conservation Corps sites.[9] In August 1935 the WPA systematized and greatly expanded work relief for unemployed artists through the establishment of Federal One, a new Federal Arts Project that organized unemployed cultural workers into separate programs: the Federal Art Project, the Federal Writers

Project, the Federal Music Project, and the Federal Theatre Project. Federal One was placed under the jurisdiction of the Professional and Service Project of the WPA. This meant financial responsibility for the arts projects rested with WPA state directors, which ensured that regional politics and local delivery became a major factor in the day-to-day running of the projects. While this impacted all regions of the country, it particularly marked the experiences of African Americans in relief programs, especially in the South, where three-quarters of African Americans lived in the 1930s.

Local delivery of federal relief programs made them palatable to white southerners and the object of fierce criticism by African American rights organizations in the early years of the New Deal. Black Americans were less likely than whites to be categorized as eligible for relief, and when they were, they received considerably less. After 1936, however, the proportion of African Americans employed by the WPA grew: in some cities African Americans WPA workers represented between three and five times their percentage of the population. Harvard Sitkoff argues that the WPA "provided an economic floor for the whole black community in the 1930s, rivaling both agriculture and domestic services as the chief source of Negro income."[10] African Americans' expectations grew: between the first and second half of the decade, black journals, including *The Crisis* and *Opportunity,* moved from scathing denunciations of WPA discrimination to cautious praise.[11] Even so, those who secured WPA employment remained dependent on and had to navigate the complex relationship between federal programs and state delivery.

African Americans' experiences with the Federal Theatre Project were also affected by the particular kind of theatre program envisaged by its creators. Government sponsorship of a national theatre program had no U.S. model on which to build. In Europe and Asia, where government subsidy for theatre was commonplace, the model was for a fixed theatre in a particular location, such as the Abbey Theatre in Dublin. By contrast, the FTP was established as a national program of work relief. While New York would serve as an important administrative center and artistic hub for the project, the relief requirement made it necessary to build a nationwide network of theatres. The appointment of Hallie Flanagan to head the program was crucial to ensuring the project reflected all of America's regions. WPA chief Harry Hopkins invited Flanagan to lead the project in part because Flanagan did not need reminding that New York was not America.[12] Midwesterners both, Flanagan and Hopkins had been classmates at Grinnell College in Iowa. Where Hopkins had gone into politics, working with Roosevelt when he was governor of New York before leading New Deal relief programs, Flanagan had built a successful career in experimental theatre, first at her alma mater and then at Vassar College.

Flanagan had a strong vision of theatre as a transformative force in American life. The first woman to be awarded a Guggenheim fellowship, she had written a book about the new workers' theatres she encountered while traveling through Europe and Russia. She also wrote and staged the experimental drama *Can You Hear Their Voices*, which attracted national attention. Respected in the world of noncommercial theatre, Flanagan was a good fit for Hopkins's vision of a program run "by a person who sees right from the start that the profits won't be money profits."[13] For Flanagan, theatre was an integral part of the changes and challenges confronting Americans:

> Our whole emphasis in the theatre enterprises which we are about
> to undertake should be on re-thinking rather than on remembering.
> The good old days may have been very good days indeed, but they are
> gone. New days are upon us and the plays that we do and the ways
> that we do them should be informed by our consciousness of the art
> and economics of 1935. . . . The theatre must become conscious of the
> implications of the changing social order, or the changing social older
> will ignore, and rightly, the implications of the theatre.[14]

The exigencies of the Great Depression, the strengthening of labor unions, and the growth of an interracial civil rights struggle prompted a good deal of rethinking by the middle of the decade. What seemed to some like exciting new opportunities to change the United States for the better, appeared to others as an existential threat that must be resisted at all costs. These challenges were reflected in the dramas developed by the FTP. FTP employees, theatre professionals, activists, and politicians fiercely contested whose vision of America should be represented on the Federal Theatre stage. When those who wrote and staged plays held different views about the social order to those who paid their wages, the repercussions rippled well beyond the stage door and the administrative functions of the WPA: writers of newspaper headlines, White House aides, and members of Congress weighed in and sought to influence the type of plays staged by the Federal Theatre.

When Harry Hopkins launched the Federal Theatre Project in August 1935, he promised a "free, adult, uncensored theatre."[15] For Flanagan, grown-up theatre meant not just freedom from government censorship but also the ability to experiment, a "many-sided theatre" that could create new theatre and new audiences.[16] The FTP had five regional centers, each with its own headquarters, in the Northeast, Midwest, West, and South, with New York City constituting a region of its own. This "federation of theatres," would be governed by "general policy and program . . . outlined in Washington"; but the implementation would be "directed by local conditions."[17] In theory at least, this meant decisions about programming and personnel would be placed in the hands of regional FTP administrators who understood the purpose and ambition of the theatre program. In practice, regional FTP administrators would need to develop good working relationships with individual state WPA administrators, who had oversight of Federal Theatre programs in their state. The relationships between the FTP and state WPA bureaucracies worked well when the two sides shared goals and understood each other's priorities. However, the establishment of two competing centers meant that when differences arose, considerable disruption ensued. State directors could—and some did—slow or even close down productions they deemed provocative or politically sensitive, even when the FTP had given them the green light. Such conflicts became a regular feature of a theatre project committed to decentralization while simultaneously pursuing national directives to develop a theatre that might change the lives of ordinary Americans.

Flanagan's vision of a many-sided theatre included not just regional variation: it also encompassed the diverse traditions and forms of American theatre. This diversity was reflected in the range of Federal Theatre drama units established in towns and cities across the United States including ethnic, foreign language, Negro, and traveling units, as well as the genre-specific units for classic, vaudeville, marionette, and experimental dramas, and Living Newspapers. Of these, it was the Living Newspapers, as well as the dramas of Negro Units, that most frequently tested Hopkins's commitment to an uncensored theatre. WPA policy mandated that Negro Units could be established wherever there were sufficient numbers of unemployed black theatre professionals who were eligible to claim relief. In practice, Negro Units were usually set up where there was already a history of interracial collaboration between white producers and black actors. Local race relations and theatre traditions determined how units worked and which were able to thrive. Negro Units were started in southern cities, including Birmingham, Alabama, and Raleigh, North Carolina, however it was in the urban centers of the Northeast, the Midwest, and the West Coast, where black theatre traditions, resources, and interracial audiences for

ck theatre already existed, that innovative, black-authored drama flour-
ed during the FTP. Of the seventeen Negro Units established by the FTP,
even maintained a production schedule for most of the four years of the
project. These were in Boston, Cleveland, Chicago, Hartford, Harlem, Los
Angeles, and Seattle. Among the seven, the Harlem, Chicago, Hartford,
and Seattle Units established reputations for developing innovative black-
authored dramas.[18] It was these Negro Units whose productions often provoked the most debate between local communities, WPA state officials,
and Federal Theatre Project administrators.

The four years of the Federal Theatre Project coincided with a growing,
bipartisan, and increasingly hostile opposition to the New Deal. From its
inception in 1935 to its premature closure in 1939, the FTP was a political
battleground. In Congress, southern Democrats and Republicans were quick
to find fault with a publicly funded theatre project that employed 13,000
theatre professionals and reached more than 30 million Americans in integrated audiences. Calling for a sweeping investigation in July 1938, J. Par-
nell Thomas, Republican congressman from New Jersey, called the Federal
Theatre "one more link in the vast and unparalleled New Deal propaganda
machine."[19] Yet the second half of the 1930s was also a period in which
African Americans' expectations grew and activism flourished. African
Americans were quick to use Negro Units to create new platforms for protest and new audiences for black theatre, for they recognized that the FTP
could be harnessed to develop black creative talent, and in particular black
dramas. Accordingly, it is the theatre manuscripts developed by black performance communities that formed around these units, rather than the
Negro Units themselves that are the focus of this book. Other studies have
documented the institutional racial hierarchies, which usually put whites in
positions of power even in Negro Units.[20] This book takes a different perspective. Rather than fitting black creativity into narratives that foreground
the actions and anxieties of white liberals, it takes black perspectives and
experiences of theatre as a starting point. *Radical Black Theatre in the New
Deal* examines black-authored dramas created during the Federal Theatre
Project. Theatre manuscripts developed by African Americans, rather than
the negotiations with white administrators, feature most prominently in
this book, for while the limits of New Deal inclusivity are now well understood, the radicality of black playwriting is not. On the pages of Federal
Theatre manuscripts, black Americans wrote of struggles past, preserved a
record of battles lost and won, and imagined a radically different future.
Theatre manuscripts are an archive of black agency, for they not only record

how and when white mastery was contested within and beyond the theatre, they also document the scope and ambition of black creativity.

Histories of Theatre, Performance, and Spectatorship

Americans have long recognized the central role of black performance and white spectatorship in maintaining white supremacy. In the middle passage, in the slave market, and on the plantation, whites sought control of black performance. The capacity to watch and control black performance was central to the construction of the white self and the maintenance of the slave system: the speculator who made slaves dance at the slave market was both displaying his "property" for potential buyers and affirming white power before black and white spectators.[21] The ability of whites to command African Americans in a spectacle of contented subjection continued to define the production and forms of black performance beyond legal emancipation, as Saidiya Hartman has shown.[22] But black performance was never reducible to the conditions of domination out of which it emerged. For if black performance and white spectatorship provided spaces for the enactment of white mastery, they also became sites of contest and resistance, where white power might be undone.

The history of blackface minstrelsy exemplifies this struggle. As Eric Lott has argued, minstrelsy was not a straightforward enactment of "racial domination": for while it embodied both white desire for, and cultural robbery of, black cultural forms, it also facilitated exchange between two tightly bounded cultures. The blackface mask was "less a *repetition* of power relations than a *signifier* for them."[23] Understanding that performance "sustained slavery *and* freedom" and could therefore be neither "trusted *nor* neglected," African Americans sought to control what was performed, by, and for whom.[24] Before the Civil War, it was a performance by Gavitt's Original Ethiopian Serenaders, one of the few all-black minstrel troupes, that prompted Frederick Douglass to theorize, "It is something gained, when the colored man in any form can appear before a white audience." Douglass was disgusted by black minstrelsy, yet he recognized that when black Americans controlled or appropriated American theatrical forms they were making a political and politicized intervention. William Wells Brown understood as much when he opened his pleasure garden theatre in New York City in 1821, the very year New York State extended male suffrage for all white men but disfranchised most African American males. Attracting a diverse audience of free and enslaved African Americans, as well as white spectators,

Brown's African Company performed original black-authored dramas as well as all-black versions of Shakespearean tragedy. When Brown moved his theatre next door to a rival white company, the police compelled him to cancel a production of *Richard III*. That the African Company challenged more than white control over the institutions of theatre was well understood. As the *Spectator* journal observed: "Thus is seems that these descendants of Africa are determined to carry into full practice the doctrine of liberty and equality, physically by acting plays and mentally by writing them."[25]

Even as African Americans pursued freedom through writing and acting plays, black performance continued to be framed through blackface minstrelsy in the nineteenth century. For some, such as William Henry Lane, (whose professional name was Juba), this required them to adapt, innovate, and work with white minstrel troupes and with managers, who controlled access to theatre venues and financial reward. By the 1870s and 1880s, some black actors stopped wearing the minstrel mask and started producing their own shows. The Hyers Sisters Combination carved out paths to freedom by presenting a number of full-length musicals, including *Out of Bondage, The Underground Railroad*, and *Urlina: The African Princess*. Bert Williams and George Walker, the famous comedy duo, teamed up with the writer Jesse A. Shipp, composer William Marion Cook, and poet Paul Laurence Dunbar to produce the hit musical *In Dahomey* (1902). African Americans continued to assert ownership of black performance, theatre, and history by writing, reading, and performing plays in the first decades of the twentieth century. Lynching dramas by black women, and college and community theatre productions fostered by the Little Theatre Movement and the Harlem Renaissance, foregrounded the concerns of black communities and connected them with struggles past. In pageants such as Du Bois's *The Star of Ethiopia* (1913) and dramas of slave resistance such as Randolph Edmonds's *Denmark Vesey* (1929), May Miller's *Harriet Tubman* (1935), and George Douglas Johnson's *Frederick Douglass* (1935), black Americans created a "performative historiography" that celebrated black heroes and reclaimed black histories from white narratives of the American past.[26]

Black ownership of black performance was fiercely resisted by white audiences, producers, and theatre makers on the eve of the Federal Theatre Project. Minstrelsy remained popular with white audiences and minstrel shows were a feature of the Federal Theatre. The New York, Massachusetts, and Chicago Federal Theatre Projects each supported a minstrel troupe, while New Orleans laid claim to producing the first full-length "black-faced marionette" minstrel show by black actors.[27] At the same time, the Federal Theatre leaned heavily on and helped cement the influence of a new generation of white playwrights—Eugene O'Neill, Paul Green, and Ridgely Torrence—who were attempting to redefine the dramatization of race. In the 1920s, Green's *In Abraham's Bosom* (1926) and O'Neill's *The Emperor Jones* (1920) appeared—at least to some—to represent a "serious" effort to engage the problems of black life. By the 1930s, however, the suffering meted out by white dramatists to African Americans in pursuit of self-determination had become a dangerous trope for many black critics. Eugene Gordon, feature editor for the communist *Daily Worker*, believed "O'Neill's, Green's and all the other 'liberal' writers' plays about the Negro serve the capitalist class better than the old minstrels . . . since their deadly influence is often fatal before it is observed."[28] This growing unease was not shared by white supervisors in the FTP, who routinely turned to this triumvirate for "Negro dramas." During the four years of the project, twenty-five productions of seventeen Green dramas were staged in nine American cities.[29] The Federal Theatre made space for a variety of genres when it came to white dramas of black life. In addition to the "old minstrels" and folk dramas, melodramas and dramas of social realism were regularly staged in the project. Differences in genre, however, were transcended by white playwrights whose "uses" of the black body had much in common, both with each other and with the commercial theatre.[30] No less than Broadway, the Federal Theatre offered ample opportunity and a multiplicity of forms through which white Americans might enact racial mastery.

But this is not the only story. Between 1935 and 1939, African Americans used the FTP to create new possibilities and push open the parameters that had contained black drama. Black and white audiences, many for the first time, came to watch black-authored dramas, performed by black casts, in integrated theatres. For Negro Units in cities with relatively small black populations, such as Seattle, performances often took place in white neighborhoods. In cities with larger and more established black performance communities, such as New York, Negro Unit productions were located in black theatres and community spaces. In both cases audiences were diverse: location, as well as the availability of free and low-cost tickets, meant that Negro Unit productions attracted black, white, and ethnic Americans who had never before seen a live performance in a theatre setting; group bookings by labor organizations and neighborhood social clubs meant that many audience members experienced theatre as an extension of their community or workplace, a place to meet old allies, forge new friendships, air grievances, and voice ambitions. While the location and makeup of the audience could vary significantly from city to city, the Federal Theatre offered a rare opportunity for audiences from diverse socioeconomic backgrounds to witness black drama in integrated spaces. It also offered black and white audiences the opportunity to perform spectatorship differently. For many Americans, a Negro Unit drama was their first experience of theatre as a black event for black communities. In Harlem, opening night of a Negro Unit production was the place to be, and be seen, for black celebrities and political figures alike. But what was embraced by black communities could be alienating and even shocking for whites: white critics and audience members who traveled uptown were fascinated, and often troubled, by the vocal manner in which African American audiences asserted their ownership of a production.[31]

In these new settings, black performance communities developed innovative new dramas that challenged the dramatic conventions that had long governed the American stage, as well as newer dogmas emerging in the interwar years, which were influenced by the theatre of Europe and the international left. Whether in melodramas, agitprop, folk dramas, or realist plays, white dramatists routinely deployed black figures to help white Americans better understand themselves. Black performance communities confronted the white gaze by adapting traditional forms and creating complex new roles for black heroes. In folk dramas, domestic tragedies, black realist dramas, Living Newspapers, and melodramas, black dramatists pushed generic boundaries and explored what it meant to be a black hero in American culture.

In the early twentieth century, dominant notions of the heroic remained firmly rooted in a white and patriarchal lineage that crossed continents and centuries. If, in the Old World, British writer Thomas Carlyle found black heroism unimaginable, the New World was little better. For white Americans, the black hero could be entertained only through reductive models of heroism and in relation to whites. But rather than insert black historical heroes into a white pantheon, black dramatists and performance communities developed new frameworks for making black heroes. It is important that these new interpretive parameters foregrounded the radical social change necessary before black heroes could be recognized on the American stage.[32] These new parameters were not exclusive to theatre. Rather, they were part of a broader exchange between playwrights, poets, novelists, essayists, politicians, and activists about the representation of black life in the arts and the role of the arts in shaping radical black politics. In the second half of the 1930s, these debates were important to black performance communities and were documented on the pages of the black theatre manuscripts they produced.

Black Performance Communities and Play Making

Black theatre manuscripts not only document the play-making process; they are also important vehicles in their own right, at the center of community debates about how race should be performed. Black theatre manuscripts served this function long before they made it to the stage, and even when they did not. As such they can offer insight into how and why dramas were changed and what was at stake. Traditionally we pay most attention to those dramas that are staged and debated in public spaces by theatre professionals, critics, and scholars. But to read black theatre manuscripts as dramatic texts and as historical sources requires we understand the communities who made them and for whom they were written. Black Federal Theatre manuscripts were the product of individual playwrights, black troupes, and a broader community of "unacknowledged collaborators" who made plays in the 1930s and thereafter.[33]

Black theatre manuscripts were made and remade in a number of settings and parallel spaces within, between, and outside the Negro Units, which I call black performance communities. The concept of black performance community draws on Richard Barr's notion of the "temporary social organization" that performance creates among spectators, actors, and actants—that is the director, author, composers, set designers, and others whose "backstage" roles shape both text and performance.[34] Although temporary, these social communities are capable of producing longer-lasting relationships and alignments both within and between the actors and actants who develop new relationships in preparing and staging a play, as well as with members of the audience. Here I understand "audience" to include those for whom the play is imagined, who imagine themselves as the audience for a drama, as well as those who turn out to watch a performance.

The idea of a performance community helps us understand the role of the unacknowledged collaborators who shape black texts. The fleeting social organizations created in temporary performance communities before and during the FTP had a long-lasting impact on how African Americans imagined the performance of theatre manuscripts. Shared experiences of performances past produced communities capable of coming together again to imagine, create, and sometimes resist new performance possibilities. In fact, black performance communities were adept at what Sandra Richards calls "writing the absent potential." Since theatre manuscripts are, by nature, collaborative, Richards argues that critics need to imagine the "latent intertexts likely to be produced in performance increasing and complicating meaning."[35] Meaning is shaped both by what is, and is not, there within the text, since the materiality of theatre, the movement, sounds, and silences of bodies on and off stage produces "competing and even opposing discourses." Black performance communities were well practiced in imagining the absent potential in theatre manuscripts dealing with race, even before they were staged. Actors on the Chicago Negro Unit, who refused to perform Paul Green's southern convict drama, could envisage all too easily the latent intertexts produced when black men appeared in chains before whites, whether in a southern work camp or on the federal stage. The black troupe of the Los Angeles Negro Unit, who were assigned "soiled and sleeveless vests" to play the role of black laborers, also understood the connection between displays of white mastery on the stages of Los Angeles and the dramatic world conjured by a white playwright. They insisted on wearing their own clothes on stage.[36]

Black performance communities exerted influence over the types of black dramas that were, and were not, staged by the FTP. They also shaped the critical reception of dramas performed by the Negro Units. Shared experience of a particular production could produce shared interpretation of its meaning. Equally, the broad audience for FTP dramas meant that performances could become sites of contestation over who got to define what that experience was. Each new production brought with it a set of "dramaturgically inscribed relationships," which might be accepted, amended, or refused by members of a performance community.[37] The reception of the Haitian *Macbeth*, staged by Orson Welles and the Harlem Negro Unit, exemplifies this. Where white critics embraced a "blacked-up" classic peopled with recognizable portraits of doomed black men, black performance communities looked past the primitive stereotypes, viewing the all-black Shakespeare play as an entering wedge for more serious black-authored drama.[38] Performance communities could encompass both homogeneity and diversity: their members might share a performance experience but take away from it different meanings shaped by competing understandings of how best to represent, and even whether to represent, the diversity of black experiences before racially mixed audiences. For example, when black audiences were invited to a staged reading of Ted Ward's *Big White Fog*, they were polite in front of the white director. Only afterward did they address their complaints, in writing, to Shirley Graham, the unit's black supervisor. Representing a range of black community groups, audience members shared certain criticisms of the play, while also articulating a diverse and often conflicting set of views about what constituted appropriate black theatre.[39]

The social transformation imagined by black performance communities was rooted in their expectations of a racially mixed audience. It is crucial that the coming together of participants in a performance community does not rely on an a priori consensus or shared social background of participants, nor does it require "exclusive commitment." Because it is fluid and not fixed prior to performance, the black performance community allows for, but never guarantees, social transformation through the process of production and performance. What a performance community creates is the possibility that participants, who may have very different backgrounds, are able to consider the relationship between the fictional society represented by the characters of the drama, the real society it purports to represent, and the "third society," including players, spectators, and actants present in the performance. As such the performance community disrupts the presumed opposition between dramatic form and content for it encourages comparison between the society portrayed on the stage and the society that produces that theatre.[40] Rex Ingram, a leading black actor who played a number of roles for the Harlem Negro Unit, articulated these connections in an interview with the *Afro-American* newspaper on his performance in *Stevedore*. Speaking of his portrayal of the fiery Blacksnake, a black stevedore who helps chase away the white lynch mob, Ingram declared: "For the first time in my fifteen years of acting, I got a chance to be myself, to say some of the things I had wanted to say for a long time."[41] Hailed as a "first" by black and white critics alike, the Theatre Union's production of *Stevedore* in New York on the eve of the FTP was understood by Harlem's black performance community as a template for how theatre could connect the fictional, the "real," and the performance society, to produce social transformation. William Pickens gave an example of how these connections might prompt social change in his newspaper account of how white audience members responded to the play: "Negro women play heroic parts. It is the first time in any American play on an American stage where a Negro woman is pictured as shooting down the white man who had insulted her and who had then led a mob to attack her people. As she fired, she exclaimed: 'I got him, I got him—I got the red-headed S.O.B.' The whites of the audience cheered wildly. Certainly this is something new."[42] The performance community that developed around *Stevedore* helped imagine into existence a society in which black women and men talk back to and confront white power in front of black and white spectators alike. It helped created the circumstances that allowed Pickens, a black critic, to tell his black readers how white spectators performed in front of black actors and audiences. That he was able to watch white spectators cheering black actors playing characters who defied white supremacy suggests this was a theatre capable of producing social transformation.

Making Black Performance Communities

Black performance communities were not unique to, or originated by, Negro Units. Before the FTP, the Lafayette Theatre and the Krigwa Players in New York; the Charles Gilpin Players in Hartford, Connecticut; the Howard Players in Washington, D.C.; the Gilpin Players in Cleveland, Ohio; and the Negro Repertory Company of the Seattle Repertory Playhouse in Washington drew from and helped grow black performance communities. However, the social and cultural agenda of the FTP helped to create and sustain a particular set of relationships that expanded their parameters and potential. The black performance communities that developed around the Negro Units drew in an array of political actors—federal agencies, unions, professional associations, and civil rights organizations—who were accountable to the constituencies they purported to serve. Through the Negro Units, the question of who black theatre was for and whose vision of blackness it should represent became a legitimate subject for political debate in both black and white communities. This legitimacy was important in binding communities together.

The performance communities that developed around Negro Units usually comprised members of the unit. They were joined by black rights, welfare, and betterment organizations, including local branches and national offices of the National Association for the Advancement of Colored People (NAACP) and National Urban League (NUL). With established methods for monitoring, advocating for, and protesting the misrepresentation of black life, these organizations were significant voices in the establishment of Negro Units across the country. Black neighborhood branches of the Young Women's Christian Association (YWCA) and the Young Men's Christian Association (YMCA), which ran a variety of cultural programs for black communities, were also strong supporters. These groups often worked together and alongside national black theatre organizations, including the Negro

Actors Guild and the Colored Actors and Performers Association. They also worked with and helped to form new organizations. Groups such as the Harlem Cultural Committee and Seattle's Colored Committee were established to coordinate action and facilitate black programming and black control of Negro Units. These coalitions drew on diverse constituencies, which included black church leaders and local cultural groups as well as interracial unions.

Although African Americans were at the heart of black performance communities, they could include white Americans and other ethnic Americans. Michael Adrian, the Puerto Rican stage designer, became a crucial figure at the Hartford Negro Unit, while the white leftist theatre director Maurice Clark worked with the Harlem Negro Unit to develop black-centered and black-authored dramas. The organized left also created new, racially mixed unions to represent the interests of workers employed by the WPA. The Workers' Alliance, founded in 1935, brought together recently formed Unemployment Councils and WPA workers to defend the work rights of the jobless and those employed by the federal agency. Black newspapers, as well as literary, performing arts, and leftist magazines, were also important to black performance communities, as they created networks of affiliation that disseminated information about and between Negro Units, documented discrimination, and lobbied for change. Theatre critics were not the only ones to cover black dramas; newspaper editors and politicians wrote opinion pieces about Negro Unit programming, productions, and performances, while celebrity news about Federal Theatre stars was a common feature on the society and gossip pages of most black newspapers.

Working in and across these settings, black performance communities were constituted by a diverse range of groups that sought to disrupt and control the parameters of black performance. As we will see, the diversity of black performance communities meant participants frequently held conflicting views about which elements of black life should be represented on the stage, and of what was meant by good theatre. Members of black performance communities did not come to a performance necessarily committed to, or even willing to share, a common experience of a particular performance or set of performances. Performance communities operated in ways that depended not only on local histories of cultural collaboration but also on the evolving set of relationships that developed around Negro Units. Crucially, these relationships were shaped by experiences of selecting, rehearsing, and staging black Federal Theatre manuscripts between 1935 and 1939.

The disagreements, compromises, and negotiations involved in the process of preparing and staging a theatre manuscript made black performance communities sites of potential social transformation.

Locating Black Radicality: The Archive of Black Theatre

Centering black theatre manuscripts, and the role of the communities that developed them, opens up new ways of understanding the radical cultural work that took place in the second half of the 1930s. The black theatre manuscripts that are the focus of this book offer an alternative history of how radical ideas and ambitions were developed in spite of, and perhaps even because of, the racial hierarchies that governed federal agencies and American theatre. The Negro Units of the Federal Theatre were not set up to drive radical social change. Social transformation, as Robin Kelley reminds us, "is the work of political education and activism," work that, by necessity, must take place outside institutions built in and modeled on the existing social order.[43] This does not mean that African Americans did not fight to change these institutions or that they were naïve in attempting to do so. Rather, it is to be reminded that if we look to the FTP and other gatekeepers of the progressive theatre in the 1930s for evidence of radical social transformation, we are bound to be disappointed. The administrative archive of the FTP is a rich and important source for understanding the history and potential of state-sponsored theatre, but it need not be the sole or primary focus of a history of black drama and theatre developed during the operation of the project. Understanding Federal Theatre administrative records as one part of a growing archive and the Negro Units as part of a broader black performance community opens up space to explore the radical potential of black dramatic texts and their unacknowledged collaborators. Locating black radicality requires that we attend to the archive and history of black theatre manuscripts.

Black theatre and its archive are contested sites of knowledge production shaped by long-standing practices of racial exclusion and omission.[44] Such a history requires us to examine unpublished, unproduced, and variant theatre manuscripts alongside dramas that were staged and published. It also requires us to recognize that all theatre manuscripts are incomplete and shaped by numerous unacknowledged collaborators.[45] African Americans' marginalization within the publishing and theatre industries means that any history focused on a "finished" or end product reinscribes the racial hierarchies of the period in question. This is not to suggest that whether a drama was published or staged is a matter of no importance. Publication and production bestow status on a manuscript, influencing the development of theatre in the 1930s as well as which dramas are available to those who come after. Yet we need to be wary of relying only on the canon of black dramas approved by white theatre producers and publishing companies for our understanding of black theatre in the twentieth century. Theatre histories that include only manuscripts that were staged and published will invariably be histories of what was considered interesting or acceptable to whites. This book examines what was important and necessary to African Americans. Although there were few black-authored dramas staged in mainstream American theatres in the first half of the twentieth century, there were many more created by and circulated among black communities.[46]

Black theatre manuscripts testify to the ambition and creativity of African American playwrights and of broader black performance communities that shaped and debated their work. These conversations are documented both on the pages of multiple, variant black federal theatre manuscripts as well as in the correspondence, memos, and letters of complaint written by black theatre workers and members of the broader performance community. They are also recorded in a set of production bulletins. Each federal theatre unit was required to produce a bulletin comprised of reports on all aspects of production, including a synopsis of the play, staging notes, audience figures, and reviews. The bulletins usually included set designs, plot summaries, and photographs of the performance. This unusually rich archive of black cultural production is spread across FTP collections held at the Library of Congress and George Mason University (GMU), as well as in the WPA Records at the National Archives. After the FTP was closed in 1939 and up to the 1970s, the FTP's official archives remained marginal to our understanding of 1930s theatre. Following a brief sojourn to Vassar College, the official Federal Theatre archive was split between the Library of Congress and National Archives. Cataloging projects were begun but never completed, and in 1964 the Library of Congress portion of the archive was dispatched to a Baltimore storage depot. The process of recovering the archive was begun in 1974 when Lorraine Brown, an English and women's studies professor at GMU "discovered" the Federal Theatre records. Securing a loan of the collection from the Library of Congress, Brown and her colleagues restored and cataloged the FTP archive at the newly established Research Center for the Federal Theatre Project at GMU. They expanded the archive too. A decade-long oral history program and the targeted collection of the personal papers of Federal Theatre participants breathed new life into the FTP collections.[47] Veterans of the FTP donated theatre manuscripts and private collections to GMU, as well as to regional public and university libraries. Yet the story of black Federal Theatre cannot be confined to Federal Theatre collections. It can be found in the collections of some of the best known figures of the twentieth century, including the papers of Shirley Graham Du Bois, W. E. B. Du Bois, Paul Robeson, Langston Hughes, Canada Lee, and Richard Wright, as well as the papers of lesser known cultural producers, including Sara Jackson (nee, Oliver), Gwen Reed, Richard Moore, Theodore Browne, and Ted Ward. Black Federal Theatre was important to a range of black rights organizations and left significant traces in the records of the NAACP and the Central Division of the Universal Negro Improvement Association (UNIA). Together with the reports, reviews, and essays published in black newspapers, communist publications, and theatre magazines, there is a rich and diverse archive documenting the role of the unacknowledged collaborators who created theatre manuscripts.

Black Literary Heritage

Just as the Federal Theatre archive was beginning its long journey of recovery in 1974, black theatre manuscripts were finally being published, many for the first time. The publication of black theatre manuscripts represents a significant achievement of the Black Arts Movement. Black intellectuals and artists of the movement were, at least initially, critical of those who came before them. With limited access to the archive of black cultural life in the first half of the twentieth century, artists judged their predecessors as having failed to question white truths or to create art inspired by black values.[48] Lacking, as they saw it, a radical inheritance, black theatre artists were determined to preserve their own radical legacy by setting up new journals and publishing their work in anthologies.[49] The first anthologies to emerge in the 1970s showcased contemporary dramas. However, in 1974, the Free Press published *Black Theater U.S.A.*, edited by theatre professor James Hatch, with playwright Ted Shine as consultant. The anthology is a landmark in black theatre history for it was dedicated to showcasing the history and evolution of black dramaturgy in America. It was the first to select black-authored dramas originating in the Federal Theatre, including both Theodore Browne's *Natural Man* (1937) and Theodore Ward's *Big White Fog* (1938).[50] In 1996, Hatch and Shine published a revised and expanded edition in two volumes: the new edition was updated to the 1990s and included an excerpt of a third black Federal Theatre drama: Abram Hill and John Silvera's innovative Living Newspaper, *Liberty Deferred.*[51]

The importance of *Black Theater U.S.A.* cannot be overstated. Anthologizing black Federal Theatre dramas has made them usable in university courses and facilitated new scholarship and productions in the United States and the United Kingdom.[52] Even a brief glimpse at the scholarship on the eve of the publication of the anthology illustrates how important published collections are to foregrounding the concerns of black dramatists and theatre communities. In 1969, black drama was represented in *Fifty Best Plays of the American Theater* by white fantasies of black life: *Uncle Tom's Cabin, Green Pastures,* and *Porgy.*[53] The same year, Doris Abramson's study, *Negro Playwrights,* was published. Willing to passing judgement on black Federal Theatre manuscripts she had not seen, Abramson's book offered an unashamedly white-centric perspective on black drama. It had been, she suggested, "unfair," to judge the technique of earlier black dramatists because they had so long been barred from American theatre. Instead, the more pertinent criterion was "whether or not they illuminate Negro life for us." For the dramatist Charles F. Gordon (Oyamo), the presumption that "Us = White" and that white people were the intended audience for black dramas was part of the reason why the "new breed of white authorities on black people" were incapable of understanding black drama.[54] This failure of understanding, however, was also predicated on, and contributed to, the refusal to take black theatre manuscripts seriously. Willingness to pass judgment on unseen manuscripts, on the one hand, and the long-neglect of the Federal Theatre archive, on the other, are a mutually constitutive force with far-reaching, ongoing consequences for American cultural history. For Abramson's study cannot be safely tucked away as a relic of the pre–Black Studies academy or serve as a comforting reminder of how far our understanding of black drama has come since the restoration of the Federal Theatre archive in the 1970s and 1980s. As the chapters of this book argue, studies of black Federal Theatre dramas before the recovery of the archive continue to shape knowledge production about black theatre manuscripts in the twenty-first century.[55]

Access to black theatre manuscripts has expanded exponentially with the advent of the Alexander Street Press digitization project, *Black Drama.* Released in 2001 and updated in a second edition in 2007 and a third in 2018, this ongoing project to digitize black dramas across a vast geographical and chronological range has made available a significant number of previously unpublished black plays.[56] Whereas only three black-authored FTP plays had been published in the *Black Theatre U.S.A* anthologies, well-resourced libraries and theatre companies are now able to pay for access to a wider range of previously unpublished and unstaged black Federal Theatre dramas. The publication of black theatre manuscripts in anthologies and on digital platforms marks a real advance in facilitating our understanding of the variety and rich heritage of black theatre making in the first half of the twentieth century. However, such an understanding remains partial without knowledge of the history of manuscripts published for the first time, and as long as we continue to view the published text as a "reified object that represents conclusion or intention."[57] *Black Theater U.S.A.* and *Black Drama* provide few clues as to the selection process for the manuscripts that were published for the first time.[58] The relationship between the texts published in the 1970s and the versions developed during the Federal Theatre period is important to the history and practice of black theatre: the variant manuscripts originating in the FTP and the broader archive of their making offer insight into how and why federal theatre manuscripts mattered to the communities that produced them; and this history continues to shape which texts are read and performed today. Understanding the history of black manuscripts allows us to consider black dramas on their own ground and examine how they were developed by African American playwrights and black troupes, as well as the ways in which they were contested, revised, and reinterpreted by broader black performance communities in the 1930s and beyond.

Black Theatre Manuscripts and the Negro Units

Positioning black theatre manuscripts at the center of our analysis foregrounds black creativity. Such an approach does not minimize the formidable obstacles black Americans faced. In fact black theatre manuscripts document both structural inequality and racist practices that underpin black theatre and performance histories within and beyond the Federal Theatre. Focusing on black theatre manuscripts, however, does represent a different approach to that taken by previous studies of race and black drama in the FTP. Early accounts of the Federal Theatre either made little mention of African American participation in the project or viewed Negro Units only from the perspective of what it revealed about the FTP and the racial "progressiveness" of its white directors.[59] Since the 1970s, scholars have done important work in documenting the prevalent, personal, and institutional racism that buttressed the project. Drawing on an ever-growing archive, revisionist accounts have pushed back against narratives of progress and good intentions. Rena Fraden's *Blueprints for a Black Federal Theatre*, the first and only book-length study of the Negro Units, examined how "work was managed and culture practically negotiated." It focused on how the FTP's "noble aim" to create a national theatre that included black Americans was undone by its insistence on separating out tightly interwoven "black" and "American" theatre traditions.[60] The recovery of the FTP archive has enabled studies of individual Negro Units and productions including in Seattle (Barry Witham, Tina Redd, and Ronald West), Birmingham, Alabama (John Poole), Chicago (Vanita Marian Vactor), and Harlem (Adrienne Macki Braconi). Collectively, this scholarship has helped broaden our understanding of the diversity of black theatre produced by the Negro Units.[61] However, scholarship on individual Negro Units and productions still tends to be studied in isolation from the history and development of black theatre manuscripts. Moreover, the focus on individual Negro Units and productions can serve to foreground a white-centric narrative in which black aspirations were inevitably thwarted by more or less well-meaning white liberals.[62] By contrast, focusing on black theatre manuscripts allows us to ask how, when, and where African Americans were empowered to create black dramas.

As the FTP archive has grown to incorporate the perspectives of African Americans, historians have begun to understand white dramas staged by Negro Units in a new light. Negro Units staged a considerable number of classic and contemporary white-authored dramas. These were often adapted in imaginative and creative ways by black designers, actors, and directors. As such, it is no surprise that as scholars have turned to reexamine how Negro Units adapted white dramas, they have been drawn to the visually rich and frequently black-originated production archive. As part of her broader study on the federal government as cultural producer, Lauren Sklaroff examines the Chicago Negro Unit production of *Swing Mikado*. Although she takes the "racial agenda" of FTP administrators as her starting point, Sklaroff examines set designs, costume notes, publicity notices, and critical reviews to argue that the Chicago Negro Unit sought to inscribe Gilbert and Sullivan's *Mikado* "with their own racial meaning." Macki Braconi also examines Negro Unit adaptations of white dramas as part of her study of Harlem's community theatres between 1923 and 1939. In productions of George Kelly's *Show Off* and George Bernard Shaw's *Androcles and the Lion,* Macki Braconi argues that the Harlem Negro Unit was able to "reinscribe" these white dramas to speak to the concerns of a black audience.[63]

Production archives have helped create new narratives that center black agency. Black theatre manuscripts, however, continue to receive minimal attention. The history of loss, recovery, and transfer of the FTP archive and the multiple, and often variant, copies of manuscripts held by the archives make the process of identifying a working script for any FTP production a difficult, but no less important, task. Although her focus is not on black theatre, Elizabeth Osborne attends to the question of variant manuscripts in her study of regional FTP productions in Chicago, Boston, and Portland, as well as touring shows that reached rural parts of the South and Midwest. In her analysis of the Chicago FTP's musical revue, *O Say Can You Sing*, Osborne draws on production materials and playbills and a comparison of scripts to determine the different purposes for which they were produced. The revisions to the manuscript, Osborne suggests, "illustrate attention to far more than simple artistic integrity," for they reveal the "volatile milieu in which certain FTP activities were inexplicably halted," as well as the creativity with which productions were altered to accommodate the demands of local communities. Such accommodation sometimes meant that the version used in production lacked the "biting, fresh, and witty" humor found in the earlier or "original."[64] Examining variant manuscripts raises questions about how and why certain avenues were foreclosed by unit supervisors and FTP administrators, and who was able to use the resources of the federal government to create exciting new dramas. In the case of black dramas, the existence of multiple versions of Federal Theatre manuscripts is of particular value, for it it allows us to move beyond understanding what was considered unsuitable for the stage by whites and toward a richer knowledge of what was important to African Americans.

In Dialogue with Black Literature

Black Federal Theatre deserves more attention. The first two editions of the *Norton Anthology of African American Literature* include only a small sampling of dramatic literature. The third edition, which was published in 2014, includes a greater number of dramas but nothing predating Alice Childress's *Trouble in Mind* (1955). Theodore Ward is the only black dramatist from the Federal Theatre to feature in the 2011 *Companion to African American Literature*.[65] This neglect reflects the uncertain status of black dramatic literature more broadly within the academy. Looking at African American literature anthologies in the mid-1990s, Sandra Richards suggested that one could be forgiven for thinking that drama was "not a species of literature."

Dramatic literature remains on the margins of criticism, a "disreputable member of the family of literature."[66] The instability of dramatic texts and the consequent challenges associated with publishing an authoritative text have contributed to making dramatic literature the poorer relation in the construction of Western literary canons. Publication has been crucial in securing status for dramatic texts, both as the legitimate subject of scholarly debate and for theatrical revival. This is particularly the case for black theatre manuscripts, whose status is also contingent on that of the playwrights and communities that produced them. For black Federal Theatre manuscripts, their marginal status has also been exacerbated by the time lag between their production in the 1930s and publication beginning in the 1970s.

Black Federal Theatre dramas have also yet to secure their place in histories of American theatre. Hill and Hatch's *A History of African American Theatre* has a chapter dedicated to the Federal Theatre. However, the *Cambridge History of American Theatre* mentions black dramas and dramatists of the FTP only in passing, while the 2013 *Cambridge Companion to African American Theatre* contains not a single reference to a black Federal Theatre drama or dramatist. More recently, the Negro Units and black-authored dramas received some attention in Kathy Perkins and Barry Witham's chapters, respectively, in the *Oxford Handbook of American Drama*.[67] Collectively, these histories of American theatre omit any discussion of variant manuscripts. Yet black theatre manuscripts are an important part of theatre history and histories of American literature: understanding their evolution puts black dramatic literature back into dialogue with the broader cultural milieu it inhabited and shaped in the 1930s. As the chapters of this book demonstrate, FTP dramas were the product of conversations with poets, novelists, and essayists about the representation of black life in the arts and the direction of radical black politics.

Choosing Theatre Manuscripts

This study focuses on theatre manuscripts authored and developed by African Americans in black performance communities as part of the FTP. As such, the choice of plays was determined by whether there was evidence of dialogue and debate over the manuscript on the part of the performance community. The nature and scope of collaboration are often documented in multiple, variant manuscripts, as well as in correspondence between playwrights, Negro Unit members, community activists, and FTP supervisors.

Because I am interested in African Americans' conversations about black drama, rather than the perspectives of the white producers and directors who often chose what would be produced, whether or not a play was staged during the lifetime of the FTP is not the determining criterion for selection in this study. However, dramas that were staged, or at least scheduled for production, tend to have both a greater number and greater variety of variant manuscripts. For example, there are multiple manuscripts for both Theodore Ward's *Big White Fog* (staged in Chicago, 1937, and New York, 1940) and Theodore Browne's *Natural Man* (Seattle, 1937; New York, 1941). By contrast, there appears to be just one Federal Theatre manuscript of Browne's *Go Down Moses* (1938), which was rehearsed but never staged. On the other hand, Abram Hill and John Silvera's Living Newspaper *Liberty Deferred* (1937–38) was never staged by the FTP yet exists in multiple drafts: it was subject to constant revision as the playwrights negotiated with the white supervisors who could give the green light to production. There are only single manuscripts for the Hartford Negro Unit's Living Newspaper *Stars and Bars* (1937–38) and Hughes Allison's *Panyared* (1939), neither of which was staged during the lifetime of the project. The book also considers variant manuscripts for white-authored dramas adapted by the Negro Units, including the multiple manuscripts of William Dubois's *Haiti* (New York, 1938) and Paul Peters and George Sklar's *Stevedore* (New York, 1934; Seattle, 1936). I also explore the relationship between dramas staged by Negro Units and subsequent collaborations developed outside the FTP, most notably Richard Wright's *Native Son*. As a member of the Chicago Negro Unit, Wright had pushed for production of *Hymn to the Rising Sun*, a chaingang drama by the white southerner Paul Green. Wright would go on to collaborate with Green in a 1941 stage adaptation of his novel. Tracing the journey of Wright's hero Bigger Thomas offers insight into the complex processes that remolded black heroes as they made the leap from page to stage.

There are a number of other black Federal Theatre manuscripts that were developed during the project but do not feature significantly in *Radical Black Theatre*, either because there are no extant Federal Theatre manuscripts or other evidence of collaboration between members of the performance community, or because they did not originate in the Federal Theatre. Ralf Coleman and Jack Bates, for example, wrote and staged a number of black folk dramas for the Boston Unit; in New York City, the Harlem Negro Unit also began its program with versions of previously staged black-authored dramas, Frank Wilson's *Walk Together Chillun* and Rudolph Fisher's *Conjure*

Man Dies; Harlem Unit supervisor Gus Smith and the white playwright Peter Morrel co-authored *Turpentine*, a labor play recognized by black reviewers as an important social document, but "not to be recommended for its dramatic integrity."[68] This book does not attend to innovative experiments in other areas of the performing arts, which sometimes fell under the remit of the FTP and which have been examined elsewhere. For example, the New York African Dance Unit featured in Harlem Negro Unit productions and also staged their own productions, including Momodu Johnson's *Bassa Moona*.[69] This project focuses on black dramas that challenged genre conventions and audience expectations, thereby expanding the possibilities for a radical black theatre in the 1930s.

Forward-Facing Radicalism

Engaging with 1930s federal theatre manuscripts in different stages of revision allows us to consider how radical ideas were rehearsed, contested, and sometimes staged in a particular historical moment, rather than through the lens of Cold War America. Accounts of black federal theatre drama tend to read backward, for they draw on revised theatre manuscripts published in the 1974 anthology *Black Theater U.S.A.* rather than those manuscripts developed during the Federal Theatre Project.[70] Barbara Foley warns against the dangers of reading backward from the standpoint of a historiography so satiated in "anticommunism" that it is "difficult to track." For her study of Ralph Ellison's 1952 novel, *Invisible Man*, Foley uses Ellison's early drafts and notes for the novel, as well as journalism and fiction in the 1930s and 1940s to "read forward."[71] *Radical Black Theatre* examines a broad collection of variant manuscripts developed between 1935 and 1939. It situates these evolving manuscripts within the context of debates within black communities and theatre circles about how to produce politically engaged art in the 1920s and 1930s. The federal theatre's rich production archive, especially the detailed production bulletins, as well as correspondence, playbills, reviews, and audience surveys, makes it possible to identify how and why manuscripts were revised, and sometimes even by whom. Rather than seek to establish either an "original" or "authoritative" text, my research into manuscripts helps us appreciate what was important to black communities involved in play making in the 1930s. At the same time, understanding the provenance, history, and relationship between multiple manuscripts helps establish which version of a manuscript was likely staged by the FTP and watched by black and white audiences in the 1930s. This is important because it illuminates not only the text, but also the conflicts that took place within black communities, as well as between black communities and white producers and directors, over which version of a drama should be presented to audiences. Where revisions to manuscripts are at the center of debates within black communities, I document my method for establishing the relationship between different versions of manuscripts within the chapters. I also include an Appendix, which describes the location, provenance, and relationship between copies of black federal theatre manuscripts held across multiple archives and, where available, the published text: for reading forward requires that we understand the relationship between the variant manuscripts and their connection to published texts.

Identifying and tracing the relationship between black theatre manuscripts not only enables us to access the history of radical black theatre, it also opens up new ways to understand histories of African American radicalism, the left, and the black Cultural Front. The anticommunist/procommunist binary of the Cold War years has crept beyond the boundaries of World War II to distort our understanding of the scope, scale, and meaning of radicalism in the first half of the twentieth century. Histories of the House Committee on Un-American Activities and Propaganda (known as the Dies Committee after its chairman) and its role in the demise of the FTP in 1939 have been partly responsible for this distortion. Established in 1938 for the purpose of investigating extremism at both ends of the political spectrum, congressional committee hearings into un-American activities in federal agencies, including the WPA arts projects, lasted through the autumn and winter of 1938–1939. From the perspective of southern Democrats and Republicans looking to dismantle Franklin Roosevelt's New Deal, the high-profile investigation into the arts projects and the acrimonious questioning of FTP officials confirmed their already strongly held belief that WPA works programs were a waste of taxpayers' money. In June 1939, Congress voted to cease funding the theatre project. Viewed through the retrospective lens of postwar McCarthyism, the Dies Committee became an important staging post in the clampdown against radical activism in all its manifestations. In some accounts, the Dies Committee has become an all-encompassing explanation for why dramas developed during the FTP were, or were not, staged. In such narratives, not just the health, but the very existence, of radical politics and culture are measured according to which dramas did or did not make it to the federal stage, and how much they were tempered by conservative forces. Dramas that were contested, altered, or outright rejected become de facto evidence of how radicalism was on the wane, crushed by the state or self-censorship in the late 1930s. Such narratives are problematic for they too easily elide attempts to delegitimize radical voices and the actual marginalization of radical politics.[72]

Congressional hearings may have encouraged some FTP administrators to err on the side of caution when it came to deciding which shows to produce in the later stages of the project. Yet there is little evidence to suggest that the Dies Committee or broader articulations of anticommunism dampened radical ambition across the FTP. In fact, as this book demonstrates, playwrights, actors, directors, and black performance communities continued to develop, rehearse, and promote radical new dramas right up until the project closed in June 1939. When we consider the ways in which black performance communities repurposed the resources of the FTP to create radical black dramas, it becomes difficult to view the second half of the 1930s as a period when radical creativity was crushed out of existence.

If the influence of the Dies Committee on radical theatre developed in the 1930s has been overstated, the consequences for subsequent histories of the project have not. As the first of the arts projects to be shut down, the taint of un-Americanism had a considerable impact on the fate of the FTP archive and the writing of federal theatre history during the Cold War. It haunted the account written by Hallie Flanagan, in 1940. In *Arena*, Flanagan offered the full rebuttal that she was not able to make when she appeared before the Dies Committee in December 1938. Disavowing the idea of the federal theatre as a radical and un-American experiment, Flanagan traced her liberal vision for the project. Certainly the national director had wanted a theatre that experimented with form; but her values were firmly rooted in a theatre that affirmed America's democratic promise and celebrated its regional and ethnic diversity. If there was room for criticism of the status quo, there was not, in her mind, space for drama that questioned the founding principles and values of the American system. Flanagan was able to use the FTP archive to help craft her story, securing a loan of the records to Vassar and a Rockefeller Foundation grant to support their processing.[73] Returned to the Library of Congress in 1940, the neglected archive did little to inform understanding of New Deal culture for the next thirty years.

By the time the FTP archive was open for business in the 1970s, historians had long been debating whether President Roosevelt's New Deal had shored up or shaken up the American order.[74] What both sides could agree on was that the 1930s had done little to develop an enduring and significant art. If conservatives believed that the socially responsible art of the

1930s held little aesthetic value, those on the left lamented what they saw as a failure to develop radical new forms capable of overthrowing the capitalist order. Such views were often contained within a dichotomous frame that positioned modernists as the vanguard of formal experimentation and leftist political artists as enemies of bourgeois "form-searchers." Irrevocably committed to a "heavy-handed documentary realism," the easily co-opted left apparently failed to develop a blueprint for an alternative future, while the Federal Arts Projects were no more than a "bland middle-brow celebration" of an America whose New Deal was the "apotheosis of the American reform tradition."[75]

In the 1990s, growing dissatisfaction with the binaries that had shaped historical studies during the Cold War encouraged historians to move away from "judging" the culture of the 1930s as conservative, insignificant, or both. Foley demonstrated that many artists on the left were committed to formal experimentation as a method for communicating radical ideas. The manifestos of John Reed Clubs, for example, included a commitment to innovation in form as part of the development of a radical new culture.[76] The new scholarship looked for radicalism beyond the Communist Party and the radical margins. Histories of the left broadened to include an array of Popular Front organizations as well as literary and cultural groups, including the Federal Arts Projects. Michael Denning's 1997 study, *The Cultural Front*, offered a bold new interpretation of the Popular Front, arguing that the growth of labor organizing had an impact stretching well beyond union members and party organizers: the Cultural Front had become the "culture of the nation."[77] For Denning and others, the significance of the Cultural Front lay in both its ubiquity and its longevity. Extending its time frame into the second half of the century, revisionists have been keen to show how the radicalism of the 1930s was not suddenly destroyed by the Soviet-Nazi pact of 1939 and the Second World War; perhaps anticommunism in the postwar era was so virulent and pernicious because radical voices were not so easily silenced.

Harder to Hear: Alternative Radicals

Some of the most radical and more difficult to silence voices in the middle decades of the twentieth century belonged to African Americans. That they have become harder to hear is, at least in part, a product of Cold War narratives of widespread and sudden retreat from the left on the part of black artists. Such narratives amplify the disavowal of former communists Ralph

Ellison and Richard Wright at the expense of other radical artists.[78] The work of Foley, Bill Mullen, Alan Wald, Nikhil Pal Singh, and Brian Dolinar, among others, has opened up new possibilities and sites for exploring radical protest in and beyond the 1930s. Crucially, it has challenged us to think about how and in what ways African Americans made, engaged and even disregarded Communist Party USA (CPUSA) and Popular Front strategies.[79] As Singh has argued, we must recognize the possibility that African Americans distanced themselves from the CPUSA, "not because they sought (or feared for) mainstream acceptance but because they perceived the party as not being radical enough."[80] In the middle decades of the twentieth century, there was a vibrant network of black international activists, intellectuals, and artists that transgressed national and organizational boundaries, and that alternately embraced and rejected the organized left. Such a list might include the writers Lloyd Brown and Chester Himes, playwright Theodore Ward, composer and activist Shirley Graham Du Bois, as well as thinkers and activists Audley Moore, Eslanda Robeson, W. E. B. Du Bois, Esther Cooper Jackson, George Padmore, Grace P. Campbell, and Claudia Jones. It is important that it neither "starts nor ends with Wright."[81] While some became, and remained, committed supporters of communism and of the CPUSA, others tired of being told that anticolonialism and the race struggle were subordinate to the class struggle. They chose to strike out in new directions independent of the organized far left. The CPUSA had no monopoly on radicalism or even the radical left in the middle decades of the twentieth century. As the century progressed, some black radicals came to believe that the black freedom struggle was more important to American communism than American communism was to the black freedom struggle.[82]

Keeping in mind that communism was not the only radicalism in town allows for more complex readings of black political theatre. Communism was not a litmus test for radicalism in black communities: representing it in dramatic terms was a discursive gesture, one that understood black political ambitions as up for debate. In other words, just because communists were not represented as the enemies of black Americans in black dramas, it did not follow that they were the only, or even the preferred, saviors. Acknowledging this fact opens up black theatre manuscripts to readings that do not privilege class to the exclusion of gender and race. It offers insight into the debates that took place within black communities about gender hierarchies in social movements, intrarace racism, and black nationalism, themes prominent in the dramas of Ward, Hill and Silvera, Allison, and Browne. Decentering communism also allows for a renewed focus on how black communities staged these debates. Just as the close association of the literature of the left with social/socialist realism has eclipsed the left's commitment to formal experimentation, it has also covered over the distinctive modes and methods for staging black political theatre in the 1930s. Political dramas such as Ted Ward's *Big White Fog* cannot be understood only in relation to the Cultural Front or black nationalism; they are also part of long-standing and ongoing debates within black communities about how to stage black political ambition in American theatres. Attending to these debates also helps us understand black theatre manuscripts as being produced by black women, as well as black men. Understanding how and when African American women were able to shape radical black theatre is especially important in the context of the gendered practices that structured which dramas were performed and preserved.

Black women have been marginalized in the archives and historical writing on black theatre and on black radicalism. Histories of black radicalism have tended to privilege black men as agents of change, and theatre history has done little to correct this.[83] Although a small number of black women found opportunities in the FTP, including Shirley Graham as a composer and Katherine Dunham as a pioneer of modern dance, when it came to developing what it saw as the serious business of drama, the federal theatre understood black playwriting as a masculine pursuit.[84] Although this reflected a broader trend that crossed racial boundaries (out of a total of 2,745 FTP productions, only 532, or slightly less than 20 percent were written by women), it is striking that black women, who had been prodigious creators of black drama and theatre in the 1910s and 1920s, received so little formal recognition as originators of drama and theatre in the 1930s. Zora Neale Hurston worked briefly as a drama coach for the FTP, but the project did not stage any of her dramatic works. The National Service Bureau, (NSB), which approved manuscripts for production, had on file a number of Georgia Douglas Johnson's lynching dramas: none were considered seriously for production by Negro Units.[85] The focus on individual playwrights as originators of black theatre manuscripts serves to confirm the narrative of men as makers of black culture. Attending instead to the collaborative process of play making in black performance communities reveals the important roles played by the many unacknowledged collaborators who were women. Rose McClendon, Edna Thomas, Gwen Reed, and Shirley Graham were supervisors, writers, directors, and play makers in Negro Units in Chicago, New York, Hartford, and Seattle. African American women were central to the development of black dramas and performance communities in other capacities, too. Sara Oliver defined the role of female leads for the Seattle Negro Unit; in Chicago, Gladys Boucree took on the difficult role of Ella Mason, a female lead who challenges male leadership in *Big White Fog*; Fredi Washington, a stage and screen actress and a founder of the Negro Actors Guild, occupied an important position as a member of the black advisory committee for the New York FTP. African American women were not encouraged to create black theatre manuscripts during the FTP, yet they played important roles in shaping their development and production: on play-reading committees and as audience members they critiqued, amended, and contributed to collaborative black manuscripts; they took on positions of leadership as Negro Unit supervisors and directors; they played lead roles in Negro Unit productions; and they led protests against discrimination and job cuts on the FTP. Black women helped forge a radical black theatre.

To Stage a Leap: Black Radical Traditions

Black performance communities explored the idea of a radical black tradition in federal theatre manuscripts. They also considered how, and if, radical ideas could be staged within an American theatre tradition. To understand these experiments in the historical moment that produced them requires that we recognize radicalism as a site of contest rather than a destination. Radical black traditions are the product of rich and disputed histories in which the very idea of tradition is seen as being in conflict with, if not the obverse of, radicalism. Yet tradition making is, like radicalism, a creative and ongoing process, "a socially embodied and historically extended discursive terrain on which the identity of a community is argued out."[86] Radicalism has too often become a way of reifying or attributing significance to the words and actions of men. To engage with a radical black tradition that is shaped by the thoughts and actions of black women as well as men is to engage with an ongoing process of contestation and creativity, rather than a singular, historically fixed notion of what it is to be radical. In using radicality as a frame through which to understand black federal theatre manuscripts, I am interested in the idea of radicalism, not so much as an end point, but rather as a place to begin.[87] New insights are possible if we start with the premise that African Americans could be architects of a radical future in the middle decades of the twentieth century. New avenues of inquiry are opened if we understand black manuscripts as a valued site for carrying and enabling radical visions.

There is a rich body of scholarship that examines the idea of a radical black tradition and asks who or what is allowed to carry its name, and who gets to decide. It explores the price, promise, and risk involved when people, plays, ideas, get categorized within or outside a black radical tradition and considers the relationship between agency and radicality.[88] One of the interventions I have found most useful has been the idea of the leap. In a conference roundtable discussion subsequently published in *Small Axe* (2013), scholars of black radicalism considered "The Idea of the Radical Black Tradition." Singh riffed on Farah Griffin's discussion of Pearl Primus, the black dancer and choreographer, who in the early 1940s persuaded the white impresario Barney Josephson to let her perform at his interracial nightclub, Café Society, in downtown New York City: "When she leaped, he had to make *space* for her. And I thought that was really interesting because the initiative comes from the *leap*. It is not that the leap is oriented toward a pre-existing horizon, like democracy or freedom or emancipation. . . . The leap itself is an *engendering* of freedom, and it creates consequences in the world that actually really matter."[89] Reckoning with this leap is, as Singh acknowledges, at least in part, an aesthetic issue, one that poses questions about how black artists showed this leap in their work. This book explores how black performance communities in the 1930s crafted black theatre manuscripts that imagined a leap. It argues that this creative practice often required its own freedom-engendering leap. Sometimes this leap was not immediately apparent or universally recognized; often it was subsumed within, or hidden among, more acceptable modes of black performance. Black theatre manuscripts and the performance communities that created them operated in the context of a history of masking and indirect critique: some reinforced stereotypes of black life; others avoided contentious subjects; still others drew on white conceptions of black music and dance to disguise their radical voices. The black federal theatre manuscripts examined in this book adapted, rejected, revised, reinvented, and satirized accepted modes of performing blackness. In the process they created space for new ways of representing black aspirations in American dramatic literature and on U.S. stages.

Black federal theatre manuscripts are part of a long tradition of radical black theatre manuscripts that defy audience and generic expectations and date back to William Wells Brown's 1857 play, *The Escape, A Leap for Freedom*. The first drama published by an African American, *The Escape* mixes melodrama with satire, minstrelsy, and the slave narrative form to dramatize the black struggle for freedom. Having escaped enslavement and become an accomplished orator and professional abolitionist, Brown understood the power and appeal of black performance: "There are some places," he reflected, "where it would take better than a lecture; people will pay to hear the Drama that would not give a cent in an anti-slavery meeting."[90] Eliding acceptable ways of performing blackness, Brown made space for black knowledge about race and slavery. *The Escape* is a hybrid drama that slips between and satirizes generic conventions for performing blackness. Although it was well received on the antislavery speaking circuit, it was more than a century before *The Escape* received a professional staging and before it was understood as something more than a "hodge-podge."[91] During the four years of the federal theatre, black federal theatre manuscripts provoked different responses from the constituencies who engaged them: many were the product of black performance communities, who cherished them; others provoked creative conflict; to white critics, black dramas could be a source of bafflement, while some never made it past white gatekeepers to reach a broader audience. But because they were kept in official federal archives and in prized personal collections, we know that between 1935 and 1939, black theatre artists leaped; and sometimes, the federal theatre made space for them. The chapters that follow explore how, when, where, and to what end black theatre artists were able to use this space to develop radical black theatre in the second half of the 1930s.

Chapter Overview

African Americans have long been excluded from the forums and institutions used by white theatre practitioners to test their ideas about form and to experiment with genre. In the 1930s, black performance communities found alternative spaces to develop methods for representing black life on the American stage. On the pages of black federal theatre manuscripts, in theatre reviews and letters to black newspapers, and through their participation as audience members in integrated theatres, African Americans mapped the contours of a radical black theatre. The first two chapters explore how African Americans tried on different forms and stretched genre boundaries. In the early 1930s, the progressive white theatre world was deeply divided over social realism and regularly debated whether realist or nonrealist theatre was best placed to stir new audiences to action. Critics of social realism saw it as depoliticizing escapism, a form of bourgeois wish fulfillment: audiences might relate to ordinary heroes who triumph over injustice, but the temporary catharsis of make-believe worlds was a distraction from the hard work of activism proper. Advocates of social realism, however, insisted that empathy rather than alienation was central to political education, pointing to the limited appeal of agitprop, whose stock villains and amateur production values did little to attract audiences who had been lured away from theatre by the slick entertainments of Hollywood. While these debates were far from settled when the FTP began in 1935, social realism was regaining a foothold in the noncommercial theatre world. The establishment of the Group Theatre (1931) and the Theatre Union (1933) in New York anchored social realism to progressive causes in the second half of the 1930s. But if the political efficacy of social realist dramas rested in their power to foster empathy and character identification, they were seldom designed with the needs of African American audiences in mind. The long history of white control of black performance and segregated audiences meant that empathy, escapism, and wish fulfillment were rarely available to black audiences of realist theatre.

The first chapter examines how African Americans influenced these debates and made space for their own ideas about realism on the eve of the federal theatre. It focuses on the production history of the immensely popular *Stevedore,* a white-authored labor drama with a "racial twist," which was first produced by the Theatre Union in New York City in 1934. When the white lynch mob arrives to lynch the black hero (who has been framed on a rape charge for being a labor organizer), the black dock workers fight back with the help of white union men. While both black and white critics regarded the drama's interracial ending as improbable, they drew markedly different conclusions as to its significance. White commercial critics mocked *Stevedore* as escapist melodrama and leftist wish fulfillment. Black critics and audiences looked past the interracial ending, and instead welcomed the opportunity for black actors to talk back to white people and publicly articulate black solidarity before integrated audiences. When *Stevedore* was staged by the Seattle Negro Unit two years later, the interracial ending was downplayed, and possibly dropped altogether. On the federal stage, black men appear to resist the white mob alone. In New York and Seattle black performance communities found ways to make social realism a politically useful tool for mobilizing audiences and building black performance communities. Blurring the boundaries between black performances on and off stage, inside and beyond the theatre walls, they developed a black realism. Black realism disrupted white racial narratives and white notions of a universal dramatic tradition; black realism gave black actors, directors, and audiences the chance to talk back and to compel whites to listen; black realism recognized that "you don't need a raised platform to make a stage."[92]

The limits of existing models of both realist and nonrealist theatre are under scrutiny in the two black Living Newspapers examined in Chapter 2: *Liberty Deferred,* developed by Abram Hill and John Silvera, and the Hartford Negro Unit's *Stars and Bars.* Hill and Silvera worked as playreaders for the National Service Bureau, where they were tasked with assessing the suitability of plays for production by units of the FTP. As African Americans, they were regularly asked to review "race" dramas, many of which were authored by white Americans. Exposed to the recurring tropes that sustained black racial inferiority in American theatre, they decided to create their own Living Newspaper in 1937. The Living Newspaper was a new form inspired by Russian and European workers theatres and remodeled for the American stage by the Federal Theatre Project. In the words of Morris Watson, who supervised the FTP Living Newspaper Unit, they "Combine the newspaper and the theatre and to hell with the traditions of both."[93] Unsurprisingly, they were contentious from the outset, not least because they dramatized America's social problems through a mixture of verbatim reportage, satire, and experimental staging. Within the Federal Theatre Project, *Liberty Deferred* was part of a broader struggle to control the parameters of formal experimentation. But it also presented a distinct challenge because it questioned how radical the FTP was prepared to be when it came to shining the spotlight on the racial practices of American theatre. White director of the NSB, Emmet Lavery, did not share Hill and Silvera's vision of what a Living Newspaper could be. When he attempted to persuade the playwrights to temper *Liberty Deferred*'s searing critique of racial injustice, the black dramatists responded by mocking Lavery's paternalism on the pages of their manuscript. Parodying the Living Newspaper's purportedly radical new form, *Liberty Deferred* documents how New Deal reformism both inspired and resisted radical new theatre. The limitations of white liberalism were also a prominent theme of a second black Living Newspaper, *Stars and Bars.* Long credited to the young white dramatist Ward Courtney, the federal theatre manuscript clearly documents the coauthorship of black members of the Hartford Negro Unit. The Hartford Living Newspaper includes a scene authored by Alver Napper, a local black activist and member of the unit. "Drama of the Slums" is an unmistakable parody of the FTP's most prized and popular Living Newspaper about America's housing crisis, *One Third of a Nation.* Examining the two black Living

Newspapers together offers insight into the variety of techniques black theatre workers deployed—both on and off stage—to compel white administrators and theatre professionals to engage with the history and practice of
black performance and white spectatorship. Black Living Newspapers shine
the spotlight on the racism inherent within all U.S. theatre, but they use
innovative techniques to show up the racist underpinnings of the Federal
Theatre Project. Although *Liberty Deferred* and *Stars and Bars* failed to make
the leap from page to stage in the 1930s, the black Living Newspaper is an
important part of the history of the FTP and the black dramatic tradition.
The protest engendered by the failure to stage a single black Living Newspaper compelled white administrators to confront their racialized assumptions about what constituted black theatre and black "reality." By making
visible the racial narrative that underpinned the performative techniques
of even progressive theatre, black Living Newspapers made space for other
black dramatists in the Federal Theatre Project.

The first half of the book considers the ways in which black performance
communities engaged with questions of form in a number of forums: through
adapting white social realist dramas; on the manuscript pages of unpublished and unstaged black Living Newspapers; and in black journals and
newspapers. The second half explores what new roles and forms were made
available for black actors and audiences when dramas devised and written
by African Americans were actually staged. Black federal theatre dramas
were the product of creative conflict between African American dramatists,
directors, critics, and audiences, as well as collaboration and struggle between black and white artists, directors, and producers who worked to put
black heroes on the stage. Harriet Tubman, John Henry, Victor Mason, Lonnie Thompson, Binnie, and Henri Christophe were heroes who spurned
white values, challenged white power, and sought no redemption for their
transgressions. Sometimes they triumphed; often they were destroyed. In
defeat, black heroes were not tragic in the traditional sense: their unravel-
ing revealed no innate capacity for self-destruction. Instead, the black self
is undone by the legacy of slavery and the dehumanizing institutions of Jim
Crow America. Black heroes who suffer in black-authored dramas do not
echo the scenes of subjection that characterize the dramas of Paul Green
and other white dramatists of black life in the 1930s: in black theatre manuscripts black heroes recount injustices past, participate in ongoing freedom struggles, and articulate the needs and desires of African Americans
in the present. While they cannot restore nor remedy what has been lost

through enslavement, they inhabit a level of black agency seldom seen on the American stage.

Chapter 3 examines one of the best known heroes of all. John Henry was at the center of debates about the role of the black hero in 1930s American culture. Theodore Browne made him the subject of *Natural Man*, a drama first staged in 1937 by the Seattle Negro Unit where Browne was playwright-in-residence. A hard-working steel-driving man, criminalized by laws designed to keep black men in their place, John Henry takes on and is defeated in a competition with a steam-drill. Though there is no triumph or redemption in his death, John Henry lives, labors, and dies resisting. Adapted four years later by the American Negro Theatre (ANT), the community theatre established in Harlem in the aftermath of the FTP, John Henry emerges as a different kind of hero. Accepting his death with the willed subjection expected of black heroes, the ANT's John Henry is rewarded with the promise of heaven and the recognition of his virtue by white onlookers. Browne's hero raised questions about who the black hero was really for and what new models must be built before he might be made anew. Such questions shaped broader debates about the role of the black hero, including the acrimonious collaboration between Richard Wright and Paul Green on the stage adaptation of Wright's debut novel. Bigger Thomas, the complex black protagonist of *Native Son*, who refused to absolve whites of responsibility for America's racial crimes, attracted large Broadway audiences at the same time that John Henry moved mountains on a small Harlem stage. As John Henry traveled from the theatres of Seattle to Harlem, and Bigger stepped out of Wright's Chicago novel onto the Broadway stage of Orson Welles, African Americans debated how they might produce black heroes legible to black as well as white audiences.

Chapter 4 examines another black hero seeking redemption. In Theodore Ward's *Big White Fog*, Vic Mason searches for, but cannot find, a better life for his family in the black nationalist Garvey movement; his son, Les, looks for answers in the interracial communist movement. Both men and both movements come undone, for they rely on the gender hierarchies that sustain racial capitalism in the United States. Focusing on the history of the Chicago Negro Unit production and the much redrafted manuscript, this chapter explores the controversy that began when Ward read a draft of his play before a South Side audience in January 1938. Drawing on variant manuscripts and the archive of black responses to early drafts, this chapter documents the role of Chicago's black performance community in shaping the version of the play first staged by the Chicago Negro Unit at the Great Northern Theatre in April 1938. The responses of the local community make it clear that it was the staging of gender and racial divisions within black families and political movements, rather than communism, that made *Big White Fog* a provocative play in 1938. Moreover, the sympathetic portrayal of the Garvey movement reminds us that communism was not the only radical path for African Americans in the 1930s. At the same time, the variant theatre manuscripts of *Big White Fog*—dating from 1938 through its first publication in 1974 and beyond—attest to the anticommunist/procommunist binary that has long shaped the knowledge production of black theatre. Viewed through the lens of the Cold War, Ward's play has been made an example of 1930s socialist realism, with its purported promise of a better future in the interracial brotherhood of the working class. Such repackaging ignores the generic codes and complexities of the play: in the 1930s, *Big White Fog* was not a socialist realist drama, but rather a black family drama that deploys domestic tragedy as a vehicle to explore black political ambition. If, as Barbara Foley suggests, we learn to read forward, then we will hear a powerful critique of race and gender, as well as class hierarchies within American society. We also see the myriad ways in which black cultural producers sought to communicate radical ideas in the 1930s.

The final chapter begins by examining the Harlem Negro Unit's immensely popular production of *Haiti*. Authored by a white New York journalist named William Dubois, white theatre critics attempted to place *Haiti* within a white dramatic tradition of black primitivism. In contrast, the black performance community worked to transform Dubois's racist play into a celebration of Haiti's founding heroes. Toussaint L'Ouverture and Henri Christophe were portrayed as powerful and self-controlled leaders, and utterly unlike the louche and lazy French generals. *Haiti* did not offer whites the reassuring portraits of failed black masculinity they had grown accustomed to seeing through Eugene O'Neill's *Emperor Jones* and Orson Welles's Haitian *Macbeth*. The Harlem Negro Unit production ends with Christophe standing triumphant before a crowd of cheering, independent Haitians and an enthusiastic interracial audience in Harlem. In the multiple drafts of the manuscript, the theatre pages of New York's black newspapers, and extensive correspondence between Harlem's political leaders and FTP administrators, we see how the black performance community was able to both resist white conceptions of defeated black heroes and stage a drama that turned out well for Harlem. The success of *Haiti* helped the black performance community push the federal theatre to invest in black dramatists.

On the eve of the FTP's closure two new black dramas were being prepared for production. Featuring complex black heroes who forced others to leap, these dramas represented a culmination of the work of black performance communities that had developed around Negro Units. The first, *Panyared* (1939), explores the origins of African slavery and was the first instalment of a historical trilogy by Hughes Allison. The second, Theodore Browne's *Go Down Moses* (1938), is a dramatization of Harriet Tubman's life that examines black agency in ending slavery. Tracing the struggle of Tubman, and other former slaves who fought for the right to fight, Browne's drama was part of a broader movement to create an Afrocentric, politically usable, record of how black Americans had brought about revolutionary changes in the past. Centering on black theatre manuscripts, and the performance communities who developed them, allows us to see how African Americans imagined radical paths to the future.

1 Our Actors May Become Our Emancipators

Race and Realism in *Stevedore*

· ·

"Nothing like it has ever appeared on the American stage before, under the management of white people." William Pickens was describing the Theatre Union's 1934 production of *Stevedore* to readers of the New York *Amsterdam News*. Harlem residents contemplating a trip to the downtown Civic Theatre were reassured that this white-authored drama was not "a play about white people and their conception about Negroes; it is primarily a setting forth of the life of the Negro: and the whites are the incidents, the 'environment.'" Declaring the stage "the best spot on earth" from which to advocate for black rights, he predicted, "Our actors may become our emancipators."[1] Written by George Sklar and Paul Peters, *Stevedore* was a welcome breakthrough for many African Americans because it offered a realistic representation of how black workers were both exploited by, but also resistant to race and class oppression. The plot traces the experiences of a black community of stevedores in New Orleans in the wake of a white woman's false rape charge against a black man. Recalling the red summer of 1919, when black communities in Chicago, Washington, D.C., and other American cities refused to flee their homes or wait passively for white lynch mobs to arrive, black dock workers in *Stevedore* fight back. Barricading their homes and arming themselves against their would-be lynchers, the play climaxes as a black woman brandishes a gun and aims a direct, lethal shot at a white man, proclaiming: "I got him! That red-headed son-of-a-bitch, I got him! I got him!"[2]

Black critics hailed *Stevedore* as a monument to black resistance even as the white playwriting team promoted a socialist realist play that celebrated interracial unionism. Sklar was already a well-known dramatist of working-class life; Peters, whose given name was Harbor Allen, was a contributing editor to *New Masses* and organizer for the American Communist Party's legal arm, the International Labor Defense (ILD). He had spent five years working as a laborer, including on the New Orleans docks, to gather material for his drama of black working-class life. Both playwrights were on the executive board of the Theatre Union, a new coalition of New York–based white playwrights and directors from across the leftist political spectrum. Housed at the Civic Repertory Theatre in Union Square, the theatre collective was dedicated to producing dramas that addressed working people's lives through a class analysis. Unsurprisingly, the Theatre Union promoted *Stevedore* as a labor play. Stage directions indicate that the black dockworkers, who are already successfully fighting off the white lynch mob, are aided by the last-minute arrival of white union men. In performance, however, the production seemed to elevate racial tensions above class conflict in ways that made the interracial ending unexpected and improbable. Outside the leftist theatre community, commentators (both black and white) overwhelmingly interpreted *Stevedore* as a play about black self-determination rather than interracial unionism. This reading shaped subsequent productions. When the Seattle Negro Unit of the Federal Theatre staged *Stevedore* two years later, it is doubtful whether the white reinforcements ever arrive. The black community appeared to fight off the white mob alone.

Stevedore is a good place to begin an examination of black Federal Theatre. Its fascinating production history offers insight into the practices and theoretical debates that framed political theatre on the eve of the FTP. Moreover, the Theatre Union served as an important model for the Federal Theatre in producing collaborative and socially relevant theatre and in developing marketing techniques for attracting new audiences. Both as a play and as a production, *Stevedore* became important to a community of black theatre critics, audiences, and performers who were willing, skilled, and increasingly able to adapt white dramas in order to develop a politically useful black theatre through the Federal Theatre. This chapter examines how black performance communities in New York City and Seattle transformed *Stevedore's* political narrative. Envisaged by its authors and production company as a labor drama that foregrounded interracial unionism, African Americans exploited the self-making possibilities of the production process and became agents of their own liberation. This transformation enabled African Americans to articulate a powerful vision of black freedom at a time when much of the progressive theatre world was consumed by debates about the political efficacy of realist theatre. In the mid-1930s, leftist theatre practitioners were divided over whether realist or nonrealist theatre provided the better spur to revolutionary change. While many were concerned by what they regarded as the escapism inherent in realist dramas, others were more sympathetic to audiences' desire to identify with the characters and scenes enacted before them on the stage. The history of radical black theatre challenges this simple binary and points to the broader range of performance strategies available to, and made possible by, African American theatre practitioners. Eschewing the narrow parameters of the realism/antirealism debate, black performance communities found ways to connect the experiences of performers, critics, and audiences in ways that inspired activism within and beyond the theatre. Examining the production history and reception of *Stevedore*, first in New York, and then on the federal stage in Seattle, reveals how African Americans reimagined the possibilities of dramatic realism and embraced its radical potential.

"A Race Riot with Class Interest":
From *Wharf Nigger* to *Stevedore*

Even before *Stevedore* opened in April 1934, Harlem was primed for a drama of black resistance. In January, the *Amsterdam News* announced that the Theatre Union was preparing "A Play to Expose the Exploitation of Negroes."[3] One of the two major black newspapers published weekly out of Harlem, the *Amsterdam News* played an important role in promoting and interpreting black theatre in New York. Among its theatre correspondents was Afrocentric historian Joel A. Rogers. His appraisal of *Stevedore* considered both its political and theatrical efficacy: "For perhaps the first time Negroes are given the opportunity on the stage to talk back to white people and say what's in their mind." Although Rogers believed interracial cooperation was "probably the only real solution to the race problem," he didn't find it convincingly dramatized in *Stevedore,* judging the play's climax, "where the white radical workers join with the Negroes at the barricade against the white mob" to be the only "unreal scene."[4] Earl Morris, staff correspondent for the *Pittsburgh Courier,* was also unpersuaded that *Stevedore* made an effective case for interracial unity: "The drama . . . fell short of its purpose to cement racial harmony and to shame whites for their treatment of dark Americans." If anything, the play was more akin to *Birth of a Nation,* in fomenting hostility between the races. It might, he prophesized, (correctly) be subject to censorship if it played in other U.S. cities.[5] The critic for the *Norfolk Journal and Guide* identified the scene where black stevedores throw off the role of victim and determine to fight for their lives as the "crowning dramatic moment." Noting that white union men arrive only after the black community have already constructed a barricade and started to fight, he continued: "fortunately for the ideal which this play intends to establish, the black man had already decided his destiny, fought, and conquered when the whites arrived."[6]

White critics were less concerned with black agency, but they agreed that the final scene was not realistic and the theme of interracial unity insufficiently integrated into the structure of the play. In the second of his two reviews for the *New York Times*, Brooks Atkinson suggested that the interracial ending was mere wish fulfilment. John Gessner argued that the play's thesis of interracial union was presumed rather than dramatized, since *Stevedore* lacked a "fully realized presentation of how the masses of white workers overcame their prejudices to the extent of coming to the rescue of the besieged stevedores."[7] The critic for *Time* magazine thought the audience's enthusiastic response to the ending had more to do with the effect of melodrama than interracial solidarity, suggesting that they cheered, "not for the symbolism of a workers' united front, but simply for a thrilling rescue." The *Nation*'s critic concurred: "Those brought up on melodrama may be reminded faintly of the old days when the marines used to get there at the last minute."[8]

The persistence of racial separatism in a play ostensibly about interracial unionism is partly explained by the fact that *Stevedore* began life as a race drama. Peters had written "Wharf Nigger" in the late 1920s after spending several months working on the New Orleans docks as a freight checker. In that southern port city he had witnessed firsthand the hostility between white checkers and black loaders.[9] According to Peters, the earlier play was unsuitable for the Theatre Union because "it dealt with the Negro problem from the race angle rather than from a Marxist approach."[10] Centered on a false rape charge, "Wharf Nigger" dramatized racial hatred: white men are shown to be ignorant, boorish, and malevolent; black men are defined by the physical characteristics attributed to black males in racist ideology. Lonnie Thompson, the hero of *Stevedore*, is called Yallah Thompson in the earlier play, while Blacksnake Johnson is described as "a huge vital Negro." The supporting cast of characters include "an awkward, grotesque Negro," and "a sporty buck." There is little attempt to explore the relationship between race and class oppression and no last-minute rescue by white union men. Distrusting of whites, the black stevedores defend themselves alone.[11]

Scenes from "Wharf Nigger" were published in *New Masses* in November 1929 and April 1930. The Provincetown Theatre in Greenwich Village came close to staging the full play in 1931, but the production was postponed indefinitely after a summer of rehearsals.[12] When the drama of the docks was reworked as *Stevedore* three years later, a number of critics recalled the earlier play. Atkinson remembered that the script had been admired, but in rehearsal it had proved "unactable," "muddled," and "unwieldy." Whereas

"Wharf Nigger" was, "primarily a race relations drama. . . . The rewriting collaboration with Sklar has made it [*Stevedore*] an exciting drama of a race riot with class interest."[13] John Anderson had also read "Wharf Nigger," and in his view the new, collaborative script compared unfavorably with Peters's earlier drama:

> With Mr. Sklar's assistance, presumably, a good deal of material about labor has been brought into it, and the mood of the play confused. In the last-act fight at the barricades, the Negroes, defending their homes against a mob of white lynchers, are saved by the arrival of the union. In franker and older melodramas this graceful duty was always performed by the Crew of the U.S.S. Olympia. It was one of the naïve touches which make "Stevedore" for adult playgoers less effective in the theatre than, for the sake of its cause, it ought to be.[14]

Writing in the New York *Telegram*, Robert Garland found the insertion of the "labor angle" confusing: "I, as an excited onlooker would rather see the back-to-the-wall Negroes win or lose standing on their own than come over the top with the assistance of the American Federation of Labor."[15]

Critics and audiences often choose to see their own politics reflected in the theatre. Ideological opposition to, or even ignorance of, interracial struggles supported by the Communist Party of the USA (CPUSA) might explain why white commercial critics preferred to see black Americans win or lose alone. Similarly, it was understandable that black critics and audiences honed in on *Stevedore*'s message of black self-determination at a time when black actors seldom got to talk back to white authority figures on stage. However, the Theatre Union production and its critical reception were more than a reflection of the personal politics of individual critics; they were also an intervention in ongoing debates about the potential for, and desirability of, genuine interracial cooperation in social movements. By the mid-1930s, moderate black civil rights organizations such as the National Association for the Advancement of Colored People (NAACP) no longer determined the parameters and possibilities of what an integrated America might look like. Since the late 1920s, the CPUSA had vied to shape the cause and course of racial justice for black and white workers. When the Sixth World Congress of the Comintern met in 1928 and declared black Americans an oppressed nation with a right to self-determination, the CPUSA enacted a two-pronged strategy that recognized the role of interracial activism and black nationalism in African American politics and culture. Even if many black Americans were unpersuaded by the CPUSA's black belt thesis—that imagined black Americans from Virginia to Texas as a separate and independent nation—the party's uncompromising defense of the Scottsboro youths and other high-profile victims of America's judicial system convinced many that here, finally, was a political party committed to the pursuit of racial equality.[16] *Stevedore* raised questions as to how far this commitment was shared by the broader organized left. In focusing on the cost to black communities of cooperating with the white labor movement, the drama spoke to broader debates within black American communities about how far existing, white-controlled institutions could be used to effect radical change. The mass appeal of black self-determination, as demonstrated by the popularity of the Garvey movement in the 1920s, and the proven benefits of organizing apart from whites continued to shape black organizing across the political spectrum in the 1930s. Du Bois's public split with the integrationist NAACP, the creation of new all-black organizations such as the National Council of Negro Women in 1935, and the growing power of the black labor union, the Brotherhood of Sleeping Car Porters, were part of an evolving black political landscape that meant that interracial brotherhood was not the only lens through which audiences might interpret *Stevedore*.

Skepticism of interracial organizing is a prominent theme in *Stevedore*. Black characters repeatedly voice their support for race solidarity and their distrust of whites. In Act 2, for instance, the black laborers gather at Binnie's lunch counter to debate the merits of interracial unionism and black self-determination. The debate is not an abstract one, for Lonnie, who is on the run from the authorities after his wrongful arrest, has arrived at the diner in need of protection. While Lonnie contemplates an offer of help from the sympathetic white union leader, his black co-workers are united in their distrust of white men: "Dar ain't no white man you can trust now, Lonnie," they tell him, "We don't want no help from de white folks."[17] Although Lonnie accepts the help of the white union leader in order to escape, his call to action in Act 3 puts race first: "Every time de white boss crack de whip you turn and run. You let him beat you, you let him hound you, you let him work yo' to death. When you gwine to put a stop to it, black man? When you gwine turn on 'em? When you gwine say: 'You can't do that. I'm a man. I got de rights of a man. I'm gwine fight like a man.'"[18]

For Lonnie, the connection between race and class exploitation is clear, but as long as the economic structures that support racial discrimination exist, there can be no peace with whites. African Americans must, in Lonnie's words "fight fo' de right to live." Lonnie's battle cry relies on the

FIGURE 1 Stevedores discuss whether to accept help from a white union leader at Binnie's restaurant. *Stevedore*, Seattle Negro Unit, 1936. Library of Congress, Music Division, Federal Theatre Project Collection, Production Records, Photographic Prints File, Container 1184.

repetition of "We" and "Dey": "Dey" are the whites who make up lynch mobs and murder black Americans; "We," are the black stevedores, their families, and the wider black community. Only at the very end of his speech does Lonnie remind his comrades that they will not take their stand alone, that the leaders of the white union will stand with them. The sole reference to white help appears tacked onto a discussion about black solidarity, black manhood, and black resistance.[19] Lonnie inspires his comrades to fight back by appealing to black pride, rather than by promising white help. Ambivalence on the part of the black stevedores is underscored by their response to the arrival of white union leader, Lem Morris. Although Lonnie lets him into the diner where his comrades are gathered, stage directions indicate that "The NE-GROES regard him with hushed suspicion, and move back from the door."[20]

Lonnie's final speech, delivered as the community prepares for battle in the climactic last scene, makes explicit its gendered, black nationalist vision:

FIGURE 2 Building the Barricade, *Stevedore*, Act 3, Scene 2, Theatre Union, Civic Repertory Theatre, New York City, 1934. Photo by Vandamm Studio© Photographs and Prints Division, Schomburg Center for Research in Black Culture, The New York Public Library.

> You all know what we hyar for. We hyar to defend our homes. We hyar to fight fo' our lives. And we hyar to show 'em dat we ain't gwine be kicked around, and starved and stepped on no mo'. We hyar to show 'em we men and we gwine be treated like men. And remember we ain't only fighting fo' ourselves. Dar black folks all over de country looking at us right now: dey counting on us, crying to us: "Stand yo' ground. You fighting fo' us. You fighting fo' all of us."[21]

The speech is accompanied by the whimpering of an elderly black woman, accentuating the gendered rhetoric of Lonnie's manifesto for black male redemption. Soon after his battle speech, Lonnie is shot down by the white mob. Retaliation is swift, triumphant, and enacted by a woman. It is Binnie, the diner manager, who shoots the white mob leader; it is Binnie who exults, "I got him." Binnie's action spurs others to continue the fight, and inspires her man, Blacksnake, to mount the barricade and declare, "They're running! They're running!" Stage directions indicate that "The shout is picked up by the NEGROES as they swarm up over the barricade and pursue MITCH's mob down the street."[22] Although sympathetic white union men show up and join in the fight, Lonnie has not persuaded his black co-workers of the benefits of the interracial cooperation: Lonnie is the only black man to place faith in the union, the only black man to consider trusting the white labor leader; and Lonnie is the only black man to die.

The growing consensus that the first two acts provided insufficient preparation for the last-minute reinforcement of the black barricade by white union men prompted the playwrights to write a public statement. Published in John Anderson's column in the *Evening Journal,* ten days after the newspaper critic first attacked *Stevedore,* the playwrights were concerned about defending their political beliefs as much as their political play:

> Both of us feel that instead of "muddying" the original play we have in reality clarified it and struck deeper into the real cause of Negro oppression. . . . The opinion has been expressed that it would be preferable to see the Negroes fight it out with Mitch's [white] gang themselves, rather than see white union men "come over the top" like the U.S. Marines. Both of us believe that the Negroes cannot fight it out alone, for that would spell certain doom. We believe that the solution of the Negro problem lies in the unity of black and white workers—a unity which, under the pressure of starvation, of black and white alike, is being welded even in the Deep South much more rapidly than most people dream.[23]

For Peters and Sklar, it was most important that they could point to real and recent examples of such unity. The interracial sharecroppers' union in Camp Hill, Alabama, the white union men who came to the armed defense of their black comrades at the lumber mill in Bogalusa, Louisiana, and the white workers who joined black Americans in resisting police enforcement of segregated bathing regulations in Denver, Colorado, were cited as evidence that Americans should dream bigger. Only at the end of their letter, and only in the loosest of terms, did the authors tie their political views to their dramatic technique: "To us, it seems not only logical thinking but sound drama that white workers, realizing how it is essential to their bitter struggle for wages and half-way livable conditions, should champion the rights of the Negro fellows."[24] Peters and Sklar imagined themselves as two more white workers engaged in the struggle to support the rights of their black comrades. The playwrights' letter suggests they understood that the politics of racial representation did not stop at the theatre door: in publishing a defense of their play in a New York newspaper, the playwrights recognized the broader community who would shape and debate the meaning of *Stevedore*.

From Empathy to Action: The Problem with Realism

Stevedore was a critical and box office success. Embraced by the black press and pronounced a hit by the *New York Times,* the show paid off its production costs of $4,654.68 and brought in a profit of $3,205.41 within the first six weeks.[25] It was regularly reviewed by leading black and white theatre critics in New York and beyond. The left, however, was deeply divided in its response. Some welcomed *Stevedore*, celebrating its contribution to the development of revolutionary theatre and its ability to engage audiences. The *Daily Worker* judged the preview performance "a tremendous advance in the realist portrayal of the life of the American toilers in the theatre," and printed headlines declaring, "'Stevedore' Ranks High in Revolutionary Drama . . . it gets you."[26] In *New Masses*, Michael Gold praised *Stevedore*'s ability to engage audience emotion through the realistic portrayal of working-class characters: "These are plain, hard-working, good humored people such as you and I know, and they are fighting for their lives. You want to help them." For Gold, *Stevedore* marked the arrival of a professional theatre that represented the workers: "here at last the American Revolutionary Movement has begun to find itself adequately expressed on the stage."[27] But even as some on the left praised the power of *Stevedore* to move audiences, others feared the emotional release it inspired during performance might take the place of mobilization beyond the theatre's walls. This anxiety was a legacy of the experiments in form that dominated noncommercial American theatre after World War I.

The development of the Workers' Theatre movement in the 1920s and 1930s challenged the place of realism as the preeminent dramatic form for radical theatre practitioners, yet it never really disappeared from view. At the beginning of the twentieth century radical theatre and realism went hand-in-hand as dramatists deployed realist techniques to expose and critique social structures. By the 1920s however, new cultural and political groupings tended to associate realism with the bourgeois art of the previous century. As Ira Levine explains in his account of left-wing dramatic theory: in these years, "Dramatic realism was especially condemned for its cultivation of an empathetic 'peephole' theatre which hypnotized its audiences with a titillating illusion of bourgeois life that distorted their apprehension of the real social world."[28] New groups such as the Provincetown Players and the New Playwrights Theatre, dramatists such as Eugene O'Neill, and leftist critics such as Michael Gold experimented with, and debated, dramatic form. As the decade progressed, experimentation in U.S. theatre was shaped by developments in Soviet theatre and the growth of American communism, as well as by the broader left movement, which clamored for a theatre that would be not just for the workers, but of and by the workers too.[29]

Agitation-propaganda, or agitprop, was to be a theatre of the people. Moving away from the idea of the stationary theatre with a professional company, workers' theatres were mobile and could play to workers anywhere from the union hall to the picket line. Often performed by amateur theatre groups, agitprop dramas were about the social, economic, and political conditions of contemporary workers. Whereas other experimental dramas in the early 1920s examined characters' inner lives, agitprop was interested in individuals and personality only insofar as they were shaped by social forces. With revolutionary themes designed to expose the worst injustices of the capitalist system, agitprop dramas usually ended on an uplifting note in which the unity of the workers heralded a better life for all. Central to conveying this message was the rejection of illusionary theatre techniques designed to trick the audience into entering a make-believe world and to "instill passivity in the spectator."[30] As FTP national director Hallie Flanagan explained in a 1931 essay on Workers' Theatre, "the theatre, if it is to be of use to the worker, must be divorced from the non-essentials which have become synonymous with it."[31] Accordingly, agitprop dramas usually abandoned the proscenium stage and the elaborate costumes and staging used to create illusion. This move reflected not only the rejection of bourgeois realism by the left but also the fact that a theatre of the workers had neither time nor money for these extras.

Agitprop groups did important work in growing theatre audiences by encouraging the production of short plays that could be performed anywhere, by anyone, and in persuading labor organizations of the power of theatre. Theatre critics, however, rejected the dogmatic format of agitprop, with its caricatures of villainous bosses, heroic workers, set speeches, and mass chants. The failures of agitprop were not only attributable to form: the amateurish production standards of many Workers' Theatre groups paled in comparison to the slick offerings of commercial theatre and the movies. As Conrad Seiller explained in an article for *New Theatre,* "Used to the smoothness of the bourgeois theatre and the films . . . the lumbering, painfully trying performances given by so many workers' groups will excite nothing but amused tolerance or derision."[32] The critical failure of agitprop was accompanied by a broader rejection of nonrealist theatre by many on the left, both in Soviet Russia, where socialist realism became state policy in 1934, and in the United States. Though theatre scholars disagree as to how far American political theatre had ever truly moved away from realism, in the early to mid-1930s, parts of the leftist theatre community began to break with agitprop and develop a professional realist theatre.[33] This shift was reflected in the essays published in *New Theatre* (the League of Workers' Theatre publication, formerly known as *Workers' Theatre*), as well as in the Theatre Union's productions of *Peace on Earth* (1933) and *Stevedore* in 1934.[34] At the forefront of the revival of realism on the professional stage was the Group Theatre. Hailed by *New Theatre* as the leading professional company in the United States, the Group Theatre was respected both for its dramas of social protest and its commitment to developing and training theatre practitioners. Founded by the director Harold Clurman and his playwright and actor friends, the Group produced two successful realist dramas in the early 1930s: Paul Green's *House of Connelly* (1931) and Sidney Kingsley's *Men in White* (1933). Members of the Group Theatre became involved with workers' theatres, ran acting studios, and offered classes to newly emerging theatre groups. Both the Theatre Union, and later the Harlem Negro Unit would host actor workshops led by members of the Group Theatre.[35]

At the same time, leftist theatre groups continued to experiment with nonrealist forms that dominated interwar theatre in Europe. Just one year after the success of *Stevedore*, the Theatre Union and Paul Peters adapted Brecht's *Mother*. A critical and box office failure, the epic drama did not translate well on the American stage. Brecht renounced the production for attempting to develop characters with whom audiences might identify.[36] Theatre historian Ilka Saal argues that a work such as *Mother* could not be transposed onto the American stage without becoming something very different. In Europe, state subsidies and the strength of the modernist movement helped forge political theatre that reflected high modernism's break from convention and encouraged the radical experimentations with form that characterized the work of Brecht and Piscator. By contrast, the strength of consumer culture, the commercial nature of American theatre, and the lack of a strong avant-garde meant that in the United States, political theatre developed within, and adapted elements of, existing theatrical traditions to accommodate the heightened political consciousness of the 1930s.[37] If, as Saal suggests, interwar theatre experimentation involved less a choice between antirealist and realist dramatization and more a continual process of adapting new theatrical forms into an American political theatre tradition, then agitprop and realism were never diametrically opposed: even those agitprop theatre practitioners who defined their project as strictly antirealist were, she argues, dedicated to persuading audiences of the verisimilitude of what they saw enacted on the stage.[38]

Saal's framework of a vernacular tradition in American political theatre reminds us that theatre is continually made anew, adapting to, shaped by, and sometimes pushing back against the conventions that frame its production. Even a Brechtian drama could have a realist production. Yet her analysis also suggests that experimentation in American theatre in this period was lacking, that it co-opted radical theatrical forms, making them more American, less revolutionary. Such a criticism echoes the anxieties felt by those on the left, who saw in the 1934 production of *Stevedore* an unwelcome return to a bourgeois form, which could only serve to pacify the workers and prop up the existing system. Realism might be successful in rousing audience emotion, but what happens after the emotional release? While some argued that revolutionary realism might produce some kind of revolutionary catharsis, how this might be effectively channeled into political action was not clear.

These questions preoccupied and divided the left during the run of *Stevedore*. Such concerns were made more acute as a result of the attention focused on *Stevedore*'s emotional appeal by both black and white commercial theatre critics, albeit from different perspectives. Where black reviewers tended to emphasize the positive and enduring impact of *Stevedore*'s capacity to bring about political change, white commercial critics seem to enjoy taunting leftist critics, insisting that the emotional energy expended by audiences for a world of make-believe replaced rather than fermented political activity in the real world. Black critics rejected such divisions, insisting that *Stevedore* "is too real to be just a play."[39] In a profession still dominated by white overseers, the Theatre Union's production provided a rare platform for black protest. Black commentators argued that the articulation of black grievances on a theatre stage could inspire black Americans to take action to fight their oppression by whites.

The idea that the boundary between "theatre" and the "real world" was an artificial one for black Americans was best illustrated through the frequent reporting of the impact of *Stevedore* on famed vaudevillian Bill Robinson. Moved by the resistance of the black stevedores to the white lynch mob, Robinson left his assigned seat in the audience, jumped on stage, and joined the black actors in constructing the barricade. Robinson's act took on heightened significance before an integrated audience that was accustomed to black Americans being confined to the stage as performers or segregated in the gallery. By breaking through the invisible wall between black and white spectators and black performers, Robinson compelled the theatre to make space for him. Robinson's leap—and the volume of coverage it attracted—made visible the unusual freedom of movement experienced by African Americans in a New York theatre. The singer, Ethel Waters, was among those who reported the story. Far from recounting an amusing instance of Robinson's eccentricity, Waters attributed political significance to the vaudevillian's actions and the impact they had on other spectators. Robinson, she suggests, embodied a collective desire to "to fight back: "During that final thrilling scene, a wave of emotion sweeps over the audience and everyone wants to heave a brick at the mob attempting to drive the Negro dock workers from their homes and to lynch their leader."[40] Writing for the *Chicago Defender,* Waters welcomed *Stevedore's* forthcoming arrival in the Windy City, and called for the play's message against racial hatred and lynching to be brought to as many Americans as possible.[41] Waters's account lent legitimacy to those who responded emotionally to the performance: it celebrated the collective coming together of audience members and presented Robinson's emotional engagement with the drama as a powerful, political investment.

Stevedore's broad appeal to both black and white audiences meant it soon became the focus of a political struggle to control and contain its political message. Bessye Bearden, the New York correspondent for the *Chicago Defender,* acknowledged as much in her review: "Stevedore Is Play for Race: But Broadway Sees It As Hit for All."[42] Whereas black commentators applauded a drama that was both entertaining and able to mobilize audiences to political ends, white commercial theatre critics appeared more troubled by its political ambitions. Some questioned whether *Stevedore* was really drama. To Richard Lockridge of the *New York Sun, Stevedore* "appeared not as a play at all, but as an emotional experience." *Stevedore* was not art, as much as a call to action: "it [was] almost as if the on-lookers were taking part . . . as if the forbidding barriers of the footlights had been magically removed." Underscoring the racial divisions enacted in the play, Percy Hammond caustically remarked that "if there had been a rope in the mildly infuriated audience, a lynching might have occurred."[43] Willella Wardorf warned that the drama swept audience members "forward on a wave of fighting hate," so that "*Stevedore* becomes an incitement to riot of the first order."[44] Reviews such as these reflected the beliefs of many white professional theatre critics that the theatre should not become a forum for public debate on pressing political issues. They also suggest a fear of political theatre, whose meaning could not be easily contained and controlled.

White critics recognized *Stevedore* as something "more" than theatre. Brooks Atkinson acknowledged that what took place in the audience might be just as important as what happened on stage, noting that "Between the audience and the play last evening was an extraordinarily interesting occasion." The *New York Times* critic understood that the vocal presence and actions of African Africans, in an integrated audience, made *Stevedore* a political event. Comparing the audience's laughs and jeers to an Elks Convention, he suggested: "Their response to the lines and the incidents gave the play an entirely fresh meaning."[45] Others noted the audience's response to the play in more patronizing tones. The reviewer for the *Christian Science Monitor* suggested the play was "so much out of the life of its audience" that they were incapable of responding to it as drama. When the character of Uncle Cato (an Uncle Tom figure) laments that the younger black generation are too uppity with whites, one black female audience member apparently responded by yelling at him to "Shut Up."[46] Burns Mantle sought to reassure readers of Chicago's *Daily Tribune*: although the play might involve a lot of shouting on the part of both cast and audience, the authorities need not become unduly worried. Indeed, the stage was "a fine outlet for the bursting emotions of the outraged radicals," for "the more chances they have to yell, the greater the release of the pressure that breeds hysteria and protest meetings."[47]

White critics had long patronized black actors and black audiences, suggesting they were neither sophisticated nor civilized enough to appreciate serious drama. Such insults were not directed only at African Americans. Mantle was also taunting those "outraged radicals" who were committed to using theatre to mobilize the masses. In suggesting that emotional release in the Civic Theatre might replace meaningful activism on the outside, Mantle struck the leftist community where it hurt. It was, however, John Mason Brown, a critic for the *New York Evening Post*, who succeeded in attracting the particular ire of the left when he suggested that revolutionaries need no longer gather in Union Square; the act of protest had been domesticated by its confinement to a theatrical arena:

With the Theatre Union angrily established in Miss Le Gallien's old playhouse in 14th St., those New Yorkers who pray for such a thing can now console themselves with the thought that they have a theatre of the Barricades. No longer do they have to stand up in Union Square to hear the inflammatory harangues which are honey to their ears. For Union Square—soap boxes, speechifiers and all—has gone indoors. At their own convenience, these indignant champions of the revolution can, without fear of rain, become as agitated as they please.[48]

Michael Gold, the easily provoked, self-proclaimed guardian of leftist theatre, was quick to take the bait, devoting an entire article (printed in both the *Daily Worker* and the *Chicago Defender*) to a counterattack. Responding directly to "the very aesthetic" critic who "allowed his class prejudice to get the best of him," he dismissed Brown as a typical southerner, a "slaveholder." However, Gold's tirade against "this fascist blast against the working class" failed to address the sensitive question Brown had posed: how could they ensure that the emotional release provoked by *Stevedore* fueled, rather than replaced, activism outside the theatre?[49]

This question continued to vex leftist theatre practitioners. In *New Theatre*, the dangers of escapism inherent in realism were thrashed out between John Howard Lawson, one of the few leftist dramatists to attempt to develop a coherent left-wing theoretical approach to the theatre in the 1930s, and *Stevedore*'s director, Michael Blankfort.[50] In a series of articles published in the summer and autumn of 1934, Blankfort defended *Stevedore*, arguing that there was a place for escapism even in revolutionary theatre.[51] Lawson responded with a robust critique:

> The real case, (as I see it) is that a large part of the audience at a revolutionary play *wants* to escape: I mean this literally; the audience (or a major part of it) wants to evade the emotional impact of class struggle. This was abundantly clear at performances of *Stevedore*. Although the Theatre Union succeeded in reaching an audience with marked working-class sympathies, nevertheless a good proportion of the audience were wavering intellectuals, people without clear convictions. I talked to many of these people. They were deeply moved by the play, but they were able to perform a very neat psychological trick—to escape from the real implications. They regarded the play as a special case of Southern prejudice: "Isn't it a shame that the South is so backward about the Negroes? But after all, it's because there are so *many* Negroes in the South. . . . it could not happen in other parts of the country." . . . In a word, many members of the audience succeeded in transferring revolutionary content into futile humanitarianism.[52]

Acknowledging that all theatre might involve some "evasion of truth," nevertheless Lawson insisted that this was not the primary function of proletarian theatre. If escapism was central to the bourgeois stage, "the function of revolutionary drama is to circumvent this escape; it is successful in proportion to its ability to *force* partisanship upon the audience."[53] In the November issue of *New Theatre, Stevedore*'s director responded by acknowledging that his use of the term "escape," even when the adjective "proletarian" was attached to it, was an unfortunate one, since it carried the pejorative connotations of bourgeois wish fulfilment. However, Blankfort argued that there was a difference between what he termed idealistic plays, which ended with a victory for the workers that had not grown out of the class and character conflict of the drama (ironically, the very charge leveled at *Stevedore*'s own unlikely interracial climax), and what he called "revolutionary idealism," which could reveal the "concrete steps . . . demonstrations, strikes, revolution" necessary to bring about that change.[54] Presumably, Blankfort understood *Stevedore*'s final scene, the building of the barricade and fighting back of black workers, as "concrete steps" in the path toward revolution.

Blankfort believed that identification and empathy had a part to play in revolutionary theatre. Characterization must be grounded in common identification between character and audience. Villains as well as heroes, he argued, should be fully fleshed out and not the stock characters of agitprop if audiences were to understand, appreciate, and ultimately resist bourgeois ideologies. Unlike the antiheroic fatalism of bourgeois realism, revolutionary realism depicted a fluid world in which characters could alter their destiny through collective action.[55] Blankfort appeared to dismiss the experiments of Brecht and Picador to create a theatre that demanded detached observation and reflection on the part of the audience. In fact, he dealt with leftist anxieties about whether revolutionary empathy imitated bourgeois forms of escapism by turning the argument on its head. Blankfort claimed that any attempt to detach audiences from engaging emotionally in the drama was itself a bourgeois misconception: "Bourgeois [e]stheticians have misused the concept of empathy to create a theory of "psychic distance" in which the audience is said *not* to be *esthetically* appreciating a play when it gets involved in it. Bill Robinson, who jumped on the stage and took part in a scene of *Stevedore,* would be described as having a non-[e]sthetic experience."[56] Rejecting the notion that theatre that engaged the emotions provided a release that forestalled any revolutionary stimulus outside the theatre, Blankfort insisted that "there is no place for 'psychic distance' in a revolutionary [e]sthetic." Much like Ethel Walters, Blankfort believed that "If it were possible, the whole audience ought to be aroused enough to jump on the stage."[57]

If psychic distance, or estrangement, was, as Blankfort claimed, a bourgeois conceit, it was surely also a privilege of whiteness: for African Americans the legitimate stage was more often a site of alienation than escapism. When you had to fight for the right to be in the theatre, to purchase a ticket in whichever part of the house you chose, when the black actors before you were fighting for equal wages and for the opportunity to play serious roles, theatre, however illusionist, was not a place of escape but rather an important arena in the struggle for black freedom. Theatre, then, was not simply something that might inspire black Americans to fight their oppression by whites outside the auditorium: rather, full participation in the spaces of American theatre was already an act of resistance to that oppression. The comments by white critics on black audiences suggest they understood as much. When Bill Robinson leaped, American theatre was forced to cede some space: black audiences and performers were co-opting the safe world of theatre and making it an uncomfortable, even threatening experience for white theatregoers.

Creating a Black Performance Community

While white commercial critics were troubled by the transformative power of *Stevedore* and white leftists worried that realism diverted class revolutions, the black performance community invested in making *Stevedore* a legitimate vehicle for public debate about black life and America's racial politics. *Stevedore* was "no mere play," to be appraised by theatre critics alone; it was a black community event. Yet establishing *Stevedore*'s credentials as a black event was not an easy task in a city where the Great White Way had a history of exploiting black theatre workers every bit as much as the stevedores in the play. The work of the black performance community therefore extended well beyond controlling interpretations of the play; the production process was also the subject of intense examination and celebration. As we have seen, *Stevedore* in performance was praised for its triumphant celebration of black self-determination rather than interracial class struggle. As a site of labor and leisure, however, the production was applauded for integrating black Americans into the American theatre. In fact, recognizing the interracial credentials of the production process was essential for *Stevedore* to become a drama of black self-determination.

Black newspapers played an important role in promoting the production and the black performance community's influence over it in three ways: as an opportunity for talented actors to participate in an integrated workforce; as an integrated black leisure activity; and as a way to mobilize support for black rights. Black reporters paid great attention to the unique opportunity that *Stevedore* offered black theatre professionals. The Theatre Union treated its black and white actors alike: all were given Equity contracts, no discrimination was made in terms of pay, and dressing rooms were integrated.[58] Black newspapers gave ample space to *Stevedore*'s cast. Rex Ingram, Jack Carter, and Edna Thomas each had feature pieces, interviews, and character photographs published, while gossip surrounding the show's stars made it into most black newspapers.[59] In an interview for the *Afro American*, Rex Ingram, who played the role of the fiery Blacksnake, declared: "For the first time in my fifteen years of acting, I got a chance to be myself, to say some of the things I had wanted to say for a long time." He compared his role favorably with those he had been asked to play in Hollywood and in other theatre productions, where he had been given: "Just a script and a director's prodding all the time; no lines."[60]

Stevedore opened up new job opportunities for black actors. By autumn 1934, leading actors Rex Ingram and Georgette Harvey had been lured away to take up new roles in the Broadway play *Dance with Your Gods,* while Alonzo Henderson was released in order to tour with *Green Pastures*.[61] Ingram's departure was a happy break for the pugilist-turned-actor Canada Lee. Taking over the role of Blacksnake, Lee would later follow Ingram into a number of roles for the Harlem Negro Unit before becoming a star in his own right, when he appeared as Bigger Thomas in Orson Welles's stage production of Richard Wright's *Native Son*. Other black actors also attracted attention as a result of the success of *Stevedore*. Leigh Whipper, who played the role of Jim Veal, captain of the stevedores' work team, was widely praised by critics for his performance. During the October revival, Whipper was contracted by the radio network NBC to narrate a scene from the play as part of a program examining the contribution of black actors to the American stage.[62]

Stevedore offered new opportunities for black theatre audiences as well as actors. Newspaper columnists frequently referred to the large number of black Americans in the audiences, the low-cost and integrated seating, and the group bookings by black organizations. In the *Amsterdam News,* Henry Lee Moon described the "more generous portion of Negroes than this reviewer has seen at any previous downtown performance."[63] It was not just that African Americans were audience members at a downtown show that was important, but the range of different groups who came to see *Stevedore*. Much was made of the truckload of twenty-four unemployed black women and men who traveled from Philadelphia to watch a matinee performance, as well as those who traveled from as far afield as Rhode Island and Massachusetts.[64] The *Amsterdam News* commended the Theatre Union's policy of distributing free tickets to the unemployed through community organizations, claiming that "the bulk of these go to Harlem organizations including the Urban League, the unemployed committees and councils of Harlem, the League of Struggle for Negro Rights, the Harlem Interracial League, various Negro clubs in Harlem conducted by the United Neighborhood Houses."[65] Under the direction of their brilliant publicist Margaret Larkins, the Theatre Union adapted the idea of using a benefit performance with group bookings to develop a regular audience. As Larkins explained: "A single night might see part of the house occupied by the New Jersey College for Women, the Fireside Club of a Briarcliff church, the Beauticians Union, a Fusion party club, a local of the Socialist party and a body of Negroes from the League of Struggle for Negro Rights." These group bookings helped fund the cost of free tickets for the unemployed. The Theatre Union collected donations at each performance to cover the cost of releasing six to seven hundred tickets each week to the unemployed.[66]

In addition to its regular programs for attracting working-class audiences to the theatre, the Theatre Union also took specific steps to appeal to New York's black community leaders. A week before opening night, the Theatre Union's executive board hosted a party for leading Harlemites. Demonstrating a commitment to integration that went beyond the professional work space, the party was held at the white home of a Theatre Union board member. Here, Harlem's great and good were entertained with music performed by members of the cast. This engagement led the League of Struggle for Negro Rights to sponsor the first preview on April 14 and its head, Richard Moore, to offer a useful endorsement for publicity notices: "This play should be greeted with the enthusiastic support of the broad masses of Negro and white workers and of all elements sympathetic to the liberation of the Negro people."[67] The Theatre Union was widely praised for being the first white theatre company to employ a black publicity man, one Ben Herb, to arrange advertisements in black publications and to book black theatre parties. In addition the black press made much of the fact that Harlemites need not venture downtown to book their tickets since the Theatre Union had opened a box office to cater to their needs in Lowenstein's drugstore on 135th and Seventh Avenue.[68]

It was not just that African Americans came to the Civic to watch *Stevedore* that mattered; their experience inside the auditorium was of equal importance. In 1934 it was common practice for black Americans to be refused access to the best seats in the house; usually they were confined to the balcony or "Nigger Heaven." Theatre Union board members penned articles in black publications to encourage black attendance and to reassure black patrons visiting the Civic they would be treated with respect. George Sklar wrote a lengthy piece for the *Amsterdam News* in which he made clear that the Theatre Union's commitment to social equality in their choice of drama would be fully reflected in the operation of the theatre: "There is no Jim Crow in the Theatre Union. Negro actors share dressing rooms with white actors. Negroes sit everywhere in the audiences. People who call up over the telephone and ask for seats apart from the Negroes are told bluntly that granting such a request is contrary to Theatre Union policy."[69] The Theatre Union, whose advisory board included the preeminent black actress Rose McClendon and the poet Countee Cullen, was one of New York's first professional theatres to have a strict integration policy. It maintained this commitment on tour, refusing offers from theatres that practiced Jim Crow seating.[70] The Theatre Union's policy on integrated audiences and support for interracial activism would prove crucial in allowing the black community to establish *Stevedore* as a black community event. As actors, critics, and audience members, African Americans were able to interpret *Stevedore* as a drama of black self-determination while working with New York's leftist theatre fraternity to make the production an interracial event.

When audiences arrived at the Civic Repertory Theatre, they were already primed to connect their experience inside the theatre with activism for social change on the outside. With advance bookings taking up the first six weeks of the run, audiences for *Stevedore* experienced the vitality of a live performance in a packed theatre alongside a group of colleagues, peers, or fellow union members, as well as the unemployed, whose tickets they subsidized. In the unlikely event that the drama did not make clear its relevance to ongoing racial problems, audience members were encouraged to make these connections at the end of the performance. One method was to stage a political fund-raiser directly after the show. The Theatre Union maintained connections with interracial leftist organizations such as the International Labor Defense (ILD) and hosted and facilitated public events on issues dear to the left. For example, after one performance, the Scotts-boro Mothers appeared at the Civic as special guests. The cast had the opportunity to meet the mothers and leading black lawyers involved in the case, while the audience was encouraged to donate toward the legal defense fund following a series of speeches. Also helping to rally the theatre audience was Ruby Bates, one of the two white women who had accused nine black youths of rape onboard a freight train in Alabama. Like the white woman who cried rape in *Stevedore,* Bates and her companion, Victoria Price, had found themselves in a position where their own whiteness was compromised by their contravention of southern gender roles. They too had deflected attention from their transgression through an attack on black manhood. Unlike the white woman in *Stevedore* however, Bates recanted her accusation against the Scottsboro Youths. Along with the Scottsboro Mothers, she became a central figure in the Communist Party's campaign to free the accused. The black press devoted considerable news inches to these events and detailed how the production had become the focus for real-life race causes. The *Afro American* went as far as to suggest that the Scottsboro Mothers were welcomed with even more enthusiasm than the play itself, which received ten curtain calls that night.[71]

After fifteen weeks, *Stevedore* finally closed in deference to the heat of a New York summer. Reopening in October for four weeks, the play was then sent on a tour of the East Coast and Chicago. In the Windy City, *Stevedore* had a Christmas Eve opening sponsored by the Drama Union at the Selwyn Theatre. According to *Pittsburgh Courier* reporter Stephen Breszka, white critics spurned *Stevedore* in favor of reviewing a musical comedy that opened the same night. The silent treatment given to *Stevedore* forced the Drama Union to start a major publicity campaign to attract an audience. When the white papers finally got around to reviewing it, they criticized the fact that *Stevedore* asked questions about race "too directly," offering "too stern a rebuke" to race prejudice. As in New York, the Chicago production challenged the racial conventions of American theatre both on and off stage. The Drama Union invited black and white audience members to join the cast in the lobby for an after-show party, a "daring stunt" that caused some white audience members to "wonder where the whole movement was heading." Toward ever more interracial mixing was the answer, according to the *Courier* correspondent. who reported on the unprecedented supper party organized by the Drama Union at Vassar House. As Breszka wryly noted, such interracial mixing, when it did occur, usually took place in the "Negro district," making it all the more notable that this after-show party was an interracial dinner for 300 guests in Chicago's exclusive Gold Coast district. Breszka could not help but remind his readers that the neighborhood was also home to the *Chicago Tribune*, the newspaper whose theatre critic had discussed *Stevedore* as if it were "a contagious disease."[72] By contrast, Chicago's black reporters praised the production to the hilt. Writing for the *Chicago Defender*, Rob Roy described the appreciative audience and the fine acting, but was also keen to stress that *Stevedore* was "more than a mere play." Robert Abbott, the editor of the *Defender*, was so moved that he included a laudatory piece in place of his regular column and encouraged readers to send in their own responses to *Stevedore*. In a piece entitled, "Finest Play on American Stage," Abbott suggested the playwrights develop a new play to dramatize the "evils" inflicted on black communities by segregation.[73]

The events that took place in and around *Stevedore*, which were organized by black activists working with the Theatre Union, showed how it was possible to channel the emotional energy released by audiences during performances of *Stevedore* directly into movements for social change. Realist drama was not destined to produce politically unengaged spectators. In fact, the black realism that developed around the Theatre Union production of *Stevedore* offered a radical departure from the American theatre tradition and inspired black theatre communities in other parts of the United States. *Stevedore* would continue to provide platforms for protest—both in the United States and abroad—even before it found its way to the Seattle Negro Unit in spring 1937. In separate productions in Cleveland, London, and Boston, *Stevedore* generated considerable debate about the representation of race and class and the role of black actors in the theatre. In London, critics' fascination with Paul Robeson in the starring role distracted from the play's racial and class politics. The critic for the London *Times* understood that the play was about the "ill treatment of Negroes in America," but like most reviewers, his admiration was reserved for the physique of Robeson and the extensive singing, which broke up the pace and immediacy of the action. Otherwise, white British critics panned the production.[74] Black Londoners objected to repeated use of the term "nigger" in the play.[75] One prominent critic was the exiled Marcus Garvey. Suggesting *Stevedore* pandered to white bigots, he classed it, together with *Sanders of the Rivers* and *The Emperor Jones*, as examples of "pictures and plays that tend to dishonour, mimic, discredit and abuse the cultural attainments of the black race."[76]

Meanwhile, back in the United States, *Stevedore* continued to provoke controversy. The profane language prompted white authorities in Boston, and black preachers and newspaper proprietors in Cleveland, Ohio, to attempt to censor the play. Although neither attempt was successful, the outcry provoked by attempted censorship fueled a broader, nationwide debate about what constituted legitimate black American theatre. Writing in his weekly column for the *Amsterdam News*, Roi Ottley expressed surprise that the preachers of Cleveland had kicked up such a fuss over the Karamu House Theatre's *Stevedore*.[77] But the Cleveland furor could hardly be dismissed as provincialism. *Cleveland Gazette* proprietor Harry C. Smith objected, not simply to the drama, but also to the fact that the direction of, and audience for, a black theatre troupe in Cleveland was overwhelmingly white. Similar criticisms would be leveled at a number of Federal Theatre Negro Units: black troupes putting on white-authored plays under white supervision were sometimes seen as obstacles that impeded, rather than helped develop, a black theatre.[78]

Stevedore opened up debates about power and politics in American theatre that revealed deep schisms within black communities when it came to the politics of representation. Sometimes these revolved around the benefits and pitfalls of working with whites. Equally contentious was the question of which version of blackness and which part of the black community could risk representation on the stage. Whether to represent working-class black life, for example, had been a central fault line of the Harlem Renaissance.[79] George Streator, writing in the *Crisis*, anticipated one possible hostile reaction to the New York production of *Stevedore* on the part of the black middle classes: "A lot of timid Negroes will object to *Stevedore*. Many nice, clean, colored people feel that a play which depicts the Negro with anything except a Harvard accent and a dress suit, is bad publicity."[80] This prediction was not borne out in New York, where *Stevedore* was widely and positively reviewed by the black press and other reporters suggested that sizable numbers of black Americans attended the Theatre Union's production. Nevertheless, the reception of *Stevedore* in community theatres outside New York reminds us that the debates that shaped theatre in New York could look very different in other localities. This difference did not mean that New York necessarily represented a more progressive or experimental arena for black theatre. On the contrary, it was often in cities and towns far from Broadway and the Federal Theatre's headquarters that the most radical Federal Theatre was developed. Moreover, a drama's meaning could change as it traveled across the United States. In New York, *Stevedore* became the focus of debates about how best to mobilize communities to activism; in Seattle, *Stevedore* arrived fully charged as a vehicle ready to drive protest forward. It was no accident that the black troupe of the Seattle Negro Unit, which would become one of the most experimental and successful Negro Units of the Federal Theatre Project, wanted *Stevedore* as its first Federal Theatre production.

Stevedore in Seattle

When *Stevedore* was put on by the Seattle Negro Unit of the Federal Theatre in 1936, the interracial ending that had troubled New York critics appears to have vanished from sight. In order to understand why and how the black performance community was able to bring about what was widely regarded as the logical conclusion to *Stevedore*, we must turn to the history of black theatre in Seattle before the establishment of the Federal Theatre. Seattle had a tradition of white-directed black theatre prior to the Federal Theatre. The Seattle Repertory Playhouse (SRP) was established and directed by Florence and Burton James, a white couple who were drama instructors at the University of Washington. Their first foray into "race" dramas occurred in 1931, when they staged a production of *Uncle Tom's Cabin*. The role of Uncle Tom was played in blackface by the theatre's white house manager, Albert Ottenheimer. It is noteworthy that theatre directors who were considered progressive in white liberal circles would have even considered staging the dramatization of Harriet Beecher Stowe's antislavery novel as late as 1931, the same year the *Theatre Guild* magazine pronounced, "Uncle Tom Is Dead." Claiming 1930 as the first year in over three-quarters of a century in which *Uncle Tom's Cabin* had not been performed, the publication declared: "Its day is done. If the play is revived, it will be as a curiosity; and no one can revive the profession of Uncle Tomming." Florence James thought otherwise, considering it "a quaint American classic."[81] The SRP's production of *Uncle Tom's Cabin* is significant to the story of *Stevedore* and the Seattle Negro Unit: it offers insight into the type of black characters Seattleites were accustomed to seeing on the stage and the type of roles available to African Americans in Seattle before the Federal Theatre. The production was also important because it marked the beginning of the relationship between the Playhouse and the local African Methodist Church, which furnished cast members for *Uncle Tom's Cabin*, and later for the Seattle Negro Unit.[82]

The Playhouse's next "race" play was a production of Paul Green's 1926 Pulitzer Prize–winning drama, *In Abraham's Bosom*. Applauded by white liberals, the play was a variation on a theme much loved by serious white dramatists: the mixed-race man's doomed quest to better himself and escape his tragic destiny. Enlivened by chorus numbers, the production proved a great hit in 1933. Larding each scene change with an "authentic" gospel song was a favorite and profitable device for white producers, and one that would come to characterize the Jameses' Seattle Negro Unit productions. From up and down the coast, white spectators came to feast on black self-destruction with music, thereby alleviating the SRP's precarious financial position.[83] The house manager recorded that the production drew "the greatest ovation in Playhouse annals." He also noted, rather grudgingly, the increasingly assertive behavior of the black cast, who insisted that Burton James make good his promise to pay the amateur troupe should the production make a profit. It did: the troupe negotiated for $1 per performance for each cast member and $1.50 for those in the chorus.[84]

It was on the back of these box office successes that the Jameses applied to become sponsors of a Negro Unit of the Federal Theatre two years later. Theirs was not the only offer: Seattle's black community had put forward their own proposal for a Negro Unit. Joseph Jackson, who had left New York to serve as the first executive secretary of the Seattle Urban League in 1930 (and in 1933 had played the part of Abe in the SRP's *In Abraham's Bosom*) and Frederick Darby, a local union man, presented an alternative plan. The Federal Theatre turned them down on the grounds that they had no appropriate theatre space and could not point to sufficient numbers of experienced black theatre professionals in Seattle. By contrast, the Jameses were armed with a ready-made theatre, a track record of producing "race" dramas, and the very same black theatre workers who could have become part of a black-led Negro Unit. The Federal Theatre accepted the Jameses' bid to sponsor a Negro Unit at the SRP.[85] However, the relationship between the Playhouse's management and the black troupe would change once they became established as an FTP Negro Unit. The black troupe who worked for the SRP had been prepared to play the tragic characters that populated Green's "race" dramas; as members of a federally sponsored theatre, they pushed for a black repertoire and, as discussed in chapter 3, created dramas of their own.

The placing of white theatre professionals in supervisory roles did not mean the Negro Unit became their toy, to play with as they desired. Historical accounts of the Seattle Negro Unit tend to emphasize the extent to which its white directors and managers exploited the company for its own purposes, relying on a black chorus to bring the crowds in, but proving to be disinterested in developing black talent.[86] Certainly in the official records, the liberal paternalism and crude racial stereotyping on the part of white directors and FTP officials ring out loud and clear. SRP house manager Albert Ottenheimer held views on black acting typical of many white liberals who believed themselves sensitive to issues of race in the theatre. Keen to be seen to reject the clichés that all African Americans could dance and sing, he nevertheless commended what he saw in the Seattle Negro troupe as a "native quality, a relaxation, a use of the body and the like which many other peoples have lost, I imagine, in a longer veneer of civilization."[87]

Correspondence between FTP and Works Progress Administration (WPA) officials offers important documentary evidence of the stated intentions and racially problematic views held by many of those who worked with and supervised African Americans on the Federal Theatre Project. Yet the voices of African Americans involved in the Seattle Negro Unit can also be heard. In oral testimonies and letters of protest, theatre manuscripts, playbills, musical scores, and posters, the creativity and quest for self-determination is manifest. Reading these together, the relationship between the white managers of the SRP and the black troupe appears complex and fluid: shaped not only by the usual theatre hierarchies between cast, managers, and directors but also by racialized theatrical conventions and local and national racial contexts, as well as the politics of the FTP. Mutual, if unequal, dependency underpinned the relationship. Members of the black troupe remembered the unit as having originated from within the community and that it was the community who "went out and contacted Mrs. Burton James."[88] The Jameses' experience, infrastructure, and networks were crucial to setting up the unit in 1936, but the testimony of other members of the company also reminds us that the black troupe brought their own skills and ambitions to the unit. Sara Oliver, who played a number of leading roles for the unit remembered that she had always acted: "Our church has always had drama. That was where you got your drama. I was in plays from the time I was five years old." Drama was, Oliver explained, a way of doing black history: "Harriet Tubman, Sojourner Truth, we did all those people. We have pageants and stuff that portrayed our people."[89]

The relief requirement of the Federal Theatre underpinned the relationship from the start. Without black actors who were eligible to claim relief, there would be no Negro Unit for the SRP directors to direct. Moreover, the Jameses were heavily reliant on the handful of black actors they were already acquainted with to spread the word about auditions and promote the project.[90] At the same time, the Jameses' willingness to flout the FTP's 10 percent nonrelief rule (which enabled units to employ a number of professionals with the experience necessary to stage a show but who were not

FIGURE 3 Cast of *Noah* with Florence and Burton James outside the Seattle
Repertory Playhouse. Theodore Browne Collection, C0225, Box 1. Special
Collections Research Center, George Mason University Libraries.

eligible for relief) meant they were able to give opportunities to talents like
Theodore Browne. Alongside other key members of the Negro Unit, Browne,
to some extent, owed his position to the Jameses' willingness to negotiate
on his behalf. This may have afforded Browne less independence than
that enjoyed by those whose relief status qualified them for the project.[91]
Yet Browne's growing status in the company as lead actor and, later, playwright made him indispensable to the Jameses. Indeed the value of a resident playwright became clear when the troupe began to make demands
about the type of plays it was prepared to perform.

Prior to the Federal Theatre Project, Seattle's black theatre community
had performed a typical white liberal program of purportedly serious "race"
drama. As a Federal Theatre Unit, this would change. Not only would the
program diversify, but the process of selecting and writing "race" dramas
increasingly became the task of black members of the Negro Unit. The Jameses had planned to begin with *Porgy* and *Stevedore*.[92] The SRP's records
document how the black troupe began a "whispering campaign" against
Porgy, which culminated in an investigation by representatives of the troupe

who called themselves the "Colored Committee." Going over the heads of their direct white supervisors, the Colored Committee submitted a formal letter of complaint to FTP state director George Hood. In it, they explained that they did not want to "jeopardize their jobs" but did object to the repeated use of the term "nigger." The community, they insisted, would not tolerate its use. The Colored Committee enclosed a list of plays they were prepared to perform: at the very top was *Stevedore*.[93] Their choice suggested a black performance community conversant in debates about radical theatre in New York and about the racialized labor politics of Seattle. Seattle's black newspaper, the *Northwest Enterprise*, had reported on *Stevedore*'s nine-month run in New York City, which had "literally set the town agog." Seattle's white newspapers also covered the play and the debates it provoked during its "long and controversial run in New York."[94] The Colored Committee might be in no doubt that *Stevedore* was a provocative drama that might put the Seattle Negro Unit on the map.

Stevedore was a timely and topical drama for Seattle, a seaport that had recently played host to a bitter, interracial labor dispute. One of the most unionized cities in the interwar years, Seattle had a small but vocal black population of around 3,000. Accounting for less than 1 percent of the city's total population, African Americans' chances of entering Seattle's industrial economy were largely dependent on white-run unions. With access to waterfront jobs controlled by the white local of the International Longshoreman's Association (ILA), African Americans were confined to lower-paying service jobs.[95] When, in 1916, the Waterfront Employers Association issued a reduction in pay, more than 21,000 dockworkers went on strike. In what became a long and bitter walk-out, the employers used African Americans to break the strike, provoking acts of violence from white strikers as well as resistance on the part of black strike-breakers. The strike was only ended when the United States entered the war in April 1917.[96] The ILA tried to incorporate the black strike-breakers into the union, but this invitation marked no period of interracial harmony on the docks. White dockworkers were the first to be hired, while African Americans spent long periods awaiting work in the union hall. Although some black dockworkers held the employers responsible for manipulating racial differences, others felt white union leaders were also to blame. Echoing Lonnie Thompson's black comrades in *Stevedore*, Horace Cayton Jr., the prominent Seattle-born sociologist, later recalled: "however desirable a mixed union was, you just couldn't trust any white man."[97] When, in 1934, the eighty-three-day maritime strike brought Seattle's Port to a standstill, the city finally had an integrated, all-union waterfront, which included 300 black workers. Nevertheless, integrated unions remained the exception in Seattle where the three largest unions, of machinists, building trades and construction, and Teamsters, continued to virtually exclude blacks until after World War II.[98] These recent racialized industrial disputes provide important context for understanding how *Stevedore* might have been presented by the Seattle Negro Unit.

Stevedore was not the first labor play performed in Seattle in the wake of the Longshoremen's strike. On the evening of January 18, 1936, the SRP staged a performance of *Waiting for Lefty*, Clifford Odets's immensely popular drama of cautious and corrupt labor unions with its climactic call to strike.[99] In New York, where both plays debuted, *Stevedore* opened a year before *Lefty*; in Seattle, *Stevedore* appeared four months after Odets's drama. Staged for one night only, *Lefty* drew an audience mainly comprised of friends and supporters of the SRP, middle-class professionals rather than working-class union members.[100] Even so, it provoked enormous controversy. Viewed by its supporters as the most exciting show to be produced in Seattle, to its detractors it was a dangerous piece of propaganda designed to stoke class warfare and proof of the SRP's leftist tendencies. In the final climactic scene, audience members, who have watched two acts of cautious union leaders, are required to consider whether collective action can end the exploitation of New York City's taxi drivers. Perhaps it was the spectacle of middle-aged university professors cheering for the taxi-drivers of New York to go on strike that made *Lefty* appear so dangerous the *Seattle Times* refused to cover it, and all subsequent SRP productions. The furor led the SRP's board to insist the Jameses schedule no further one-off productions without their "express authorization" and prompted Florence James to reflect in her memoir: "when you incite people in evening clothes to riot, you are really climbing into revolution."[101] Fired up by *Waiting for Lefty*, and confident that *Stevedore* commanded the respect of the black troupe, Florence and Burton James started work on a second labor drama, this time under the auspices and, they hoped, protection of the Federal Theatre.

Opening on May 14, 1936, *Stevedore* ran for eight nights at the SRP, before appearing at Seattle's annual Summer Drama Festival for nine performances in June and July. The following year it was revived for a further four performances and moved downtown to the more capacious Moore Theatre.[102] When it was first staged, critics raved about the exciting drama and noted the "tense and fascinated audience," who "crowded in the rear of the house and remained to watch the play standing up," and hissed at the white villains.[103] They praised the script, the professional production, and the fine performances of Theodore Browne, who played the lead role of Lonnie Thompson, and Joe Staton as Blacksnake. The adjectives "brilliant," "perfect," "effective," "rousing," and "profoundly moving" filled the review pages of Seattle's newspapers.[104] In their uniformly positive reviews, the Seattle critics made no reference to the white union men who, in the New York production, arrive at the last minute to save the day. The interracial ending, which had been a provocative feature of the production on the East Coast, passed without comment. Black resistance was the theme most prominently featured by Seattle's critics. One headline declared: "'Stevedore' Depicts Negro's Fight against Whites in the South," and the accompanying review explained that "the intoleration of the negro by the white became the main themes of the play."[105] Another thought that "*Stevedore* shows with straight, hard body punches, the plight of the black race in America."[106] Bill Hollomon, who wrote positively about *Stevedore* for the *Seattle Star*, but who was wry in his judgment of its effect on the audience, understood it to be a drama about black life rather than interracial cooperation, and advised his readers: "if you like to clinch your fist with emotion, and laugh and maybe sob a bit at the life of a southern Negro, then don't miss this performance." The reporter for the *Argus* commented on the play's dogged pursuit of its thesis and its "bold stand," which "makes no compromise with straddling controversial matters."[107] Such analysis stands in stark contrast to the widely panned interracial ending of the Theatre Union's New York production.

Theatre critics in Seattle were well aware of debates about the efficacy of leftist political theatre that filled the pages of theatre journals on the East Coast. In what was surely a reference to the strong opinions voiced by leftist critics of the New York production, Ellen McGrath writing for the *Argus*, reflected on the production's impact on the Seattle audience: "Are they sufficiently aroused by the dominating theme of injustice to react with warmth and vigor rather with a calm air of emotional detachment?" Pointing to the bulging preview audience, many of whom had to stand at the back, the *Argus* reporter reasoned, "It's far easier to feel outraged getting your own toes stepped on in the crush of a group." Joe Staton remembered audiences were inspired to participate in the show: "People became so engrossed in that last scene that they came up on stage and helped us build a barricade. That was really something! Really something!"[108] While Staton offers no clues as to who leaped up on the stage, it is intriguing to speculate whether the actions of the Seattle audience delivered the playwrights' much longed-for interracial ending.

The Federal Theatre's Los Angeles Regional Bureau held a copy of *Stevedore* which is available at the National Archives. It is however, very close to the published version and so offers few clues as to changes that may have been made to the manuscript during the development of the Seattle production.[109] There are, however, a number of documents that help us reconstruct what audiences would have experienced. Perhaps the most significant of these is the multiple-authored production bulletin, which included a director's report, synopsis of the play, costume and set photographs, a program, and a technical report. When read alongside critics' reviews, the production bulletin for *Stevedore* suggests the Seattle Negro Unit may have changed the ending of the Sklar and Peters script so that the stevedores and their families fight off the white mob alone. The photographs, director's report, and technical report offer no evidence to suggest that Seattleites witnessed the original New York ending. Tellingly, the synopsis indicates that the Seattle Unit made this a drama about the plight of *black* working men, as Peters had intended in "Wharf Nigger," rather than a dramatization of workers coming together across the racial divide to fight for justice. The synopsis offers a detailed scene by scene account of key developments in the plot. The description of the final scene makes no mention of the white union men or their leader, Lem Morris: whites are mentioned only as enemies coming to march on and burn black homes. The concluding sentence of the synopsis describes how "the negroes succeed in fighting off the mob."[110]

The idea of a revised Seattle ending is hinted at in a 1976 interview between the historian John O'Connor and George Sklar. O'Connor, who was part of the Federal Theatre Oral History Project at GMU, put it to Sklar that the Seattle Unit changed the ending so that white rescue party "doesn't show up at all. It leaves them at the black barricade and fighting when the curtain comes down."[111] Sklar's reaction is instructive: "That's interesting as hell. There was a lot of controversy about that ending, I mean about the Marines to the rescue. But of course at the time you had to take it in context of what was happening." Forty years later, Sklar seemed unsurprised that the play had been changed, recalling the controversy the original ending provoked, and still defending as realistic the representation of interracial cooperation in his co-authored play: "actually the chances for blacks being admitted into a union which had not existed before were becoming a reality too, although the bigotry was still prevalent—I mean, there was no question about that, . . . [but] the unionists were being educated to some degree, to the degree to which, in an isolated instance, a thing like this could happen, that whites could come in and fight with a bunch of blacks who were being attacked."[112] Sklar's fellow dramatist remembered things rather differently. In an interview in 1978, Paul Peters admitted that the ending of *Stevedore* "diminished both the honesty and the quality of the play," and called the interracial ending "sheer wish dreaming."[113] Whether white men come to the rescue or whether the Seattle Negro Unit changed the ending so that the black stevedores win their fight alone may never be known with absolute certainty: what is more certain is that from the East to the West Coast, black performance communities made *Stevedore* a drama of black self-determination rather than the interracial "wish dreaming" its authors had envisaged.

"Speaking Their Own Mind"

The Theatre Union's production of *Stevedore* and the leftist theatre traditions out of which it developed served as an important model for the Federal Theatre. Like the Theatre Union, the Federal Theatre produced new contemporary dramas that reflected the lives and aspirations of ordinary Americans. Set in the workplace rather than the parlor rooms of high society, the new dramas developed by the FTP appealed to working women and men who had not previously participated in the world of theatre. Adopting many of the Theatre Union's techniques in its efforts to create a more accessible and relevant theatre, the FTP solicited group bookings and invited political and labor groups to sponsor after-show events. Like the Theatre Union, the FTP would also offer cheap seats as well as free tickets for the unemployed. The Theatre Union also paved the way for integrated seating: the Federal Theatre only played integrated houses even when touring the South. According to George Sklar, so effectively did the FTP take over the mission of the Theatre Union that the latter's doors closed in 1937. As Sklar explained: "it had no reason for existence once the Federal Theatre came into being . . . because the Federal Theatre was doing a much better job . . . than we could ever begin to do."[114] The FTP recognized the legacy of the Theatre Union and its contribution to the development of black theatre. In a press release to the *Afro American* in 1937, the FTP traced the development of "an authentic Negro theatre" in the United States, praising the Theatre Union productions of *Stevedore* and *They Shall Not Die* as "straightforward, realistic plays dealing with acute problems of the American Negro" which "brought a permanent Negro Theatre one step closer."[115] However, it would be black performance communities, rather than coalitions of leftist theatre practitioners, who would shape the new possibilities for black theatre in the second half of the decade.

The black performance community in New York that mobilized around *Stevedore* and reclaimed realism as a politically useful tool maintained its momentum with the establishment of the Negro People's Theatre (NPT). The new theatre was led by Dick Campbell, a former vaudeville star who went on to become an important manager and producer, and Rose McClendon.[116] A veteran black actor, McClendon had served as a board member of the Theatre Union and was well known for her support for activist theatre. Outlining the purpose of the NPT, McClendon explained the new group would present "plays that [were] vital to Negro life, thereby developing the creative and artistic talents of the Negro, fostering the high ideals of the race, and illuminating the forces of social realism through the medium of the theatre."[117] Their first play, which was sponsored by the Friends of Harlem, a united front coalition, was Clifford Odets's *Waiting for Lefty*.[118]

The Group Theatre's original production of *Waiting for Lefty* was still running at the Longacre theatre on 48th Street, when between four to five thousand people crammed into Rockland Palace to watch the first black production of *Waiting for Lefty* on the evening of June 1, 1935. The NPT's production was intended to fulfil McClendon's vision for a black theatre that was socially and politically relevant and that offered a realistic portrait of black life. Though they struggled to hear much in a stadium more suited to basketball and dances than dramas, black reporters welcomed an adaptation of a white drama that reflected the prominent role played by African Americans in the New York taxi strike.[119] The leftist press was quick to mark the production as a political event. Writing in the *New Masses*, Alan Chumley compared it to the Harlem Riot earlier that year: "In the Negro cultural field it was no less an event than the spontaneous upsurge of March 19; for it proclaimed decisively the beginning of Harlem's emancipation from the false and degrading picture of the Negro perpetrated by the commercial theatre and film. It laid the foundation for a theatre of and for Negroes which will present their real problems."[120] Others similarly celebrated the opportunity the NPT afforded the black community to present its own problems in its own ways. Noting that much of the cast of *Lefty* came from the Broadway production of *Green Pastures* (as well as *Porgy* and *Stevedore*), Joe Foster in the *Daily Worker* welcomed the attempt at realism: "For several years their theatrical talents have been occupied with a play [*Green Pastures*] far removed from social realism and protest. But in discussing the perspectives of this new theatre, they voice an excitement and interest they have never felt before. . . . Many prominent social and cultural leaders in Harlem joined this united front, in the realization that once the Negro developed his own activities on the basis of his own mores, customs and social problems, UNDER HIS OWN DIRECTION, a cultural movement of untold significance was possible."[121] McClendon claimed the large audience for *Lefty* as evidence that African Americans did support black theatre. If black communities had been shy of attending black theatre in the past, this was due to the misconception on the part of many a director, that "the use of an all-Negro cast constituted the creation of a Negro theatre." By contrast, *Lefty* had shown that a "Negro theatre operated by Negroes as a cultural experiment and based upon a program of social realism could be established on a permanent basis." Here was a tradition upon which a new black theatre could build.[122]

The NPT would host just one more show, a benefit performance at the end of June, before its leaders joined the Harlem Negro Unit. McClendon would serve as guiding spirit and co-director of the Harlem Negro Unit until her premature death in 1936.[123] Stories of the founding of the Harlem Negro Unit have given McClendon credit for its foundation. However the significance of African Americans' relationships with professional leftist theatre groups in the early 1930s has been obscured by the role of McClendon's prominent, longer-lived co-director, John Houseman. Accounts of the Harlem Negro Unit's origins usually attend to the role of the Hungarian-born British producer who engaged Orson Welles to direct a version of *Macbeth* set in Haiti. In such narratives the boy genius becomes instrumental in discovering "untrained," "unknown" black actors—Jack Carter, Rex Ingram, and Canada Lee—for the Harlem Federal Theatre.[124] Black theatrical creativity is often narrated through the lens of powerful white figures who were able to harness it. However the history of *Stevedore*—in New York and in Seattle—reveals the importance of the connections forged between the leftist, interracial, and professional theatres of the early 1930s. It also draws attention to how African Americans made their own space within the left-wing theatre movement. As McClendon told an audience after a performance at a communist summer retreat: "we belong in the left-wing theatre and only in the left-wing movement can we build and maintain such a theatre."[125] *Stevedore's* production history also foregrounds the development of black performance communities who claimed *Stevedore* as their own in the making of Negro Units. Finally, *Stevedore* illustrates the problem for white administrators, playwrights, and directors who sought to control and contain the representation of black life on the American stage. The growing assertiveness of black troupes and nurturing of black talent by black performance communities meant that Negro Unit productions could be the product of interracial collaboration and black ambition as much as, and sometimes more than, they were the product of white imaginations. White playwrights such as George Sklar and Paul Peters took considerable pains to educate their audiences through program notes and newspaper articles, yet they were unable to control the meaning of their dramas once they were let free on the American stage.[126]

Negro Units across the United States could, and did, change the meaning of the white-authored dramas staged during the Federal Theatre Project. These struggles took place on and off stage. In an interview in 1976, Joe Staton offered a vivid account of an encounter with Burton James, who directed him as Blacksnake in *Stevedore*. Accused by a preacher of being a godless man whose faithlessness put him on a direct path to hell, Blacksnake responds by shrugging it off. Three times he retorts: "That's right." In performance, Staton altered the line so that instead of dismissing the preacher's threat, he replies: "I think you've got something there." Whether Staton was simply playing the line for laughs or affirming the importance of religion to black communities is unclear. What is clear, however, is that Staton and his fellow cast members challenged the authority of white directors and felt empowered to speak their own lines. In an oral history interview nearly forty years later, Staton recalled the reprimand he received from Burton James as if it were yesterday. "This is Stevedore, not a minstrel show." He turned right around and walked right out. Nobody said a word 'til he got out the door and then, on, boy! There was about 20 men in that room and each one of them got up and imitated how he came in and spoke to me, you know. Oh boy, Oh, boy. I'm telling you it lasted until I finally got mad enough to fight him."[127] Staton did not fight him directly. James had a reputation as an autocrat: fellow troupe member and playwright Theodore Browne called him "a very arrogant man . . . bent on doing things his way"; Charles Monroe, an actor and stage manager for the Seattle Negro Unit, remembered the long lectures he would give the cast in the middle of rehearsals on the causes of the Depression.[128] Monroe also recalled his own subversive backstage act during a performance of *Stevedore*, when he was in charge of the public announcement system. During a scene change the audience was supposed to hear a voice from a policeman's radio saying, "Calling all cars." Monroe played the line for laughs, changing it to "Calling Car 51. There's a report of a naked woman walking on Rampart Street. All other cars stay in your district." Florence James rushed backstage to scold him for breaking the spell.[129]

Florence and Burton James were part of a cadre of white theatre professionals who controlled the purse strings, administrative structures, and cultural capital that made them gatekeepers of American drama and theatre in the 1930s. Willing to work with African Americans, they were prepared to exploit racial stereotypes and the minstrel tradition to attract a predominantly white theatregoing audience. As Tina Redd points out, Burton James's insistence on putting "Negro" songs in between each scene of *Stevedore* reflected a broader racist ideology that positioned black Americans as "natural performers," who came armed with a ready store of black folk music. For Redd, the unequal power dynamic between the Jameses and the Seattle Negro Unit members left African Americans with "little room to negotiate."[130] Clearly the vision, ambition, and race privilege of white dramatists, directors, producers, and Federal Theatre administrators matter: their access to the funds and resources required to bring a drama to life was rooted in the history of the SRP and the conventions of white–controlled theatre. But the recorded desires and plans of white directors and administrators are not the only or last word on how Federal Theatre operated. We risk reinscribing racial hierarchies when we rely on white accounts of what black theatre was or should be; and we risk erasing the ways in which black Americans shaped the theatrical processes and dramas in which they performed.

The production records of the Federal Theatre and Seattle Repertory Playhouse, as well as black newspapers, letters of complaint, and oral histories, offer rich evidence that African Americans understood theatre as an eminently contestable site through which to explore and assert black autonomy. As troupe member Charles Monroe recalled much later, it mattered that many of those who acted in *Stevedore* experienced the play as "speaking their own mind about it." For Monroe, his performance "came right out of his stomach."[131] Such experiences helped to mobilize black performance communities and open up new possibilities for black theatre practitioners within the Federal Theatre. The production history of *Stevedore* also helps us to see how African Americans influenced debates among theatre communities on the eve of the Federal Theatre about the limitations and possibilities of realism. Working within and around the Negro Units, African Americans in the FTP were able to develop black theatre traditions and experiment with new dramas, birthing an activist black theatre movement that would continue well into the century. This birth was a painful one: the national and local politics of Federal Theatre bureaucracies and the politics of those plays that did and did not make it to the federal stage were mutually constitutive. The next chapter examines the battles that occurred over which dramas were produced on the federal stage. These struggles help us understand the evolution of a black dramatic tradition and the role of the Federal Theatre in the story of U.S. theatre.

2   They Love to Watch Us Dance

Exposing the Mask in Black Living Newspapers

· ·

When Burton James admonished Joe Staton for changing his lines in *Steve-dore*, fellow cast members enacted the exchange, parodying the white director until Staton "got mad enough to fight him."[1] In the early days of the Seattle Negro Unit, the troupe tested the boundaries and conventions of American theatre practice, rewriting the lines of white dramatists and acting out for each other the unequal power relations they experienced with white directors. Later on, they created dramas of their own. The evolving relationship between black performers and white and black spectators is central to the story of black Federal Theatre. As described in chapter 4, the creativity and conflict sparked by these relationships shaped the writing, performance, and reception of Ted Ward's *Big White Fog* in Chicago. This chapter looks at what happens when black performance and white spectatorship become the focus of the drama itself. *Stars and Bars* and *Liberty Deferred* were two radical black Living Newspapers that were developed, but never produced by the Federal Theatre. Living Newspapers, as their names suggests, combined the techniques of newspapers and theatre to explore pressing social and political issues. With roots in the Russian Revolution and the efforts of the Bolshevik government to disseminate news, education, and information, the Living Newspaper was taken up by the international workers' theatre movement in Europe before reaching the United States in the 1930s. Responsive, eclectic, and flexible at the outset, the model adapted by the FTP for the American theatre changed during the four years of the project. At the start of the FTP, the Living Newspaper was an experiment in nonrealist theatre that drew on staging techniques designed to emphasize the artificiality of theatre. Symbolic props were favored over naturalistic staging and newsreels were introduced, as well as the new device of the Voice of the Living Newspaper, a narrator of sorts who interrupts the action and offers critical commentary. While many of these devices continued to appear in American Living Newspapers, the FTP's Living Newspaper Unit increasingly adopted elements of realist staging. Many, but not all of the project's newspapers, were products of the Federal Theatre's new

Living Newspaper Unit. Based in New York City, it was staffed by journalists from the Newspaper Guild and led by playwright Arthur Arent. The first Living Newspaper to be staged by the FTP explored the problems of the farmer during the Depression. *Triple-A-Plowed Under* opened in March 1936, just two months after the U.S. Supreme Court struck down the Agricultural Adjustment Act (AAA), a 1933 law that allowed the federal government to pay farmers to reduce their crops and acreage in order to increase their value.[2] It was followed by versions in Chicago, Los Angeles, Milwaukee, and Cleveland. In January 1938 the FTP opened what would become the best known and most popular Living Newspaper. Taking its title from President Roosevelt's second inaugural address, *One Third of a Nation* examined America's housing crisis. The New York production ran for nearly a year and was seen by over 200,000 people. Unlike *Triple-A-Plowed Under*, which used film projection and amplified voices to create visual tableaus, the saga of the slums was "a masterpiece of stage illusionism."[3] When the FTP was shut down in 1939, its champions judged the Living Newspaper to be its crowning achievement. Critics, on the other hand, alternated between outrage at what they saw as New Deal propaganda disseminated at taxpayers' expense, and charges that the Living Newspaper called for a communist revolution. It is no surprise that the Living Newspaper would become a central focus of the Dies congressional committee's investigation into un-Americanism within the Federal Theatre Project.[4]

Both contemporary and historical accounts of the Living Newspaper have been influenced by the criticisms advanced by opponents of the FTP in Congress. Within a year of the project's demise, its director, Hallie Flanagan, wrote an account of the project in which she took pains to stress the Living Newspaper's American antecedents. According to Flanagan, the development of the Living Newspaper Unit was the product of a casual conversion between herself and Elmer Rice, soon to become the director of the New York FTP. Wondering how to find plays with casts large enough to employ the "hordes" of people on the project, Flanagan suggested he use them in Living Newspapers: "We could dramatize the news—without expensive scenery—just living actors, light, music, movement."[5] In Flanagan's account, the Living Newspaper owed nothing to the European form: "to the best of my knowledge," she claimed, "they did not resemble anything hitherto seen on the stage." Living Newspapers, she insisted, were as American as "Walt Disney, the March of Time, and the *Congressional Record*." A well-traveled theatre professional who had studied the theatre of Russia and Germany firsthand and written an important book on the subject, Flanagan's claim was disingenuous.[6] But if scholars have easily identified the direct influences of European workers' theatre on the FTP's Living Newspaper, that Flanagan chose not to do so in 1940 was hardly surprising given the charges of communist infiltration being leveled against the Federal Theatre Project.

The recovery of these much-maligned, but hugely popular, documentary dramas has been a slow one. The continued appeal of the Living Newspaper format, especially in times of economic recession, was evident in the 2011 revival of *One Third of a Nation* by the Metropolitan Playhouse in New York's East Village.[7] However, scholarship on white Living Newspapers is divided over whether they heralded a radical new form or remained mired in what some see as a resolutely "unradical" vernacular. For scholars of left-wing theatre such as Ira Levine, the Living Newspaper represented a decisive break with bourgeois realism.[8] The Living Newspaper introduced theatrical devices to break down the barrier between actor and audience by "disclosing" and "uncovering" events rather than simply "reproducing them."[9] Ilka Saal casts doubt on the notion that the Living Newspaper marked a significant shift away from realism, however, arguing that the U.S. tradition of commercial theatre flattened any radical impulses in interwar American theatre. Sparse sets, a documentary style, and mass casts reflected the parameters of FTP budgets rather than any new embrace of modernist political theatre. They were, she argues, "stylistic innovations that remained firmly embedded in a native concept of realism, one that privileged fact and experience over theory and abstraction." In fact, Saal views the Living Newspaper as exemplary of American vernacular theatre: it combined elements of European workers' theatre, such as devices to interrupt the plot, but remained reliant on naturalist staging and identification with individual characters. It did not represent a decisive break from American theatrical tradition.[10] The problem with this debate is that it is modeled on white Living Newspapers. As such, it is preoccupied with the realist/antirealist binary which shaped the white progressive theatre world which birthed many, but not all, of the Living Newspapers.

Scholars have identified up to four black-authored Living Newspapers that were in varying stages of development when the FTP closed in 1939. About three of them we know little and have no extant manuscript. These include: "Negro Script," a Living Newspaper by George Norford and Max Gandard; a second, on the history of slavery, which was under development; and a third examining slum housing in Harlem, which probably emerged from research for *One Third of a Nation*. The fourth was *Liberty Deferred*.[11] Written by Abram Hill and John Silvera under the supervision of National

Service Bureau (NSB) director Emmet Lavery, *Liberty Deferred* is ostensibly a history of black progress since Africans were first captured and forcibly brought to American shores. In tone and form, it has much in common with what we should understand as a fifth black Living Newspaper: *Stars and Bars*, a collaboratively devised newspaper that examines the racial discrimination and poverty of life of the northern "Negro" in Hartford, Connecticut. Although it is usually attributed solely to the young white playwright Ward Courtney, I argue that it should be included in any discussion of black Living Newspapers. It might seem axiomatic that a collaborative Living Newspaper, in which African Americans played a role in researching and writing should not be attributed to an individual white author. In fact, the contribution of African American members of the Hartford Negro Unit to the newspaper is recorded in the extant manuscript. Yet the drama continues to be attributed to the white dramatist in ways that reflect racial histories of American cultural production and deny black creativity. Privileging the individual white practitioner also obscures the collaborative process of both the Living Newspaper format and the working methods of the Hartford Negro Unit.[12]

Stars and Bars and *Liberty Deferred* were written between 1937 and 1938. The newspapers have much in common: both examine the relationship between black performance and white spectatorship and both parody the theatrical devices of the FTP's Living Newspaper. While satire can be found in white Living Newspapers, black Living Newspapers inhabit the form they intend to mock, appearing, at least initially, to legitimate its innovative techniques. In this sense they might be viewed as a form of what Sonnet Retman calls "modernist burlesque," a mode of satire that "occupies its subject from the outside in by pushing its most theatrical and technological elements to spectacular excess." What makes it modernist is the starring role played by technologies of mass production and media in communicating and upholding dominant narratives.[13] *Stars and Bars* and *Liberty Deferred* draw attention to the technologies that sustain cultures of lynching and deny black bodily integrity; they also unmask performative devices used within white Living Newspapers that consolidate, even as they critique, the racial discourses that enforce black subordination. Both black Living Newspapers mock the innovations of the white Living Newspaper for their perpetuation of racial capitalism in which black bodies become commodities to be consumed by liberal—and not so liberal—white audiences. By contrast, black Living Newspapers position white and black spectators as objects of the black gaze. *Liberty Deferred* deploys multiple onstage audiences and onlookers—a white couple, an interracial pair, and a black couple,—to draw attention to the performativity of blackness and the expectations of white spectators. Black audiences of minstrelsy were experienced in looking at themselves through white eyes; *Liberty Deferred* offered black audiences the opportunity to observe black figures looking at being looked at on stage. At the same time, it embraced the potential interracial audience made possible by the FTP, inviting white audience members to look at images of whiteness and blackness through the eyes of the "other." Perhaps most daring of all, it asked white audiences to "look at being looked at." Such multiple, and shifting perspectives not only position actual white and black audience members in the "strange situation of looking at one's self through the eyes of others," but also hold out the promise of inhabiting what Brechtian feminist Elin Diamond has called the "enlivened position of looking at being looked at ness."[14] Critical distance is also facilitated in *Stars and Bars* as the racial hierarchies that underpin the Living Newspaper's theatrical devices are ceremoniously unmasked: the Voice of the Living Newspaper is removed; black actors reject their lines and refuse to "perform" subordinate roles; white actors performing the roles of empowered whites are revealed to be complicit in perpetuating racial privilege.

Black Living Newspapers extended their parody of American theatre beyond the confines of the Federal Theatre Project: they also turned their attention to the truth claims of documentary and social realism, cultural vehicles long positioned as the engine of 1930s liberal social reform.[15] Numerous scholars have unsettled reductive ideas about Depression era genre by exploring the proliferation and popularity of hybrid texts. Sonnet Retman, for instance, demonstrates the porosity of satire and documentary, genres both driven by truth claims, while Denning argues that Popular Front arts pushed genre to excess, undoing established forms and narratives to disrupt audience expectations of passive reception. One example is the deployment of the "proletarian grotesque," a revolutionary "way of seeing" that "realigns our categories of allegiance" and "wrench[es] us out of the repose and distance of the aesthetic" through the juxtaposition of the incongruous.[16] Black Living Newspapers might be understood as part of a growing subgenre of hybrid texts that help us understand the power and reach of 1930s realism. Imitating the style and tone of 1930s documentary reportage, black Living Newspapers relate horrific details of bodily disease and of lynching in a manner that contrasts starkly with the grotesque absurdity of bodily mutilation. Collectively, the techniques deployed in black Living Newspapers might be understood as a form of "afro alienation."

In Daphne Brooks's conceptualization, "Afro-Alienation Acts" use the tactics of "heterogeneous performance strategies" to disrupt the narratives of blackness written into minstrelsy. Such disruption may take the form of experimentation with new techniques that eschew realist representation and defamiliarize black bodies in order to subvert and reinterpret dominant narratives of blackness.[17] This chapter argues that black Living Newspapers experimented with alienation techniques to undo master narratives and to wrench audiences out of passivity; in so doing, they created the space and devised the techniques necessary to build black culture anew.

Black Living Newspapers remain largely absent from studies of the Federal Theatre. This is partly a product of the FTP's enduring reputation for having produced few worthwhile black-authored dramas of any kind, a reputation that has, in turn, shaped access to manuscripts. There are complete, unpublished manuscripts for both *Stars and Bars* and *Liberty Deferred* in Federal Theatre archives at George Mason University and the Library of Congress. In 1989, a later, considerably revised, version of *Liberty Deferred* was published in an anthology of Federal Theatre Living Newspapers, while the first half of *Liberty Deferred* is also available in the 1996 edition of *Black Theatre U.S.A.* When black Living Newspapers feature in histories of the Federal Theatre, it is usually to lament the fact they were not staged. As such they have become no more than useful illustrations of how congressional opposition to the Federal Theatre made it impossible to produce radical theatre.[18]

Liberty Deferred and *Stars and Bars* are important to the history of the Federal Theatre, not simply because they were not staged: they are also literary artifacts in their own right. The manuscripts document the history of black artists in the Federal Theatre: they tell us about black dramatists and performers who worked in Negro Units, how they developed their craft as theatre practitioners, as well as their strategies for engaging with white power brokers. As we will see, black theatre workers used a variety of techniques, both in their dramas and also behind the scenes, to force white administrators and theatre professionals to engage with the history and practice of black performance and white spectatorship. These included experiments with form that shaped debates about how audiences might be encouraged to adopt a position of critical distance. As described in chapter 1, white leftist theatre practitioners debated theoretical innovations in theatre journals and left-wing magazines; African Americans critiqued theatrical form and suggested radical innovations on the pages of theatre manuscripts. The manuscripts of *Liberty Deferred* and *Stars and Bars* suggest the Living

Newspaper was neither the radical brainchild of a few white radicals nor a shoring up of New Deal reformism; in African American hands, the Living Newspaper became a highly self-reflexive vehicle that challenged, and sometimes changed, the ways in which power was brokered between white directors and black creatives within the Federal Theatre. Along this journey, black performance communities in New York City and in Hartford, Connecticut, played an important role in shaping the parameters and form of the Federal Theatre's Living Newspaper. This chapter begins with an examination of those white Living Newspapers which established the Federal Theatre's reputation as a producer of new theatre and considers the various theatrical devices which have come to be most associated with the Living Newspaper format. This sets the framework for a critical analysis of the development and dramaturgy of *Stars and Bars* and *Liberty Deferred*.

White Living Newspapers on the Federal Stage

When *One Third of a Nation* opened at New York's Adelphi Theatre in January 1938, Hallie Flanagan proclaimed it "one of the greatest successes in New York City Federal Theatre" and "the most mature living newspaper we had done." Versions of the "Saga of the Slums" soon opened in other cities, including Cincinnati; Detroit; Hartford; New Orleans; Philadelphia; Portland, Oregon; San Francisco; and Seattle; while in 1939, it was made into film by Paramount Pictures. Musing on its contemporary popularity, Eleanor Roosevelt also predicted the longevity of its appeal, speculating that the newspaper "will mean a tremendous amount in the future, socially, and in the education and growing-up of America."[19] She was proved right: *One Third* has dominated the scholarship on the Living Newspaper. Ilka Saal's verdict that the Living Newspaper offered no radical new form capable of challenging the conventions of American theatre rests on the presumption that the Living Newspaper story starts and ends with the popular success of *One Third*.[20] Surveying a broader range of Living Newspapers, Stuart Cosgrove considers the ways in which the form of the Living Newspaper developed over time. *Triple-A Plowed Under* had deployed nonrealist staging and was directed by Joseph Losey, who was interested in epic theatre and would later direct Bertolt Brecht's *Galileo*. The second Living Newspaper, *Injunction Granted*, examined the history of organized labor in the United States and its relationship with the judiciary. Popular with trade unions, it included a direct quotation from U.S. Communist Party leader Earl Browder and indicted the Roosevelt administration for failing to protect organized labor.

In the wake of complaints of propaganda and biased editorializing from both supporters and critics of the New Deal, Flanagan closed the production prematurely, in October 1936. Radical directors were pushed out and the Living Newspaper Unit was brought under closer supervision by Flanagan.[21]

One Third appeared to mark the shift of the Living Newspaper away from nonrealism and closer to New Deal liberalism. Some of this transition took place as the newspaper was developed. In 1937, the FTP funded a summer school at Vassar College, where Flanagan had taught drama prior to her appointment as national director. The summer school represented a significant investment of time and resources on the part of the FTP, as it brought together actors, directors, playwrights, designers, and technicians to learn and debate new theatre techniques and to collaborate on a new piece. *Housing* was a short, one-act Living Newspaper for a cast of ninety-nine people that was devised by the Living Newspaper Unit. The early versions reflect the Living Newspaper's experiments with nonrealist form. Director Howard Bolton recalled attempts "to discard conventional scenery and props and substitute an object background equivalent to the subjective, psychological material used by surrealist painters." Rather than attempting to recreate a realistic slum on stage, broken toilets, trash, old beds, and fire escapes were suspended above the stage so that the audience would see "people actually living under the shadow of these horrible objects."[22] However, when the Living Newspaper opened on January 7, 1938, New York audiences instead were presented with an intricately constructed tenement building. *"Housing"* had undergone significant alteration at the summer school, becoming a full-length Living Newspaper with a new title, written, as one advertisement explained, by the president himself. "One third" was a reference to the president's second inaugural address, in which he promised to root out the injustices that had made "one-third of a nation ill-housed, ill-clad, ill-nourished."[23] Allied closely to the administration that funded it, the Living Newspaper had retreated from its earlier flirtation with radical politics and form. In Cosgrove's view, "The Living Newspaper had not abandoned its investigative and oppositional campaign to change social conditions, but it had compromised on its role as the formal and political vanguard of the depression stage. It had moved a step back towards the safe terrain of naturalism."[24]

This "step back" was also apparent in the characterization. The most striking innovation is the introduction of the Little Man, a new character who interacts with the Loudspeaker or Voice of the Living Newspaper. The Little Man is the lens through which we experience the suffering and horror of countless generations of poor Americans living and dying in New York

FIGURE 4 Set for the New York production of *One Third of a Nation*. Library of Congress, Music Division, Federal Theatre Project Collection, Production Records, Photographic Prints File, Container 1181.

City's slums. At the same time, the Loudspeaker role has developed from that of simple narrator to all-knowing chronicler of America's past. Together they guide us through New York's real estate history, introducing the elderly, the infirm, the young, and all the vulnerable who are victims of cholera, speculators, landlords, and inept officials. Appeals to emotion propel these scenes: deaths, especially those of young children and the frail, are frequently staged; young adults are tragic figures who despair of bringing new life into a sorrowful world.[25] The Little Man, too, can scarcely watch the horrifying scenes that unfold before him.

For all its exposure of New York's miserable slums, *One Third* offers little in the way of solutions. Those individuals and corporations who make money out of the suffering of their fellow citizens are let off the hook. As the play reaches a climax, we learn that the "inertia" of tenement residents, of politicians, and of landlords is to blame. Low-cost housing cannot be provided by the private sector because there can be no profit in renting decent homes. Money must be taken from the armed forces in order to subsidize low-cost housing. Such a proposition might have been provocative to some, given the looming war in Europe— but it represented no existential threat, just a reordering of priorities within the existing system. *One Third of a Nation* ends with a call to action of a very general kind: "We're going to holler. And we're going to keep on hollering until they admit in Washington it's just as important to keep a man alive as it is to kill him."[26]

Although *One Third* would come to be regarded as the definitive Living Newspaper, Federal Theatre records suggest it was, in fact, the source and site of contestation about whether there was a role for realism within the Living Newspaper. Just as the show opened at the Adelphi Theatre in New York, the staff of the Living Newspaper Unit compiled a manual for students and theatre practitioners on how to write a Living Newspaper. It emphasized the form's flexibility while seeming to defend the reversion to realist staging in *One Third*: "the complex and many-sided nature of Living Newspaper subject matter does not actually prohibit but limits the use of stark- or quasi-realism in design and production." It went onto explain that audiences should not be surprised by the realistic staging they would encounter in *One Third*: "Almost from the very start the Living Newspaper was destined to go through many changes because no theatre medium had yet been developed with such unlimited capacity for transmitting subject matter of large proportions in crisp and efficient form."[27] This resistance to rigid categorization on the part of the Living Newspaper Unit draws attention to the hybridity of Popular Front arts in general and the fluidity of the FTP's Living Newspaper in particular. It reminds us that the direction of the Living Newspaper was still up for grabs when *One Third* was staged in 1938.

The Negro Dramatists Laboratory: Learning to Write a Living Newspaper

Two African Americans participated in the six week Federal Theatre summer school that developed *One Third of A Nation:* Shirley Graham, a composer, playwright, and supervisor on the Negro Unit in Chicago, and Byron Webb, the technical director at the Harlem Negro Unit. He was the only African American employed as a staff member at the summer school, where he ran classes on lighting technique. A third Negro Unit was connected to the summer school through the Puerto Rican set designer and Hartford Negro Unit supervisor Michael Adrian, who spent time at Vassar in summer 1937.[28] Just as prominent Federal Theatre professionals retreated upstate to plan a new Living Newspaper, African Americans devised their own summer school in New York City. The Harlem Negro Unit launched a summer session of the Negro Dramatists Laboratory (NDL) to develop a black Living Newspaper.[29] The NDL was a collaboration between the Harlem Negro Unit, the Living Newspaper Unit, and the FTP's Play Bureau, which was established shortly after black theatre professionals Gus Smith, Carlton Moss, and Harry Edward took over the management of the Harlem Negro Unit from John Houseman in 1936. The NDL aimed to address the "dearth of good plays dealing with the American Negro" and avoid the "spirit of defeatism" manifest in many of the plays presented to the unit.[30] One hundred black playwrights were invited to a meeting to discuss the aims and purpose of the laboratory in November 1936. By invitation of the Negro Unit management, George Zorn (Houseman's company manager) drew up a schedule of lectures and classes designed to develop a collective play and to provide a forum for writers to develop and get feedback on their work. The first NDL program ran from November 1936 to March 1937. It consisted of evening classes held two to three times a week and attracted an impressive lineup of guest speakers, including the black dramatist Frank Wilson, black set designer Perry Watkins, and white director of the Federal Theatre's Play Bureau Frances Bosworth. Fifty members enrolled and work began on a collective class play entitled "If the Townsend Plan," which was inspired by Francis Townsend's proposal to introduce a federal state pension for all people over age sixty. Later renamed "Granny," it was submitted to the FTP for experimental production. In his report Zorn explained that membership had dwindled by the end of the four-month course to twenty-five: playwrights returned sporadically, seeking constructive criticism from the group when they had something to show. Zorn estimated eighteen full-length and five short dramas had been submitted to a range of production sources following the course. Two had been accepted by the Federal Theatre and one by a professional theatre; other NDL participants had gone on to act on Broadway or receive further instruction in New York schools. Though there was something tangible to show, Zorn concluded that the success of the first NDL program in developing new black-authored plays was limited on account of the difficulty in engaging experts on playwriting.[31]

The NLD summer school was designed to address this issue. The stated aim of the 1937 summer school was to develop a new black Living Newspaper on the theme of "Negro Youth," with sessions led by Living Newspaper Unit chief Arthur Arent, black actors Edna Thomas and Wardell Saunders, and George Zorn. Open to all black dramatists, regardless of whether they were employed by the WPA, evening classes were scheduled to run twice a week over the four months of the summer.[32] There are no attendance records to indicate whether the creators of *Liberty Deferred* and *Stars and Bars* participated in the NDL summer school. As NSB employees living in New York City, Hill and Silvera knew about the summer school, and we can speculate that they may well have attended, given that the pair developed their own Living Newspaper shortly afterward.[33] While it is not clear whether members of Hartford Negro Unit participated in the NDL summer school (we know they regularly traveled to New York for Harlem Negro Unit productions, so they may have attended some sessions), it seems likely that they were aware of the ideas emanating from Federal Theatre headquarters and disseminated at the Vassar summer school. Along with other participants at Vassar, Michael Adrian had been instructed by Flanagan in her opening lecture to think of himself as representing 200 Federal Theatre Project workers. Indeed throughout their time at Vassar, Federal Theatre employees were repeatedly reminded of the important task that lay ahead in transmitting their training to the units back in the regions.[34] The Hartford Negro Unit appears to have shared this view of the responsibilities of their director. Gwen Reed, a leading actor for the Hartford Negro Unit, suggests the company saw Adrian as their delegate. In her account recording the history of the Hartford Unit, Reed describes how Adrian spent the summer of 1937 "absorbing any and all material necessary or valuable to bring back to the company," while the company "made plans and suggestions of their own for summer activities."[35]

The Hartford Negro Unit and *Stars and Bars*

The Hartford Negro Unit offers an interesting example of an amateur African American troupe that collaborated successfully with white supervisors and playwrights under the auspices of the FTP. The Negro Unit grew directly out of the Charles Gilpin Players, a long-established, independent black community theatre. Since 1921, the company had met in each other's homes, in churches, and in community halls, and had staged and directed their own work. For example the Gilpin Players put on company actor Ethel Goode's *There Is a God* as part of a race relations program at the Hartford YWCA. They also performed new work by white writers, including *Homage to Shiva*, a drama in verse written for them by the poet Lindley Williams Hubbell. From the outset they looked for opportunities to engage with, and actively solicited the involvement of, experienced white theatre professionals. In the 1920s they worked with Hallie Gelbart Reynolds, a white drama instructor, producing *The Merchant of Venice,* as well as plays by Ridgely Torrence and Paul Green. They were the first company to perform at Hartford's new Bushnell Memorial Hall, where they staged *In Abraham's Bosom.* A regular fixture in the Hartford theatre calendar for much of the decade, the Gilpin Players developed a reputation for performing the classics as well as producing their own dramas at community venues across the state.[36]

The death of Reynolds in 1930 and economic stresses of the early 1930s adversely affected the group's fortunes. This changed in 1935 with the establishment of the Federal Theatre Project. The Gilpin Players grasped the new opportunities on offer: three of their members, Service Bell, Theodore Howard, and Harold Taylor, performed in the Harlem Negro Unit's production of *Macbeth* in 1935, while the Gilpin Players approached Connecticut state FTP director Gertrude Don Dero with a proposal that the Federal Theatre sponsor a Negro Unit in Hartford. It took two volunteer productions before the Gilpin Players were formally established as a Federal Theatre Unit with paid workers. In the meantime, and at the group's request, the set designer Michael Adrian began working with the Gilpin Players as a supervising director in September 1936. Adrian was born Victor Ecchevaria to Spanish parents in Puerto Rico. He had spent time in New York as a researcher and technical assistant for Rudolph Valentino before moving to Hollywood, where he worked as art director for a number of film production companies. On his return East he was employed by the Civic Repertory Theatre in Bridgeport, Connecticut, and became part of the Hartford Federal Theatre as a designer and director.[37]

The Gilpin Players retained their strong identity as an independent community theatre in the second half of the decade. When the troupe produced two volunteer productions under Adrian's direction, *The Sabine Women* in December 1936 and *Noah* in May 1937, theatre reviews in the black press still referred to them as the Gilpin Project. Even after they became part of the Federal Theatre, reviewers continued to regard the company as being under the leadership of Lillian Tillman and W. Earle Smith, veteran actors who had been at the heart of the company since its foundation.[38] By this time Adrian had become a valued member of the black performance community, who understood the needs of the troupe. He held rehearsals in the evening since many of the actors held day jobs, and offered biweekly workshops and lectures on the history of theatrical form. Attracting an average attendance of fifty, the workshops were open to the public and "draw people from the Negro population of the city who are, as yet, not connected to the CHARLES GILPIN PLAYERS."[39] The hard work paid off. The

Gilpin Player's critical and box office success, as well as the eligibility of a number of the cast members to claim relief status, allowed state director Gertrude Don Dero to help this already well-established volunteer group achieve recognition and funding as an official unit of the Federal Theatre.[40]

In 1937 the Charles Gilpin Players became the Hartford Negro Unit. Adrian was made supervising director, but he also designed costumes and stage sets as well as directed a number of the Negro Unit's plays. In this he was supported by S. Iden Thompson. A white director who had worked with the Provincetown Players in the 1920s, Thompson directed the troupe in productions of *The Field God, The Emperor Jones, Jericho*, and *Porgy*. The Gilpin Players had a broad range of talents: Mariette Canty and Theodore Howard were actors who went on to work on Broadway; Gwen Reed came from the tobacco fields of Connecticut to become the secretary for the Gilpin Players, and later, a playwright-actor who performed leading roles in Negro Unit productions, and Alver Napper, who wrote one of the most striking scenes of *Stars and Bars*, would become an associate editor of the *Hartford Advocate* and leading figure in the Connecticut NAACP.[41]

The Hartford Negro Unit knew of, and sometimes adopted the repertoire of higher-profile Negro Units. For example they staged popular dramas by Paul Green. But they also worked with the white Federal Theatre Unit in Hartford to stage new dramas. In October 1938, under Adrian's direction, the two companies put on a production of *Haiti*, the wildly successful drama of black resistance first performed by the Harlem Negro Unit.[42] The two Hartford units came together for a second time a few months later. In January 1939, under the white director Daniel Reed, the Hartford Federal Theatre put on a production of *One Third of a Nation*, which pulled together talent from both white and Negro Units and required some rewriting of the scenes to accommodate the large, racially mixed cast. Staged at both the Bushnell and Avery Theatres in Hartford as well as the Schubert in Bridgeport, *One Third* was a sellout.[43]

Although *One Third* was not staged in Hartford until January 1939, nearly two years after the Negro Unit first began devising their own Living Newspaper, the influence of the FTP's most successful Living Newspaper on *Stars and Bars* is clear. The black Living Newspaper was still under development when *One Third* first opened to rave reviews in New York in January 1938.[44] Originally titled "The Hartford Negro," it was renamed "Bars and Stripes," and approved for development in April 1937. Director of the Federal Theatre's Play Bureau, Emmet Lavery, had signed it off, suggesting it "should be a good show" and a production was scheduled for the fall. The Hartford

Living Newspaper then disappeared from view until after the opening of *One Third* in New York City. Still called "Bars and Stripes," between February and June 1938, it appears in the monthly programming schedules for Connecticut Federal Theatre.[45] The Hartford Living Newspaper was never staged, and there is no record of how and why the decision was made to cancel its production.[46] Perhaps using the white and Negro Units to stage the tried and tested *One Third* seemed a safer bet than the collaboration between the little known Courtney and the Hartford Negro Unit.

It is impossible to know the precise parameters of the relationship between Courtney and the members of the unit but it seems that the well-established troupe chose to work with the aspiring young playwright. Certainly the Gilpin Players were a better-known quantity to the theatre-going public of Hartford than the white playwright. Shortly after becoming the Hartford Negro Unit, the troupe commissioned him to write *Trilogy in Black*, a black version of the Atreus Cycle, which they staged at the Avery Memorial on June 18, 1937. Separate from their Federal Theatre work, the troupe put on their own volunteer production under Courtney's direction, staging the Danish drama, *Jeppe on the Hill*, at the Avery Memorial in June 1938.[47] This close relationship and Courtney's frequent association with black dramas have led to some confusion over his racial identity, both at the time and subsequently. Irwin A. Rubenstein, manager of the Federal Theatre's NSB, which housed the play department, assumed, incorrectly, that he was African American. Rubenstein, it seems, had not troubled to inform himself of the actual racial identity of a number of playwrights whose work was performed by Negro Units. In a letter to a theatre manager, Rubenstein boasted that "most of the negro units have negro playwrights on their staffs" and went on to misidentify Frank B. Wells (the white southerner who wrote the racist John Henry play for the Los Angeles Negro Unit), William Debois (Dubois, the white author of *Haiti*), and Ward Courtney as "Negro" playwrights.[48] Yet in his preface to *Trilogy in Black*, Courtney describes the "Negro" actor in terms that make his own racial affiliation clear: "he [the Negro actor] has the universal feel of Love and Hate that one of our own race can seldom put across the lights."[49]

The Hartford Negro Unit, and Courtney's role as a dramatist within it, comprise a significant, if overlooked, part of the history of the Negro Units, as well as the history of dramatic collaboration between black and white playwrights. The fact that Courtney is usually, and mistakenly, assigned exclusive authorship of the Living Newspaper is hardly surprising: when black and white theatre professionals worked together to develop a black-originated script, it was usually whites who reaped the artistic and financial rewards. Langston Hughes learned this the hard way when his drama *Mulatto* was turned into a sensational Broadway show in 1935 by the white producer Martin Jones.[50] There were plenty of whites in American theatre who wanted to work with black creatives; there were few able to work collaboratively with and for the mutual benefit of both parties.

The record of collaboration between Negro Unit members and white directors and playwrights in the Hartford Negro Unit is patchy, but we are able to get sense of how the relationship worked through WPA publicity notices. Press releases issued by the administrative office credited the work of African American members of the troupe in a range of roles. They often began by recounting the history of the Gilpin Players, "who were well known throughout Connecticut as a dramatic troupe of unusual talent and ambition," before moving onto mention Adrian's expertise as a stage and costume designer and director. Responsibility for fulfilling his artistic vision was invested in the workshop on Main Street where the "Negro staff" were led by stage manager W. Earle Smith and James "Rastus" Walker, who "headed" the "acting personnel." According to one WPA publicity notice, "Negroes" on the Hartford Negro Unit "are not content with being the best natural actors in the world they persist in some of its best playwriting as well." While there were no black playwrights formally employed by the Hartford Negro Unit, troupe members apparently found other ways to become co-creators of theatre manuscripts, through impromptu revisions to the script in rehearsal:

> Nearly always the substitutions are so much better than the original parts that a wise director writes them into the script and they are acted that way from then on. This fast and loose and healthy playing around with an author's work was responsible for some of the best touches in "The Sabine Women" which the Negro Unit of the WPA Federal Theatre Project presented at the Palace Theatre in December. Michael Adrian, supervising director, not only welcomed these spontaneous revisions during rehearsals of that show but very early in the proceedings he began to watch for such improvements.[51]

An illustration of this was the unit's second production, *Noah*. Written by the French author André Obey, the Hartford Negro Unit remade *Noah* with "original delightful bits" and "words called from the wings" by cast members awaiting cues. The press notice concluded that these were natural adjustments, "which just seem to happen when stage-minded Negroes are in production with a show they believe in."[52] Casting African Americans as both "natural" actors and spontaneous playwrights, WPA publicity notices for black and interracial theatre on the FTP were paternalistic at best; at worst they pandered to and reinforced harmful clichés about African Americans as talented but untrainable. The manuscript of *Stars and Bars* provides an alternative account of the central role played by African Americans in devising new theatre manuscripts.

The *Stars and Bars* manuscript contains a number of clues as to how the collaborative process worked. The title page acknowledges its multiple collaborators: "Based on research compiled by the author with the cooperation of the Negro Unit of Connecticut Federal Theatre." Elsewhere in the manuscript, authorship as well as credit for material is attributed to individual Negro Unit members.[53] Understanding *Stars and Bars* as a collective venture, rather than the product of a sole author, helps us appreciate its significance as a Living Newspaper. For *Stars and Bars* does not offer the conventional liberal critique of racial inequality; instead, it unmasks the role of Living Newspapers in reproducing the racial fictions that sustain white supremacy. Such unmasking is achieved by inhabiting and satirizing the Living Newspaper format. Divided into two acts, the first follows the formula of *One Third of a Nation*: the Loudspeaker or "Voice" of the newspaper leads the Little Man (a Connecticut Yankee) through a potted history of milestones in the black freedom struggle. Although Hartford Negro Unit members were involved in developing the first act, and its transformational final scene, African American voices are more prominent in Act 2. Here the Living Newspaper diverts from its earlier progress narrative and toward a pointed assault on racist attitudes, practices, and structures that have conspired to keep black Americans poor.

Stars and Bars opens with a black janitor and elevator operator chatting. Soon they are called off stage by the stage manager and assistant manager because the formal drama is about to begin.[54] Foregrounding onstage black spectators from the outset serves to remind the audience that performances of race are already mediated by the racial discourses that connect the lives of Hartford's citizens with their membership of this temporary theatre audience. Typically Living Newspapers drew attention to the mediated nature of theatrical performance through the role of the Loudspeaker, and *Stars and Bars* is no exception. In *Stars and Bars*, the Loudspeaker has a prominent editorial role right from the start. In the first scene, which is set in 1850, he introduces the slave ship "bearing slaves for the Land of the Free" and explains the United States' relationship to slavery: "The United States of

America, first of the republics of modern times: founded on Revolution, established on the principles that all men are created equal, last great patron of slavery in Western Civilization. America shuddered at the horrors of slave ships—outlawed them, but continued buying their cargoes. America so loved Liberty that she enslaved another race that her citizens might have more Freedom!"[55] The Loudspeaker is quickly established as a probing interrogator of American racial narratives. Yet the narrow parameters of the Loudspeaker's reformism are soon revealed. Believing civil rights are enshrined in the constitutional amendments passed after the Civil War, the Loudspeaker maintains that African Americans need only insist upon the enforcement of the amendments to achieve their freedom.[56] With the Loudspeaker's liberal reformism clearly established, the limits of such an approach are soon made clear.

In *Stars and Bars*, the Loudspeaker is exposed as one more theatrical technique that serves to consolidate, rather than challenge, the power of American racist discourse. In Act 1, Scene 4, entitled "Milestones," the Loudspeaker narrates a familiar story of how black Americans have been gradually incorporated into the American Republic, covering Connecticut's outlawing of the slave trade, Crispus Attucks's role in the War of Independence, and the abolition of slavery in Connecticut in 1790. When the Loudspeaker turns to southern slavery, his authority is challenged by the character of the "NEGRO": "NEGRO with microphone [is] SPOTTED at one end of stage." Interrupting the Loudspeaker, he reflects on the hypocrisy of northern whites:

Negro: For the most part discrimination and prejudice went hand in hand with the sentiments for abolition. To this day the South treats her Negroes like children. But children are human. In the North Negroes are regarded as not quite human. I do not want to condone the attitude of the South toward my race, I merely wish to point out the singular fact that the Southerner thinks and acts consistently, while most Northerners think and talk sympathetically while they discriminate and exploit.
Loudspeaker: That's about enough from you.
Negro: In the North the free Negro is debarred from fellowships not of his own race; he has been ruthlessly excluded from the more profitable occupations.
Loudspeaker: Please leave the stage, and permit me to go on reading from my history book.

Negro: History book! The trouble with you is you can be liberal until you come down to your own times—your own generation! Are you willing to admit that discrimination and prejudice are not by any means dead right here in Connecticut?

Loudspeaker: I am not in a position to admit that. I am not required to admit such things. Any newspaper has the right to be conservative.

Negro: I'm going to ask for a change of Editors for the Living Newspaper!

Loudspeaker: Black him out!

(Blackout)

Now let us go on with our Milestones in the history of the Negro in America. No doubt this Negro is a Communist.[57]

Following this exchange, NEGRO is picked out by a spotlight: he is holding a red herring on a string, a mocking response to the Loudspeaker's attempt to dismiss him as a communist agitator, which was the charge frequently used to discredit attacks on American racism in the 1930s.

The exchange between the Loudspeaker and NEGRO serves to implicate directly the imagined audience for FTP Living Newspapers. Developed mainly in New York and other northern cities, white Living Newspapers usually targeted the hypocrisies of inhabitants of other places and others times, such as southerners or unenlightened ancestors. When they examined problems closer to home, the focus was often on powerful elites. Greedy bankers, corrupt officials, and exploitative corporations, all served to help audiences better understand the injustices wrought against the Little Man. By contrast, the Hartford Living Newspaper refused to settle responsibility on outsiders, or to reserve its criticism for elites. Instead, it pointed the finger directly as its audience. Unlike *Stevedore*, *Stars and Bars* does not allow American racism to be viewed as a sectional problem. Rather, it directly targets the complacent northerner, the white Yankee from Connecticut who refuses to recognize the racial sins of his own community. This critique is delivered through a challenge to the very form of the Living Newspaper, and in particular the device of the Loudspeaker. Typically the Loudspeaker served to guide the Little Man, helping him understand the historical roots and contemporary causes of a major social ill. In *Stars and Bars*, the Loudspeaker becomes part of the problem. Conceived as white and male, the Loudspeaker lends authority to the reformist agenda of the New Deal and helps to avert a more radical restructuring of American society. In critiquing the Loudspeaker, *Stars and Bars* challenges the newly emerging conventions that governed the Federal Theatre's Living Newspaper.

The role of the American theatre in sustaining racial hierarchy emerges as a central theme in *Stars and Bars* as the audience witnesses a dramatic work that self-consciously replicates the very hierarchies it claims to challenge. In a scene ostensibly about the relationship between white employers and black workers in Connecticut, NEGRO refuses to play the role written for him. When YANKEE offers NEGRO his henhouse as a family home, NEGRO steps outside his assigned character to play the role of the black actor. NEGRO/Black Actor not only rejects the offer to house his family in a chicken hut, he challenges the scene that has been written for him. "Do you know what's wrong with that?" he asks the white actor who plays YAN-KEE. But the white actor is unable to deviate from the script. Instead he simply repeats his line, insisting that the henhouse is a good deal. "To you cheap," he tells NEGRO, as if his fellow actor had simply forgotten his lines. Black Actor/NEGRO is no longer prepared to respond to the white man's cue. Instead, he demands the White Actor playing YANKEE recognize the connection between his white ancestors' exploitation of black Americans and the White Actor roles he is empowered to play on the contemporary stage. Stepping out of "character" again, Black Actor insists: "I'm an actor. I'm not here to work for men like you. That's what you gave my grandfather 'cheap' that's just about what you gave all the Negroes you sent for to come up here and work for almost nothing! Your imaginary henhouse over there would be a palace compared to what I see all around me here in Hartford's North End."[58] Black Actor articulates the frustrations of African Americans whose performative labor was often enlisted in order to shore up racial hierarchies established in plantation slavery and adapted to control millions of black Americans who left the South hoping for better jobs in northern cities. He also draws attention to the alienation experienced by black performers and audiences on encountering narratives of white domination in which black subjugation is assumed, rather than fought over. Crucially such alienation not only makes visible the condition of alterity experienced by black performers and audiences, but converts this alienation into "self-actualizing performance." To paraphrase Brooks, the performance of alienation has become the means to liberation.[59] For a moment it appears that Black Actor's challenge might only consolidate white power on and off stage. NEGRO is quickly categorized by whites as "uppity" for his refusal to play out his assigned part as grateful recipient of the white man's beneficence.

The Loudspeaker insists he "get into your part." When he refuses, the Loud-speaker engages STOOGE (a black "yes man") to replace NEGRO. But he will not be dismissed so easily. When the Loudspeaker attempts to continue his narrative, NEGRO returns to challenge the Loudspeaker's authority with the announcement that he has an order to change the Voice of the Living Newspaper. Under pressure, the Loudspeaker's 'real' attitudes are made apparent: "Why you impudent African! I'm intrenched in this job. The editorship is beyond criticism. You're an unappreciative sort: why tonight I'm going to show these good people the heroic qualities of your race. How they have progressed in the Arts, Music, Theatre, Education! I shall make them weep with tears of sympathy for the Negro's guileless soul. I shall teach Hartford to love and cherish her 8000 Negroes like little children."[60] This is the last we hear of the Loudspeaker. His racist views uncovered, he is swiftly replaced by a "more vital, younger" character, Voice of the Living Newspaper. The new Voice expels STOOGE and YANKEE, summoning the stage managers to come and "move these 'milestones' out of the way." The new Voice announces a change of direction: "From now on this Living Newspaper will be concerned with the City of Hartford only." With the title "DISCRIMINATION" projected in large letters on to the stage, the Living Newspaper turns to examine how racial injustice operates in present day Hartford.[61]

The closing scene of Act 1 marks a departure from the historical milestones depicted in the first four scenes. Whereas earlier scenes follow a typical Living Newspaper format, tracing America's progress from the dark days of slavery, under new management *Stars and Bars* showcases examples of current racial discrimination and the experiences of slum housing provided by members of the Hartford Negro Unit. Its targets are wide-ranging, and indictments are leveled against bankers, landlords, and local politicians, as well as ordinary white residents of Hartford who profit from the city's black slums. Act 2 opens with Alver Napper's extraordinary poem, "Drama of the Slums," a parodic citation of *One Third of a Nation*, which advertised itself in regional productions as a "Saga of the Slums."[62] Featuring Tuberculosis, Infant Mortality, and Syphilis, characters who snatch women, men, and children and dance them, off stage, to their death, the poem dramatizes the catastrophic consequences for those forced to endure inhuman living conditions. The characters representing diseases associated with slum housing reappear in Act 2, Scene 4, where they are joined by Pneumonia. Together they vie for control of the ill and vulnerable, shooting dice to determine who will get the privilege of seizing the remaining victims.[63] This nod to *One Third*, and the light-hearted personification of diseases that disfigure and destroy black bodies, signals that *Stars and Bars* is not only a burlesque of the FTP's most popular Living Newspaper, but also of the performative mutilation of black bodies that made lynching the defining spectacle of the Jim Crow South. As Susan Glenn has argued, burlesque is both a "parodic imitation of literary and theatrical texts and styles . . . as well as contemporary social, culture and political fashions and foibles."[64]

Act 2 represents a shift in focus, for it foregrounds black experiences and the representation of slum housing. Napper's authorship and authority to represent black living conditions are clearly recorded in the manuscript. Napper was an activist experienced in protesting substandard housing for black Americans. He was elected secretary of the statewide, interracial Negro Social Conference, which met in New Haven in June 1938 to address black social problems and was part of a delegation to the mayor of Hartford to protest the exorbitant rents faced by black Hartford citizens. Napper was also a member of the North End Tenants Association, whose reports on slum housing feature in *Stars and Bars*. Napper himself features as a character in *Stars and Bars*. In the penultimate scene, Napper's character delivers a report on behalf of the Tenants Association calling for greater tenant protection against exploitative landlords and the establishment of a Federal Housing Unit to ensure higher quality housing. By the end of Act 2, African Americans are no longer alienated spectators to white narratives of black subordination; instead, they are becoming agents of their own liberation.[65]

Napper was not the only member of the Hartford Negro Unit to feature in *Stars and Bars*. Donald Wheeldin, a lead actor for the unit who was active in the Communist Party, and Ward Courtney, the white playwright, appear as NEGRO and AUTHOR respectively, in Act 2, Scene 3. It is one of the most self-reflexive scenes to appear in a Federal Theatre Living Newspaper. The two men are "looking for material for the Living Newspaper," and they have come to a crowded slum to interview a female tenant whose experiences with an exploitative landlord were dramatized earlier in the scene. The audience has already witnessed the landlord warning his tenant against reporting her miserable living conditions to the authorities. In telling her story to NEGRO and AUTHOR, and to the Living Newspaper audience, the tenant is taking a risk. The Loudspeaker acknowledges as much when he tells the audience: "the characters are not fictional—this woman lives in Hartford's North End." A footnote affirms that the scene is based on the "author's experience," and that it was "witnessed" by a Negro Unit member,

Mr. Wheeldin. It is interesting that it is the black man who is needed to le-gitimate the white author's account, in an inversion of publishing practices begun in slavery and continued through the Harlem Renaissance, in which black authors required a white authority to validate their work.[66] Other unit members also contributed material, including whole scenes, to *Stars and Bars*. In Scene 5 of Act 1, a sketch dramatizing discrimination against a black patron of a café is footnoted as being "based on the experience of Miss Jones with her permission," while the title page for Scene 5 records that Gwen Reed wrote the sketch about the second-class medical treatment received by black Americans. Reed, who performed her first role for the company in Courtney's *Trilogy in Black*, would go on to play a number of roles on Broad-way and Hollywood as well as Aunt Jemima for the Quaker Oats Company. She also wrote her own dramas and kept a record of the Hartford Negro Unit's experiences.[67]

Like most Living Newspapers, *Stars and Bars* was a collaborative work rather than the vision of one dramatist. Partly written and devised by the Hartford Negro Unit, it reflected the priorities of its members and the broader black performance community that had been developing since the establishment of the Gilpin Players in 1921. It was also a parody of white Living Newspapers, and especially *One Third of a Nation*. By inhabit-ing the Living Newspaper format, *Stars and Bars* was able to show up Amer-ican theatre practices that reproduced rather than challenged America's racial codes, and to mock the idea of the white Living Newspaper as a radi-cal force in American culture. *Stars and Bars* was an important theatrical experience for black Americans: members of the Hartford Negro Unit had the opportunity to dramatize their experiences and to work collaboratively with a white playwright to undermine the racial fortress that guarded American theatre making. But it promised something new for white Amer-icans too: a rare opportunity to look behind the curtain that separated them from black Americans. Such a glimpse was vital to the creation of a black theatre, according to Napper. In an essay outlining his theory of "Ne-gro Theatre" and its relationship to the Federal Theatre, Napper explained why Americans needed this kind of black theatre: "America should be given a chance to look behind the scenes, to see for herself why and how the Ne-gro thinks and thus appreciate the Negro's contribution, his hopes and am-bitions which too frequently meet the rebuff of unsympathetic, uninformed sophistication of whites who live and move in a world they mistakenly think as apart from the Negro."[68] If the first act of *Stars and Bars* positioned its audiences as familiar with liberal critiques of American racial narratives, the second act reveals the performative nature of racial knowledge. *Stars and Bars* allowed its audience to observe the "apparatus of representation," both by pulling back the curtain on black performativity and through unmasking the "uninformed sophistication of whites."[69]

Black Performers, White Spectators, and Liberty Deferred

In her 1969 study, *Negro Playwrights in the American Theatre, 1925–1959*, Doris Abramson argued that "Writing a Living Newspaper demanded a theatrical sophistication that was probably beyond John Silvera and Abram Hill. It would have been beyond most of the Negro playwrights."[70] The idea that black dramatists were incapable of writing scripts that merited production was widely held during and after the Federal Theatre. Such a narrative relies, at least in part, on the repeated assertion that black-authored dramas do not address universal themes. But it also rests on an untroubled ignorance of black theatre manuscripts: Abramson had never seen a manuscript of *Liberty Deferred* or several other black dramas about which she wrote.[71] The charge that black dramas lack universalism and the inattention to black theatre manuscripts are mutually constitutive forces that have inhibited analysis of the development and evolution of black theatre manuscripts and black dramatic form. This is a problem, not least because black theatre manuscripts are one of our main sources for understanding how African Americans understood, debated, and theorized black theatre in the first half of the twentieth century. Although black Federal Theatre dramas often failed to get as far as the tryout stage, some, like *Liberty Deferred,* did make it through a number of stages of revision, rewriting, and resubmission. These processes are worthy of careful consideration. Reports from Federal Theatre's play reading department reveal that white Americans often judged black dramas unsophisticated and unproducible when they eschewed or challenged white perspectives. The negotiations which took place between black dramatists and white Federal Theatre administrators over *Liberty Deferred* suggest that black dramatists mastered, critiqued, and even parodied white conceptions of theatre. This resistance is evident in the manuscripts of *Liberty Deferred*.

There are five closely related Federal Theatre manuscripts of *Liberty Deferred*. Two, almost identical, drafts are held at the Library of Congress, while George Mason University holds another two that are essentially the same, as well as a further manuscript with an altered ending. I have named these the "early drafts." All five manuscripts are undated, but we can be fairly confident that one of them, or at least something quite similar, was the working draft under discussion by Hill, Silvera, and the white director of the playreading department, Emmet Lavery, in winter 1937 and spring 1938. This is because the correspondence between the men refers to key characters as well as the overarching structure found in the early drafts. Since there was no Federal Theatre production, my concern has not been to establish which version was performed or even the last version to be approved by the authors. Rather, I am interested in how the early draft manuscripts developed in relation to the revisions recommended by Lavery to the authors. Accordingly, my analysis of *Liberty Deferred* will be based on the early drafts held at the Library of Congress because they correspond mostly closely to the written negotiations between the authors and Lavery about the direction of *Liberty Deferred*.[72] However, there are, in addition, a number of other, later draft versions of the manuscript. These include a version held by the New York Public Library for the Performing Arts, as well as two published versions. These versions contain significant variation and offer a fascinating epilogue to the struggle for control that took place between Lavery and the playwrights in the winter of 1937 and the following spring.[73]

Between 1937 and 1938, Hill and Silvera wrote a black Living Newspaper for the FTP with the encouragement of Emmet Lavery.[74] In addition to directing the playreading department, Lavery was a recognized playwright and strong advocate for the Federal Theatre. He frequently defended the right of the FTP to operate free from external pressures.[75] Hill was an aspiring young playwright, who had previously worked as a drama coach for the Civilian Conservation Corps, while Silvera, a self-proclaimed "adjectives man," had organized publicity for black shows, including the road tour of the Harlem Negro Unit's hit version of *Macbeth*. It seems that Hill, the more experienced dramatist, was the driving force in dramatic terms, though both men were experienced readers of white-authored "race" dramas in their roles as playreaders for the National Service Bureau.[76] As Hill recalled, their job in the playreading department required them to analyze scripts "with Negro characters or Negro themes to see that these were true to honest portrayals of Negro life or whether they were the stereotyped kind of plays." Hill read plenty of cliché-ridden, white-authored dramas of black life. He later wondered why none of the plays he recommended was ever produced.[77] Although there is no record of Hill and Silvera having reviewed the Hartford Negro Unit's *Stars and Bars*, their role as playreaders make it likely that they would have availed themselves of the opportunity to do so.

In fact, *Liberty Deferred* uses tropes very similar to those deployed in *Stars and Bars* to dramatize how whites imagine black life.

The manuscript of *Liberty Deferred* that was presented to Lavery in December 1937 demanded that the entire American white public be held to account for its part in the oppression of black Americans. This represented a stark contrast with white Living Newspapers, which appealed to a white everyman by targeting special interests such as slum landlords, utility companies, and monopolies. In common with *Stars and Bars*, however, *Liberty Deferred* offered no unifying figure around which the audience might unite. On the contrary, the motivations of white spectators who enjoyed watching African Americans perform are called into question and placed front and center of the Living Newspaper. The first scenes of *Liberty Deferred* are set before an onstage audience consisting of a white couple: a southern belle, Mary Lou, and her northern counterpart, Jimmy, who wants to show her the sights of Manhattan. In the first scene Jimmy persuades Mary Lou to come uptown to experience black entertainment: "come the Harlem moon and their day is begun . . . gin, swing, trucking and sin . . . that's all they ask. . . . they like their fun straight. . . . just a happy-go-lucky, devil may care bunch of God's chillun. . . . I know these people, I know 'em."[78] A series of pageants designed especially for white consumption unfold before the white couple. They include a team of Big Apple Dancers; a railroad porter, bowing and scraping for his meager tips; bandana-wearing cotton pickers of the Hollywood variety; "noisy, vulgarly dressed blacks playing at craps—the Hollywood version of the Negro's favourite pastime"; and a traditional vaudeville act. Stage directions indicate that they should be accompanied by: "platitudinous music with all the clichés one might expect: snatches of banjos twanging, raucous trombones, occasional fragments of torch-singing voices, wailing saxophones, spirituals—in other words, it is a sound background for the visual scenes. "[79] These are the images of black life expected by white Americans who "know their darkies." Stage directions indicate that the flashes should be done in a satirical manner, "the object of which is to portray the Negro as he too often is shown on the screen, stage and over the air; in fact, as he is seen through the eyes of JIMMY and MARY LOU, who represent white supremacy."[80] But just as audiences are settling into looking at black entertainers through a white lens, the white perspective is abruptly interrupted. As the music slows, we see a young black couple, Linda and Ted, dancing quietly across the stage. The couple's slow movements are in stark contrast to the noisy scenes that precede them, which serve to emphasize the distortions required in any presentation of black "reality" before a white audience. Aware of the white onlookers, Linda asks her boyfriend, "Don't they see anything else?" Ted replies: "Nope. They have blinders attached to their eyes—blinders that are made out of stuff which is a combination of news—print, movie film, and essence of microphone, with just a dash of grease-paint. . . . You can buy those blinders any day of the week."[81] An indictment of the news and cultural industries' perpetuation of racial stereotypes, Ted's list is also a swipe at the Living Newspaper, whose technical innovations are simply the most recent mechanism for the mass communication of America's racial codes: newsprint for "factual" stories; film projection, microphone, and the character of the Loudspeaker to break up the action; a spot of makeup to sustain make-believe. These are the "blinders" through which white Americans view black Americans, regardless of dramatic form. Whether realist, agitprop, or Living Newspaper, American dramas are always consumed within a racist, capitalist society, in which black bodies are just one more commodity. As Ted explains, the only fields of "achievement" open to him as a black man are those chosen by, and for the amusement of, whites. "Maybe if I trained as hoofer I'd get a job. Maybe if I had the numble [nimble] feet of a Bill Robinson or a Jessie Owens I'd get along."[82]

Having invited white audience members to look at being looked at, the next scene is a flashback that takes in early European immigration to the New World, the roots of slavery, and the eventual abolition of the U.S. slave trade in 1806. Here the narrative is interrupted by Mary Lou and Jimmy. They have not been enjoying the history lesson: Jimmy complains: "I came here for entertainment—is this what they call entertainment?" When Mary Lou blames Jimmy for exposing her to such "downright insolence," he tries to explain it away: "It's probably a gag, honey. It's probably just a new routine."[83] Coming from the mouth of Jimmy, the line is an ironic comment on the inability of any theatrical form to dismantle the "blinders" through which whites view African Americans. Foregrounding whiteness as an American problem was a bold and unprecedented move for a Living Newspaper: *The South*, an early Living Newspaper, which was developed but never staged by the FTP, had limited its analysis of race to one part of the U.S. racial problem; *Stars and Bars* turned its focus on the northern city. *Liberty Deferred* took a broader view: the entire white American public should be held to account for America's racial sins and black Americans must be prepared to lead the reckoning. In *Liberty Deferred*, black Americans do not naïvely support the American creed. They have learned that black freedom requires revolutionary change. The climax is a convention of the National Negro Congress (NNC), the national coalition of former Garveyites, trade unionists, socialists, communists, and those disillusioned by the NAACP's leadership, who came together in 1936 to reject the remedies of the New Deal and channel black activists toward a more radical route to freedom.[84] In *Liberty Deferred*, the radical potential of this new coalition is realized: NNC delegates resolve to boycott the American Constitution, dismissing it as "a scrap of paper in the hands of unscrupulous politicians."[85]

Liberty Deferred closes with a typical socialist realist ending, one that appears to parody the unexpected interracial alliance that often closed Depression-era labor plays such as *Stevedore*. At the conclusion of *Liberty Deferred*, white unions, which had previously excluded black workers, become sudden converts to black liberation. This surprising change of heart is accounted for by the defeat of Jim Crow, a character who dominates the last eight scenes of the newspaper. Introduced initially as a "distinguished citizen," who is singlehandedly responsible for discrimination against black Americans, Jim Crow's true identity is revealed when he appears at the NNC convention to counter the arguments for black equal rights. Jim Crow turns out to be none other than the White American Public. Arrested and threatened with a lynching by NNC delegates, Jim Crow/White American Public finally consents to the passage of an anti-lynching bill and an end to segregation. There is a jubilant finale in which black leaders, including W. E. B. Du Bois, Mary McLeod Bethune and James Ford, sing the Negro National Anthem and call for "a place in the Sun."[86] The final scene, however, appears to parody the socialist realist tradition by deliberately undercutting the optimistic ending. Just as the great and good of black leadership parade toward a nebulous place in the sun, stage directions indicate that Jim Crow viciously cracks his whip as if to underscore the fantasy we are witnessing.[87] It is an ending that appears to mock, more than it proposes solutions. Jim Crow is not some dramatic character, easily conjured and soon dispelled, but rather a way of life constructed for the benefit of, and controlled by, white Americans.

The preponderance of scholarship on *Liberty Deferred* has focused on why it was never produced by the Federal Theatre. A number of scholars have speculated that any attempt to stage the black newspaper would have prompted cries of outrage from the congressional "guardians of Americanism" who would begin their assault on the New Deal under the auspices of the Dies Committee in late summer 1938.[88] Certainly Living Newspapers were controversial from the outset, not just because of their political content, but because they were viewed by some as an attempt by the Federal

Theatre to make theatre politically. Political pressure on the Living Newspaper Unit dated back to its first aborted production, *Ethiopia*. Scheduled to open in January 1936, *Ethiopia* explored the recent Italian invasion of Abyssinia. The Living Newspaper's claims to be politically impartial because based on documentary sources was first tested in *Ethiopia*, which featured speeches by Benito Mussolini and Haile Selassie. Senior officials in the White House feared there might be diplomatic repercussions if a speech by a foreign head of state was placed in the mouth of an actor employed by the federal government. The White House's intervention led to a ban on the dramatic impersonation of any foreign head of state on the federal stage, the resignation of Elmer Rice as director of the New York Federal Theatre in protest at censorship, and the cancellation of *Ethiopia*.[89] Attempts by politicians to shape Living Newspapers did not end there. When *One Third* opened in January 1938, it soon became clear that U.S. senators took a dim view of seeing their own speeches delivered by actors in front of the footlights, even when they were "exact quotes from the Congressional record."[90] A group of senators who had voted against the Wagner housing bill and who appeared as characters in *One Third* went on the attack after newspapers reported that theatre audiences had booed and hissed at their characters on stage. Arthur Arent publicly denied having heard any booing. Insisting that *One Third* merely presented facts, he refused to alter it, even after one senator was quoted in the *Motion Picture Herald* as saying "foreign elements" must be behind such un-American shows.[91] Arent's defense of the Living Newspaper was supported by senior Federal Theatre administrators who were prepared to take risks to defend the project's flagship new drama. They neither amended nor apologized for *One Third*, even in the face of public criticism from congressmen. In seems, then, that the Federal Theatre still felt strong enough to defend its Living Newspapers in spring 1938, when Hill, Silvera, and Lavery were discussing the new black Living Newspaper.

Liberty Deferred was a more radical and provocative drama than the pro–New Deal *One Third*, and there is no doubt that it would have upset southern senators and, down the line, the Dies Committee. Yet it is hard to concur with speculations that *Liberty Deferred* was scuppered by anti–New Dealers in Congress. The Dies Committee was not established until May 1938, and congressional investigations did not get underway until late summer and early autumn 1938. Lavery's problems with *Liberty Deferred* dated back to December 1937. *Liberty Deferred* shone a spotlight on southern lynching, but it also targeted, albeit from a different political perspective, many of the same forces that animated those hostile to the New Deal and the progressive pretensions of the FTP. Reading the manuscripts of *Liberty Deferred* alongside the correspondence between Lavery and the playwrights allows us to grasp what was at stake: the black Living Newspaper was at the very center of a hard-fought contest over the representation of race on the Federal Theatre stage. As such, the interesting story about *Liberty Deferred* is not how it became another piece of ammunition to anti-New Deal forces in Congress. *Liberty Deferred*'s significance lies in its ability to reinvent and creatively critique the Living Newspaper form at a time when its radical potential was being undercut from multiple directions.

Abram Hill understood that *Liberty Deferred* risked alienating not only Lavery and other powerful white sponsors in the FTP, but the broader constituency that supported the New Deal's reformist agenda. The black Living Newspaper, Hill recalled, had been based on the enormously successful *One Third of a Nation*; however, they had tried not to "follow that specific format," wanting instead to offer something "unique and different." Hill remembered welcoming the opportunity to experiment with form and "Break away from the basic format of the well-written play." Part of the experiment, for Hill, was to do with how he imagined his audience. He wanted *Liberty Deferred* to be staged downtown so he could reach the audience who would find it most uncomfortable, for although it was about black people, Hill insisted it was not a black play.[92] Black critics agreed. In his review of the manuscript for the *Amsterdam News*, Dan Burley was struck most powerfully by the spotlight the drama placed on the white spectator: "The philosophy of the American white man and what gives him his viewpoint," he proclaimed, "has never been so graphically discussed for theatre purposes as in this script."[93] It was the newspaper's "graphic" focus on whiteness and the Living Newspaper techniques that were used to dramatize the racial hierarchies of U.S. theatre that became the site of contest between the playwrights and their supervisor.

Following his first reading of *Liberty Deferred* in late December, Lavery wrote to Silvera, indicating that he liked the material but that it needed to be adapted to reflect Living Newspaper techniques more closely. He also communicated his enthusiasm to Living Newspaper staff worker Ira Knaster, asking him to "supervise him [Silvera] in the actual technique of converting this material into Living Newspaper form." Lavery also suggested changes to the story line, including "occasional consideration of the advancement which has been made by the Negro people, even in the face of all the deferred liberties." Lavery went on to provide instruction as to how this might be achieved: "this could be nicely pointed out throughout by the inference that the Negro has been given prominence in the arts, in the sciences,—in fact just about everything—except liberty." Although he did not mention the Federal Theatre directly, Lavery's language suggests he was keen that the authors of *Liberty Deferred* acknowledge the debt African Americans owed the Federal Theatre, one of those things "the Negro has been given." Accordingly, he recommended a number of significant changes designed to water down the critical focus on whiteness. These included a detailed plan to change the opening. In Hill and Silvera's manuscript, the juxtaposition of the racist white couple, Mary Lou and Jimmy North, and the young black couple, Ted and Linda, is important in establishing the hierarchical relationship between white spectatorship and black performance from the outset. Although Lavery presented his proposals as a simple strengthening of structure, in reality the changes would have reworked the meaning and purpose of *Liberty Deferred* by deflecting the criticism of white Americans implicit in the script.[94]

Lavery wanted to abandon the focus on white spectatorship. Instead of the young white couple sipping cocktails while they watched black entertainers, Lavery suggested that the narrative of black progress be performed before black spectators. In the revised scene, the newspaper would open in a schoolroom where black children were reciting the pledge of allegiance, guided by their black teacher. An Uncle Tom figure, the schoolteacher presents a positive picture of black progress to his young charges, only to be interrupted by the Voice of the Living Newspaper, who shows that the optimism of this "pathetic figure" is not borne out by recent history. Changing the race and age of the spectators who were to witness the journey through American history would have completely altered the satirical tone of the script. No longer would *Liberty Deferred* point a finger of accusation at the White American Public; rather, blame would be redirected at the black schoolteacher. In this schema, the Uncle Tom character would serve two purposes: on the one hand, he is implicated in the failure of black Americans to achieve equal rights; but on the other hand, he could be admired for his faith in the American system and his determination that individual black achievers could overcome the more universal experiences of black hardship. Lavery's proposed changes would turn *Liberty Deferred* into a traditional didactic play, one in which the education of the audience was facilitated through the process of watching the learning experience of a naïve and innocent group. It was a million miles away from Hill and Silvera's attempts to position the white theatre audience as the subject of critical investigation.

Just as significant as Lavery's advice to recast the identity of the spectators was his suggestion that the authors pay greater attention to black achievement in the arts and sciences. The trumpeting of black success in the arts was comfortable territory for many white liberals and a source of frustration for black creatives. As already described, it was mocked directly in the Hartford Negro Unit's Living Newspaper when the Loudspeaker promises to show white audiences how African Americans "have progressed in the Arts, Music, Theatre, Education."[95] Lavery sent Hill and Silvera a follow-up note with a suggestion of how they might showcase black success. The schoolchildren, he imagined, had become weary of the demoralizing scenes of black suffering and asked their teacher to "beg" the editor of the Living Newspaper to show black America's achievements. What if the Living Newspaper "matches each picture of accomplishment with a vivid picture of defeat?" he asked. Lavery's idea was to juxtapose kaleidoscope projections of vaudevillian Bill Robinson dancing and the image of a black man hanging from a tree. Through this means, he suggested, the schoolchildren would learn something important: not under the tutelage of their hopelessly optimistic teacher, but from the Living Newspaper. As Lavery put it: "The majority of the little group is silent. The LIVING NEWSPAPER has raised some real questions for them."[96] In his version, it is the Federal Theatre's Living Newspaper, fostered by Lavery himself, which has offered hope and instruction to the ignorant black children and their incompetent instructor. The paternalism of Lavery's vision is breathtaking.

Hill and Silvera responded to Lavery's recommendations through a combination of parody and checkbox inclusion. As we have seen, *Liberty Deferred* opens with a satirical sketch, accompanied by "platitudinous music" and featuring a traditional vaudeville act for white spectators who "know their darkies." The authors also include brief vignettes of the black achievers Lavery desired: the poet Phyllis Wheatley, the inventor Benjamin Banneker, and the actor Ira Aldridge. These scenes appear far removed from Lavery's intention to showcase the opportunities for black Americans, however. Introduced by our black guide, these exceptional characters underscore how rarely white Americans recognized black achievement. "Plenty that had what it takes," Ted muses, adding, "all they needed was a chance for recognition . . . which here and there they got. Not often, but here and there."[97] Lavery would need to have been wearing the "blinders" that Ted claims warp the white understanding of black life not to recognize a parody of his recommendations. Perhaps he did. In April 1938, Lavery read a revised script. His response suggests that nearly four months later, Hill and

Silvera were still resisting his advice that they present a "balanced" picture. From Lavery's perspective "two big defects in the story," remained: "Except for a footnote, no adequate provision seems to have been made to preserve achievement and set-back and you will remember we discussed in detail how important it is to show the Negro's achievements in the arts at the same time that he is meeting reverses in the field of civil liberties."[98] The second problem, as far as Lavery was concerned, was the fact that the manuscript lacked a character common to the whole story, other than the Loudspeaker. At the opening of *Liberty Deferred*, the white and black couples serve as interlocutors who witness, comment on, and contest the scenes enacted before them. Though these characters reappear at intervals, their functions are usurped, first by a pair of schoolteachers, one white and one black, and later by the characters of JIM CROW and the FRENCHMAN. Changing the character of onstage spectators invites the actual audience to consider how performativity and spectatorship help consolidate racist discourses. Such a "triangulated dynamic of looking"—in which the audience watched the onstage audience as they watch the performance—was made more powerful by switching around the positions of those involved in the triangle.[99] For if perspectives were the product of racialized experiences, recognizing how and why they were produced was the first step in tearing them down. As a way of getting the audience to think about the constructed nature of race within and beyond the theatre, the use of multiple viewpoints had potential. Lavery seemed to understand this to some extent. For example, he entertained the possibility of a change in the editor of the Living Newspaper, as happens in *Stars and Bars*.[100] By this point, however, Lavery had become wedded to the idea of having black children as spectators, and added, more firmly, that without this change, the script was more "old school" Living Newspaper and "not the thing we are shooting for."[101]

Lavery's notion that there was a clearly defined and well understood Federal Theatre Living Newspaper genre is questionable. As Paul Nadler has argued, the playreading department had little idea of what to look for when it came to reviewing Living Newspapers.[102] Moreover, as Douglass McDermott has suggested, although we might retrospectively identify an "orthodox" format, there were up to five variations on the format, one of which included the historical chronicle, a category that *Liberty Deferred* appears to be partly modeled on.[103] Lavery's demand for a central, connecting narrative, as with his desire for a permanent, unchanging interlocutor, may also be suggestive of his desire to fashion a Living Newspaper more akin to *One Third* than the more radical "old school" Living Newspapers that preceded it.

Above all, it reveals Lavery's concern to make Hill and Silvera's Living Newspaper a liberal critique of racism rather than a critique of liberal racism.

Recognizing that Lavery's approval was a hurdle they must clear if they were to bring their manuscript to life, Hill and Silvera made further revisions. Crucially, however, they did not reframe the Living Newspaper in the manner Lavery suggested. *Liberty Deferred* continued to shine the spotlight on white spectatorship. Another three months passed before Lavery delivered his verdict: "I still feel that the second part lacks a certain continuity between the episodes, most of which have been lumped in without any connecting thread." In spite of his reservations, Lavery promised he would "urge its production in several units of the Federal Theatre."[104] In fact, however, in the months that followed, Lavery slowly and carefully withdrew his support for what might have become the first production of a black Living Newspaper.

Lynchotopia

For all his concerns about the framing of the Living Newspaper, surprisingly, Lavery makes no mention of what is still the most shocking and powerful sequence in *Liberty Deferred*. Appearing in the final third of the newspaper, Lynchotopia is a satire on southern lynching. It deploys the grotesque to disrupt normalizing narratives that present lynching as an unfortunate but explicable form of racial control, but also to challenge practices of passive reception in the theatre. It portrays an afterlife for victims of lynching, ghostly citizens who are competitive about their experiences of the lynch mob. The scene opens on January 1, 1937 as the Keeper of Records, who wears a black rope round his neck, reviews the intake from the previous year. The arrival of thirteen new members in 1936 has brought the total membership to 5,107 since 1882. As the scene unfolds, the Keeper of the Records admits new lynch victims, and, using a microphone as a device for communicating with officials in the land of the living, ascertains the circumstances of each new admission. Invariably, the victims have been neither tried nor convicted at the time of their murder. Although 1937 gets off to a slow start, a new member from Alabama soon arrives, causing the Keeper to remark, "Dear old Alabama, they would be first." When another two victims, this time from Mississippi, are sent to Lynchotopia, the Keeper is impressed by the "modern" methods used by the lynchers, including "blow torches." More victims come in, and at the end of the year, the

Keeper compares the scores of the various states. Mississippi wins first place, followed closely by Georgia. Florida comes in third.[105]

The climax of each year is the New Year's Eve Review, when a prize is awarded to the victim of the most horrific lynching. As in the previous two years, Claude Neal, a Lynchotopia resident since 1934, is awarded the privilege of narrating his "winning" story to the assembled victims. Notorious even within the history of lynching, Neal was a black farmhand from Florida who was accused of murdering a white woman in 1934. After being dragged across state lines into Alabama, Neal was strung up outside the county courthouse. Advance notice of the lynching was given by radio. Special trains were laid on to carry spectators to the site. Women and children helped mutilate the corpse after the mob had tortured him.[106] In *Liberty Deferred*, the tone changes from the macabre to the surreal as Neal leads his fellow lynch victims on a march to Washington, accompanied by the dwarfs' tune from the 1937 animated Disney film, *Snow White and the Seven Dwarfs*: "HI HO, HI HO, off to Washington we go." Eating popcorn, smoking cigars, and chewing gum, the ghosts of lynching victims are in "typical holiday mood" as they arrive at the Senate. Once in the chamber, they heckle southern senators who are attempting to derail the Costigan-Wagner anti-lynching bill with a filibuster. Their jovial participation as onlookers is a parody of the carnivalesque atmosphere that accompanied the increasingly ritualistic nature of southern lynching in the early twentieth century.[107]

The Lynchotopia scene was not only a burlesque of the horrific spectacle of lynching: it also lampooned the Living Newspaper's reliance on "facts," "evidence," and "statistics." Victims of the lynch mob often failed to make it to trial for their alleged crimes, and there was little regard for legal evidence. By contrast, beginning with Tuskegee Institute in 1882, anti-lynching campaigns relied on the collecting of statistics and documentary evidence.[108] Yet as historians of lynching and anti-lynching campaigns have demonstrated, the awareness of facts, statistics, and evidence was not enough to change the culture of racial violence that made the burning and mutilation of black bodies a popular form of entertainment for white Americans in the late nineteenth and early twentieth centuries. Audiences for mainstream U.S. theatre and the lynch mob shared a common lexicon, which Koritha Mitchell calls the "theater/lynching alliance": "the way that mobs relied on theatricality, and the mainstream stage relied on the mob's themes, characters, and symbols." By contrast, the task of African American lynching dramas was to expose "the ways in which theater and lynching worked together to conceal evidence of black humanity and achievement."[109] For

Abram Hill, Lynchotopia was an attempt to reveal the meanings and motivations of lynch mobs which often lay buried beneath the statistics and rituals of early twentieth century lynching:

> The scene to me is symbolic and it's a symbol of the worst thing that has happened in society, to us in society. For years and years . . . we kept statistics on the number of blacks that are lynched every year. . . . But the point there that we were trying to make was that this becomes a symbolic scene because it represented the worst thing that could have happened. But you see, the lynching pattern underwent transitions in the 20th century. They didn't hang you to a tree, but they hung you on many other limbs in the housing and education and job opportunities. . . . You read an application and see on there "Black." "Can't use you." You see, that's a lynching. You move into Detroit into a white neighbourhood. They bomb the house. That's a lynching.[110]

The Lynchotopia scene was not the first time Hill had attempted to address lynching from a dramatic perspective. In fact, both Hill and Silvera had considered the question of how to dramatize racial violence when Silvera, in his role as playreader had rejected Abram Hill's *Hell's Half Acre* for production by the Federal Theatre. Written and revised a number of times between 1936 and 1938, the play tells the story of a southern lynching. Though the members of the lynch mob are brought to trial and found guilty, the judge passes a sentence that effectively renders them free.[111] Silvera's fellow playreaders found it to be a mixture of good and bad, with much melodrama and some gruesome scenes alongside some good writing and dramatic tension. Although Silvera was, by some distance, the most positive reviewer—he called it an "excellent play"—he did not recommend it for production: "Such gruesome realities as the old cracker Granny who has pickled as souvenirs the left ear of every Negro lynched for the past twenty years, and the fighting over parts of the victims body have no place in Federal Theatre offerings. There is a much more wholesome job to be done."[112] Perhaps Silvera believed his satirical treatment of lynching in his collaboration with Hill constituted a better approach.[113] An older Silvera certainly believed "nothing is more effective than ridicule and humour." Recalling Lynchotopia many years later, he reflected "people get tired of the serious preaching about some of the things that are wrong. . . . if you can laugh them out of existence maybe you'd do a more effective job."[114]

In an earlier scene of *Liberty Deferred*, Hill and Silvera deployed humor to expose the absurd pretense of democracy in the American South. To explore the politically sensitive issue of black disfranchisement, they used the device of a large map of the United States in which southern states were painted black with white lettering and northern states painted white with black letters. Each of the southern states has a door large enough to accommodate a human head. A comical barker named Joe Lilly White questions each southern state in turn to ascertain whether black Americans can vote in their state. One by one the door to each state opens and a man pops his head through and confirms, "Not here." Although Texas has already been called, the man representing Texas opens his door a second time and repeats the negative answer, much to the consternation of the barker. When called on to explain his deviation from protocol, Texas explains, "I'm such a helluva large state I deserve two answers." But any transgression from the established system is unwelcome, and Texas is reprimanded: "For breaking your routine—you can't have no lynchings this year." Suddenly all the doors open and the talking heads bellow: "Rah—rah—rah—Texas can't have no lynchings." Texas wails in response. Cracking his whip to restore order, the barker orders the state representatives to shut their doors, suggesting that the same whip that controls African Americans who agitate for the vote can also be used against the white man who steps out of line. But the action is interrupted by VOICE from the audience who asks the barker, "what is a Negro?" A discussion ensues in which Joe Lilly White gets caught up in tautological definitions of race based on skin color and hair texture. Challenged on the ambiguity of these categories, eventually the barker falls back on, "well anybody can tell a Negro when they see one." Echoing civil rights activists in the 1930s who drew parallels between Nazi Germany and southern racial justice, VOICE replies, "I thought only a Nazi could tell a pure race bred."[115] The scene reaches a climax when a black man rushes from state to state on the map, demanding from each the right to vote, only to be turned down on the grounds of his race.

The sketch was based on a real case of a black doctor who brought a suit against electoral judges in Texas. In *Nixon vs. Condon*, the Supreme Court initially struck down a Texas statute that allowed the Executive Committee of the Texas Democratic Party to grant membership only to whites. In spite of the court ruling, the Texas Democratic Party continued to hold white-only primaries by giving state party executive committees the power to determine qualifications and thereby exclude black participation in state nominating conventions. Nomination to the Democratic ticket meant certain election, and black Americans continued to be disfranchised from voting in Texas.[116] In *Liberty Deferred*, Nixon is mocked for his faith that the Supreme Court will guarantee his Fourteenth Amendment rights. The scene ends with the Loudspeaker reading out the Fourteenth Amendment, at the conclusion of which all the panels on the map swing open to reveal the talking heads, now dressed in white graduation caps. Stage directions indicate "they lower their heads and the tops of their caps [spell] out: D-E-M-O-C-R-A-C-Y." Finally the Barker cracks his whip and shouts "DEMOCRACY" to the accompaniment of much laughter.[117]

Situated within a satirical framework, *Liberty Deferred* still retained some of the "gruesome realities" that had marked Hill's grim portrayal of black subjugation in *Hell's Half Acre*. Nevertheless, in summer 1938 it appeared to be a strong contender for imminent production. In June, the Federal Theatre decided to participate in a national program of rededication to the American ideals of democracy and liberty. The idea was to promote plays that spoke to these themes, and Lavery seemed to believe that *Liberty Deferred* would be both appropriate and ready in time for the new program. In a letter to Blanding Sloan, regional director for the Eastern Region, Lavery promoted *Liberty Deferred*. Calling it "a play on the lost causes of the Negro," Lavery promised that a script being prepared by his department would be ready for December production, in time to commemorate the anniversary of the ratification of the Bill of Rights.[118] Meanwhile, a joint press statement issued by George Kondulf and Paul Edwards about New York's black theatre made positive mention of *Liberty Deferred*, leading several reporters to conclude it would soon be scheduled for production. The *New York Times* reported that it was in the "final draft stage."[119] In July 1938, Lavery wrote to Hill and Silvera explaining that while he still held certain reservations, he would push for production.[120] However, just one week later, Lavery reported to George Kondulf, director of the New York Federal Theatre Project, that the completed script was not yet ready to be sent out because it was "pending certain revisions."[121] A couple of weeks later Hill and Silvera submitted another revised draft to Lavery. In an accompanying note the authors outlined their revisions to the ending of the first half, the strengthening of characterization throughout the second half, and strikingly, given debates around form and realism in the Living Newspaper, a "more realistic" final scene.[122]

At what point in the development of the manuscript Lavery chose to send it out to units in the field cannot be ascertained, and how far he truly carried out his promise to "urge" production is unclear. In September he seemed to be hedging his bets, sending Kondulf the latest draft but insisting, "I am not at all satisfied with it yet, but the authors were anxious to get your reactions to it. I believe it still needs a firmer thread to hold the various episodes together. But the general scheme, has, I think, fascinating possibilities."[123] Nevertheless, Lavery continued to believe that his ideas for the Living Newspaper should have been followed and that the manuscript suffered as a result. In October, at the authors' request, he sent the latest draft to John Gibbs of the playreading department, commenting, "I still feel that the script lacks a great deal but perhaps a different perspective would save what is basically an intriguing idea. I once provided a story outline which both Howard Miller and John McGee liked but which the authors never followed."[124] By November it would appear that Lavery had finally sent *Liberty Deferred* out for the units to consider, reporting to Knaster that he had heard nothing back from the Eastern region, which had expressed interest in the script, and nothing definite from New York: "At the moment there doesn't seem to be any interest there."[125]

With progress stalled, Hill took matters into his own hands. Beginning in September 1938, Hill sent a series of letters to Hallie Flanagan, making the case for *Liberty Deferred* in terms designed to appeal to the national director. Explaining that their Living Newspaper was not a finished product, but rather a work in progress, he urged Flanagan to assign a director and troupe of actors to try out the script and promised their full collaboration in making necessary amendments. Hill made direct reference to *One Third of a Nation* and the investment of time and resources into the Federal Theatre Summer School at Vassar that had supported the work of white theatre practitioners. He also reminded Flanagan of the FTP's commitment to the national rededication effort and suggested a play on black history would make a timely contribution toward the February 1939 Negro History Week. He sought to reassure Flanagan that he had been, and would continue to be, open to guidance: "we have made efforts to carry out the suggestions made by Mr. Lavery, Mr McGee and yourself to the fullest degree."[126] Hill's letter is interesting, both because it suggests that Flanagan had already read it and proposed amendments, and also because it suggests that Hill and Silvera had accepted the revisions suggested, not only by Flanagan, but also by Lavery. What revisions were put forward by Flanagan and McGee and how far they were incorporated into the manuscript is not documented, but Lavery's own correspondence makes clear that the playwrights continued to resist his substantive changes.

If Flanagan replied to Hill's September plea, there is no record of it. In early December 1938, Hill again wrote asking the Federal Theatre director for help in bringing their Living Newspaper to production. Busy testifying before the Dies Committee in Washington, Flanagan wrote back promising to read the script when she had more time. This time Hill appealed to Flanagan's pride in the FTP. Hill informed Flanagan that the New Theatre League (the left-leaning federation of little theatres and amateur groups) had praised the manuscript and recommended it to its affiliated theatres. However, *Liberty Deferred* was, Hill explained, a work that only the Federal Theatre, with its substantial labor force and technical facilities, was capable of delivering. Hill now pushed for a production at the Lafayette. Suggesting that Harlem was the natural home for *Liberty Deferred*, he enclosed a clipping of a positive review printed in the *Amsterdam News,* Harlem's most vociferous advocate for black Federal Theatre drama.[127]

Hill's change of tactics in choosing to push for *Liberty Deferred* as a black history play suitable for Harlem reflected the growing pressure faced by the Federal Theatre from Harlem's theatre community. In July 1938, the New York FTP made the decision to move the Harlem Negro Unit's hit show, *Haiti,* downtown, to the consternation of many in Harlem. In December 1938, George Kondulf penned a defensive letter to one such complainant, a Mr. Edgar Brooks of West 152nd Street. Insisting that both the playreading department and the New York Production Board were giving serious consideration to *Liberty Deferred,* Kondulf committed himself so far as to suggest, "It is our very definite feeling that we will be able to get it in suitable shape for production very shortly." The manuscript was still listed as a work in progress in the playreading department's roundup of manuscripts on December 31, 1938. Pressure came, too, from the black press. The *Amsterdam News* published a glowing review of the manuscript the same month.[128] In spring 1939 more complaints came in, this time from the Negro Arts Committee Federal Arts Council, a recently formed coalition that included the NAACP, the National Negro Congress, the Urban League, and the Brotherhood of Sleeping Car Porters. They produced a fifteen-page brief that they sent to Lavery protesting racial discrimination within the FTP, and in particular the failure to develop black playwriting talent. They singled out the fate of Hill and Silvera's Living Newspaper as symptomatic of the treatment of black playwrights on the projects.[129] In his reply, Lavery denied the serious charges made against him and defended his role in *Liberty Deferred*: "while originally I did have high hopes for the play I did not recommend it for production for I felt distinctly that it did not bear out the high hopes I had for it."[130]

If the Negro Arts Committee had consulted Hill, Silvera, Kondulf, or McGee, they could be forgiven for thinking Lavery had in fact recommended

Liberty Deferred for production, for he had communicated as much in his earlier correspondence with them. But in his response to the Negro Arts Committee, Lavery backtracked further, denying that the release of advance publicity for a production constituted a commitment to actually produce a play: "It is true that, in order to encourage the authors, I allowed some publicity to be released regarding the preparation of the script, but you will see this in no way committed the project to a production." Lavery presented himself as someone who had neither blocked nor encouraged the project, preferring to place responsibility on individual production units: "As soon as this particular script was finished I advised the authors that it did not come up to my expectations, but that I would not keep them from submitting it to the New York project. Surely, therefore, the disinclination of the New York project to produce a script far from completion is no indication of the discrimination against Negro plays." Finally, he rejected the charge that the fate of *Liberty Deferred* signified a broader disinclination to stage black-authored plays in the Federal Theatre and pointed to the fact that his office was already "in close contact" with Hughes Allison from the Newark Negro Unit on developing a black trilogy.[131]

In an interview forty years later, Lavery suggested that the fate of *Liberty Deferred* was the result of the uncertainties of theatre. "The ultimate decision to produce or not to produce isn't necessarily a matter of discrimination," he explained, but rather, "there are so many questions of taste and style involved that the ultimate acceptance or rejection of a script may have nothing to do with the personality of the author, or even the worth of the enterprise. So many peripheral factors."[132] The process of adapting any script into a fully fleshed production is, as Lavery points out, a precarious one. Hill believed it was only possible to bring a Living Newspaper to life through a process of tryout with a cast and director. Previous histories of the Federal Theatre suggest that *Liberty Deferred* was either dramatically too weak to merit development through the production process or that it was killed off by the Dies Committee. Federal Theatre records indicate otherwise. In spring and summer 1938 the Federal Theatre could still afford—politically and financially—to put on Living Newspapers. But in terms of both content and form—or in Lavery's words, "taste and style"—*Liberty Deferred* posed too great a challenge to the liberal politics of Federal Theatre administrators. Though he had failed to persuade the authors to change their manuscript, Lavery played an important role in the development of *Liberty Deferred*. Lavery's correspondence with the authors and the evolution of the manuscripts suggest that rather than being forced into abandoning the black Living Newspaper for the sake of political expediency, Lavery chose to withdraw his support from a play he could not control. The manuscripts of *Liberty Deferred* capture, and even parody these episodes. As such, *Liberty Deferred* documents and is an important part of the history of the Federal Theatre's Living Newspaper.

Liberty Deferred Lite

Liberty Deferred did not end with the Federal Theatre, however. The Performing Arts Library of the New York Public Library holds a later manuscript of unknown provenance, cataloged under Silvera's name. The manuscript is undated but was probably revised between October 1938 and the closure of the FTP in June 1939.[133] The Performing Arts Library version begins with a two-page synopsis, which appears to reflect the changes Lavery demanded: "The complacent old school teacher Professor Hat-in-Hand" gets upset when his star pupil, Douglas, refuses to pledge allegiance to the flag because "With Liberty and Justice to all" does not apply to black Americans. Professor Hat-in-Hand is the black figure Lavery had long desired, an instructor who teaches his young charges an "Uncle Remus" history: "A scene of dancing and singing Negroes dramatizes in entertaining fashion the type of plantation life that the Professor wishes to tell about." Out of the dancing emerges Sam, a young black man who interrupts the Professor to tell the children the "real story of American slavery." Tracing the history of American slavery from the British slave trade through the Civil War, Sam appears as a Civil War veteran, and later as a witness to the events of Reconstruction and the terrors of the Ku Klux Klan, and as a soldier in World War I. Unlike the earlier versions, the Performing Arts Library manuscript has the two central characters Lavery had wanted. The synopsis also appears to outline a more optimistic ending than the early drafts. Although Sam is lynched, and becomes a resident of Lynchotopia, he is nevertheless able to preach a message of peaceful change. Sam exhorts the young students to use constitutional methods to enforce their rights: "Not Black Americans but just American (takes off rope from his neck and holds it up) there'll be no more of this if that constitution is enforced. We've got to enforce it. Then we'll have real liberty until then our Liberty is deferred." Read alongside the revisions to the manuscript, the synopsis might suggest that Silvera and Hill had finally accepted Lavery's demands. The closing sentences of the synopsis, however, suggest otherwise: "dancing, singing and music is so placed throughout the play as to provide light entertainment following heavy spots. The achievements of Negroes as well as the defeat of their ambitions are so designed as to give offense to no sector locale. Ample opportunity is provided for a Negro chorus."[134] Encapsulating what many white liberal Federal Theatre administrators, and Lavery especially, expected from black playwrights and Negro Units, the authors make clear that this version, a *Liberty Deferred* "lite", is one envisaged by and for whites.

During the Federal Theatre Project, black dramatists carved out spaces for black representation in diverse ways. Parodying the Living Newspaper allowed black theatre professionals to try on and show up the FTP's most prized and innovative new genre. It also allowed them to explore the relationship between white spectatorship and black performance through devices designed to disrupt the white gaze and position white audiences in a state of "being looked at ness." In looking at white spectators observing black performers, both on and off stage, the actual audience is asked to consider when and where black performance begins and ends. As the black guide, Ted, explains in *Liberty Deferred*, "They love to watch us dance. Dancing on the levy. Dancing on the old plantation. Dancing in the floor-show. Or, dancing on the end of a rope."[135] So powerful was the black image in the white mind that black-controlled performance could be deemed suspect, inappropriate, or even inaccurate. Black claims to authenticity and the realistic representation of black life had to be filtered through white administrators. Though many black performers and artists did not accept the assumptions implicit in their performances for whites, if they wanted to be heard, and if they wanted to earn a living, they had to "wear the mask that grins and lies."[136] *Stars and Bars* and *Liberty Deferred* exposed that mask. The Hartford Negro Unit used the devices of the Living Newspaper to reveal the mask, while Hill and Silvera positioned black spectators as observers of the mask. When the somber black commentators Ted and Linda look upon the black entertainers who perform for Mary Lou and Jim North at the opening of *Liberty Deferred*, it is, crucially, the black gaze that pries off the mask: "As they [Ted and Linda] reach this position, every one of the characters, hitherto playing his part as the white expects them to, suddenly stops in his tracks and stares, almost accusingly, at JIMMY and MARY LOU. It is almost as if each one had dropped his clownish mask in self-disgust."[137] Confronted by the black gaze of Linda and Ted, the black performers acknowledge their shame in wearing the mask. If the early drafts of *Liberty Deferred* attempt to resist and reveal the "clownish mask," by contrast, the heavily revised manuscript in the Performing Arts Library calls attention to white demands for black Americans to put the mask back on.

The failure to make it to production and the existence of the revised manuscript might suggest that the legacy of the Federal Theatre was to secure the mask that protected black theatre and made black dramas safe and acceptable to whites. When it became uncomfortable, there were always music and dance to take the sting out of the "heavy spots." To draw such a conclusion, however, not only limits our understanding of cultural production to those small number of dramas that make it to the legitimate stage at the time they were written; it invariably reinscribes and legitimizes the power of institutions and individuals, invariably white, who had the authority to decide what was worthy of production. Though neither *Liberty Deferred* nor *Stars and Bars* were produced by the Federal Theatre, they were debated by black dramatists, performance communities, and Federal Theatre administrators. Black Living Newspapers exposed the racial narrative that underpinned the codes and techniques of even the most progressive theatre, paving the way for new ways of telling stories about black and white Americans.

Black Living Newspapers showed a leap to freedom by subjecting white spectators to the black gaze. In the process, they generated debates that had a significant impact on the writing, production, and possibilities for black drama in the FTP. As described in chapter 5, the fallout from *Liberty Deferred* mobilized black critics of white authority within the FTP, impacting the relationship between the Harlem community and the white-run New York Federal Theatre Production Board. *Liberty Deferred* also had a positive influence on how white theatre practitioners within the FTP thought about the representation of black life on the U.S. stage. Lavery went to considerable lengths to ensure that the next black manuscript to come his way did not meet the same fate as the black Living Newspaper, while other black dramas under development in the Federal Theatre were hastily scheduled for production, including Hughes Allison's *Panyared* and Theodore Browne's new drama, *Go Down Moses*. African Americans were unable to create the space for radical Living Newspapers to be staged by the FTP, but they broadened the parameters of what might be portrayed on the American stage by other black dramatists. African Americans on the FTP subverted and adapted white visions of black life; but they also found spaces to create radical roles of their own. The chapters that follow examine how, when, and with what success black communities created and staged radical black dramas.

3 Wrestling with Heroes

John Henry and Bigger Thomas from Page to Stage

. . . .

John Henry is the most celebrated of all American folk heroes. A black steel-driving man who labored on the southern railroads, he is a contest hero, whose strength is exhibited in a competition with the steam-drill. In most versions of the tale, he dies as a result of his extraordinary exertion, but not before he has beaten the machine. As Lawrence Levine explains, "it is the glory of his victory not the tragedy of his demise that dominates."[1] This victorious trajectory is usually traced through Depression-era America when John Henry gained new traction as a folk hero for the left: "frequently inserted in the red line of African American history," he was, Barbara Foley argues, "a figure at once tragic and victorious, containing in his Herculean body the dialectic of resistance to oppression and the promise of this class's ultimate triumph."[2] In Theodore Browne's Federal Theatre drama *Natural Man,* John Henry does not triumph. Victory eludes the black hero: the steam-drill cannot be beaten, and John Henry dies a defeated man.

This chapter, and the two that follow, consider how African Americans imagined, debated, and dramatized the black hero in Federal Theatre dramas. Black performance communities debated what needed to be dismantled, and what new interpretative parameters built, in order to create black heroes that were legible to black as well as white audiences. Such debates were shaped by contemporary politics: the continuing appeal of black nationalism, on the one hand, and new alliances between black and white leftists, on the other, inspired, and in many ways expanded what was possible for black heroes on the American stage. At the same time, the vexed question of black heroic agency was entangled in long-standing traditions in which the act of witnessing black suffering reinforced white mastery.[3] Such established ways of looking had created theatrical conventions that governed who could create, stage, and perform black heroes, and who was allowed to watch. In the 1930s these ideas were challenged by black communities, who questioned both the American heroic tradition and the function of black suffering in constructing narratives that were morally legible to white audiences.[4]

Who the black hero was for and how he might be made anew were questions that consumed black performance communities and lay at the heart of many of the black dramas that made it to the stage during the FTP. It was the central dilemma of *Natural Man*. From its first staging by the Seattle Negro Unit in January 1937, *Natural Man* shaped conversations among black writers and dramatists on what Richard Wright would later call "The Problem of the Hero." Browne's drama subverted the mode of representing race that was expected and well understood by American audiences. Unlike *Uncle Tom's Cabin* or *Stevedore*, both of which were staged by the Seattle Negro Unit, in *Natural Man* the black hero's suffering is not rewarded by a recognition of his virtue on the part of white figures, nor is it redeemed through a triumphant death. In fact, the quest for a hidden truth is never resolved in the Seattle production of Browne's drama. This absence confused white critics, who were accustomed to the melodramatic mode in which protagonists "share the common function of revealing moral good in a world where virtue has become hard to read."[5] Because virtue was hard to read, the "spectacle of racialized bodily suffering" had come to serve as the necessary prelude to what Peter Brooks calls "moral legibility."[6] Such legibility required audiences not only to witness the suffering black body, but ultimately, to recognize the virtue of the victim-hero. John Henry's virtue in *Natural Man* was not easily discernible to white spectators. Writing for the *Seattle Star,* the white critic, Ann Wilson, encountered a "braggart character" rather than the "lovable destroyer" she had understood John Henry to be: "the most difficult problem with which Browne was faced in writing the play was that John Henry, a negro man who wanted to be left alone by white men to drive his sledge hammer and throw his shoes in any door he pleased, is a character of the imagination and cannot be portrayed on the stage without objections."[7] The white critic for the Seattle *Argus* was similarly perplexed: "If the play had been better known or more universally appealing audience reaction would undoubtedly have been more encouraging." As it was, "many were quietly puzzled."[8]

If white critics could not, or would not, imagine a black man who wanted to be left alone by whites, black critics understood only too well. John Henry's disregard for whites was a reminder of the Garvey movement in Seattle, which had attracted a cross-class membership in the 1920s. Black nationalist movements and ideas remained popular, if contentious, in the 1930s. As recently as 1934, the Seattle chapter of the NAACP had sponsored a political meeting to debate whether black Americans should fight for a forty-ninth state, to be run for and by black people.[9] Although the city's black newspaper, the *Northwest Enterprise,* avoided editorial comment on the play's political content, it printed a reader's critique of Browne's militant new drama.[10] The author was Frederick Darby, a local black union leader who believed black theatre had a duty to "strive for the continued betterment of interracial feelings." Theatre, he believed, must project positive images of black life, images that would not frighten whites. Performed before a racially mixed audience, in which whites were in a majority, Darby was troubled by "an implied plot of the play on the part of the Negro, that of vengeance."[11] In *Natural Man,* John Henry defies the criminal justice system, the black church, and the racist labor movement. He also defies the expectations of critics, who came to watch Browne's drama at the Metropolitan Theatre in Seattle, for there is no clear-cut moral affirmed in John Henry's unnecessary death. In portraying John Henry as a defeated hero in a society where black men who fight back are always punished, Browne's drama questions the price exacted for performing the role of victim-hero. Such a message was unsettling and challenging for American audiences; in the context of Depression-era culture, when John Henry was the "closest approximation to *Narodnost* on the American left," it was also radical.[12]

Natural Man received a new staging in 1941 as the second major production of the American Negro Theatre (ANT), the community theatre established in Harlem by Abram Hill and other Federal Theatre veterans in 1940. The ANT version contained significant revisions, including a new ending and musical score. Whereas in Seattle the hero dies defeated, in Harlem John Henry emerges from the tunnel victorious and reconciled to death. It is important that the black hero's virtue is recognized by a white figure and the implied plot of black vengeance is replaced with the promise of black redemption. What was puzzling to Seattle critics was made legible when the play moved East. White critics in New York recognized this John Henry: the white critic for the *New York Post* applauded its "heart," its "dancing feet," and "a throat which never tires of bursting into agreeable song." Yet the black critic for the *Afro-American* lamented this version of the John Henry legend, arguing that the "play fails to give the audience a leading character it can either hate intensely or love immensely—or at least sympathize with—it rarely ever rings the bell."[13] Scholarly analysis and recent restagings of *Natural Man* have drawn on a version of the revised manuscript staged by the ANT and published in *Black Theater U.S.A.* in 1974.[14] Accordingly, scholars have found in *Natural Man* a "strategic triumph over white oppression." Although he dies, John Henry appears as "the prophet for a new ethic of redemption that survives his own demise"; his victory over the machine offers "hope of transcendence beyond the fog of modern mechanized society."[15] The earlier performances and variant manuscripts of the Seattle Negro Unit, however, reveal a different kind of hero and a different ending. There is little triumph or transcendence in the hero who lies dying on the Federal Theatre stage. John Henry's final remarks "No, I ain't whipped that guy. . . . He's going right on," are accompanied by the sobs of Polly-Ann; Seattle's *Natural Man* offered no easy resolution to the black man's struggle.[16]

To understand the journey of these manuscripts and what was at stake in their revision, I turn first to the variant manuscripts and productions of *Natural Man* from the years 1937–1941. This chapter situates the manuscript and staging of the drama at the center of broader conversations about the problem of the hero. These discussions filled the arts pages of journals, newspapers, and left-leaning magazines and occupied the black performance communities that gathered around Federal Theatre Negro Units. They also took place in novels and collaborative theatre manuscripts authored by black and white dramatists beyond the Federal Theatre. When the revised version of *Natural Man* opened uptown at Harlem's 135th Street Library, the stage adaptation of Richard Wright's *Native Son* was already running at the St. James Theatre downtown. Wright's interest in staging the black hero dated back to at least 1936. Employed as a publicity agent for the Chicago Negro Unit, Wright attempted, unsuccessfully, to persuade the troupe to perform Paul Green's chain-gang drama, *Hymn to the Rising Sun.* Four years later, Wright chose Green to collaborate on the stage adaptation of his 1940 novel into a Broadway play directed by Orson Welles. The tussle over the manuscript and the differences between the published play and the drama staged in March 1941 revolved around conflicting understandings of Wright's protagonist, Bigger Thomas. Whereas the black author insisted that tragic heroes required a level of agency unavailable to the black man, the white dramatist believed that "every man is responsible for what he becomes."[17] Wright thrashed out these differences in a dramatic sketch entitled "The Problem of the Hero."

This chapter considers Wright's sketch, and the struggle for control of the black hero, in light of the revisions made to Browne's *Natural Man*. The Seattle manuscripts of *Natural Man* and the novel of *Native Son* offer little hope of redemption through individual heroic acts and the suffering of black heroes. By contrast, however, John Henry and Bigger Thomas serve a redemptive purpose in the ANT version of *Natural Man* and in Green's stage adaptation of *Native Son*, respectively. In the revised versions, the victim-hero has become morally legible: with his virtue recognized and the "true villain" identified, a solution is found that restores, rather than challenges, the moral certainty that underpins the American system.[18] In exploring the making of heroes on the American stage, we see how black playwrights and performance communities responded to, and sometimes pushed back against, the racialized assumptions that underpinned so-called universal theatrical conventions and heroic traditions. We also see how black performance communities created theatrical models and heroes of their own.

Actors Become Writers: The Seattle Negro Unit

> These people left a lot of the things to us
> because it made them look better.
>
> —Joe Staton

An actor and aspiring playwright from New York, Theodore Browne found his way to the Seattle Repertory Playhouse (SRP) soon after his arrival on the West Coast in 1935. There he developed a relationship with Florence and Burton James, white theatre professionals who ran the playhouse and sponsored the Seattle Negro Unit, often called the Negro Repertory Company, between 1936 and 1937. While Browne later gave credit to the Jameses, saying, "I thought the Seattle Unit owed them a great deal," he also recorded his own role in recruiting actors to the unit at the outset: "of course, knowing me, they got me to interview the Negroes, you know, who were on relief at that time and had possibilities."[19] From its inception in 1936 until his return East in 1938, Browne was a key member of the Seattle Negro Unit. Charles Monroe, an actor and stage manager for Seattle Negro Unit productions, recalled Browne's influence: "We were just the Indians. He was the chief and we were the Indians."[20]

As described in chapter 1, the Jameses' authority as directors and producers did not go unchallenged. Members of the troupe found ways to adapt white plays and space to develop new black dramas. Sometimes this meant asserting their cultural capital as guardians of black culture and skilled improvisers. Improvisation played an important role in navigating relationships with white supervisors, who understood black creativity as spontaneous. "It didn't look like anything rehearsed," Staton recalled, adding:

> We would listen to the comments that different people would make
> and those who were directing us would listen because out of the
> mouths of babes come pearls of wisdom. And after all, if I were to

direct a white group in a show, how in hell could I tell them how to react to certain situations. You see what I mean? So these people left a lot of the things to us because it made them look better in the sight of those who watched the show and those who wrote about it and everything else.[21]

Joe Staton and Theodore Browne began their Federal Theatre careers playing lead roles in white-authored, white-directed dramas including *Noah*, *Stevedore*, and *It Can't Happen Here*. Attracting critical acclaim as a performer was a well-trodden path for black theatre professionals wanting to create new black roles on the American stage. As the celebrated actor Ira Aldridge discovered in the nineteenth century, such a route was neither linear nor easy, yet it could provide a crucial stepping stone for black theatre professionals who aspired to write, direct, and promote black dramas. The Seattle Negro Unit was officially run by a series of white directors and producers between 1936 and 1939. The Jameses were important in shaping the unit in its genesis, yet it was a relationship that evolved, from their first involvement in early 1936 to their departure in November 1937. To replace them, Hallie Flanagan appointed her protégée, Esther Porter, as assistant director, assigning her to work on the Seattle Children's Theatre and the Negro Unit.[22] Four decades later, Porter remembered her experiences on the Negro Unit. In particular she recalled unit members strongly resisting her attempt to dress a female member of the cast in an Aunt Jemima–style red kerchief. What Porter thought looked "adorable," the black troupe found to be a disturbing echo of how some white Americans liked to imagine slavery.[23] She also remembered the troupe trying to educate her. In the winter of 1937–1938, Porter directed the unit in a production of *Is Zat So?*, a drama about a prize-fight boxer who helps a white socialite out of a fix. Porter recalled the troupe "insist[ing]" she come along with them to watch a boxing match: "they thought I shouldn't direct the show unless I came and saw what a fight was really like."[24] Another white director, Richard Glyer, who directed the black troupe in a Federal Theatre production of *A Dragon's Wishbone* in May 1939, learned that "Although the negro has a keen sense of rhythm, it must be his own rhythm."[25]

Both white directors, like the Jameses before them, quickly discovered that their own vision of black drama would be resisted and reframed by this tight-knit and talented group of emerging theatre professionals. When Browne left for the East Coast in May 1938, Staton became the driving force behind the unit. He devised and directed *An Evening with Dunbar* in

October 1938 and, alongside troupe member Herman Moore, played a key role in adapting *The Taming of the Shrew* for the company in June 1939.[26] The experiences of Seattle's Negro Unit were not unique. Members of the Hartford Negro Unit wrote sketches for the Living Newspaper, *Stars and Bars*; in Harlem, Negro Unit supervisors Gus Smith and Carlton Moss wrote and acted in unit productions; and in Chicago, Theodore Ward also performed in Chicago Unit productions before and after he wrote *Big White Fog*.

In Joe Staton, the Seattle Negro Unit found a talented artistic director and actor; in Theodore Browne, a bold and gifted dramatist. Browne's first formal writing for the Seattle Negro Unit was an adaptation of *Lysistrata*, Aristophanes's comedy, in which the women of Athens and Sparta refuse to have sexual relations with their warring men until they sign a peace treaty. By all accounts, Browne's version was faithful to contemporary translations and received rave reviews when it opened at the Metropolitan Theatre in September 1936. Situated near the University of Washington, the theatre seated well over a thousand, a considerably larger house than the 250-seat Repertory Playhouse. The move from the SRP to the Metropolitan reflected high expectations for a long run, but *Lysistrata* was closed after just one performance. When news of its risqué theme reached Don Abel, state director of the Works Progress Administration (WPA), he promptly shut it down. His action sparked a controversy that culminated in Hallie Flanagan sending senior FTP official Howard Miller to Seattle with instructions to reopen the play immediately. Once in Seattle, however, Miller felt the play had been "badly cast" and "badly directed," explaining in his report to Flanagan that, "The James' always seem to fall down on anything experimental." Though Abel admitted he had exceeded his remit (the decision to close down a Federal Theatre show was not the responsibility of the WPA), Flanagan did not order the show to reopen.[27]

The cancellation of *Lysistrata* and the lack of push back from the usually resolute FTP director caused considerable anger and frustration among members of the Seattle Negro Unit. Styling himself as the chair of the Seattle Negro Repertory Theatre, Robert St. Clair wrote a letter to Hallie Flanagan, charging racial discrimination against the Negro Unit.[28] Overtly political plays about lynching and race riots were acceptable, but a drama in which black sexuality was represented as legitimate, and even a source of political authority on the part of the women, caused some white Seattleites to feel moral outrage. Forty years later, Charles Monroe recalled how it "broke our hearts: I remember some of the people almost crying about it because they'd worked hard on that thing and it was a good play."[29] Following the *Lysistrata* fiasco, Monroe, Browne, and Staton, as well as Sara Oliver, Albert Walker, and several other members of the unit, appeared in the Seattle version of *It Can't Happen Here*, part of a nationwide FTP staging of Sinclair Lewis's cautionary antifascist drama, in October 1936. Drawing a cast from both white and black Seattle Units, it was directed by Florence James, who rewrote elements of the drama to set it in Seattle's black neighborhood. Browne and others received critical praise for their performances, but it was clear from the production bulletin that both the company's directors and the critics understood Lewis's work as being for and by whites.[30]

Accounts of the premature cancellation of *Lysistrata* have gone some way toward shaping historical accounts of the Seattle Negro Unit and FTP Negro Units more broadly. In his analysis of the fiasco, Ron West concludes that the sponsorship of black theatre by white liberals was indicative of the broader problems faced by Negro Units. The units were, he argues, "a form of surrogate and a location for the playing out of the political aspirations of both liberal and conservative sides of the white power structure." Ultimately this left little room for black agency: black actors were "confined to representing the exclusively white vision of the conditions of black Americans . . . restricted to or exploited in, roles conceived and assigned by a white power structure."[31] Such a conclusion overstates the power of white directors in the Seattle Unit. It also takes little account of the changing and complex power dynamics between white directors, Federal Theatre administrators, and black performance communities. In the aftermath of *Lysistrata*, the black troupe of the Seattle Negro Unit wrote and staged dramas that reflected their own political aspirations.

John Henry Takes to the Stage

It was in this context that Browne developed his masterful drama for, and about, African Americans. In black folk-heroic tradition, John Henry is a rebel who defies white attempts to control black labor and black bodies. His actions become heroic because they challenge the validity of laws made by and for white men.[32] For artists and activists on the left, John Henry became a useful vehicle to articulate the relationship between race and class exploitation during the Depression. A familiar figure on posters and magazines, John Henry was a "mascot" for both *New Masses* and the *Daily Worker*. The muralist Thomas Hart Benton sang "The Ballad of John Henry" at the opening of his exhibitions, and soon the musicologist Charles Seeger, folklorist Lawrence Gellert, and his artist brother Hugo Gellert all adopted John Henry. In leftist culture, John Henry's plight came to present both the intensification of the clash between workers and the capitalist system wrought by advanced capitalism, and the racial chain that bound together the labor and criminal justice system in the United States.[33]

If John Henry soon became an icon of radical protest in folk song and popular art, he did not translate so easily to the stage. White dramatists struggled to conceive of a John Henry unshackled by the racial conventions of American theatre. Roark Bradford (whose earlier novel was the basis for the Broadway musical *Green Pastures*) wrote a 1931 novel that became the musical *John Henry* (1939). Even with Paul Robeson in the title role, Bradford's play with music flopped spectacularly in 1940. Featuring terrible dialect and disreputable women, Bradford recast the steel-driving hero as a cotton-rolling man. Critics welcomed the return of Robeson after a seven-year spell away from the New York stage, but thought him "wasted" in a drama that "Never rises to the stature of its hero."[34] Zora Neale Hurston, who recorded a John Henry ballad for the Federal Writers Project, found Bradford's work as frustrating and cliché ridden as that of other popular white dramatists: "it makes me furious when some ham like Cohen or Roark Bradford gets off a nothing else but and calls it a high spot of Negro humor" she wrote to Walter and Gladys White.[35]

In the Federal Theatre, the Los Angeles Negro Unit staged a production of Frank B. Wells's *John Henry* in autumn 1936. There was considerable resistance to the white dramatist's portrayal of the black hero both among members of the black troupe of the L.A. Unit and in other parts of the project. Initially scheduled for production by the New Jersey Negro Unit, it was postponed on account of "local objections to some of its scenes."[36] Playreaders at the National Service Bureau (NSB) offered clues as to what these objections may have been. Black playreader C. C. Lawrence compared the white drama to black-produced knowledge of the folk hero. Working on the railroads and construction gangs of the South, Lawrence had "heard the saga of 'John Henry,' told around many campfires and in many shantys, after the day's work was through. To these people John Henry, was hero, a giant in strength [*sic*] and the friend of the downtrodden." By contrast, the white newspaperman "takes a legendary heroic folk character of a people and distorts him into a villainous, murderous cutthroat."[37] Wells's version, which is set in 1851, casts John Henry as a slave, rather than an icon of resistance to the Jim Crow South. This John Henry blames the condition of enslave-

FIGURE 5 "A Stone Quarry in Mississippi," scene from *John Henry*, Los Angeles Negro Unit production, 1936. Library of Congress, Music Division, Federal Theatre Project Collection, Production Records, Photographic Prints File, Container 1178.

ment on black passivity. African Americans must learn to fight like natural-born men. From Big Boy to Granny Lou to John Henry's promiscuous wife, Wells's script exemplified the narrow range of demeaning roles available in white-authored dramas of black life. Disdain for the humanity and history of African Americans drips from the pages of Wells's manuscript as well as the directors' reports contained in the production bulletin. White critics praised the singing. *Variety* welcomed what it called an "episodic account of highlights in the life of [a] negro who seeks freedom." Members of the black troupe were more wary and found ways to circumvent the roles they were expected to perform. Some of the black actors cast as miners were na-ked to the waist, while the chorus wore "old undershirts, not too clean, or old, soiled, and sleeveless vests." According to the director's report, the greatest problem they faced in staging *John Henry* was encountered after opening night when cast members performed in "garments that they them-selves wished to wear."[38]

"Serious" white dramatists were also fascinated by the John Henry legend. Paul Green was one of them. His 1934 drama *Roll Sweet Chariot* (a reworking of his earlier *Potter's Field*) featured both a southern chain gang and a John Henry figure who moves from confidence man to deity during the course of the play. Opening on Broadway in October 1934, it lasted less than a week. The *Amsterdam News* caustically observed that in Green's play, "The life of the Negro in the sunny South is just one dance and song after another."[39] Green, however, was not just one more would-be white dramatist looking to cash in on John Henry. By the mid-1930s he was regarded as an authority on black dramatic heroes. Green's reputation for writing complex black heroes extended well beyond *Roll Sweet Chariot* and dated back to the 1920s. Howard University professors Alain Locke and Montgomery Gregory included three of his dramas in their 1927 anthology *Plays of Negro Life*.[40] In the same year, Green was awarded the Pulitzer Prize for what would become one of his best known and most performed plays, *In Abraham's Bosom*. A drama of a mixed-race man's doomed attempts to lift himself and his people up from ignorance and poverty in the aftermath of slavery, Green's hero was unable to escape the fate of tragic mulattoes in southern literature. Although white critics welcomed this "tragedy charged with primitive emotion," and Locke and Gregory continued to support Green's "folk" dramas, other black critics were more skeptical. The writer and leftist activist Eugene Gordon despaired of the white dramatist's "false fatalism," while Du Bois lamented that Green's dramas always ended with "lynching, suicide or degeneracy." Frustrated by Green's perpetuation of the tragic mulatto, Langston Hughes reputedly wrote his own play, *Mulatto*, in response to seeing a rehearsal of Green's play.[41] White Federal Theatre administrators turned eagerly to Green's plays, even when their own playreaders questioned the value of his work. Playreader reports for Green's John Henry drama were damning. John Rimassa described *Roll Sweet Chariot* as "a negative, false, sadistic conception of the Negro's past, present and future," while John Morris described "Four long talky acts, called scenes. . . . Summed up I should say nauseous."[42] Playreaders seemed well aware of Green's status as a leading dramatist of Negro life. One noted that "the exploitation of negros has long interested white dramatists, but most of them have allowed themselves to be seduced by the emotional and dramatic qualities of the mumbo-jumbo of spirituals and superstitions to have written as yet, a really strong dramatic story of these injustices." Another, unnamed playreader placed Green firmly in the past, viewing his latest drama as a retrograde step: "Regarding the negro question, Green is still too subjectively Southern; he is inclined to regard the negro as static and seems to be unaware of the changes going on among the negroes of his locale." Notwithstanding the negative assessments of NSB playreaders, the New Orleans Negro Unit staged *Roll Sweet Chariot* in June 1936.[43]

Paul Green's work was a staple of both Negro and White Units in the Federal Theatre Project. Between 1935 and 1939 there were twenty five productions of seventeen Green dramas in Chicago, Boston, New York, Hartford, New Orleans, Jacksonville, Wilson and Manteo in North Carolina, and Seattle.[44] In Seattle, the Negro Unit's genesis could be traced back to Green: members of what would become the unit's regular troupe had first played together in the SRP's 1933 production of *In Abraham's Bosom*. It was a great success both at the box office and with Seattle's white critics, who appreciated the tragic mulatto: "His [Abraham's] mixed blood gives him the desires of the white man's mind, but with a black man's body. His sudden uncontrolled tempers lead him to his tragic end. His squalid surroundings and the Rodinesque pull of the soil downward, holds him from rising with his fancies towards greatness."[45] Encouraged by the profits to be had in staging Green's dramas, the SRP's managers also considered staging *Hymn to the Rising Sun*. They were not alone. As we will see, the aborted attempt to stage Green's 1936 chain-gang drama was the source of considerable controversy on the Chicago Negro Unit.[46] By the time Browne began writing his version of the John Henry legend for the Seattle Negro Unit, Green was the most frequently produced contemporary playwright of "Negro" drama. In fact, the white folk tradition of what a black hero should be owed much to the white southerner. *Natural Man* can be seen as rebuttal to that tradition.

The Making of *Natural Man*

Natural Man was staged at the capacious Seattle Metropolitan Theatre. The first production opened on January 28, 1937 for three nights and a revised version played for a further three nights beginning February 18. The archive of the Seattle productions is rich: manuscripts for both the January and February productions survive in the Federal Theatre archive alongside photographs and a playbill; the archive also holds the production bulletin, including a play synopsis, reports on staging, lighting, music, and costuming, as well as on critical reception and audience response. Taken together, these documents establish that the manuscripts, which I call "January Seattle" and "February Seattle," were the basis for the two Federal Theatre productions: they detail the sequence of episodes, including the northern labor scene, (a scene excised in later scripts) and, for the February production, confirm the addition of a new scene set at a religious camp meeting.[47]

With the exception of the religious scene introduced into the February staging, the two Seattle manuscripts and productions are very similar. John Henry is established as a rebel early on, in Episode 3. On the chain gang John Henry finds it hard to accept that his labor is owned by others, and struggles to keep the pace of his hammer slow enough for his fellow convicts. Nevertheless he is able to sympathize with co-workers who lack his physical strength. When a young black convict perishes on the chain gang, it is John Henry who defends his body. What begins as a small act of resistance to the white guard mercilessly whipping the lifeless body of the young convict quickly escalates. John Henry kills the guard and flees the chain gang. The guard's inhumanity is successfully resisted, but at a cost. A rebel and a fugitive, John Henry's refusal to obey American racial codes initiates a sequence of events that lead back to the chain gang. In a series of retrospective scenes, first in a bar on Beale Street, Memphis, (Episode 4) and then in a hoboes' camp (Episode 5), John Henry is unable to find the freedom he desires as a natural man. Forced to flee Memphis when he is recognized as the killer of a white man, he cannot accept the emptiness of living on the edges of society, where he is denied access to productive work. Hearing of work opportunities in the North, John Henry rides the rails to a northern city where he finds employment as a steel driver. In Episodes 6 (the labor scene) and 7 (the jail scene), John Henry defies the racial expectations of whites, first as a fellow worker and then as a fellow inmate. It is in these episodes, where John Henry challenges the systems that both control and privilege working-class white men, that Browne develops John Henry as a distinctly black folk hero. Accused of being a scab, John Henry cannot identify with the cause of white workers who have for so long excluded black laborers from their union. John Henry's decision not to strike for men who deny his manhood is validated when his white co-worker tells him: "You ain't wanted in the north. You can stay, if you want to, but you ain't allowed to do this kind of work. Building and construction belongs to white labor. You niggers have to black boots or swing a mop, if you want to remain up north."[48] John Henry's resistance to the work identity that whites impose on black men soon provokes a fight, which leads to John Henry's arrest and incarceration in a northern jail.

The penultimate episode, which is set in jail, is the climax in the Seattle versions of the play, for it is here that Browne's hero reflects on the nature of white power and the consequences for black men who challenge it.

John Henry refuses to identify with his white inmates: "You got everything. Got the world in a jug and the stopper in your hand!" he tells them.[49]

FIGURE 6 Joe Staton as John Henry, Seattle Negro Unit production of *Natural Man*, Seattle Repertory Playhouse, 1937. Federal Theatre Project Photograph Collection, C0205, Box 49, Folder 25. Special Collections Research Center, George Mason University Libraries.

Nor will he perform the role of black man for them, as is clear when he rejects their demands that he sing a "coon" song. For John Henry, sharing time in jail with white inmates does not diminish racial hierarchies: in fact, it highlights the very different meaning of freedom for those whose history has included enslavement:

> White man's country. White man's world. Big Mister Great-I-Am!
> Make all the high and the mighty laws and rulings. Change every-
> thing to suit hissef. Black man got to bow and scrape to him, like he
> was God Almighty Himself. Black man to go to him with his hat in
> his hand and ask for the right to live and breathe, sleep and eat, sweat
> and slave! Got to go to Almighty White Boss for every little thing.
> Even down when it comes to thinking. Black man got to go to him

for that, too! Nothing he say or do what white man ain't got something to say about it!⁵⁰

John Henry articulates the double bind of the formerly enslaved, who after the Civil War faced the responsibilities, but few of the privileges, of freedom. The regulation of black labor and black bodies written into American racial laws and customs during and after Reconstruction ensured that black self-mastery often looked very much like subjugation to the will of former masters.⁵¹ The racial coding of freedom is reinforced by stage directions. While we both see and hear John Henry, who is positioned center stage, we only hear the voices of the white inmates, who are placed offstage.⁵² His fellow jailbirds are fascinated by Henry's difference. How does it feel, they wonder, to be a "Sambo," a "nigger"? Shrugging off these racial slurs, Henry replies: "Like a giant in a straight-jacket! . . . Like a natural man mongst a heap of muscle bound sissies! . . . Like a great king without a throne to sit on!"⁵³ Defining his masculinity against the effeminate indolence of whites, John Henry locates his identity in his productive labor. But rather than stake a claim to participate in a corrupt, capitalist system, or be integrated with whites, John Henry's labor fosters independence and the ability to create his own values:

> You tallow-faced sissies may be sitting on the throne, but that don't make you king cause you sit there. Nossir! I built that throne. Built that stone palace you live in. Yes, even down build roads so you could travel from place to place. And I ain't asking you all to thank me for what I do. I ain't asking you to be my friend. Ain't wishing to eat at the same table with you. Ain't wanting you to put yourself out of the way for me at all, understand? All I ask is that you let me be. You can have that swell place and the golden throne, but don't mess up with my crown. I'm going strut the earth with that crown on my head till old Gabriel sounds his trumpet for me to go on up to Glory! And I'm going walk right smack into Glory Kingdom with my crown still on my head.⁵⁴

It is in defending this crown that John Henry has the chance to become heroic. Plucked from jail by Captain Tommy to work on the Big Bend Tunnel, he has come full circle. Though no longer bound by physical shackles, John Henry is neither free nor enslaved. When a white Sales Agent attempts to sell the Captain a steam-drill, the Captain is driven to prove the "superiority" of coerced human labor. He pits John Henry in a contest with the

FIGURE 7 Episode 8, Theodore Browne, *Natural Man*, Seattle Repertory Playhouse, Seattle Negro Unit. Federal Theatre Project Photograph Collection, C0205, Box 69, Folder 25. Special Collections Research Centre, George Mason University Libraries.

machine. This is not a competition John Henry can win: his employer has promised to send him back to the chain gang if he loses, and if he outperforms the machine, he will remain only a nominally free laborer whose liberty depends on the whim of white employers. In the contest with the machine, John Henry pushes himself to the utmost, and his maniacal hammering helps him progress through the tunnel more quickly than the steam-drill. Although he is in the lead, John Henry puts aside his hammer to duel with his mechanized rival, who is represented on the Seattle stage as a full-size robotic man. Man and robot wrestle, and John Henry appears to have won, throwing his opponent into the dark tunnel. John Henry's friends and co-workers celebrate his triumph. But it soon becomes apparent that his is a pyrrhic victory: as he lies exhausted, we begin to hear the renewed chugging of the steam-drill, the machine that cannot be beaten. John Henry's defeat is made plain in the stage directions: "Cheering from the crowd and shouts of 'John Henry beat that steam drill on down!' In the midst of the wild cheering, intrudes the rising chugging of the steam drill, as if it had suddenly regained its vitality." John Henry's girlfriend Polly-Ann tries to reassure him: "Just listen to the folks. They all talking about how you beat that old steam drill down." But as the lights dim and death approaches, John Henry cannot deny the truth: "No, I ain't whipped that guy. Listen! Hear him? He's going right on."[55] A rebel to the end, he resists the pretense that his life and death can be turned into a hero's victory. Although John Henry dies knowing he cannot win, he is granted a dignified stage death in the arms of his grieving woman. Like his enslaved ancestors who committed suicide on the Middle Passage or escaped the plantation knowing it would likely lead to capture, punishment, or even death, John Henry refuses the life offered him by the white man.[56]

Three weeks later, a second version of *Natural Man* opened with the same cast and an additional scene. The new scene in "February Seattle" is inserted as Episode 4. Set at a religious camp meeting, it examines the church as a source of moral leadership for black Americans. Audiences were introduced to a new character, the black minister preaching to his followers. But his ministry offers neither a haven from, nor resistance to, the racial codes that govern black lives. Teaching respect for the laws of man as before the laws of God, the pastor and his congregation do not offer to aid the escaped John Henry, who is seeking refuge from the forces of the law. Instead, they encourage John Henry to give himself up. John Henry cannot submit to this dogma, for he knows laws made by white men are not just laws.[57] The Federal Theatre archives contain no clues as to why the extra scene was added, but one possibility is suggested by a review in the *Northwest Enterprise*. Shortly after the January production, the Seattle black newspaper published a critical review from a reader demanding to know why black playwrights did not "write around the lives of men who have given to the world at large something outstanding?" Worthy examples might include "the overworked doctor of a Negro community," and "the minister trying to teach and lead his flock."[58] Though there is no evidence to connect this review directly to the new scene, the changes visible in "February Seattle" appear to correspond with the thoughts expressed here though not in the sympathetic manner suggested by the reviewer. Notably, the author of the review was one Frederick Darby. A local labor organizer, Darby's plan to establish a Seattle Negro Unit had been passed over in favor of the SRP's sponsorship in 1935.

John Henry Comes to Harlem: The ANT's *Natural Man*

Natural Man and Theodore Browne attracted attention beyond Seattle as well. The *Chicago Defender* noted the play's success, while the composer and jazz pianist James P. Johnson, who had secured the rights for a "grand op-era" of *Natural Man*, began negotiations with Langston Hughes to supply a libretto. Although a contract was signed this project never came to fruition. In May 1938 the *Pittsburgh Courier* reported that Browne was leaving Se-attle for New York to talk with Rex Ingram about a new production of the play. On the East Coast, Browne soon found himself in demand as a Fed-eral Theatre dramatist. In April 1938, John Silvera tried to get him assigned as a playwright to the New York Federal Theatre so that Browne might be enlisted to help with the black Living Newspaper, *Liberty Deferred*.[59] Mean-while Browne had written a new, two-act drama about Harriet Tubman. *Go Down Moses*, which is discussed in chapter 5, was cast and scheduled as the major new production of the Harlem Negro Unit in spring 1939. Rehearsals with the white director Maurice Clark were well under way but the Federal Theatre was wound down before it could be staged. Meanwhile, Browne had relocated to Massachusetts, where from March 1939 he was engaged as a playwright on the Boston Negro Unit. The FTP's premature closure in June 1939 shut down one tried and tested path for Browne, just as he was gaining in reputation and experience as a playwright. Nevertheless, his career as a dramatist seemed to be taking off at the start of the 1940s. Along-side other former Federal Theatre playwrights, he joined the new Negro Playwrights Company (NPC) in New York, and in April 1941 he secured a prestigious $1,000 Rockefeller Grant, which he would use to develop a new drama on the history of minstrelsy and black performers. In May of the same year, *Natural Man* was chosen as the second full-length drama to be staged by the most promising new black theatre group to emerge after the FTP, the American Negro Theatre (ANT) in Harlem.[60]

The ANT was organized by FTP playreader and playwright Abram Hill, Frederick O'Neal, and their theatre friends in 1940. Their purpose was to provide a people's theatre that might function as a "spur to citizen ambition." This commitment was reflected in its playreading committee. Playreaders were asked to consider whether the drama contained "a spe-cial message which will benefit the audience" and whether "we [are] in sym-pathy with the message." Moreover, they were asked to consider whether the resolution to the play was "clear cut" and "gratifying."[61] Perhaps these priorities were inspired by Hill's ambition to avoid replicating the failure of the NPC. Ward, Browne, and Hughes Allison, as well as Langston Hughes, Powell Lindsay, and Frederick O'Neal, had founded the company with Hill in 1940 with a view to producing the work of black playwrights. Within six months, Hill had resigned. The NPC closed after just one production at the

Lincoln Theatre in Harlem—a revival of Ward's *Big White Fog*. As will be described further in chapter 4, when *Big White Fog* was staged, first by the Chicago Negro Unit in 1938 and later by the NPC, it proved controversial and provocative rather than "clear-cut" and "gratifying." Hill recalled feeling increasingly uncomfortable with what he saw as the NPC's promotion of theatre with a "social message" at the expense of artistic merit.[62]

Unlike its predecessor, the ANT was able to establish itself as a real force in black theatre through the 1940s. It maintained a strong record of production in the first half of the decade, producing black-authored plays including Hill's own very successful *On Striver's Row* (1940), Owen Dodson's *Garden of Time* (1945), and Browne's *Natural Man*. The ANT also adapted white-authored dramas, the most successful of which was *Anna Lucasta* (1944), a domestic tragedy authored by Philip Yordan, a little-known American playwright of Polish descent. Greatly revised by Hill and the director Harry Gribble for a black cast, *Lucasta* ran for five weeks at the 135th Street Library before transferring to Broadway in late summer 1944, where it would run for two years. In 1947 the company took the production to London where it played at His Majesty's Theatre and helped to develop the nascent black British theatre scene. Like the black theatre professionals who worked for the Federal Theatre and the NPC, the ANT looked for and encouraged black-authored dramas. However, as the 1940s progressed, the company increasingly turned to the work of white dramatists.[63]

Natural Man was the first serious black-authored drama staged by the ANT. With its prominent critique of the criminal justice system, it is not difficult to see why it appealed to the author of the *Liberty Deferred* and *Hell's Half Acre*. Yet Hill was now responsible for running a theatre company, and wanted dramas that would attract an audience and grow the ANT. Accordingly, for the ANT's first full-length production, he chose his own drama, *On Striver's Row*. A bourgeois comedy of manners, the drama is organized around a Harlem debutante's coming-out party that becomes riotous when the low-down folk arrive. Hill saw his drama as a necessary adjustment to the stream of white-authored dramas of black life that featured the "underdog, the lower depth, the ne'er do well, [and] the criminal element."[64] *On Striver's Row* was first produced by the Rose McClendon Players in 1939, where, under the direction of Dick Campbell it received favorable reviews. Revived by the ANT in 1940 and then again as a musical in 1941, Hill's comedy was a hit with Harlem audiences. Not everyone was enamored of the ANT revival, however. Writing in the *Daily Worker*, Ralph Warner insisted: "Nothing is to be gained by pitting one class of Negroes against the other.

Nor by ignoring the universal problem of Negro discrimination. Nor by imitating white playwrights by producing a comedy of manners."[65] Examining earlier versions of the drama, Jonathan Shandell found that for the ANT production, Hill had cut some of the overtly political speeches and "softened the defiant political tone of his comedy."[66]

It is interesting to consider that Hill tempered the political tone of his own work when he staged it for the ANT. The version of *Natural Man* staged by the company in 1941 can also be seen as representing a softening of the defiant tone of the Seattle manuscripts. The ANT's *Natural Man* did not ignore problems of racial discrimination, but neither did it set out, as Hill's earlier FTP dramas had done, to directly confront the racial prejudices of white liberal audiences. Crucially, in the ANT version, John Henry's virtue is recognized, and he is rewarded by the promise of redemption in the next life. There are no records documenting when, why, or who made the revisions to *Natural Man*. It is possible that Browne himself revised the manuscript for the ANT or that he authorized Hill and the ANT to make their own revisions, much as he granted Johnson and Hughes the rights to adapt his drama into a folk opera without his input in 1938. Hill worked closely on the project as assistant director alongside Benjamin Zemach, whom he brought in as guest director. A Russian Jewish director and dancer, Zemach had worked for the Moscow-based Habima Theatre before coming to New York in 1926. Whether the manuscript was revised by Hill and Zemach or by Browne, or whether it was a collaboration between the three men, is impossible to know. What is clear is that when it came to staging *Natural Man* in Harlem, Browne was not involved. Thirty and more years later, he recalled his discomfort with the ANT's production: "I didn't go near the place until they actually produced it. But I was sorry for that, too, because they had done things with it that I didn't think they should have done. I mean, they got some criticism for it. Instead of sticking to the folklore quality of it, they wanted to give it a meaning."[67]

We can only speculate as to what Browne was getting at when he hinted that the ANT "politicized" his folklore drama. Each of the variant manuscripts is packed with speeches that might convey a whole host of political meanings. We do know that at the time of his oral history interview, Browne had become a firm advocate of less overtly political drama and distanced himself from what he saw as the unnecessarily antagonistic dramas of the Black Arts Movement.[68] Moreover, it is not clear whether it was the revised manuscript or the staging that Browne says he regrets in his oral interview. Whichever it was, Browne's reservations were not sufficient to prevent him

FIGURE 8 Cast listing from Episode 1 from the theatre program for the American Negro Theatre production of *Natural Man*, 1941. Manuscripts, Archives and Rare Books Division, Schomburg Center for Research in Black Culture, The New York Public Library.

from donating the ANT manuscript version of *Natural Man* to the FTP collection at George Mason University. The ANT manuscript was also the version Browne authorized for publication in the Hatch anthology, *Black Theater U.S.A.* In fact he was "very pleased," that "they used the text that I wanted them to use."[69]

Browne's authorized version is one of five extant manuscripts of *Natural Man*. In addition to the two earlier Seattle Federal Theatre manuscripts and the later ANT manuscript, there are two further manuscripts of *Natural Man* held by the New York Public Library: one at the Schomburg, the other at the Performing Arts Library (PAL). Of the later three manuscripts, the ANT version has the greatest variation—in both nature and number—from the Federal Theatre manuscript "February Seattle," the manuscript that appears to be the basis for all subsequent versions.[70] The ANT program helps clarify that the manuscript held at GMU corresponds most closely to that used by the ANT in its two-month run starting on May 7, 1941. The ANT version

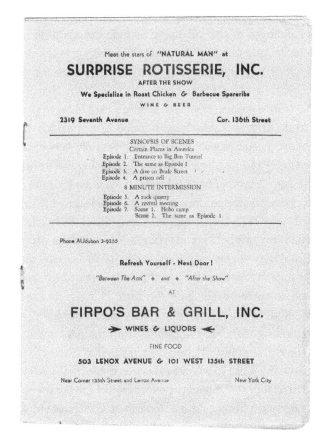

FIGURE 9 Synopsis of scenes from the theatre program for the American Negro Theatre production of *Natural Man*, 1941. Manuscripts, Archives and Rare Books Division, Schomburg Center for Research in Black Culture, The New York Public Library.

at GMU (ANT-GMU) is the only extant manuscript that follows the same sequence of scenes as laid out in the ANT program. Newspaper reviews of the ANT production also confirm this sequence of scenes. Taken together, these documents corroborate that the ANT production eradicated the northern labor scene (Episode 6), which had been featured in Seattle and placed the new Beale Street bar at the center of the drama.[71]

The changes made for the ANT production are extensive, and include the removal of the racially tense northern labor scene, the commissioning of new music, the restructuring of the scene order, and a new ending. New characters are also introduced, most notably, the Creeper. A sinister figure, the Creeper knows John Henry's past and predicts his fate. Serving as a one-man chorus, he takes on some of the lines spoken by spectators in the Seattle production. He also intervenes in the action. In the jail scene, which appears as the penultimate episode in Seattle, but is moved forward to Episode 4 and entitled 'A prison cell' in the ANT version, the Creeper sings to calm John Henry and to placate the white prisoners' demand for black entertainment.[72] Other changes to the jail scene include the addition of two extra characters, the Jailer and a Sheriff, who are necessary to the development of the new plot.[73] The jail scene is central to all versions of *Natural Man* because it contains the strongest articulation of John Henry's political outlook. In the Seattle manuscripts, John Henry uses abusive language to address the white prisoners who have taunted him since his arrival, calling them "tallow-faced sissies." In the ANT version, however, John Henry avoids the racialized-gendered epithet, addressing them simply as "You."[74] The language is tempered elsewhere as well. In Episode 3 of the Seattle manuscripts, black convicts are verbally abused by the white chain-gang guard, who calls them "niggers" and "black bastards." The convicts also use the term "nigger" among themselves when the white guard is out of earshot, and they deploy racialized language to describe the guard. When this scene appears as Episode 5 in the ANT manuscript, the controversial terms have been removed: here the term "nigger" is used only once, by the white jailbirds who taunt John Henry in Episode 4.[75]

Toning down and removing racialized language from the ANT manuscript serves to lessen the racial animosity between white and black characters. It also complements the more extensive revisions made by the ANT: the removal of the northern labor scene, and the expansion of the bar scene, as well as a significantly revised ending, all serve to promote a different kind of hero. The remodeled John Henry is untroubled by interracial labor disputes that were central to the Seattle production. He is too busy fighting black Americans in a Beale Street bar. Moved forward from Episode 4 to Episode 3, the expanded bar scene replaces the labor scene to offer an alternative narrative of how John Henry ends up at the Big Bend Tunnel. In the ANT version, the bar scene becomes the site and explanation for John Henry's arrest and incarceration. When a fleeing pickpocket enters the bar looking to offload his loot, the black hostess obliges, placing the stolen jewels in the pocket of the drunken John Henry. Crucially, it is the deceptive act of a black prostitute in a den of iniquity, rather than John Henry's defiance of racist white labor leaders in the workplace, that leads to his arrest and incarceration. In eliminating the labor scene, the 1941 production removed Browne's critique of a racialized, capitalist system supported by organized white labor.

The new ending devised for the ANT production dilutes interracial antagonism by staging the white man's recognition of black suffering. In his furious competition with the steam-drill, John Henry sets the tunnel on fire.

When it becomes clear that his life is in danger, it is, significantly, the white Sales Agent who speaks on John Henry's behalf. Appealing for empathy, he asks the Captain: "Why the hell you threaten him? He's a human being, same as you and me. And a mighty damn fine human specimen, you ask me." It is important that the Sales Agent learns that for the Captain, the contest was never one between mechanized and manual labor, but rather a way of proving his mastery over the physically stronger John Henry: "You think you can break his spirit?" he asks. The Captain responds: "Think? I did break his spirit. He was cringing. He pleaded and begged. I twisted him round my little finger, because I'm his master. That's why he beat that steam drill! You've got to make them fear you."[76] The Captain's excess establishes him as a monstrous Simon Legree figure harking back to *Uncle Tom's Cabin* and the horrors of American slavery. His enjoyment of spectacular black suffering appears in stark contrast to the Sales Agent's recognition of black sentience. Yet the character of the Sales Agent embodies the ambiguous line between witness of, and spectator to, the violence done to black bodies: his recognition of the black man's humanity is dependent on the system of domination that allows white men to watch and place wagers on black suffering.[77] John Henry emerges from the tunnel in surrender: "I comes out peaceful," he tells the waiting audience. The Sales Agent responds with compassion: "There is something we can do for you," he reassures, "Whatever it be, we want to do it, Believe me." John Henry does. The ensuing dialogue builds toward a racial reconciliation and redemptive ending that would have been unimaginable in the Seattle productions. In the ANT version, John Henry addresses the white Sales Agent as "Brother'" and appears reconciled to death. Though at first he struggles, gets mad and "sets them rocks-afire," "Then I come to my senses. I gits still and quiet and very peaceful inside. I don't mind a thing, no, not a solitary thing in this world!" His face lighted by a smile, the ANT's John Henry is transfigured, his oppressors absolved. He does not die blaming the cruel and unjust world that has paid to watch him suffer; he does not die resisting. John Henry has become "as free as the Blue Ridge Mountain, the Mississippi River, the Tall Lonesome Pine." With a shaft of light shining down on him, his hammer on his shoulder, John Henry has faith in an afterlife where he can drive steel to his heart's content: "They say they got mountains and rocks up there." Thus, John Henry "symbolically sets out for parts unknown."[78]

On the Harlem stage, Browne's hero dies, but he dies a victor, full of hope. John Henry takes responsibility for his lack of self-mastery in a Beale Street bar. Having failed to perform the duties required of the burdened individual, he has accepted the punishments that are his due. His redemption lies precisely in his ability to fulfil the only form of agency allowed to the formerly enslaved. As Hartman explains, in the aftermath of slavery "to be responsible was to be blameworthy. . . . the exercise of free will, quite literally, was inextricable from guilty infractions, criminal misdeeds, punishable transgression and the elaborate micropenality of everyday life."[79] When the curtain falls in Harlem, John Henry has been redeemed and is already on his way to a better next place: "If the other boys should ask for me, just tell them the last thing you see of him was his coat-tail flapping in the wind! Tell 'em, say, he long-gone from here to drive hell out of steel!"[80] Scholars who have based their analysis of *Natural Man* on the ANT version anthologized in *Black Theater U.S.A.* agree that it offers a redemptive and hopeful ending. Director and playwright Henry Miller argues that "In the final episode of the play, Browne makes John Henry's death a Negro triumph over racial prejudice," while for Harry Elam Jr. the hero "walks off into a glowing white light, he becomes symbolically linked to a higher cause of black social consciousness and resistance." Such triumph and transcendence seem a world away from the production first staged by the Federal Theatre in 1937. In Seattle, John Henry's acknowledgment that the machine goes on and the mournful sobs of Polly-Ann that accompany his death suggest the heroic acts of individuals offer little in way of resolution.[81]

Critical reception of *Natural Man* in Harlem was mixed. Widely reviewed in the dailies, white critics compared *Natural Man* favorably to the John Henry musical starring Paul Robeson that had flopped the previous season. Writing in the *Brooklyn Eagle*, Arthur Pollack thought *Natural Man* had paved the way for the ANT to become "Something very important in the theatrical life of New York City." Brooks Atkinson, unable to get over the woefully small stage of the 135th Street Library, compared it negatively with the Seattle production. He noted that *Natural Man* had come from Seattle with a "considerable reputation," but that it had not been handled in a manner likely to enhance the reputation of the ANT.[82] Ralph Warnes, the critic for the *Daily Worker*, found it a stirring revival but picked up on its residual black nationalism. John Henry, was, he regretted, "weakened by nationalism" in his response to the taunts of white jailbirds in the prison cell. *Natural Man* risked becoming a "rallying cry for hatred of all white men and for Negro nationalism." However, he had warm praise for the camp scene in which white hoboes extended a hand of friendship to Henry. With a correction to the interracial hostility on display in the jail scene—an adjustment that he felt could easily be made—*Natural Man* would be "a fine piece of

Negro theatre."[83] Black critical reception was also mixed. The *Amsterdam Star News*, a longtime champion of Harlem community theatre, judged it "by far the best that has been produced by a little theatre group in Harlem" and urged Harlemites to show their support. The *Atlanta Daily World* noted the play's "enviable reputation" after the Seattle production and judged it to have gone down well in New York. The *Afro-American* found this John Henry a rather pathetic character, and insisted it was "about time that Hollywood's version of how colored people act in church, should be discarded."[84]

The new redemptive ending of *Natural Man* took on particular significance when viewed in the context of other black heroes treading the boards. By the time John Henry began hammering away at mountains on a Harlem stage in May 1941, Bigger Thomas had been smothering a white woman in her bed for over six weeks at a downtown theatre. Indeed, the parallels between the two productions and the two black heroes did not go unnoticed. To the white critic Arthur Pollack, John Henry appeared as "a kind of Bigger Thomas."[85] For its part, the ANT was more than happy to be connected to the popular *Native Son*. The night before *Native Son* opened, the ANT hosted its first social event to which it invited the entire cast of the Broadway play.[86] It proudly proclaimed that members of the ANT company had played in *Native Son*: "we have constantly supplied Broadway with talent; such as Jacqueline Gant Andrew, and Helen Martin who are now appearing in 'Native Son.'" Canada Lee, who starred as Bigger Thomas, was a stalwart of the Harlem Negro Unit and served as a critical link between Harlem's theatre community and the Welles-Houseman Mercury Theatre, which had staged *Native Son*. Lee had played a range of heroic black figures: in addition to staring as the triumphant Henri Christophe in the Harlem Unit's *Haiti*, he had recently performed the role of Vic Mason, a tragic Garveyite, in the NPC production of Ward's *Big White Fog*. With a diverse portfolio of black heroes in his repertoire, Lee could be trusted to deliver a complex Bigger Thomas.

It was more than a coincidence of timing and a shared troupe that made the comparison between *Natural Man* and *Native Son* apt: both dramas were the product of deep-rooted and ongoing debates about what a black hero might look like on the American stage. These debates played out in, and shaped, the manuscripts used for both productions. For *Native Son*, the transformation of Bigger Thomas from novel to stage play reflected conflicting visions of the black hero held by the white southern dramatist and the black novelist. These differences resulted in a published text and stage production that featured different, even incompatible, heroes. For *Natural Man*,

John Henry was similarly made over into a different type of hero when the play was transferred from Seattle to Harlem. In both cases, the black hero's transformation involved the recognition of his virtue by whites and the reward of a better next life; in both cases, the revised climax offered a swift and facile resolution to the complex problems staged in each drama.

Many factors influenced the journeys of these two heroes to the New York stage in spring 1941 including long-standing debates about black suffering and white spectatorship as well as the growing influence of black-run community theatres. It is a story also shaped by the competing priorities of those involved including Orson Welles and John Houseman as well as Wright's evolution as an artist and changing relationship to communism. Yet it is a journey that cannot be understood without the Federal Theatre. Browne and Hill developed their reputations in the FTP, but WPA theatre was also important to the careers of Green and Wright. The white dramatist and black novelist both bore witness to, and became directly involved in, the divisive but sometimes creative conflicts over what types of hero should be staged by Negro Units and who was, or should be, empowered to make those decisions. These experiences would have a direct bearing on the kind of Bigger Thomas who left the pages of Wright's novel to try his luck on the stage.

Richard Wright, Paul Green, and the Chicago Negro Unit

Richard Wright took up his post on the Chicago Negro Unit of the Federal Theatre Project in January 1936. The same month, Paul Green's new drama, *Hymn to the Rising Sun*, was published in *New Theatre* magazine and staged by the Let Freedom Ring Company in New York City.[87] Wright had transferred from the Federal Writers Project to work as a publicity agent for the theatre unit. Here he penned a couple of essays on Chicago theatre. Increasingly interested in "dramatic realism," Wright approached the white Jewish director Charles DeSheim with the suggestion that he direct the Negro Unit in Green's new chain-gang drama. DeSheim appeared to have the credentials to stage the type of realist drama Wright was after: he had come out of the Group Theatre in New York and had recently staged a production of Odets's *Waiting for Lefty* in the Windy City.[88]

Green wrote *Hymn* as a direct response to a recent and particularly brutal case of prisoner abuse in the North Carolina Prison System. Shropshire and Barnes, two black men sentenced to the chain gang for petty crimes, were left chained in an unheated building as punishment for their slow work. When their legs froze and developed gangrene, the prison officers in charge instructed that their feet be amputated. On trial for the part they played in this tragedy at the time when Green was writing his play, both officers were acquitted.[89] *Hymn to the Rising Sun*, takes place on the fourth of July on a railroad chain gang. In the version of the play published in *New Theatre* and held in manuscript form in the Federal Theatre archive, the action takes place in the present, "somewhere in the United States." In subsequent published versions, the urgency of the drama is diluted and particularized: set "some years ago," it takes place "somewhere in the southern part of the United States."[90]

Although Green had originally envisaged black convicts at the center of his drama, the main speaking characters are white and the action revolves around the chain-gang Captain and Bright Boy, the newly interned white youngster.[91] The centerpiece of the drama is a long monologue delivered by the Captain to mark Independence Day. He believes the chain gang will turn failed citizens into men by reaffirming the relationship between manliness and productive labor, a relationship threatened by the temptations of the consumer age. Mothers are to blame for their failed manhood: "they didn't know how to train you, petted and spoiled you." The chain gang will reverse this damaging process: "you won't be petted here. . . . when I turn you loose you'll be hard as iron, you'll be men."[92] Directly referencing the case of Shropshire and Barnes, the Captain articulates the ties that bind together the southern racial system: black Americans' perceived refusal to work without coercion and propensity to criminal behavior, and the demand for cheap labor to drive forward industrialization. The chain gang ensured that African Americans who had failed to fulfil their assigned role in this racial hierarchy would learn how to do so in prison. Prison would redeem their manhood, the Captain promised, by teaching them the importance of productive labor:

> For if you don't get hard you can't make your time, and if you don't make your time you can't pay your debts to the state. And the only way you can pay it is by work. You can't pay by playing sick, by getting beat, by being shut up in the sweatbox, by being chained up till your feet fall off. That don't do nobody no good. It's work we want. Work the state wants. It's for that the great railroad company has hired you from the governor.[93]

To reinforce this message, the Captain concludes his speech with a public whipping of Bright Boy, the white prisoner who dared voice concern over the ill-treatment of his fellow inmate, a black prisoner named Runt. Confined to the "sweatbox" for masturbating, Runt is unable to pay his debt to society, he does not make his time. The play ends with the white cook cleaning out the sweatbox following Runt's death.

The incident that leads to the black prisoner's punishment was a deliberate and controversial choice on the part of the playwright. In the opening lines of the play, a fellow prisoner, who is white, reflects: "Reckon when Runt gets out of that box he'll quit going behind the tent to love himself."[94] Although it is the punishment, rather than the original act, that drives the dramatic action, the passing reference to this rare opportunity for self-love within the confines of the dehumanizing convict camp was significant both for Green, and for readers and audiences of the play. In creating Runt, Green drew on dangerous racial myths of black men's uncontrollable sexuality. Green, however, insisted he chose a sexual act, above all other examples, because it allowed him to examine the individual black man, and in particular, the agency of the tragic hero who must play some part in his own downfall.

In autumn 1935 Green sent a draft of *Hymn* to Percival Wilde, who had commissioned Green to write the play for his volume of one-act plays on social themes. The editor suggested that the sensationalism of masturbation would distract from the central issue of the chain gang and proposed, with an editor's tact, that Green's play would be "more tremendous if Runt's offense were a triviality which would not be punished anywhere else. . . . masturbation is not the issue; the chain gang is."[95] Green agreed. The chain gang was the central concern of *Hymn,* but for this reason Runt's punishment could not be as a result of what might be viewed as a triviality:

> For then the darker, more disastrous nature of convict life would be but once again illustrated by a pathetic and not tragic incident—and tragedy is what I'm after in this piece, since the lives I'm telling about are tragic. Suppose the Negro were put into the sweatbox because he had been caught smoking in his bunk, or talking back to one of the guards. Then the dramatic result would be to point the finger of accusation at the system while it put an arm of sympathy around the abused individual.[96]

Green was a southern liberal who campaigned for prison reform. But his belief in personal redemption also informed his understanding of the relationship between individuals and society. Green insisted that there was room for individuals to shape their own lives in meaningful ways, however flawed the system: individual striving must accompany social change.

To blame the system without acknowledging personal choice would be, he believed, a simplification that denied truth and obscured tragedy. In Green's words, it would be the "old sheep-and-goat method now a little dear to our younger radical writers, and not true to the infinite complexity and shades of difference of human nature." For Green, his portrayal of Runt's "crime," was part of his broader commitment to revealing the "darker" and "more disastrous nature of convict life." To Richard Wright, it suggested a dramatist prepared to push the boundaries of what could be presented on the American stage.[97]

Actors on the Chicago Negro Unit felt differently. Reluctant to perform white-authored "Negro folk dramas" in which black protagonists were invariably victims of "lynching, suicide or degeneracy," they voiced strong objections to playing the role of chain-gang prisoners.[98] The resistance of the black troupe put Wright in a difficult position as intermediary. In *Black Boy*, Wright's "Record of Childhood and Youth," which was published in 1945, the author recalled how the troupe questioned his support for the play and the authenticity of Green's dramatization as soon as they began their first read-through. They apparently did not get far before one of their number confronted Wright and DeSheim, saying, "we think this play is indecent. We don't want to act in a play like this before the American public. I don't think any such conditions exist in the South. I lived in the South and I never saw any chain gangs. Mr. DeSheim, we want a play that will make the public love us." Wright's account strikes a paternalistic note. Responding to the troupe's complaint, Wright refuses the possibility that they might have had legitimate cause to question the liberatory potential of white-authored folk dramas:

> I could not believe my ears. I had assumed that the heart of the Negro actor was pining for adult expression in the American theatre, that he was ashamed of the stereotypes of clowns, mammies, razors, dice, watermelon, and cotton fields. . . . Now they were protesting against dramatic realism! I tried to defend the play and I was heckled down. . . . I felt—but only temporarily—that perhaps the whites were right, that Negroes were children and would never grow up. DeSheim informed the company that he would produce any play they liked, and they sat like frightened mice, possessing no words to make known their vague desires.[99]

Wright articulates a false binary: presented with the choice of minstrelsy or white-authored "dramatic realism," black actors, he contends, chose familiar minstrel roles. The boundary between the two was more blurred than Wright suggests. If, as Hartman argues, the spectacle of white mastery and the enactment of a willed subjection underpinned both minstrelsy and melodrama, it was no less a defining feature of white dramatic realism. Realist dramas of the 1930s frequently required black troupes to participate in "scenes of subjection."[100] On this occasion, members of the Chicago Negro Unit felt empowered to resist. They were not alone: the troupe's ambivalence toward Green's work was, as we have seen, widely shared among black critics. Although some, such as Montgomery Gregory, welcomed the "fidelity to the actual life of these people" other black critics were weary of white audiences and playwrights who insisted that the only "authentic" Negro was a dead one. Writing in *New Theatre*, the black communist Eugene Gordon argued that: "Negro workers who know the 'stark realism' of, say, O'Neill's, Green's and Heywood's plays look upon it not as the kind of realism the black man actually encounters, but as another and a more 'civilized' method of attack." Gordon believed that only "upper class Negroes" were capable of believing that the "fatalism" of southern white imaginations was "true to Negro life."[101] What Wright saw as truthful "adult expression" often appeared to black actors as one more vehicle for white mastery.

FTP records attest to the conflict that arose within Negro Units when black actors were presented with Negro "folk" roles. Correspondence between white administrators suggests that they understood the "folk" play as a site of contestation between white dramatists and Negro Units as well as within black performance communities. Negro Units frequently objected to performing in folk dramas. Blanding Sloan, the director for the Eastern Region, informed the director of the NSB that it was "difficult to sell negro groups in federal theatre on doing folk stuff. The words 'darkies' 'coon' and 'nigger' are objectionable to the negro race almost regardless of how used." In Chicago, Wright was not alone in observing the Negro Unit's reluctance to perform folk plays. In June 1936, Mid-West regional director Thomas Wood Stevens wrote to Hallie Flanagan that "The Negro Theatre has been in 'hot water' ever since it started because of the factional battles of the negro community. There is a very strong feeling there against anything in the way of a Negro folk play."[102] Whether expressed by white administrators or Chicago Negro Unit actors, Wright found the concerns about Green's play parochial. In response, he requested and was granted a transfer back to the Federal Writers Project. Reflecting on the episode in a letter to Green in 1940, Wright confided: "I had to fight both Negroes and whites to get them to see that the play was authentic."[103]

Hallie Flanagan shared Wright's view of actors in the Chicago Negro Unit, recalling in her book-length account of the FTP how the play's closure caused "such demoralization and timidity on the part of the Negro group that it was months before we finally got them to face another audience."[104] Rushed out within a year of the project's closure, Flanagan's account glossed over the fierce opposition from black actors and the broader community that FTP regional directors had communicated to her, recording simply that "the Negroes were ready to open with Mr. Green's play, which they felt to be . . . serious drama."[105] Putting Flanagan's unusual forgetfulness to one side, the account of the Mid-West regional director confirms that there was some hostility both within the Negro Unit and in the wider black community as to the suitability of *Hymn* for a Negro Unit.[106] Notwithstanding these concerns, the Chicago Negro Unit came very close to staging Green's drama. Exactly how, or even if, the concerns of the troupe were overcome is not documented in the FTP records. We know that at some point after Wright's departure, the play was rehearsed and made ready for production. The final twist in *Hymn*'s troubled Chicago career came when Robert Dunham, the white head of the Illinois Works Progress Administration (WPA), stepped in and banned the play on opening night on account of its "moral character."[107] Outraged that a Negro Unit production had been closed down by white authorities, the black community rallied to its support and demanded that the play be allowed to open. The outcry that white censorship provoked suggests that some in the black community supported the play, or perhaps that a play censored by white authorities was worth defending after all.[108] *Hymn* never opened in Chicago. The Federal Theatre's defeat at the hands of the WPA prompted the resignation of a number of FTP officials and directors in Chicago, including the director Charles DeSheim.[109]

Hymn to the Rising Sun was eventually staged by the FTP. Six months later, the white, New York Experimental Unit put on a version of the play in the city where it had premiered in January 1936. The Experimental Unit's April 1937 production offered the provocative theatre that was much admired by the New York critics. Arthur Pollack called it a "little masterpiece," "written with the beautiful, compassionate simplicity. . . . it is a stinging attack on inhumanity."[110] The circumstances that led to the cancelation of *Hymn* in Chicago and its warm reception on the East Coast would, in time, lead Wright to several important conclusions: the Windy City was a cultural backwater; New York was the only stage for radical theatre; and Green was the only playwright capable of adapting Wright's shocking novel for Broadway.[111]

FIGURE 10 Scene from New York Experimental Unit production of Paul Green's *Hymn to the Rising Sun*. Photograph four of six, Library of Congress, Music Division, Federal Theatre Project Collection, Box 1217.

Adapting *Native Son* for the Stage

Native Son, was published on March 1, 1940. Achieving sales of 215,000 copies in three weeks, it was the first novel by an African American to be featured by the Book of the Month Club.[112] Wright received and turned down numerous offers to adapt his book for the stage before settling on Paul Green. In a letter to the white dramatist, he explained why he had accepted Green's offer of collaboration: "because of the manner in which you handled the Negro character in your play, 'Hymn to the Rising Sun' . . . because of the kind of insight you displayed for the Negro character in that play, I think you can handle a boy like Bigger."[113] Over the summer 1940, Wright traveled to Chapel Hill, North Carolina, to work with Green on adapting his novel for the stage.[114] Although Wright had approved of Green's characterization of black prisoners in *Hymn* and admired his skill as a dramatist, the two men soon proved to have very different ideas about Bigger. Green was determined to produce a tragic hero. Accordingly, he revised the original plot of *Native Son* to allow Bigger to express sorrow and take responsibility for his murderous actions. No longer the rebel who resists to the end, who feels like a man in the act of killing and being pursued, Bigger was reconfigured to become one of the Christ-like figures who populate Green's dramas: black victim-heroes who suffer and die so that others, usually whites, might be saved. The most significant changes included reworking the character of Mary Dalton, the white girl Bigger murders, as a brazen hussy rather than a well-meaning leftist, as well as diluting the effect of the murder scene, which is so graphic in the novel, by staging the white woman's death in a retrospective dream sequence. Bigger was softened. His girlfriend, Bessie (renamed Clara), was no longer the intended victim of Bigger's newly focused and powerful hatred, but rather the unfortunate victim of police cross fire. Crucially, Green wanted a new ending. Instead of closing the play with Bigger facing the death sentence, Green imagined the hero taking his own life, but only after his attorney has won him a life sentence. Rather than blame society for Bigger's execution, Green's hero would absolve society by taking responsibility for what he had done: his death would be recast as an enactment of "black will."[115] The new, redemptive ending risked undermining the central message of Wright's work. As *New Republic* critic Malcolm Cowley noted in his review of the novel, "If Mr. Max had managed to win a life sentence for Bigger Thomas, he would have robbed him of his only claim to human courage and dignity."[116] If Green got his way and had made Bigger commit suicide, it would have made the play a spectacle of white mastery and black subjection.[117]

Wright initially agreed to Green's revisions. However, between the early stages of collaboration in June–August 1940 and the opening night of *Native Son* in March 1941, the established white playwright and rising black star came to very different positions on the role of Bigger. It is clear from Green's correspondence and the published version of the play he endorsed that the white dramatist had always been keen to create a tragic hero with responsibility for his own downfall. Rejecting "the old familiar whine that the reason I'm a dead beat, or I'm mean, or I can't get anywhere in the world is that the world treats me wrong," Green insisted that "Every man has something to do with what he becomes."[118] Just how far and for how long Wright went along with Green's revisions has become the subject of considerable debate among Wright scholars. In particular, there are conflicting interpretations of Green's reworking of Bigger Thomas, the extent to which Wright initially supported Green's vision, and the role of Houseman, who, in his memoir, presented himself as the savior of Bigger in his journey from page to stage. Drawing heavily on the diaries, recollections, and autobiographies of Green and Houseman, scholars have debated how, when, and why Wright and Green began to disagree to the extent that their ambitions for the play became irreconcilable.[119] The question is not one of which white man's public recollections we should credit. As Rowley notes in her account, both Houseman and Green too frequently spoke for Wright, particularly after his death.[120] In this chapter, I am less interested in the tug-of-war for influence over Wright and more interested in Wright's voice and his need to publicly defend his work in 1941. In particular, I want to examine how Wright conceived of and struggled with the stage Bigger Thomas, a character who exemplified the difficulty of constructing a black tragic hero in the American theatre. In this endeavor, Wright was part of a broader debate within the black community about the problem of the black hero.

The problem of the black hero would become the subject of an increasingly public and bitter debate in late 1940. In the months that followed the completion of the first working draft in August 1940, Green quickly and publicly committed himself to the idea that the stage Bigger would accept responsibility for his crimes. In a letter defending his decision to take on the project to a white member of the North Carolina Interracial Commission, Green insisted that his play contained a "basic human truth," albeit one "shorn of its surrounding hate and evil." Green reassured this prominent white liberal that "It is only incidental that he [Bigger Thomas] is black" and that "of course we have to take account of the individual's moral responsibility."[121] Between late summer 1940 and the opening of *Native Son* in March 1941, the script was subject to numerous, conflicting revisions. These were made not only by Green, but also by Wright, who worked on the script in New York with Houseman. Wright and Houseman's revisions would directly contradict Green's public statements about Bigger's moral responsibility and "incidental" racial identity. Placing Bigger's race, once again, at the center of the drama, Wright and Houseman's revisions made it clear that white guilt, rather than Bigger's acceptance of responsibility, is what leads directly to his death.

Wright would trace the struggle for control of Bigger and the limitations placed on the black dramatic hero in a seven-page drama entitled "The Problem of the Hero."[122] Written shortly before *Native Son* was due to open in mid-March and intended for publication in the *New York Times*, Wright envisaged his sketch as "an attempt to reconstruct the general sense of the central problem we faced in dramatizing my novel." Over four short acts, the protagonists, "White Man" and "Black Man" gradually reveal the difference that race makes in how they approach the question of individual agency within a system of structural inequality. "White Man: (graciously but seriously) I wasn't quite satisfied with your novel when I read it, but I liked it. I felt it was the best piece of fiction written by a Negro in America. Now, in dramatizing it, I would like to make your character, Bigger, a hero in the tragic sense. As he stands now, he seems a figure of pathos, more acted upon than acting." The Black Man responds, "Yes, I know what you mean, Bigger is not heroic in the sense that he determines his own destiny."[123] The rest of the play draws out the differences between the two men's approach to the hero. Whereas the White Man sees in Bigger a Christ-like figure who could bear the sins of the world through an act of suicide, the Black Man is concerned that such an act of self-destruction was not truthful, for "he must be made out of the debris and trash and muck of our American scene."[124] Green's proposed ending serves as a troubling reminder of the many white-authored dramas in which "bad" black men were punished by taking their own lives. As the Black Man explains: "a suicide ending, in my opinion, runs parallel to so many suicide endings about Negro characters that ours will be counted as just another trip down the same stereotype road."[125] The Black Man also admits to his fear "that many Negroes will feel that our hero—after his bloody deeds—is simply obligingly removing his carcass from the presence of respectable people because of the awful things he has done."[126] Whereas Green had claimed that Bigger's racial identity was not central to the play, Wright affirmed its importance when he has the Black Man explain to the White Man: "western civilization for 300 years has strenuously sought to keep its principles, its learning, it culture and its political power from the hands of black men; therefore I am afraid that if we went through with this idea of a black hero, a black God, we would be but gratuitously endowing a black hero, the American Negro, with qualities that he has never been allowed to possess in America."[127] The final act takes place a month later in New York, following the Black Man's rewriting of the play.[128] In January and February 1941, Wright had worked with Houseman to amend Green's latest draft, and he wrote to Green to warn him: "I don't know just how you will like the last scene, but we recast it in terms of the book." The new version, he assured Green, was "short, effective, I think, and forms a good conclusion to the play."[129] In Wright's dramatization of these events, the White Man disagrees with the revisions, believing they rip out the heart of the play and destroy a hero who might have brought unity and hope to black and white Americans. The Black Man resists this type of hero, fearing "it might fill the defenceless with false hope." Though the white man makes a final plea: "But there must be heroes!" this time it is the Black Man who has the last word: "There shall be heroes, when men are *free!*"[130]

Wright sent "The Problem of the Hero" to Brooks Atkinson, the drama editor at the *New York Times* and a longtime supporter of Paul Green. Hoping it would appear in print before the play opened, Wright took the precaution of warning Green in a telegram on March 12th: "Wrote article for NY Times on our collaboration discussing problem of hero in US drama. Gave your views and mine. Tried desperately to be objective and fair. Maybe they wont use it then will publish elsewhere see you over weekend regards—Richard Wright." Green responded immediately and firmly. Questioning the wisdom of airing their disagreements publicly, Green advised Wright against publication, suggesting that "we had better stand or fall together on the production." He later recalled Atkinson warning him of Wright's "dramatization of their collaboration," which the theatre critic described as "an attack on you." Much later, Green offered an account that contradicts his contemporaneous correspondence. Claiming it was common practice for the author of a forthcoming show to be invited to comment on the adaptation, he suggested that he had advised Atkinson to publish Wright's sketch. Whether Atkinson's friendship with Green or a change of mind on the part of Wright was responsible, "The Problem of the Hero" was not published.[131] However, the official version of the play was. On March 28, four days after a twice-postponed *Native Son* finally opened, Harper and Brothers released a version of the play under both men's names. Much to the annoyance of Orson Welles, the publishers tied the published text to the Mercury production.[132]

There was considerable variation between the version of *Native Son* that was staged and the version published in March 1941. One thing they had in common, however, was that both were the result of compromise. With Houseman, Welles, and Wright united against him, Green had backed down and let them get on with the stage production. He did not relinquish control over the published version, however. In the final scene that Green authorized for publication, Bigger accepts responsibility for his crimes, saying, "I didn't give myself no chance," and concedes he was "wrong and crazy." Finally, "becoming more of a man," Bigger walks to the death chamber on his way to a better place. The promise of Christian redemption is heavily implied as the play ends with a priest's voice intoning "I am the resurrection and the life."[133] Green did not get the tragic hero he wanted, however, in the version that ran for fifteen weeks at the St. James Theatre. Mary

Dalton's murder was staged realistically, rather than in the dream sequence he had proposed and audiences were left in no doubt that Bigger was not ready to die to take away their sins. With Bigger insisting: "I'm more alive now than I ever was in my life. Goddamit. I'm alive now and they're going to kill me!" the stage version closes with him grasping the prison bars awaiting his execution. No priests in sight.[134] Even so, Green's alternative vision for Bigger persisted. Most crucially, the Bigger who appeared before audiences at the St. James Theatre is not an intentional killer. Bigger commits only the accidental murder of the white girl. He does not commit the second, deliberate murder of his girlfriend.

Whether the stage adaptation adhered more closely to Wright or Green's vision rather depended on the viewer. Deferring to Green's status as the senior member of the collaboration and the established playwright, white critics tended to foreground Green. Such a focus served to emphasize the changes to Bigger in the stage version and to minimize Wright's involvement. For example, in his review, Burns Mantle referred only to the "help" offered by Wright and suggested that Green's adaptation had served to "soften, rather than to intensify the novel's body blows." With the exception of the defense attorney's speech in the final scene, there was, in Mantle's view, only a "casual effort" made to remind audiences that Bigger was a victim of society.[135] For Wright, however, these final scenes were crucial in terms of establishing white society's responsibility for creating Bigger. Wright lost control of his creation when he became a character in a play, but he had not lost his desire to control the characterization of his hero in print. Having failed to publish his dramatic sketch documenting the collaboration with Green, Wright took pains to ensure that his vision was recorded for posterity. Accordingly, excerpts from the stage version of the drama were reproduced in the playbill with an accompanying program note by Wright in which he explained why Bigger could not find redemption in a society that denied his humanity.[136] It is important that Wright chose to reproduce in the playbill the prologue, along with scenes 7, 9, and 10: these were the scenes that had caused the most conflict between the collaborators; they were also the scenes that contained the greatest variation between the published play and the Broadway production that ran in spring 1941.

Following Wright's lead, black critics made the vision of the black author and black actors central to their reviews. In contrast to the white critics, black critics tended to mention Green only in passing, as the co-author of the script. Of the whites involved with *Native Son*, only Welles, who had helped focus attention on black theatre and actors when he directed the

Harlem Negro Unit's *Macbeth*, was given credit for the success of the production. The role of civil right organizations, which had sponsored preview performances, was also given ample coverage.[137] Most of all, however, black reviewers concentrated their attention on Richard Wright, Bigger Thomas, and Canada Lee. A former prize-fight boxer, Lee had risen to stardom as an actor on the Harlem Negro Unit. Black newspapers were invested in Bigger as a black creation and were particularly interested in Lee's portrayal of the character. The *Afro-American* published an exclusive interview in which the actor explained his interpretation of Bigger. Describing his view of Bigger as "A creation of hate and fear," Lee understood his character as "the result of forced idleness, a home devoid of privacy, of a society which either ignores or patronizes him." In playing the role, he said, he hoped to make "an eloquent plea for the thousands of black boys who will lose their souls and their lives, unless given the opportunity to work."[138] Like Lee, black theatre critics tended to interpret the stage Bigger in keeping with the spirit of Wright's novel. The *Amsterdam Star News* saw the stage play as "a sympathetic expose of the corrupt conditions which create Bigger Thomases," while the *Chicago Defender* found in Bigger Thomas a protagonist who embodied "the dejection and desperation, the stunted expression of a considerable part of the Negro race." The Atlanta *Daily World* declared the play "pretty much faithful to the book" and affirmed that "added weight is definitely given that part in which Bigger, in jail, finally speaks out."[139]

When the original novel, *Native Son*, was first published in March 1940, fellow authors and some black leaders welcomed it as a "great piece of work," praising its "emotional power," and delighting in Wright's success. But others worried about how whites would perceive a character who desired, and killed, a white woman, fearing it was a book that "could do a great deal of harm."[140] As white America's fascination with Bigger followed him into the theatre, black critics became more vocal. Wright's fellow playwright and friend Langston Hughes called for a debate about the role of the black hero in American culture. In an article in the June 1941 issue of the *Crisis* entitled, "The Need for Heroes," Hughes questioned how far *Native Son's* continuing appeal to whites relied upon its portrayal of black abasement and the affirmation of white power. "If the best of our writers continue to pour their talent into the tragedies of frustration and weakness, tomorrow will probably say . . . 'No wonder the Negroes never amounted to anything. There were no heroes among them. Defeat and panic, moaning, groaning, and weeping were their lot. Did nobody fight? Did nobody triumph? Here is that book about Bigger. The catalogue says it sold several hundred thousand copies. A Negro wrote it. No wonder Hitler wiped the Negroes off the face of Europe.'"[141] Cognizant of the need to name and expose injustices, nevertheless Hughes argued that a black culture that was knowledgeable of and celebrated black heroes of the past would be better placed to resist those injustices in the future. Surely if black artists continued to present spectacles of black suffering, as his friend Wright did, they would serve to undermine cultures of black resistance and reinforce white domination.

Hughes's essay was published just as *Natural Man* was in the middle of its two-month revival by the ANT at the 135th Street Library in Harlem. Although Hughes does not mention Theodore Browne in his *Crisis* article, in another essay for the *Chicago Defender* he drew on *Natural Man* as an example of the kind of play black theatre groups should be producing. Hughes had long admired the character of John Henry and had agreed to write the libretto for an opera version of the play several years earlier. Although the project was never realized, Hughes used the legend for his own musical play, *De Organizer* (1940).[142] In *De Organizer*, the black union leader's manhood is validated through his woman's comparison of him to the black folk hero John Henry, albeit a John Henry who has given up steel driving to organize the poor.[143] John Henry the union man strikes a very different note to the hero Browne developed in the Federal Theatre production of *Natural Man*. In Seattle, John Henry has no time for unionism, which has historically not only excluded African Americans, but served to maintain the racial hierarchies on which American capitalism had come to depend.

Another *Natural Man* Manuscript: A Path Not Taken

The fate of black heroes in black-authored dramas was determined by a host of competing and sometimes contradictory imperatives. Interaction between authors, playwrights, directors, and producers, as well as theatre hierarchies, critical reception, and the audience for different types of theatre, all shaped the journey of black heroes from the page to stage. On such journeys heroes could be transformed: on the Seattle stage and in Wright's novel, John Henry and Bigger Thomas indict white Americans; in the ANT's adaptation of *Natural Man* and Paul Green's reworking of *Native Son*, they offer racial redemption. The parallel endings in these 1941 adaptations are notable: just as the ANT's John Henry dies dreaming of the mountains and rocks and the tunnels he will forge "up there," Bigger Thomas starts calling to the overhead planes—"Riding through-riding through, I'll be with you! I'll . . . Keep on Driving! To the end of the world-smack into the face of the sun" Fly 'em for me—for Bigger." With a priest chanting the last rites, at the play's close Bigger has become a Christ-like figure who dies to save us from our sins.[144] The parallels between the two dramas are all the more striking if we consider briefly a fifth, as yet undiscussed, *Natural Man* manuscript. The version held at the Performing Arts Library in New York, ("PAL") appears to represent an earlier draft of the ANT manuscript." Although it includes a new scene: "Revised Final Episode of Natural Man," it is unlikely to have been the version used in production by the ANT as its structure does not match the sequence of episodes outlined in the ANT program. It remains a fascinating text, however, and helps explicate the transition from the Seattle version to the ANT manuscript.[145]

The PAL manuscript has a unique ending: it includes a flashback to Episode 2, which is set at the entrance to the Big Bend Tunnel and comes directly after the "Hobo sequence.'" Stage directions refer to the "original script" and detail the deviation: the hobo scene ends with John Henry angrily demanding that the hoboes cease their mockery.[146] The action then moves directly to the Big Bend Tunnel. John Henry walks into the tunnel which appears to be on fire as a result of his hammering. The speech in this version is considerably longer than in the ANT manuscript: John Henry talks of leaving his spirit behind, in the Big Bend Tunnel, the dive on Beale Street, the Jail House, the Chain Gang, and even the Hobo-Jungle. In common with the ANT manuscript, John Henry is peaceful in his newly discovered spirituality. But this time he is also evangelical. Stage directions indicate that his face is lighted by a smile, and that he looks up to heaven and declares: "'You my spirit reaching up outta the earth. Great God Almighty, what would it be like if all the natural folks of this earth was to reach up at the same time? They could reach to high heaven and ease it down to earth,' (John Henry proudly raises his hammer over his shoulder one last time.)"[147] With repeated references to heaven and to God, the PAL manuscript fully embraces the interracial, peaceful co-existence that is hinted at in the version staged by the ANT. Whereas the Seattle manuscripts promote a radical black self-determination, or even a "note of vengeance," the ending in the PAL version offers a path to redemption for white as well as black Americans. By contrast, in the ANT manuscript, John Henry's closing words are directed at his community—"the boys"—and not at the blossoming interracial community imagined in the "PAL." Assured of a heaven full of mountains and rocks in the "PAL," a contented John Henry sinks to the floor, and dies onstage. This alternative version represents an even greater departure from Browne's earlier hero than the version performed by the ANT in spring 1941. Although the John Henry staged by the ANT is significantly altered from the hero first conceived by Browne, the version held at the Performing Arts Library reveals both the full extent of that reworking and the fact that somewhere in the process of adaptation, the decision was made not to transform John Henry into a symbol of interracial union.

Unfortunately, the records of the ANT and of the individuals closely associated with it contain few clues as to exactly how and why the ANT settled on the version now held at GMU for their production of *Natural Man* in May 1941. Yet the very existence of multiple manuscripts with their different characterizations of John Henry and revised endings is important, as are the battles to control Bigger Thomas's journey from page to stage and on to published dramatic text. Taken together, they reveal the way in which theatre manuscripts in the late 1930s and early 1940s were able to contain and facilitate broader debates about the black hero that would shape black literary culture well into the 1940s. The mutability of text and character within these manuscripts also draws attention to the particular function of unpublished theatre manuscripts as a laboratory for radical ideas: Wright used a dramatic sketch to challenge Green's notion of universal heroes and black agency in "The Problem of the Hero"; Hughes, wanting heroes that black Americans could celebrate, was inspired to write his own John Henry drama; and Browne explored a different kind of hero in his next play, a dramatization of the life of Harriet Tubman. The new possibilities for the black American hero were also tried out in black dramas that made it to the Federal Theatre stage. Both *Natural Man*, and, as is described in chapter 4, *Big White Fog*, present black victim-heroes whose sacrificial deaths defamiliarize the spectacle of black suffering found in the work of Paul Green and other white dramatists. Featuring black heroes who recount injustices past, and articulate and attempt to meet the needs and desires of black women and men in the present, black Federal Theatre dramas constitute a form of redress. For while John Henry's enjoyment of his physical strength and Victor Mason's empowerment as a member of the Garvey movement can neither restore nor remedy what has been lost through enslavement, they do, however, suggest a level of black agency seldom seen on the American stage.[148]

Garveyism, Communism, and Gender Trouble

Theodore Ward's *Big White Fog*

· ·

When Shirley Graham invited South Side community leaders to the YWCA to hear Theodore Ward read his new drama, she was hoping a black-authored play would win the Chicago Negro Unit new friends. As supervisor of the unit, Graham was pleased to find that the audience was "courteous" and "showed intelligent interest" on the night of the read-through.[1] But in the days and weeks that followed, complaints poured in. Summarizing their tone and content for Chicago Federal Theatre director Harry Minturn, Graham explained that South Siders were troubled more by Ward's portraits of defeated black men and transgressive black women than by his depiction of communist activists:

> People have said to me, "This play is *not* representative of us. We *do* have many successful business men in Chicago—our sons *do* get scholarships—we *do* support our own businesses—black *men* are respected not only in their own homes, but throughout the community—our respectable women do not keep all kind of rooming houses—and our girls *do not* have to sleep with white men to get fifty dollars." Except for a few exceptions, whether or not the play was communistic seemed to be of minor importance.[2]

The criticisms expressed by representatives of South Side organizations and the response of Federal Theatre administrators offer a window onto how black performance communities were able to shape Federal Theatre dramas in the rehearsal and production process. Contemporaneous commentaries also contradict the historiographical consensus that has come to shape our understanding of *Big White Fog* as a socialist realist drama that privileges the communist "solution." Instead, the response of the first black audience to encounter *Big White Fog* draws our attention to the play's bold use of domestic tragedy to stage gender conflict within the black freedom struggle.

Big White Fog examines black masculinity in relation to three political movements and ideologies with competing visions for black progress in the years between 1922 and 1932. Garveyism, capitalism, and communism are each represented by a male member of the Mason family, all of whom embody the promise of redeemed black manhood. Each ideology, in turn, offers to restore the pride, dignity, and status of black men, who have long been excluded from hegemonic notions of manliness; each, in turn, is shown to be dependent on the very gender hierarchies that divide black communities and help sustain white supremacy. Ward's portraits of failed men (and the movements they represent) offered a stark critique, not only of hegemonic masculinity, but also of those who worked to achieve it for black men. *Big White Fog*'s reception on the South Side calls attention to what was distinctive about Ward's drama and the significance of its staging by the FTP. Federal Theatre units facilitated, and even required, engagement with the communities in which they operated, but because there was no commercial imperative or dependency on community sponsorship, new dramas did not necessarily have to be approved by the widest possible audience. In fact, the Federal Theatre could produce challenging, provocative, and radical dramas that divided black performance communities. By focusing on the manuscripts and production developed for and by the Chicago Negro Unit, this chapter explores the controversy surrounding *Big White Fog* in January 1938 and the role of the black community in shaping the version performed at the Great Northern Theatre three months later. Analyzing the evolution of Federal Theatre manuscripts alongside community responses enables us to construct a performance and manuscript history of *Big White Fog* alive to, but not overshadowed by, the anticommunist imperative that for so long shaped our understanding of 1930s culture in general and Federal Theatre drama in particular.[3] The long shadow of anticommunism has helped to sustain two, interdependent arguments about Ward's drama. The first is the widely held notion that *Big White Fog* is a socialist realist drama that stages communism as the solution to the black man's problems; the second suggests that this "pro-communist" message was what made the play controversial when it was first produced.[4] Such retrospective privileging of an anti/pro-communist binary overlooks the significance and provocation of staging a realist black family drama before a mixed audience and distracts from Ward's powerful critique of race and gender hierarchies within black communities. By foregrounding the responses of the local black community, it can be clearly seen that it was the Negro Unit's staging of gender and racial divisions within black families and political movements, rather than communism, which made *Big White Fog* a provocative play in 1938 and a drama of enduring significance in American theatre history.

Garveyism, Communism, and Gender Trouble   165

Revived as a major production for the Guthrie Theatre in Minneapolis in 1995 and in London by the Almeida Theatre in 2007, *Big White Fog* is the best known black drama of the Federal Theatre. It also represents a landmark in American theatre history: whether viewed as crucial to the development of black drama in the twentieth century or part of Popular Front culture, *Big White Fog* is an early example of what has become a powerful black theatre tradition that takes the black family as an allegory for black political life.[5] The black man's dream of a better life and failure to achieve hegemonic manhood in his domestic and work life are themes that, as shown in chapter 3, informed the stage adaptation of Richard Wright's *Native Son* (1940). The racial and gendered limitations imposed on black manhood and the gender conflicts this provokes within families are also at the heart of Hansberry's *Raisin in the Sun* (1959) and August Wilson's Pittsburgh Cycle plays.[6] *Big White Fog* is also an important play within the history of what Michael Denning calls the "Cultural Front," by which he means the popular, leftist, and frequently masculinist culture that nurtured the political and social movements of the 1930s. Both on- and off-stage, labor unions, political groups, and cultural institutions of the Popular Front have long been criticized for privileging male struggle. Underpinned by a workplace, rather than community unionism, male workers "forged a web of symbols which romanticized violence, rooted solidarity in metaphors of struggle, and constructed work and the workers as male."[7] By contrast, *Big White Fog* focuses on the mutually destructive consequences of racialized gender hierarchies for black women and men, both in the workplace and in the home. It not only critiques Popular Front gender politics, it also complicates historical narratives of a cultural front shaped only by masculinist imperatives. Moreover, *Big White Fog* was never only about the politics of the left. Listening to the voices of its first black audience reminds us that the play was equally concerned with, and occupies an important place within, the history of Garveyism. Written in the decade after the Universal Negro Improvement Association (UNIA) had reached its peak, but when black women were at the forefront of black nationalist politics, Ward was one of the first to offer a serious, if critical, dramatic treatment of Garveyism.[8] Male characters espousing Garveyite beliefs are accorded considerable dignity, even if they eventually fail. But they are also challenged by women. *Big White Fog* raises serious questions about strategies for black male redemption that rely on the subordination of women.

Resisting Communist Plots

Ward rejected attempts to pigeonhole *Big White Fog* as a communist drama. "No impartial critic or writer or historian can say that Big White Fog advocated Communism," he declared in a 1976 interview.[9] In the 1970s Ward frequently argued that *Big White Fog* was a drama that explored the complexity of the black experience, rather than a play that revealed the solution to racial problems. In a chronological index to his works, Ward suggested that "what the play discloses is the obscurity of the outlook of black America in its pursuit of freedom in America."[10] The positioning of *Big White Fog* in the 1960s and 1970s reflects the arc of domestic anticommunism and its impact on historical accounts of the 1930s. In the postwar period, the Federal Theatre would be swept up into a broader narrative that depicted social justice movements of the 1930s as part of a communist conspiracy to undermine the American way of life. It is important that *Big White Fog*'s reputation as a communist play was not cemented until the late 1960s when scholars such as Doris Abramson began to examine the black dramas of the Federal Theatre. Ward repudiated her analysis: "I don't think she understood what Big White Fog was about . . . . she thinks I was advocating that the Negro should go Communist . . . it was twisted around because a Communist boy was in the play and the son is being led towards Communism."[11] The appearance of "Communists" on stage in the final scene of *Big White Fog* has been crucial to analysis of the play in the late twentieth and twenty-first centuries. It is almost as if every character in Ward's play—even those hostile to the left—are tainted by association with the handful of reds who enter the stage in the climactic last scene.

At this stage an outline of the plot is required to explain why it is that a drama that critiques Garveyism, capitalism, and communism, is so frequently analyzed solely in terms of its apparently "pro-Communist" ending. Victor Mason is the tragic hero of *Big White Fog*. Trained in agriculture at Tuskegee Institute, Vic can find no homestead to support his family in the South. Like many black southerners in search of better opportunities, he moves to the urban North. Vic's experiences of racial discrimination in Chicago lead him to Marcus Garvey and the UNIA where he finds a respect and hope seldom available to black men in America. When his son Les loses his college scholarship on account of his race, Vic is moved to invest the family savings in the faltering black nationalist organization. Without savings, the Mason family struggle when the Depression hits and Vic is temporarily laid off due to a construction strike. His wife, Ella, becomes increasingly critical of his failure to bring home a family wage and resentful of the sacrifices her children must make in order to fulfill their father's Garveyite dream. Though the wages of their eldest daughter, Wanda, keep the family afloat for a time, as the strike continues Vic asks Les to give up college so he can contribute to family finances. Still their combined earnings are insufficient to cover the rent on the family house. With the threat of eviction hanging over them, Wanda has sex with a white man in order to raise funds for a new home. On discovering Wanda's act, Vic accepts the help of Les and his communist friends in resisting eviction. In the final scene this interracial group of men stand together, against the white bailiffs, to defend the family home. Such resistance comes at a cost. In the ensuing struggle, Vic is fatally shot. The ending offers little in way of redemption: Vic dies a disappointed man, the wife he has alienated unable to reconcile with him even on his deathbed.

Big White Fog has often been read as though it were a socialist realist drama which offers a Marxist vision of triumphant class struggle. Commentators have regarded the gathering of communists at the end of a play as offering an uplifting solution to the problems staged therein. Alternately viewed as hopeful, naïve, and perplexing, this view has been central to the dominant interpretation of *Big White Fog* as a "pro-Communist" drama," while its "pro-Communist agenda" has been held responsible for upsetting the local community out of which it emerged. Such interpretations have been shaped by, but not confined to the Cold War era. If anything, *Big White Fog* appears to have grown more firmly "pro-Communist" over time. In the first decades of twenty-first century, scholars such as Harry J. Elam Jr. have seen in Ward's drama "the ultimate victory of socialism over both pan-Africanism and capitalism." Alan Wald, who considers the drama's different meanings in the 1930s and in the later Cold War context, agrees that the ending of *Big White Fog* is clear: "the implication of *Big White Fog* is strong that the course of the son and his Communist friends offers the only way out of the "Big White Fog," that had hitherto obscured all choices."[12] A decade earlier, however, scholars saw Ward's portrayal of the left in less definitive terms: Rena Fraden and James Hatch focused less on the handful of communists who appear on the stage at the end and more on what they saw as a call for populist unity and broad coalitions of the labor movement. But what appeared to Fraden a "hopeful," if "naïve" ending, represented for Hatch a "powerful emotional and political statement."[13] Though commentators across the political spectrum differ as to the political and dramatic efficacy of the ending, there is a consensus that Ward offers a socialist realist ending with a "hopeful" resolution.[14] This privileging of communism in Ward's play tells us more about the enduring legacy of twentieth century anticommunism and the dominance of particular genres than the making and staging of *Big White Fog* in the late 1930s. It also pushes *Big White Fog* into a socialist realist tradition where it does not belong: in Federal Theatre manuscripts, *Big White Fog* is subtitled "A Negro Tragedy"; the responses of Chicago's black performance community suggest it was understood as such in 1938.[15] A black political family drama, which deploys the domestic tragedy to critically analyze problems within black communities, *Big White Fog* is more akin to the classic realist dramas, which sought to tear down established beliefs, than socialist realist dramas, which promised audiences they might easily construct new ones.[16] In turning to the production and manuscript history of this provocative Federal Theatre drama, we see that it was precisely this critical lens and ambiguous resolution that first troubled black audiences in Chicago.

Rehearsing *Big White Fog*

Production plans were well underway by the time South Side community leaders gathered at the YWCA to listen to Ward read his new play. A first draft of the manuscript was made ready, and rehearsals begun in October 1937. However it was not until late December that the New York–based National Service Bureau (NSB) gave its official, retrospective, and "limited" approval to an "experimental production" of Ward's drama by the Chicago Negro Unit.[17] Even then it was another three months before the play made it to the Great Northern Theatre on the Chicago Loop. Consultation with the South Side community, rewriting of the manuscript, and negotiations with the local censorship board would be necessary before the play could open on April 7, 1938. Shirley Graham was hopeful that *Big White Fog* would mark a turning point in the Negro Unit's fortunes. Following the controversy that surrounded the aborted production of Green's *Hymn to the Rising Sun*, the troupe of the Chicago Negro Unit developed a reputation as a lost cause. Between the cancelation of *Hymn*, in October 1936, and the development of *Big White Fog* in the winter of 1937–1938, the unit had failed to bring to production a number of dramas, including several Paul Green plays. In fact the only play to make it into production between July 1936 and the opening of *Big White Fog* in April 1938 was *Mississippi Rainbow*. The work of white playwright John Charles Brownwell and featuring original music by Shirley Graham, it ran for fifteen weeks and seventy-nine performances. FTP administrator George Kondulf believed it to be "one of the best scripts for a Negro company that I have run across in years," and added, "It has no social significance." The critics were not so kind. The production was described by one white reviewer as "a comedy so innocuous that the suddenly play conscious city hall may never know of its existence."[18]

In its first two years the Chicago Negro Unit did little to inspire the community it was supposed to serve. In May 1936, the *Chicago Defender* lamented the poor record of a theatre that faced relatively few risks compare to the commercial theatre since it had "no prejudices to cater to."[19] Aware of the Chicago Negro Unit's low standing, and beginning with *Mississippi Rainbow*, Graham made a concerted effort to gain community support. Such efforts were by no means unique to Chicago: Federal Theatre Units frequently looked to community partners to support its productions. Sponsorship could take the form of helping with publicity, building audiences through group bookings, or providing a performance venue. On Graham's part, the desire to secure sponsors was also connected to a wider ambition to stage black productions in black neighborhoods. Both Graham and Chicago FTP head Harry Minturn believed African Americans could be drawn to the theatre if the costs of time and travel were reduced.[20] Graham's view that black theatre should be not just about, but also by, of, and near, the people it claimed to represent, was a view she shared with W. E. B. Du Bois, who had articulated this principle in a manifesto statement in the 1920s and the man Graham would later marry.[21]

Keen to test the potential of a black-authored production based in the community, Graham initiated a range of measures designed to solicit the views and sponsorship of black organizations and leaders in January 1938. Most significant was the decision to send out copies of the draft manuscript and to invite the community to attend a read-through. Graham's strategy appeared to pay dividends when the Federal Theatre secured the support of the University of Chicago's International House to host two consecutive performances of *Big White Fog*, on February 17 and 18. In the meantime, Graham arranged for the playwright to perform a read-through of the play at the local YWCA on the evening of January 5. Aware that a play that included any reference to communism might prove problematic for black churches, Graham had purposefully invited secular organizations, though none of them could be considered particularly sympathetic to communism or the Communist Party USA (CPUSA). In the event, communism did not define the audience's response to the reading of *Big White Fog*. Given the communist frame in which later critics have understood *Big White Fog*, it is striking how few complained about, or even mentioned, the "C word." Out of twenty respondents, only three referred directly to the discussion of communism within the play. B. B. Church, of the South Side Boy's Club, had both read the manuscript and attended the YWCA reading. He found the play "well-written" with "tremendous possibilities for a strong dramatic presentation." However, and without wishing to go into the "merits, or demerits, of communism," he felt the author's "swing into full diapason to the theme of communism" was in "bad taste," for an organization sponsored by a democratic government. Clubwoman Bertha Lewis, who was impressed by the play, found it "very communistic," but thought the propaganda "skilfully handled." The most sustained criticism of the play in regard to communism came from A. C. MacNeal, executive secretary of the Chicago branch of the NAACP, the national civil rights organization whose bitter dispute with the CPUSA over the handling of the Scottsboro case several years earlier had entrenched the distrust and rivalry between the two groups that had long been apparent.[22] Insisting that "some of the worst phases of Negro life seem to have been deliberately selected," he made clear that the NAACP "would not under any circumstances sponsor the presentation of the 'Big White Fog,'" and indicated that he would resist any further attempts to present it on the South Side, explaining: "I suppose you are aware that this play was written largely for the purpose of being a vehicle for communistic propaganda, rather than for the purpose of presenting some 'Realistic' phase of Negro life."[23]

As Graham noted in a report to the director of the Chicago FTP, with few exceptions, "whether or not the play was communistic seemed to be of minor importance." Instead, and to Graham's initial surprise, the most common complaint concerned the representation of the racial and gender politics of black families and its pessimistic ending. Robert Anderson, who represented a college men's club, found the play "dangerously realistic," and believed that "Many of our members would be offended by the color question as discussed in this play," while Corrine Smith, director of the South Side YWCA objected to the characterization of women in the play and "Considers the long discussion on 'color' as pointless." Pearl Pachoaco of the Richard B. Harrison Dramatic Club agreed, believing the play would "Tear down unity between the races as well as within the race." Parsing these criticisms for Minturn, Graham pointed to examples of the play's treatment of racism within black communities. The scene in which the "very black" Vic is called a "monkey chaser" by his "brown" brother-in-law because of his support for Marcus Garvey would antagonize West Indians, she suggested, for "it is even more bitterly resented by people from the West Indie Island (from whence Garvey came) than is "nigger" by the American Negro."[24]

Community responses drew Graham's attention to the inter- and intrarace tensions that might be inflamed by the exchange between Vic, Ella, and her mother in Act 2. Ella is shocked when Vic describes his mother-in-law's mixed-race heritage as "a badge of shame" inherited from "your raping ancestors." Graham reported that a white man had singled out for criticism the line: "Every time a nigger girl goes riding with a white man it can mean but one thing." It is hardly surprising that rumors circulated about the possibility of race riots: in *Big White Fog*, white men are either sexual predators, pawnbrokers, bailiffs, or "bastards" who destroy black lives. Only Piszer, the Jewish communist, and his allies do not inflict injury and violence intentionally on the Mason family, though their protest leads to Vic's death.[25] If later commentators found Ward's interracial ending hopeful and naïve, African Americans in 1938 Chicago found it disturbing and bleak. Leaders of the South Side Motion Picture Club found little resolution in the ending, concluding, "The one ray of hope is too uncertain to lift general gloom," while Delta Sorority member Jeanette Triplette felt it lacked "inspirational value" and that "The general trend is downward."[26]

With the complaints of the read-through audience fresh in her mind, Graham was sensitized to the gender conflicts staged in *Big White Fog*. Specifically she saw that Wanda's exchange of sex for money from a white man was difficult for black audiences, arousing feelings of "shame" in black women and "resentment" in black men. Graham understood the play's representation of intrarace racism and interracial hatred made for uncomfortable viewing, especially in front of whites. This discomfort was heightened, Graham reported, when the white director, Kay Ewing, announced on the night of the read-through that "This play is so absolutely typical of the Negro family in Chicago." Ewing's view, and the fear that white audiences would see the characters in this black-authored drama as representative of all black Americans, provoked a strong reaction among South Siders. In their letters of complaint to Graham, they contested *Big White Fog*'s depiction of gender trouble within black families, and, as we saw in the opening quotation of the chapter, insisted that black men and women could, and did, fulfill hegemonic gender roles: black men were successful, respected businessmen, while "our respectable women" were not reduced to transgressive sexual transactions with white men.[27]

Few of Graham's correspondents made explicit mention of Wanda's disreputable act, referring instead to the problematic characterization of women and the lack of an uplifting or inspiring tone. Positioning herself as an intermediary between sophisticated theatre professionals and the black performance community, Graham explained the community's responses to her supervisors. Making clear that as a theatre professional she was able to look at the dramatic qualities of *Big White Fog*, Graham also represented herself as an authority on "the community" and warned of the potentially damaging intracommunity rift that might undermine her efforts to draw the broader black community to the Negro Unit: "I had read the play as a 'play' and as 'theatre.' I am used to going to the theatre, perhaps I have fewer inhibitions that people whose lives have been more limited. But certainly my second reading did reveal dangers of which I had not thought before."[28]

Shirley Graham was not the only recipient of complaints about *Big White Fog*. International House, which had earlier agreed to host two performances of Ward's drama, withdrew from its contract following protests from a number of black organizations and individuals concerned that the play might incite "inter-racial hatred."[29] Federal Theatre records suggest that administrators took seriously the concerns of the black performance community and that their complaints had direct consequences for the production. Minturn had been surprised to learn of the "the resentment of some of the Negro groups," and in particular, that the incitement of race hatred was a major concern. However, in a letter to Hallie Flanagan he concluded that "if the script could be rewritten to eliminate that, then I can see no reason for its not being done."[30] *Big White Fog* was rewritten. Its evolution from read-through to production is documented in the surviving Federal Theatre manuscripts and production materials. Together they offer fascinating insight into how, and how far, a black Federal Theatre drama could be responsive to the needs of the community it was written by, for, and about.

Revising the Manuscript

The production notebook for *Big White Fog* documents the process of revision. Submitted on behalf of the Negro Unit by white director Kay Ewing, it records the play's evolution from page to stage and includes reports from the director and technicians as well as critical reviews from the opening night. The director's report confirms that Ward was very much involved throughout the lengthy (four-month) rehearsal period. Ewing notes that Ward had written the play for the troupe of which he was a member and with particular actors in mind. Though absent from the first casting try-outs, he was involved in the "final stages" of casting as well as the "cutting, telescoping, and some rewriting" of this "untried script."[31] For his part, Ward later remembered Lieutenant Harry Costello, chair of the Chicago Board of Censors, raising objections to the play following the dress rehearsal. Whereas newspapers reported that the attempted ban had been due to the "theme of racial prejudice between whites and blacks," the playwright recalled a meeting in which the Costello had suggested that obscenity was the problem. Apparently Costello was able to point to just one example of blasphemy, the phrase "God damn," which Ward obligingly cut.[32] Federal Theatre records and variant manuscripts suggest, however, that concerns about interracial tension and profanity were not the driving force behind the rewrite; instead, revisions centered on the representation of intraracial and gender conflict.

We need to turn to the variant manuscripts to understand the precise nature of the revisions and the difference they made to the play that was staged at the Great Northern Theatre in April 1938. As theatre, and as a piece of dramatic literature, interpretations of *Big White Fog* are usually based on the version of the manuscript published in *Black Theater U.S.A.* This version, published in 1974, contains significant variation from the play staged by the Federal Theatre in 1938. There are five Federal Theatre manuscripts: four are held at the FTP Collection at the Library of Congress and a fifth is at the National Archives. Since I am interested in the version of the drama that was developed and debated by the Chicago Unit in 1938, these manuscripts are the focus of my analysis. However, other manuscripts are also important, not least because they shaped the history of *Big White Fog* after Chicago. Versions of the play are also held at the Schomburg and Performing Arts branches of the New York Public Library, as well as the Hatch-Billops Collection, which is now housed at Emory University. There is also a second published version, which was used in the Almeida Theatre's 2007 production.[33]

Federal Theatre archives include: one long and unwieldy manuscript, "Early Draft"; three intermediate versions, which are very similar and are labeled "FTPa," "FTPb," and "FTPc"; and there is a fifth, labeled "Last Version," which is likely to be the most recent existing Federal Theatre draft.[34] The "Last Version" manuscript corresponds most closely to the production records. In particular, photographs of opening night and the playbill's cast list provide compelling evidence that "Last Version" or something very like it was performed at the Great Northern Theatre in spring 1938. Handwritten annotations as well as typed amendments confirm that this is the latest of the drafts in the Federal Theatre archive. The notation, "Last Version" is handwritten in pencil alongside the instruction to "Return to NSB." The most compelling evidence, however, is found in the frequent handwritten revisions to this manuscript, which correspond to the complaints made by members of the black performance community following the read-through in January.[35] Together, the typed and handwritten revisions that are visible in "Last Version" support a reading of *Big White Fog* that foregrounds racial and gender conflicts within black families and political movements, rather than anxieties about the discussion of communism. The amendments made to "Last Version" also reveal how, and how far, black performance communities were able to shape the writing and production process of the Negro Unit.

The most frequent revision in "Last Version" is to the language used to dramatize gender and racial conflict. As mentioned, the representation of women's sexual activity in *Big White Fog* was not well received on the South Side. The modified language used by Wanda in the later draft appears to respond to these complaints. When, in the earlier drafts, her friend Claudine suggests she consider earning money by offering her body to an interested white customer at the store where she works, Wanda demurs: "I'm no whore" she tells Claudine. In "Last Version," the term is replaced by the less incendiary "streetwalker." Similarly, in "Last Version," Wanda's mother, Ella, avoids explicit mention of the act. However, in earlier manuscripts, Ella directly confronts her daughter: "Is it true, too, you were laying up with a white man?" In "Last Version," however, her query peters out: "Is it true, too, that you were . . ."[36] Early Federal Theatre manuscripts include a plot line in which a young black mother and her child are evicted for nonpayment of rent after her husband has run off with another woman. The sexual betrayals of men are minimized in the rewrite, however. In "Last Version," the victimhood of the young mother is uncomplicated by the moral failings of her husband. In this manuscript, the husband's absence is explained by his premature death, rather than his betrayal.

Racially abusive language is also modified or removed altogether in the later manuscript, in ways that seem to correspond directly to community complaints. For example, where, in earlier drafts, the mixed-race Grandmother repeatedly refers to her son-in-law as a "nigger," in "Last Version" the phrase is consistently crossed out by hand and replaced with the term "black fool."[37] It seems likely that these revisions were carried over into the performance since black newspaper reviews made no mention of the term at a time when the black press was alert to racially offensive language and the use of "nigger" in particular.[38] Although the language is toned down, the intrarace racism articulated by Vic's mother-in-law remains central. Similarly, although "Last Version" tempers the language used to describe Wanda's sexual act, it does not seek to minimize the conflicted responses it provokes within the Mason family. In fact, in this version alone, Vic dies unreconciled, not only to his wife, but also to his eldest daughter. In earlier manuscripts Vic acknowledges that he was too hard on Wanda. "I spoke a little hard about you but I didn't mean it, because I understand." There is no such concession in "Last Version." Vic does not acknowledge Wanda's sacrifice on behalf of her family. Instead, in a revision incorporated into the typed manuscript, Vic addresses all his children on the subject of conflict and unity: "I want you all to try and be true to yourselves and one another. You'll find it pretty hard." Stage directions indicate that: "Wanda turns away and walks up to table beneath stairs." Her silence is in direct contrast to earlier manuscripts, in which she calls to her father to "Come back, come back." In "Last Version," Wanda cannot find a way to forgive Vic.[39] The consequences of Wanda's act in "Last Version," are even more disastrous for the Mason family, creating an irreconcilable rift between sacrificing women and wounded men. Such an emphasis is difficult to square with the softening of racial and sexual language in the same manuscript. Perhaps in performance the toned-down speech may have served to deflect community criticism that "our girls do not have to sleep with white men to get fifty dollars."[40] But any attempt to pacify community critics through a change of language worked alongside a determination not to compromise on the central message.

There is only one instance in which the community's anxieties about communism could be seen to be reflected in the revised manuscript. In "Last Version" the political affiliation of the white men who help the Masons resist eviction is made less explicit. No longer described as "comrades," as in earlier versions, here the white supporters are referred to as "men" and later "buddies." For their part, they address the fallen Garveyite hero as "Mr." rather than "Comrade," as in earlier drafts. Although no longer directly referenced in the final scene, "Communists" are still included in the list of characters in "Last Version," as they are in all Federal Theatre manuscripts, and in the playbill for the production.[41] Perhaps Ewing, Ward, Graham, or all three in combination, hoped the more oblique references to communists in the final scene would diminish the role of communism and allay criticisms such as those proffered by the head of the local NAACP branch. Whoever was responsible for the changes, they suggest an alternative narrative of the role of communism in *Big White Fog*: rather than staging a "Communist solution," communist characters decrease in importance as the manuscript is revised for production in order to prevent communism from overshadowing the other ideologies discussed in *Big White Fog*. This trend continued after the end of the FTP: when the Negro Playwrights Company staged *Big White Fog* in 1940, the "Communists" had become a "mob"; by the time *Big White Fog* was published in 1974, they were listed as "white and Negro workers"; and in the 2007 Almeida production, they were called "workers." If, in historiographical terms, *Big White Fog* has become progressively more "pro-Communist," in manuscript and production the role of communists diminished in importance.

Producer Masculinity and the Garvey Movement

Taking "Last Version," as the performance text and attending to the responses of the South Side community to an earlier version of the play opens up alternative readings of *Big White Fog*. Records of revision allow us to see the central importance of gender conflict in Ward's dramatization of race and class politics in 1930s America. Gender conflict is embedded in and central to the structure, content, and characterization of *Big White Fog*. The play is organized into three acts, each of which revolves around two conflicts: one is between two male characters, who debate competing ideals of manliness and black progress, and the other is between a male and female, in which black manliness is performed in front of, and defined in contrast to, black womanhood. In Acts 1 and 2, Vic debates the merits of black nationalism over capitalism with his brother-in-law Dan Rogers. In each of the first two acts a second conflict arises in Vic's struggle to assert his authority over women: in Act 1 he battles with his wife, Ella, while in Act 2 he takes on both Ella and her mother. Significantly, by Act 3, it is Vic's son, Les, who has been newly converted to communism, who challenges Dan's faith in capitalism. In this final act Les also comes into conflict with, and increasingly exerts authority over, the Mason women. At the end he even takes charge of, and instructs, his father. In each act the conflicts give way to a monolog from Vic. In Acts 1 and 2, Vic's closing speeches are calls to action: to redeem black manhood and fulfill the black nationalist dream; his final speech in Act 3, however, is one of resignation and defeat. Vic's failure to achieve manhood is reinforced by the fact that it is the speech and actions of women, and more particularly those of Ella, that both open and close the play.[42]

Character development in *Big White Fog* draws attention to the gender conflicts of the black home and of black political movements. In the opening scene, black men's quest for autonomy is explored from the viewpoint of women. Set in 1922, at the height of the UNIA's popularity, *Big White Fog* opens with a discussion among female members of the family: wife and mother Ella, teenage daughter Wanda, sister Juanita, and Grandma Brooks. The women discuss the difficulties that have followed them in their migration from the South. It is from them that we learn of the obstacles faced by hard-working black men like Vic, whether in the rural South or the urban North. While Vic finds employment as a construction worker in Chicago, his claims to manhood are undermined by the limited range and low pay of the jobs available to black men.

Black male vulnerability is staged in the opening scene of Act 1, when Vic's status as the sole breadwinner is challenged by the actions of his daughter. According to middle-class ideals of manliness, the family wage meant men could provide for and claim authority over their families. Wanda, however, makes decisions without consulting her father. Her female relatives are the first to learn that she is leaving school in order to start earning. Believing that the adults around her are "kidding" themselves with their dreams of progress abroad and at home, Wanda tells her mother: "There's nothing in this country for a Negro girl to look forward to. . . . I'm going to make it for myself, and you and Papa might as well get used to the idea, because whether you like it or not, I'm going to live my own life."[43] Wanda's angry exit is followed by the first entrance of her father, Vic. Informed second-hand of his daughter's decision, Vic responds with resignation: "Let her quit," he tells his furious wife. Unable to comprehend her husband's reasoning, Ella doubts his judgments: "I don't want to hear any explanations or promises either. I've had enough of them— 'A stack of lies, the whole world's a stack of lies'—You brought me out of the South with one; you and your fine talk about freedom and happiness and giving the children a chance to be somebody." But in the first of his lengthy speeches, Vic tries to get Ella and his family to understand his dream:

> Wanda's just reached the point where she sees what a girl her color is up against in this country! Be patient a little longer. We'll soon be out of this rut and on our way to Africa. I can see her now, like a mother weeping for her long lost children, calling to us to return into our own. Soon, and it won't be long now, You're going to see the black man come out of the darkness of failure into the light of achievement, wearing the cloak of human greatness about his shoul-

ders. . . . Yes, Lord! And our enemies shall tremble when he stretches forth his mighty hand to gather in his share of the God given stars of glory![44]

For Vic, the road to redemption is paved with manly glory, glory that will be achieved through conquering and defending a feminized homeland. Vic figures Mother Africa as maternal and nurturing, but denied access to her offspring. She weeps for her boy children to return as men and restore her to greatness. In redeeming Mother Africa, the black man will achieve his manhood; he will reclaim, by force if necessary, his "God given share," his destiny, his ancestral home. Vic's imagined home is a refuge for black men from the slights and humiliations of everyday life, "the darkness of failure."

Vic's dreams of a new start in Africa are kept alive by the lived experience of the new home he has found in the Garvey movement. Denied the respect and power accorded heads of white households, in the second scene of Act 1, Vic looks to affirm his status elsewhere. It is through his membership in a community of committed black nationalists who will one day return home to Africa and restore black rule that Vic finds respect and comradeship. In Scene 2, audiences are introduced to Vic's fellow Garveyites, who visit him at home. They are dressed in the Garveyite uniform, and stage directions indicate that they move with dignity. Addressing Vic as "Brother" and "Captain," their presence indicates the comradeship and respect Garveyites share.[45] Here, within the welcoming embrace of the homosocial UNIA, Vic finds a place where black men respect each other and are rewarded for their efforts. The protective, racially autonomous environment of the Garvey movement provides a home, a place of safety where men can recover from the wounds of the outside world, and a site of resistance where manliness is revered and men and women's apparently separate spheres celebrated.[46]

The Garvey movement is the home to which Vic retreats when his manhood is denied by the outside world. In Act 2, Vic's eldest son, Les, loses his college scholarship after the benefactors discover his racial identity. Unmanned by white control over his son's destiny, Vic reasserts his authority through the Garveyite community. He invests his life savings in the UNIA's steamship in spite of reports that the ship has been refused permission to sail and that Marcus Garvey has fled to Canada. Similarly, when the strike at the construction site where Vic is employed puts pressure on the family finances, he takes refuge in the Garvey movement. Vic immerses himself in a proposal to develop cooperative farming in Africa, preparing a speech

FIGURE 11 Vic Mason is celebrated by members of the UNIA in the Chicago Negro Unit's *Big White Fog*, 1938. Library of Congress, Music Division, Federal Theatre Project Collection, Production Records, Photographic Prints File, Container 1173.

on the subject for the UNIA's annual convention in New York City. Vic's efforts are acknowledged in Act 2, Scene 2, when UNIA officials award him the title of Lord of Agriculture of the Provisional Republic of Africa. In contrast to the world run by whites, in the Garvey movement, honest endeavors and loyalty are rewarded.

Significantly, the ceremonial presentation of Vic's new title by his fellow Garveyites is performed at home in front of his wife and children. His wife, Ella, and eldest son, Les, are proud of his work for the movement. Although Vic's temporary unemployment means that resources are scarce, Ella spends their last few cents on ingredients for eggnog so that her husband's hour of glory will not be undermined by the reality of his "failure" to provide for his family. Even as she creates this illusion of home comfort, Ella knowingly sacrifices and risks the well-being of the household, for the money was needed for her sick children, who require new winter shoes and the attention of a doctor.

Vic's status within the Garvey movement commands, for a time, the respect of his son and consent of his wife. Indeed, Ella is complicit in Vic's acting out of the Garveyite ideal of manliness, where true men provide for their families, make important family decisions, and protect their children's dreams. It is Ella who chides her husband for his failure to find another decent-paying job; Ella, who fails to give credence to the role racism plays in denying black manhood. Indeed she places some of the blame on black men themselves. She is especially critical of the Garveyites' reliance on rhetoric, complaining: "I'm sick of listening to nothing but talk, talk! For twenty years that's all we've had in this house—And ain't nobody done nothing yet!"[47] Garveyites may mimic the language, costumes and ceremonies of white imperial power, but they do not possess white power. Garveyism fails to deliver redemption for Vic because its promise of manhood cannot be fulfilled by performance alone.[48] The Garvey movement cannot defend its leader, let alone its rank-and-file membership, from a system that denies black men access to justice, employment, housing, and education. Self-belief and racial pride are difficult to maintain when faced with the reality of unemployment, racial discrimination, and sick children. Following Garvey's arrest and imprisonment, Vic's support for the movement only serves to reinforce his lack of authority at home. Ella increasingly questions the sacrifices demanded by the Garvey movement and Vic's devotion to it, while her mother and sister ridicule UNIA plans as "Nothing but bunk to catch more suckers like Vic."[49]

Consumer Capitalism and Unmanly Men

Women are not the only ones to challenge the Garveyite vision of manliness in *Big White Fog*. Garveyism's gender politics are also held up against a capitalist vision of the male consumer. The consumer capitalist who is able to purchase and provide is represented by Vic's assimilationist and individualistic brother-in-law, Dan Rogers. The most consistently outspoken critic of Vic's black nationalist dreams, Dan believes that: "There's chance enough for anybody in this country if he's got get-up enough to take it." Black Americans have only to pull themselves up by their bootstraps and learn the ways of whites to access the American dream. After all, the dream belongs to black Americans as much as whites, for they too built America. For Dan, the idea of working outside the American structure is tantamount to giving up, an abandonment of a home that is as much his heritage as it is that of white Americans.

(*Defensively*) *Vic*: You don't understand the new spirit, Dan. We're out to wrest our heritage from the enemy.

(*Challengingly*) *Dan*: What our?—My heritage is right here in America!

(*Quietly*) *Vic*: What?—A lynchrope?[50]

Dan refuses Vic's presumption of a shared black struggle, African heritage or ancestral homeland. Contemptuous of UNIA costumes and ceremonies, he is in search of a different kind of black home. Dan's solution is to create new homes of a more literal kind. He plans to purchase a lease on a block of flats, divide them up into cramped apartments, and rent them out to poor black families at a profit. He invites Vic to join him, but Vic does not believe that they can build homes for black Americans using the master's tools.

Big White Fog stages a series of confrontations between Vic and Dan, and later between Dan and Les, that would have been familiar to South Siders. The play dramatizes the different ways black men position themselves within and against competing ideologies of black nationalism, capitalism/ assimilationism, and communism, and explores how and why these ideologies appeal to black men. In the first confrontation in Act 1, Vic defines his manliness in opposition to his accommodationist brother-in-law, who has modeled himself on white ideals at the expense of his community. For Vic, their different approaches to education encapsulate their conflicting ideology. Where Vic sees his own education as contributing toward the betterment of the race, for Dan, education is, "like a pair of kneepads . . . it enables you to crawl through the gravel and mud of white prejudice without the least sense of pain or dishonor." While Vic boldly demands "freedom here and now," like a coward, Dan crawls on his belly.[51] Dan's kneepads, Vic suggests, might protect his knees, but not his manhood. As a Garveyite, Vic views political ideology as a measure of manliness: Garvey's followers were manly men who challenged the ideology and practical manifestations of white supremacy; their opponents appeased their white oppressor and accepted notions of black racial inferiority.[52]

Dan, by contrast, believes black men must learn how to achieve manhood in the white world rather than waste time creating a separate black one. Accordingly, he dedicates himself to learning how to succeed by the white man's rules. For a while his scheme to make money is successful. Act 2 opens one year after Vic's refusal to join Dan in his get-rich-quick scheme. Dan's success as a slum landlord is apparent when he arrives at Vic's home in his new Cadillac. His prosperity contrasts sharply with his brother-in-law's recent impoverishment. Vic's investment in Garvey's doomed Black Star Line, as well as his participation in the construction strike, have placed serious strain on family finances and relationships. The two men's contrasting fortunes invite the audience to reflect on the impact of growing economic stratification among African Americans in Chicago. In the decade preceding the production of *Big White Fog*, black-owned businesses in the retail, wholesale, and service sectors of Chicago grew by nearly 80 percent.[53] This growing economy became the source for a new vision of masculine identity based on consumption. As Martin Summers has explained: "middle class Americans increasingly unlinked manhood from the market, at least from the orientation of the producer, and began to define it in terms of consumption. One's manhood became more and more defined by the consumer goods one owned, the leisure practices one engaged in, and one's physical and sexual virility." Yet positioning consumption as a path to masculine identity was problematic at a time when more than half of black Americans in Bronzeville were on relief. Moreover, it posed a challenge to traditional markers of respectable manhood to which many Garveyites subscribed.[54] Producer values continued to define manliness, as one Garveyite supporter explained: "[the NAACP] appeals to the Beau Brummel, Lord Chesterfield, kid-gloved, silk-stocking, creased-trousered, patent leather shoe element, while the UNIA appeals to the sober, sane, serious, earnest, hard-working man, who earns his living by the sweat of his brow."[55] Whereas the Garveyite is a hard-working producer, unashamed of manual labor, the integrationist is a consumer, who, lacking in race pride, apes the effeminate costumes and conspicuous consumption habits of his oppressors.

Vic questions whether Dan's identity as a prosperous consumer can really be the basis for redeemed manhood. A true Garveyite, Vic sees himself as a producer whereas Dan increasingly comes to define himself and others in terms of consumption. Vic is a builder of homes, but Dan has made money out of offering substandard homes to the most vulnerable. When Dan boasts of spending thousands of dollars on a new car as a "little present" for Juanita, Vic expresses doubt in the relationship between consumption and manliness, particularly when that consumption is dependent on "living like a leech on the blood of your own people." Dan has evicted a female tenant and her baby, causing Vic to question the manhood of his brother-in-law, who would put his own gratification before the protection of a vulnerable young black mother and the future of the race.[56] Vic, by contrast, exhibits his manliness in his refusal to join in his brother-in-law's moneymaking scheme and through his ungrumbling acceptance of hard labor, shoveling snow for dimes while waiting for the strike to end. Dan might provide handsomely for his wife, but his success is built on the misery of those he regards as "weak and shiftless," and is unwilling to protect.

Big White Fog explores the gendered nature of capitalist exploitation by juxtaposing Dan's bestowing of an expensive new Cadillac on his wife, with his unfeeling eviction of an abandoned mother and child. But the play also offers a gendered critique of black economic nationalism. Vic's investment in a black economic venture might have struck a chord in a city such as Chicago where "Don't work where you Can't Buy" boycotts attracted widespread support through the Depression. Yet in having Vic purchase Black Star Line shares only after his son's scholarship disappointment, audiences are encouraged to see his actions as desperate and reckless.[57] Later, in Act 2, when Vic is unable to bring home a wage on account of the construction strike, he refuses to listen to his wife and brother, who urge him to sell his UNIA shares. Indeed, he prefers to ask his son, who is working to pay his way through college, to suspend his education in order to contribute to the family finances. Vic's actions appear to place his own pride before his family's needs. "It's a mighty poor slave," he tells Ella, "that'll give up trying to break his chains just because there's a knick in the hammer!" Resisting their pleading, Vic attempts to exert an authority he feels is rightly his as the head of the household. "I've had my say," he tells them.[58]

Women Bear the Burden and Men Suffer

Both Dan and Vic appear to have had their say by the opening of Act 3. It is now 1932: Vic has lost his savings, his Garveyite dream, and his patriarchal authority. The Mason household is fragmented: Vic's mother-in-law has gone to live with Dan and Juanita, and though Ella remains, she can no longer bear to speak to her husband. Not only has Vic been unsuccessful in his attempts to build a better home for his family, he has squandered the family savings on the now-desiccated Garvey movement. Its leader, Marcus Garvey, has been arrested and imprisoned and Vic has come to realize that not only the Garvey movement, but also his dreams of a better home, have been destroyed. Dan's fortunes have also declined following the 1929 stock market crash. He no longer owns a car, and his wife, Juanita, who has taken over the running of the real estate business, is renting out the apartments to prostitutes.[59] Dan's demise suggests that reliance on consumerism as a basis for masculine identity is not only precarious, but also rooted in, and sustaining of, racial capitalism. For both Dan and Vic, the failure to redeem their manhood through capitalism and Garveyism, respectively, leads to the resumption of responsibility by women. However, in assuming control of the family, the female Masons, in turn, inspire the reassertion of manly struggle in the form of the communist brotherhood. It is this struggle that is explored in the final act.

In Act 3 women now head the family: they exercise authority, provide food and money, and make key decisions. Ella works to ensure the survival of the family home by discarding those parts they can no longer afford. She tries to sell her furniture to Mr. Marx, a Jewish pawnbroker, in order to raise the funds necessary to avoid eviction. But this outsider does not share Ella's valuation of her home, offering her only a fraction of the value of precious household items. Witnessing her mother's desperation, Wanda takes charge and forces the white stranger from their house. Wanda's action reflects the fact that she has taken on the burden of supporting and protecting her family who, since Act 1, have increasingly come to rely on her wages. Wanda's employment in a white-owned drugstore also furnishes her with a clear sense of her sexual worth to white men. A young, light-skinned, and attractive woman, Wanda comes to the conclusion that her body might be the price of keeping her mother and family from being thrown out on the street. Having witnessed the sacrifices made by her family in service to her father's Garveyite faith, Wanda wonders whether her family can afford for her to maintain her own moral code.

The final act of *Big White Fog* reveals the challenges black men face when they must step back and allow women to take charge of the family. Black women's ability to support their families has historically provoked conflict between black men and women because it is too often used as evidence of, and explanation for, black men's "failure."[60] Black political movements have often countered these dangerous ideas by insisting that black men's salvation rests on, and can be measured by, black men's ability to protect, and sometimes control, black women. *Big White Fog* explores this damaging cycle by comparing the gender politics of black nationalism and communism. Communism is presented as a putative avenue toward black male redemption at precisely the moment when Wanda is about to sell her body to save her family, in the first scene of Act 3. The ultimate signifier of male disempowerment during slavery, the inability to protect black women from sexual exploitation by white men, occurs at just the moment when Les's growing involvement in, and understanding of, communism offers hope of redemption. This is a powerful combination that allows the eldest son to usurp his father and take control of the family.

FIGURE 12 Les reckons with Wanda in the Chicago Negro Unit's *Big White Fog,* 1938. Library of Congress, Music Division, Federal Theatre Project Collection, Production Records, Photographic Prints File, Container 1173.

Although formerly an admirer of Garveyism and proud of his father's position within the movement, by Act 3 Les has embraced the promise of communism. Rejecting his father's failed black economic nationalism, it is Les who now debates political ideology with Dan, and Les who steps forward to reassert male control over the women of the family. Spotting Wanda emerging from a white man's car, Les suspects that his sister is on the verge of a major transgression: Wanda has stepped outside her temporary wage-earning role to support her family in a time of crisis and has assumed the position of household head. In this role she (unlike her father) will sacrifice anything, even her honor, in order to protect the family. "I said I wanted to talk to you, and I don't mean tomorrow," Les barks at his sister. Accustomed to the authority her breadwinner status has given her, Wanda is not easily cowed: "I won't sit down. You can't bully me."[61] But Les is determined to find out just how far Wanda's sense of responsibility has taken her. Crucially, Les does not use the language of brotherly protection. Rather he frames his interrogation in terms of injured manhood, pointing to the damaging impact of Wanda's wage-earning capacity on the men of the family: "I don't suppose you realise it, Wanda. But it's been pretty painful to me and Papa both, sitting around here day after day, allowing you to bear the whole burden of the house."[62] Les and his father are wounded by their inability to provide for the family and their reliance on Wanda, who cannot appreciate the burden she has placed them under by becoming the principal breadwinner. Les is no longer willing to "allow" Wanda to bear what he sees as a man's responsibility for his family; from now on he will control the fate of the family and the actions of the Mason women.

Les exerts his authority immediately. When Ella begins to suspect her daughter might be up to something, Les reassures her in authoritative terms, saying, "I've already put my foot down." He will take charge and find a way through, as he explains to his mother, telling her that "a bunch of folks like myself" will go to see the Governor of Illinois to protest housing evictions and unemployment.[63] Warned by his Uncle Dan of the brutal force with which the state will greet their protest, Les welcomes the prospect of violent confrontation. Appropriating both the confrontational role and the masculinist rhetoric that characterizes his father's relationship to Dan, he retorts: "Let them. The quicker the better. . . . The disinherited will never come to power without bloodshed." Les informs Dan that the old capitalist America is finished, saying, "Your world has crashed. But you're so full of capitalist dope, you don't even know we're building a new one."[64]

Communism's Failure to Redeem Black Manhood

In the final scene of *Big White Fog*, Les and his communist allies appear to take up the mantle of black male redemption from Vic and the Garvey movement. Black Chicagoans would have been familiar with communists' claims to be the "legitimate heir of Garveyism."[65] Although initially dismissive of what they saw as the bourgeois nationalism of the Garvey movement, the CPUSA paid increasing attention to the appeal of black nationalism from the late 1920s onward and adopted policies designed to attract former Garveyites. Following the Communist International's recognition of African Americans as an oppressed nation with the right to self-determination in 1928, the CPUSA encouraged black cultural nationalism, mobilized thousands of Americans against a justice system designed to uphold white supremacy, and publicly repudiated instances of racial discrimination within its own ranks.[66] The CPUSA also offered tangible strategies to tackle the extreme economic hardship that disproportionately impacted African Americans: they set up groups to meet the specific needs of local black communities, organized integrated unions to defend black workers' jobs, and brought the jobless together into Unemployed Councils to protest the lack of jobs and fight tenant evictions.[67] As Robin Kelley has argued, "African Americans who joined the [Communist] Party in the 1920s and 30s were as much the creation of American Communism as of black nationalism."[68]

Former Garveyites did not have to renounce their black nationalist past in order to switch their allegiance to the CPUSA, nor were they called on to rethink the gender politics of black nationalism. Both the CPUSA and the UNIA reinforced dominant notions of men as worker-providers and women as nurturers. Barbara Foley's study of the "woman question" in the American communist movement has shown that although women in the early 1930s were frequently figured as class warriors, both as workers and housewives, the new search for a Popular Front in the struggle against fascism meant that "in the late 1930s Communism was held up as a means of preserving the traditional family rather than of challenging or destroying it." Popular Front politics and Marxist economic determinism offered reassurance that a radical restructuring of gender roles would not be required, at least not until after the overthrow of the capitalist state.[69]

In Act 3 communists replicate the gender hierarchies of Garveyites in their appeal to black men. In the final scene of *Big White Fog,* men resume control of the home, resisting the white state and wresting authority from women. When a white judge orders the Masons evicted from their home, Wanda finally crosses the line, raising money to rent another apartment through prostituting her body to a white man. Her family's willingness to believe her implausible story that she borrowed fifty dollars from her white boss implicates them all. Les, however, appeals to his weary father to resist the temptation to use Wanda's "tainted" money. Wanda's cash might temporarily solve their problems, but not those of the race, as Les tells his father, saying: "You can't afford to take this way out." He has a duty, not only to himself, but also to "the thousands of others who're facing eviction this morning." Vic, who has been driven by a sense of duty to his race for much of the play, now needs direction from his son. No longer certain he should risk his family's security for the sake of an ideal, he asks his son, "What duty?" Les explains that "Our only hope is in resistance" and promises that his communist comrades will help defend their home from the bailiffs who will execute the eviction order.[70] Significantly, it is not this promise of interracial solidarity that persuades Vic to defend his home. Rather, the crucial turning point is the moment in which Vic discovers his daughter's prostitution. In Vic's eyes this revelation is a shocking signal of his complete emasculation, for he has failed to protect his female relatives and thereby fulfill the responsibilities of hegemonic masculinity. For Vic, the actions of his daughter, whom he calls "a little tramp," "changes the face of everything." Now determined "to stand my ground," Vic asks his son to accept his comrades' help. However, his decisive action has come too late to redeem himself in the eyes of his wife and eldest daughter. "Raging" that her husband would talk of his own daughter in such derogatory terms, Ella insists he bear the blame, telling her family: "now that I've lived to see my child ruined on account of his fool ideas, there's nothing I'd like better than to see him dead!"[71]

In the final confrontation between the white state, represented by policemen and bailiffs, and the black home, represented by the former patriarch, Vic's pride reemerges temporarily and he is spurred to action once more. With his wife's taunts of failed manhood ringing in his ears, Vic confronts the bailiffs who have come to dismantle his home. Vic is no longer cowed: "I'm not going to stand no eviction!" he tells the bailiff.[72] Rejecting the advice of the cowering Dan, and commanding his family to go back into the house, Vic stands his ground while his son's communist allies attempt to return his furniture to his home. In the ensuing struggle, Vic is shot by a police officer. Falling to the ground, his life ebbing away, Vic is returned to the family home in the arms of his son. The positions of Vic and his son have been reversed. Where once Les's disappointment in losing his scholarship on account of his race meant he could see nothing but a "big white fog," now it is the father who can see no way through. Les, on the other hand, believes he has found a path that will lead to the redemption of black manhood: "There is a light," he tells his dying father, pointing to his friends. Les and his black and white communist allies have prevented the eviction and the police and bailiffs have left. For Les, at least, the fog has lifted. Through the interracial class struggle of the Communist Party, he has found a path to the redemption of his manhood.[73]

Struggle appears to have been reestablished as a man's job. But a careful reading of the play suggests that Ward is doing more than adopting the customary ending of 1930s social dramas in which comrades routinely gathered on the stage as willing fighters in the battle to defeat the villainous boss. I suggest that rather than being "naïve" or simply following convention in his choice of ending as some critics have suggested, *Big White Fog* disrupts precisely this easy formula.[74] Les's youthful idealism may enable him to see a path through the fog, but it is not a vision shared by the rest of

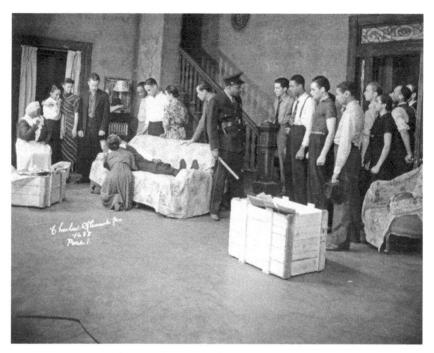

FIGURE 13 Vic Mason dies, unable to see through the "big white fog," 1938. Library of Congress, Music Division, Federal Theatre Project Collection, Production Records, Photographic Prints File, Container 1173.

the family. Vic "can't seem to see" the light as clearly as his son. Vic's final utterance, "I guess my sight is gone," does not suggest a final and triumphant restoration of black manhood, nor a celebration of the power of interracial alliances of workers. As one black audience member put it, even "the one ray of hope is too uncertain to lift general gloom."[75] Vic, who once shared his son's sense of newfound manhood through his own involvement in the Garvey movement, no longer sees so clearly; communism cannot offer him a path through the fog—it cannot save him. He dies a bitter man, unreconciled with his daughter and wife. The play ends, as it began, with Ella. Unable to forgive her husband, Ella remains silent during the final confrontation. Though her husband lies dying before her, she is unable to respond when Vic calls her name. It is only after his death, in the closing line of the play, that Ella is finally able to speak her husband's name and begin to grieve for all that she has lost.

Ella's silence at the climax of the drama points to a broader theme that runs throughout *Big White Fog*. Women are frequently silenced, particularly at moments of confrontation between men, but they step up and play their part to maintain the family when their men are down. In spite of this, men and women are seldom represented as partners working together in the struggle for race redemption. Collaboration and support occur between and among men or between women, but seldom across gender lines. When women cross into the "male" sphere of breadwinner, they soon take over, rather than share, the burden of black men. But if Ward is sympathetic to the particular difficulties facing black women—and they are given space to explain their frustrations with men—women are also implicated in the construction of oppositional and dangerous gender identities. When Vic is finally driven to action, in part by his mocking wife, it costs him his life. His son offers an alternative avenue for the redemption of black manhood in the interracial fraternity of the Communist Party. Yet the appeal of the communist movement is repeatedly undercut by Les's masculine language, invocation of violent imagery, and assertion of control over women. It appears that communism, like Garveyism, is also fractured by gender and race divisions, which could make for an equally unstable foundation on which to build a black home in America.

"Radical Plays Should Be Allowed": Reception and Reputation

For all the rumors that *Big White Fog* might provoke race riots, there was no outcry when the play opened. In Chicago, the new play was generally well received by critics. While the presence of communist characters was often mentioned, communism could hardly be said to define the play's critical reception in the Windy City. The Chicago *Daily Tribune* was typical in its account of *Big White Fog* as a play that focused on black family life, and in particular, the Garveyite aspirations of protagonist Vic Mason.[76] Among reviewers who commented on the ending, few were persuaded that the play offered a clear-cut communist solution. In describing the "sort of communistic brotherhood of the underdog," Claudia Cassidy of the *Journal of Commerce* found that the "closing tableau . . . is too vague to dominate memory of the riot squad's encounter with unarmed protestants at an eviction. Perhaps the author meant it so, as a dim flicker in what he calls the "big white fog" of the white man's domination." Lloyd Lewis noted the ambiguous nature of Ward's drama in the *Herald and Examiner*. While the play's title seemed to indicate "the modern Negro's inability to see his future . . . at the end Mr. Ward seemed to glimpse a new society in which the proletarians of both races would join in taking over the world on the Marxian basis." *Daily*

Times reporter Gail Borden was a little more certain that Ward was "probably" advocating communism, and referred to "letters passed around suggesting that the mayor do something about stopping the production of 'Big White Fog' on the grounds that it is 'Communistic.'" She was, however, staunch in defending the Chicago Negro Unit's right to put on a play uncensored: "Radical Plays Should Be Allowed," was the headline in the *Daily Times*.[77] Borden may have been misinformed about the source of any potential censorship, for other newspapers reported that Harry Costello, head of the Chicago Censor Board, had attempted to ban the play because of the "theme of racial prejudice between whites and blacks." Sterling A. Brown also cited "Mr. Ward's frankness in discussing the race problem" as the source of controversy, while Ward remembered talk of blasphemy.[78] Other reviewers, however, made no mention of communism, focusing instead on the portrayal of Garveyism and the "realistic detail" of black domestic life.[79] *Variety* paid the communist conversion of Vic's son no heed. Describing its "fundamentally strong theme," it summed up *Big White Fog* as a "Negro show based on theme of racial prejudice, being built around the Garvey movement."[80]

In spite of positive reviews, after six weeks the production was moved from the Loop to a South Side school auditorium, where it promptly closed after just a few nights. Ward always regarded this as a deliberate act of sabotage and blamed Chicago Federal Theatre head Harry Minturn. It is hard to establish exactly why *Big White Fog* was moved. Certainly it had attracted considerable support from Federal Theatre administrators including Minturn and Susan Glaspell, then director of the Mid-West Play Bureau, as well as from Hallie Flanagan. Official correspondence suggests that the next Federal Theatre show scheduled for the Great Northern Theatre, a Living Newspaper on syphilis, required that the theatre be closed well ahead of the opening to allow the set to be built.[81] Ward's claims notwithstanding, the decision to send *Big White Fog* to the South Side after a successful run on the Loop might have made sense to Graham and Minturn, who wanted black theatre to be experienced in and by the black community. Ward, however, was already preparing the ground for *Big White Fog* to make its New York debut.

Negro Playwrights Company, Harlem, 1940

Big White Fog was the first and last production of the Negro Playwrights Company (NPC), one of the new black theatre companies that brought to-

Negro Playwrights Company, Inc.

LANGSTON HUGHES

GEORGE NORFORD

THEODORE BROWNE

OWEN DODSON

Active Members

POWELL LINDSAY

THEODORE WARD

GEORGE B. MURPHY, Jr.

Officers

FIGURE 14 Members of the Negro Playwrights Company. Negro Playwrights Company program, Theodore Ward's *Big White Fog*, Lincoln Theatre, New York, 1940. Theodore Ward Collection, Box 1, Folder 21, Camille Billops and James V. Hatch archives at Emory University, Stuart A. Rose Manuscript, Archives, and Rare Book Library, Emory University.

gether the talent and training of black veterans of the Federal Theatre in Chicago and New York following the FTP's closure. The networks and friendships that connected black intellectuals and artists in the two cities were important to the development of black drama after the Federal Theatre Project. Ward's friend Langston Hughes had first seen a read-through of *Big White Fog* in Chicago, and his admiration for the "best drama yet written by a black American" was reported in the black press.[82] Hughes followed through on his statement of support by sponsoring a public reading at his new theatre in Harlem. Aided by Louise Thompson, Hughes set up the Harlem Suitcase Theatre with the sponsorship of the New Theatre League at the International Workers Order Community Centre on 317 West 125th Street. Its inaugural production in April 1938 was Hughes's new theatre piece, *Don't You Want to be Free*, which would help launch other radical theatres, including in Chicago, where Ward would produce it alongside Fanny McConnell.[83] The Suitcase Theatre was still very new when Broadway star Mercedes

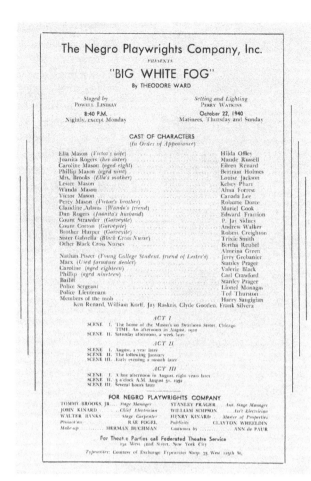

The Negro Playwrights Company, Inc.

PRESENTS

"BIG WHITE FOG"

By THEODORE WARD

Staged by	*Setting and Lighting*
POWELL LINDSAY	PERRY WATKINS
8:40 P.M.	October 22, 1940
Nightly, except Monday	Matinees, Thursday and Sunday

CAST OF CHARACTERS
(In Order of Appearance)

Ella Mason *(Victor's wife)*	Hilda Offley
Juanita Rogers *(her sister)*	Maude Russell
Caroline Mason *(aged eight)*	Eileen Renard
Phillip Mason *(aged nine)*	Bertram Holmes
Mrs. Brooks *(Ella's mother)*	Louise Jackson
Lester Mason	Kelsey Pharr
Wanda Mason	Alma Forrest
Victor Mason	Canada Lee
Percy Mason *(Victor's brother)*	Roburre Dorce
Claudine Adams *(Wanda's friend)*	Muriel Cook
Dan Rogers *(Juanita's husband)*	Edward Fraction
Count Strawder *(Garveyite)*	P. Jay Sidney
Count Cotton *(Garveyite)*	Andrew Walker
Brother Harper *(Garveyite)*	Robert Creighton
Sister Gabriella *(Black Cross Nurse)*	Trixie Smith
Other Black Cross Nurses	Bertha Reubel
	Almeina Green
Nathan Piszer *(Young College Student, friend of Lester's)*	Jerry Grebanier
Marx *(Used furniture dealer)*	Stanley Prager
Caroline *(aged eighteen)*	Valerie Black
Phillip *(aged nineteen)*	Carl Crawford
Bailiff	Stanley Prager
Police Sergeant	Lionel Monagas
Police Lieutenant	Ted Thurston
Members of the mob	Harry Sangigian
Ken Renard, William Korff, Jay Raskris, Clyde Gooden, Frank Silvera	

ACT I

SCENE I. The home of the Mason's on Dearborn Street, Chicago
TIME: An afternoon in August, 1922
SCENE II. Saturday afternoon, a week later

ACT II

SCENE I. August, a year later
SCENE II. The following January
SCENE III. Early evening a month later

ACT III

SCENE I. A late afternoon in August, eight years later
SCENE II. 3 o'clock A.M. August 31, 1932
SCENE III. Several hours later

FOR NEGRO PLAYWRIGHTS COMPANY

TOMMY BROOKS, JR.	*Stage Manager*	STANLEY PRAGER	*Asst. Stage Manager*
JOHN KINARD	*Chief Electrician*	WILLIAM SIMPSON	*Ass't. Electrician*
WALTER BANKS	*Stage Carpenter*	HENRY KINARD	*Master of Properties*
Promotion	RAE FOGEL	*Publicity*	CLAYTON WHEELDIN
Make-up	HERMAN BUCHMAN	*Costumes by*	ANN de PAUR

For Theatre Parties call Federated Theatre Service
132 West 42nd Street, New York City

Typewriters Courtesy of Exchange Typewriter Shop, 75 West 125th St.

FIGURE 15 Cast List for Negro Playwrights Company Production of *Big White Fog*. Negro Playwrights Company program, Theodore Ward's *Big White Fog*, Lincoln Theatre, New York, 1940. Theodore Ward Collection, Box 1, Folder 21, Camille Billops and James V. Hatch archives at Emory University, Stuart A. Rose Manuscript, Archives, and Rare Book Library, Emory University.

Gilbert and Harlem Negro Unit veteran and screen actor Daniel Haynes gave a public reading of *Big White Fog* there on May 13, 1938.[84] When the NPC production of *Big White Fog* finally opened at the Lincoln Theatre in Harlem on October 22, 1940, it featured Harlem Negro Unit star Canada Lee as Vic Mason. Edward Fraction of the Chicago Negro Unit reprised the role of Dan Rogers for the new production. Powell Lindsay directed.

The NPC production, and specifically Ward's recollection of its critical reception, played an important role in shaping the reputation of the play.[85] From the vantage point of the 1970s, *Big White Fog* became part of the American narrative of anticommunism in which all leftist politics was delegitimized and discredited at the end of the 1930s. Central to the way in which the NPC production has been reconstructed is the testimony of Ward himself. Keen in the 1970s to defend his reputation as a playwright and resurrect his Federal Theatre–era dramas, Ward took pains to distinguish the critical reception of the Federal Theatre production from the NPC production two years later, attributing the New York reviews to the "retreat . . . of the American intellectuals" that followed the Nazi-Soviet pact. One of the problems with such an analysis is that it is unclear which version of the play was performed by the NPC in 1940.[86] What is clear is that the NPC, unlike the FTP, did not list "Communists" as characters in its cast list published in the playbill in 1940. Rather, they are described as "members of the mob."[87] The less explicit reference to communist characters suggests that the NPC gave some thought as to how the play would be received in terms of its representation of communism in autumn 1940. However Ward's argument that the critics slammed the apparently communistic slant of his play "enough . . . to kill the New York production" is hard to sustain.[88] Though the critical reception accorded *Big White Fog* in New York in 1940 was mixed, it was not dominated by fears of, or antipathy toward, communism.

The city's black newspapers paved the way for a positive reception of *Big White Fog* by recalling its success in Chicago. In April 1939, the New York *Amsterdam News* had reported on the play's reception in the Midwest, noting that critics had hailed it as "as one of the finest plays written last year" but that most thought the play "too honest." Ward, they warned, "pulled few punches" and let the "chips lie where they may."[89] The *New York Age* reported that *Big White Fog* had troubled the censors in Chicago and suggested it was the Chicago Negro Unit troupe who had ensured the play went on. It also reported Hughes's endorsement of the play.[90] When *Big White Fog* opened at the Lincoln, most black critics made little or only passing reference to the appearance of communist characters. The *Afro-American* declared in a headline that Ward's play was a triumph of "art, faith and sincerity." The *New Journal and Guide* called it "the most outstanding play of the year or any year," and reported on the repeated curtain calls from an audience reduced to tears. Les's conversion to communism was mentioned but seldom regarded as central. The *New York Age* called it a "fine drama" that offered a picture of black life that was "accurate in detail," even if there "are those who will quarrel with the political ideology at the conclusion." Alain Locke was one of those. He found an otherwise admirable play limited by its "solution": "Instead of holding to its excellent posed character conflicts, over money and race loyalty, Americanism and Garveyism, it swerves to a solution by way of radical social action for its denouement." Locke's insistence that the play had presented a compelling, if misguided, solution was contradicted by those who might be expected to find an empowering communist message in the play.[91] Ralph Ellison, not yet disillusioned with communism, regarded the play's ending as disappointingly inconclusive. In his *New Masses* review, Ellison questioned Ward's failure to develop communism as a serious alternative to Garveyism comparing the play's lengthy consideration of Vic and black nationalism to the limited exposition of Les and his communist allies. Rather than favoring the communist solution, Ellison thought Ward had left "the solution of the play undramatized," with its hero seeing life as "just a big white fog." Ellison later confided to Richard Wright that the editors of *New Masses* had asked him to drop the discussion of tragedy in *Big White Fog* from his review. If *Big White Fog* did not quite cut it as a pro-communist play, its serious analysis of Garveyism was nonetheless appreciated. Ellison noted that "The Negro people long ago discarded the utopianism of the Garvey movement," yet he recognized Ward's respectful portrayal of the Garvey movement, "a movement which has been passed off as a ludicrous effort by Negroes to ape British royalty and reveals in it that dignity of human groping which is characteristic of all oppressed peoples." Similarly, Sterling A. Brown noted not only the "sympathy" with which Victor's Garveyite faith was portrayed but also that it was developed "more fully than the son's conversion to radicalism."[92]

Few white critics paid much attention to communism. Two who did were at opposite ends of the political spectrum. Writing for the *Daily Worker*, Ralph Warner was more concerned with analyzing political movements than interpreting plays. He explained to his readers that Garveyism had "diverted the Negro people from their vital struggle." Determined to cement *Big White Fog* as a play sympathetic to communism, Warner, in contrast to Ellison, claimed that when Vic dies at the end, he "understands for the first time that the big white fog can be lifted, but lifted only by the unity of the minority of the Negroes with the majority of the working-class." Even so, Warner conceded that "the transition of young Les from a bitter defeated youth to a socially conscious and dynamic fighter for justice is accomplished with too great haste."[93] In his review for the *New York Times*, Brooks Atkinson understood Ward's drama as containing the "usual ailments" of socially significant drama, including the "regulation Communist finish." Though acknowledging it as a matter of form, Atkinson nevertheless took pains to point out his disagreement with what appeared to the "message" of the play: "If Mr. Ward believes that alliance of insurgent Negroes with the Communist party is the way to social and economic liberation that is his privilege. But most of us will believe that he is moving toward a system of slavery more stifling than anything his race has yet experienced in America. For Communism is no longer a mystic dream, but Soviet Russia, which is a hard, brutal, treacherous reality." With his antipathy to the Soviet Union clearly stated, Atkinson was then free to admire the "best serious play of Negro authorship about race problems" he had seen, and a playwright who had something "bold, hard and disturbing" to say. He understood that Ward's drama was not designed to satisfy "the white man's taste": "Big White Fog eschews spirituals and hot dancing, which are the only two things Broadway knows about the Negro theatre."[94] John Mason Brown, writing for the *New York Post*, loved finding fault with dramas of social protest; he found that in its "final Communist solution, the melodrama seems for all the world like an echo of every playwriting fault omitted in the worst of the scripts presented down at the erstwhile Theatre Union." Other influential critics paid little heed to the portrayal of communism. Burns Mantle thought *Big White Fog* "not a good play by Broadway standards" but the "best play written by a Negro dramatist to date," and the best production by a black organization in Harlem. He agreed with Atkinson that it was a drama for the "colored race." Unlike Atkinson, however, he saw, not a soapbox for communism, but "the story of Victor Mason," a Garveyite idealist who attempted to free himself from white domination. Though he discussed the plot, he made no comment on communists or communist solutions, beyond mentioning that the son "turns Communist." Richard Watts Jr. admired the "sheer force of its embattled bitterness," but thought it an incompetent, badly produced drama. Arthur Pollack similarly made no mention of communism, praising the characterization in Ward's drama but questioning the quality of the production. Louis Kronenberger, writing for *PM*, pronounced it a "decided failure" but thought the "over-ambitious" production was "evidence that the company may go on to better things."[95]

In New York, as in Chicago, the representation of communism was sometimes described, often critiqued, and frequently ignored. Although Atkinson linked the play to Soviet Russia and reminded his readers of the brutalities of the Stalinist regime, what is more striking is the mundane way in which critics responded to the discussion of communism in the play, whether in 1938 Chicago or 1940 New York. Dating the moment at which rational discussion of the role of communism in American life ceased is perhaps an impossible task. Even efforts to chart the historiography of anti-communism and communism in the United States have proved contentious.[96] As Martha Biondi has shown for New York, the Black Popular Front continued during and after World War II. In some cities CPUSA membership grew after the war.[97] At the same time, the trajectory of civil rights insurgency cannot be neatly mapped onto the rise and fall of the CPUSA.[98] The anti-communism/communism binary has not only blurred the chronology, but also obscured the diversity of progressive-left politics in black and interracial communities across the United States during and after World War II. The construction of such a narrow range of radical possibilities for African American distorts our understanding of the relationship between the black freedom movement and the organized far left. African Americans and the "race" question were important to, and influenced by, the CPUSA, but as Singh has argued African Americans had commitments to other ideologies and movements, including black nationalism, and radical diasporic traditions that shaped how they understood and engaged with Marxist ideas and communist organizations.[99] The critical reception of *Big White Fog* suggests African Americans had considerably more scope than is often assumed (and perhaps more than Ward himself remembered) to include communism in discussions of American political ideologies in the late 1930s. If reviewers' casual responses to the portrayal of communism in *Big White Fog* do not help in establishing the chronological parameters of when (and even if) Americans moved from discussing communism as a political ideology to treating it as an infectious disease, they do, however, help us appreciate that *Big White Fog* was understood to be about something more than communism. The play's reception in New York opens up discussion of other important themes explored in the drama and enables us to better understand the appeal, provocation, and power of Ward's drama.

If the New York critics did not push *Big White Fog* into an early communist grave, we are left with two fascinating questions: why did Ward date the communist interpretation of *Big White Fog* to the 1940 production and why did the play emerge in the second half of the twentieth century as an example of a (failed) communist play? The reputation of Federal Theatre drama and Popular Front culture in the second half of the twentieth century makes it understandable that Ward would view *Big White Fog* as a victim of obsessive anticommunism. In a 1976 oral history interview with Federal Theatre historian Lorraine Brown, Ward made a direct connection between the New York reviews, the play's communist reputation, and the lack of interest in a revival. He singled out Atkinson's *New York Times* review for insinuating that both he and his play were communist: "It hasn't been done since most people think it's a Communist play."[100] Ward attributed particular significance to the time frame between the two productions, since the New York production occurred after the Nazi-Soviet pact of 1939.[101] While the two-year alliance between Soviet Russia and Nazi Germany had a profound impact on the Popular Front coalition, alienating many of those who were broadly sympathetic to the antiracism and social justice causes promoted by the CPUSA, it hardly marked the end of organized left or its representation in American cultural and political life.[102] Moreover, contemporary accounts suggest a range of factors contributed to the closing of *Big White Fog* in December after sixty-four performances. Funding and sponsorship were, as for all noncommercial and, especially, black theatres, a major issue for the NPC. It was never really able to pay the cast or technicians, which led to a good deal of disharmony in the company. Newspaper reports regularly reported on the actors doubling as janitors, having to clear the stage between performances, and threatening to beat up Ward unless he paid them. Hill later remembered that "the playwrights . . . felt that they would have a better possibility of developing a theatre if they approached from the playwrights' point of view and not the actors and other personnel in the theatre."[103] Perhaps actors and backstage theatre professionals felt their perspectives were not taken into account, or perhaps they found more lucrative roles elsewhere. Certainly the company found it difficult to hold onto lead actors and suffered from regular cast changes. Canada Lee, their biggest star, left after just a few weeks because of a previous booking. He was replaced in the role of Vic Mason, first by Henry Walker and then by Virgil Richardson, who was playing the "comical prof" in *On Strivers Row* for the American Theatre.[104] Even the end of the run occurred amid acrimony. The *Amsterdam News* reported that the closing night after-party was a washout, due to the "lack of community support," which had meant stagehands and cast were never paid, while the *New York Times* reported on ticket prices of four dollars, forty cents, "the highest in many years."[105] General anxiety about anticommunism may have kept audiences away while disaffection with the Popular Front among liberals did not make it easier to attract funding. Yet those who were concerned about potentially radical plays were perhaps not ever likely to visit Harlem to sit in a cramped library basement to watch a bold new drama. Meanwhile, differences of opinion between NPC's founding playwrights were already beginning to weaken the company. The departure of Abram Hill was compounded by systemic problems that made it (and still make it) very difficult to sustain an independent black theatre in New York. Of one thing we can be certain: while Ward and many critics did not see *Big White Fog* as a communist play in 1940, by the 1970s it had become one.

Conclusions

Ward blamed the neglect of *Big White Fog* in the second half of the twentieth century on its erroneous communist reputation.[106] Perhaps this explains
why, in the version of the play Ward gave to James Hatch to publish in *Black
Theater U.S.A.* in 1974, "Communists" were no longer named in the list of
characters. Though anyone who read through to the end of the play would
not have been in doubt as to the political affiliation of the "Negro and white
workers" who prevent the eviction of the Mason family, removing communists as named characters was not without significance. Beginning with
the Dies Committee's investigations into the Federal Theatre, the House
Committee on Un-American Activities had a history of targeting plays
and playwrights whose titles sounded risky or included potentially un-
American-sounding characters. Ward had learned caution when it came to
representing the radical left.[107] By contrast, some of the issues that had inflamed South Side community leaders in 1938 and were removed from the
Chicago Negro Unit production were reinstated in the version of *Big White
Fog* published thirty-six years later. The published version does not follow
the "Last Version" in modifying the language used to describe Wanda and
sexual acts: Wanda is called a "whore" and the direct reference to "Laying
up with a white man" is reinstated, even though both phrases were omitted from the version performed by the Negro Unit in Chicago. By contrast,
in the anthologized text, Wanda receives forgiveness from her father and
racial divisions within the black community are minimized. For example,
Wanda places responsibility for the lack of teaching opportunities for
black teachers directly on the system of Jim Crow, rather than blaming the
black community for "kicking against colored teachers," as in "Last Version."[108] In the 1974 published text, the term "nigger" is used, once, by Vic,
when challenging his mother-in-law's assault on manhood.

The 1974 anthologized version of *Big White Fog* was the basis for the only
professional U.S. revival of Ward's drama. In 1995, the Guthrie Theatre in
Minneapolis–St. Paul staged *Big White Fog* under the direction of Penumbra's Lou Bellamy. It is also the version most often used by scholars and has
been made more widely available as part of the Alexander Street Press digital resource *Black Drama*.[109] *Big White Fog*, like all dramas, has evolved
as it has been rewritten, reinterpreted, and adapted for theatrical production. It continues to provoke controversy about whose histories are being
re-presented and who is empowered to re-present them. Michael Attenbor-

ough's Almeida production in London played amid a bitter dispute with Ward's daughter over copyright and allegations of unauthorized use of the play in 2007. Attenborough was quoted in the London *Evening Standard* as saying, "Because it has never been staged outside America, it's almost like doing a new play." He credited the Almeida's creative director with having "discovered" the play in the *Black Theater U.S.A.* anthology. A discourse that involves the "discovery" of "neglected" black dramatists is often problematic: it risks elevating the "discoverers" and glossing over the struggles of those who ensured that black dramas survived so that they could be rediscovered.[110] The Almeida Company produced and published its own version of the play, which it described as "an amalgamation of two original drafts of the play not enormously different from each other."[111] The undocumented elision of manuscripts also has a cost if dramas like *Big White Fog* are to be kept alive theatrically and recognized as important artifacts of black dramatic heritage. *Big White Fog* is more than "a remarkable historical document" or an "imaginative footnote to recent Negro history," as theatre critics claimed.[112] From the Federal Theatre and NPC productions in Chicago and New York, survival through the Cold War to become a published text, and eventual production by major theatre companies in the United States and the United Kingdom, the history of *Big White Fog* is an important part of the story of how black Americans fought to create the world anew.

The dominant narratives of the twentieth century can be read through the manuscripts of *Big White Fog*. But if we also remember to read forward, we will encounter a richer and broader set of ideas about how black liberation could be achieved in the 1930s and 1940s. Reading forward, as Barbara Foley suggests, provides a way to navigate the almost invisible anticommunism that has shaped what we look for and are trained to find as historians of black culture.[113] Reading forward allows us to attend to other radical ideas with which African Americans engaged and to explore how they developed in the 1930s. Instead of squeezing black cultural texts into a set of narrow generic boundaries that have come to be associated with the radical left, reading forward foregrounds the ambitions of black cultural producers searching for new ways to communicate radical ideas in the 1930s. Reflecting on the problems of black theatre history in a 1979 interview, Amiri Baraka argued: "The history of Afro-American literature, of Afro-American drama is still not clearly outlined according to its own traditions. Black theatre history is always told in terms of its relationship to antithetical forms."[114] The radical provocations that animated the South Side audience for *Big White Fog* are easier to hear when we consider the processes that shaped its development as both theatre manuscript and Federal Theatre production. In turn they draw our attention and help tune our ears to the genre experiments and debates about the black hero that were taking place in and around the Negro Units. On tuning in, we encounter dramas that defy both the genre expectations of black and white audiences in 1930s America and the historical narratives constructed to keep black drama in its place; we encounter a black theatre busy making its own traditions.

5 Free at Lass!
Plays That Turn Out Well for Harlem

· ·

African Americans who fight back usually pay for it with their lives in 1930s dramas: in *Natural Man*, John Henry is driven to an early grave for resisting the violence of the white guard; in *Big White Fog*, Vic Mason stands his ground against an attempted eviction from the family home, only to be fatally shot by the police in front of his family. In *Stevedore*, black men who stand up for their rights at work are soon called to account by the mob. If physical resistance by black men is a constant refrain in black theatre, so too was their inevitable death. In the final year of the FTP, the Harlem Negro Unit developed two new dramas in which black heroes fight and win: *Haiti* told the thrilling story of the first independent black republic and was based on a drama by the white *New York Times* journalist William Dubois; Theodore Browne's *Go Down Moses* dramatizes the life and career of Harriet Tubman, the self-liberated slave who led African Americans to freedom on the Underground Railroad and worked for the Union Army during the Civil War. The two dramas present contrasting measures of success. While *Haiti* became the longest-running show in the Harlem Negro Unit's nearly four-year history, *Go Down Moses* was cast and rehearsed, but not staged before the FTP was shut down in summer 1939. Nevertheless, Browne's drama represents a successful culmination of the many demands for black control and black-authored plays both from within and outside the unit since 1935. *Go Down Moses* also marked an important moment in the histories of the Federal Theatre and American drama. Featuring a gun-toting black heroine, who leads from the front and is victim to no man, it offered a radical counter to visions of black liberation that privileged the muscular resistance and suffering of black men. Tubman, the resolute leader of fugitives, and Granny, a stationmaster on the Underground Railroad, draw their authority from experience and expertise in forging networks of resistance to undermine American slavery.

This chapter examines *Haiti* and *Go Down Moses* and the black performance community in Harlem that developed these two dramas. The Harlem Negro Unit was the first FTP unit to stage a production, and it would go on to produce the greatest number and variety of black dramas between 1935 and 1939. As the largest employer of African Americans on the project (over half of those employed by the FTP worked on the New York Project), it also appointed more black supervisors than any other. Beginning in spring 1936 with comedies by black dramatists—revivals of Frank Wilson's *Walk Together Chillun* and Rudolph Fisher's *Conjure Man Dies*—it was John Houseman and Orson Welles's sensational "Voodoo *Macbeth*," that really put the Harlem Negro Unit on the map and subsequently shaped the reputation of the Harlem Unit and the Negro Units in general.[1] Yet the Harlem Unit staged other provocative dramas that had implications, not just for the Harlem theatre, but for the Negro Units and black theatre more broadly. The Harlem Negro Unit's production history was shaped by its proximity to FTP headquarters, which were located, at least from 1937 onward, in New York City. It also reaped some of the advantages of being in the nation's theatre capital. The New York City Project was the largest in the country, with eleven production units, including the Negro Theatre, Negro Youth Theatre, African Dance, and Drama Units, as well the Experimental Theatre and Living Newspaper Units. New York was also home to the FTP's National Service Bureau (NSB), where plays were submitted, reviewed, and sent out to units across the country. The location of the playwriting department within the NSB meant the black playwrights and readers who worked for it, including Abram Hill and John Silvera, were well placed to connect with the Harlem Negro Unit as well as with various cultural groups that advocated for black arts in Harlem. New York was also the headquarters for many national black rights groups, including the National Urban League (NUL) and the NAACP. Regarded as the epicenter of WPA Negro theatre, and often pressing for formal recognition as such, the Harlem Negro Unit fought publicly and formally for black autonomy in ways that contrasted with some of the "behind-the-scenes" rebellions of other Negro Units. Whereas in Seattle, Chicago, and Hartford, an understanding of black priorities and resistance to white directives must be teased out of theatre reviews, manuscripts, production bulletins, and oral histories, in Harlem, demands for greater independence and black control over the Negro Unit feature prominently in the FTP's administrative records and production archives, as well as in the records of racial justice campaign groups.

Drawing on all these sources, I examine, first, the production and manuscript history of *Haiti*. Thought originally to have been a drama in the mold of *Birth of a Nation*, by the time the Harlem Negro Unit came to stage William Dubois's play, *Haiti* had become a commemoration of Haitian independence and a symbol of black self-determination. This transformation was due in no small part to the work of the members of the black performance community, whose demands shaped the process of adapting and interpreting the play from rehearsal through the seventeen-week run at the Lafayette Theatre. The black performance community used *Haiti* to demand greater autonomy for African Americans and Negro Units within the Federal Theatre Project and to position these demands as part of the broader black freedom struggle. The second part of this chapter considers how debates inspired by *Haiti* pushed the Federal Theatre to invest in two black dramatists, Hughes Allison and Theodore Browne. When *Haiti* was moved from the Lafayette Theatre in Harlem to Daly's Theatre downtown, it prompted speculation that the unit would be closed and charges of racial discrimination. Coming so soon after the failure to see through the black Living Newspaper and the reduction in black employees on FTP payrolls, Federal Theatre administrators were forced to respond. The pressure on the Federal Theatre to stage black-authored dramas in Harlem was maintained through a multipronged campaign. It involved black Federal Theatre employees who worked on the Harlem Negro Unit and for the NSB, black newspapers, and local and national black rights groups. Taken together, these campaigns reveal not only what was made possible through intense and continuous negotiation, but also the radical role the Harlem performance community envisaged for its theatre.

Establishing the Flagship in Harlem

Characterizing the Federal Theatre's regional centers in dramatic terms, its national director saw Chicago as melodrama, Los Angeles as musical comedy, the South as a folk play, and New York as a Living Newspaper.[2] How far Hallie Flanagan's characterizations drew on her knowledge of the Negro Units is not clear, but in the case of the New York Negro Unit, the analogy is appropriate: the Harlem Negro Unit, like the Living Newspaper, experimented with form and tried to change the dynamic between audience and performers; it also became one of the most politicized units, in terms of both the content and the process through which plays were staged. Acutely aware that the Harlem Unit was seen by the Federal Theatre as its "flagship" Negro Unit, employees of the unit and the wider Harlem community that supported it exploited the Federal Theatre's desire to showcase its liberal aspirations in order to promote their own agendas. Actors, technicians, stage managers, directors, and the black supervisors who ran the

Harlem Unit between 1936 and 1939 were acutely aware that they were part of, and responsible to, a broader African American theatre community. Located at the Lafayette Theatre at 2227 Seventh Avenue between 131st and 132nd Street, the Negro Unit was situated "in the heart of Harlem" though not in Harlem's "theatre district," which was on 125th Street between Lenox and Eighth Avenues. In a policy and planning document written in the summer and fall of 1936, the Negro Unit styled itself a "true community theatre" at the heart of a black community of churches, fraternal organizations, civic and social clubs, YMCAs, and YWCAs, whose work was promoted and scrutinized by three local newspapers. Its goal as a community theatre was "to provide facilities by which community leaders may raise funds for the propagation of their ideas and ideals."[3] Such an ambition would be realized through various engagement programs that drew the community into the theatre and took theatre to the community. One such endeavor was the Suitcase Theatre. Actors from the Harlem Unit would bring live entertainment to community members in their own organizational settings. Engaging with communities through a Suitcase Theatre would enable the unit to develop independent research on what audiences wanted, which could then be used to shape FTP production policy. Moreover, plays suitable for a Harlem audience would be created through a series of playwriting classes designed to address the dearth of black-authored dramas.[4]

The Harlem Negro Unit was initially set up under the co-directorship of black theatre veteran Rose McClendon. Apparently at McClendon's request, Hallie Flanagan also appointed the Hungarian born British-educated theatre producer John Houseman to lead the unit. In 1934 Houseman had directed an all-black cast in Virgil Thomson's opera *Four Saints in Three Acts*. As a foreign-born white man with experience of working with a black troupe, Houseman was expected to open doors that had been closed to black theatre practitioners. McClendon, who was diagnosed with a terminal illness in late 1935 and died the following summer, was never able to share the direction with Houseman. Up until August 1936, when Houseman resigned to pursue new projects, the Harlem Negro Unit operated under white direction.[5] The benefits and limitations of Houseman's leadership were tested early on when he engaged the mercurial Orson Welles to direct the unit in a Haitian-themed *Macbeth*. The decision to stage a black classic proved successful in terms of attracting the attention of prominent theatre critics as well as curious Harlemites to the Lafayette Theatre. After it was transferred downtown, *Macbeth* went on a 4,000 mile tour before returning for a final run at the Majestic Theatre in Brooklyn.

Macbeth was, however, just one in a series of successes for the unit: within the first twenty months it had produced nine dramas, in nearly 600 performances, to an audience of over 400,000. It had also survived a number of administrative reorganizations. Employing over 500 personnel at its peak in May 1936, the Negro Unit offered opportunities, not only for black actors, but also for stage managers, shop carpenters, and timekeepers, as well as jobs in the technical department, and clerical and publicity work. According to the FTP's Department of Information, the Harlem Negro Unit was a "play factory" that included many of the ingredients necessary for play making and was "more self-sufficient than any other to be found within the project."[6] This included a playreading committee consisting of Gus Smith, Edna Thomas, Thomas Mosely, and Dewitt Spencer. The committee read and recommended plays that might be suitable for the unit; they also commented on and often firmly rejected play recommendations of white FTP administrators keen to find another hit for the Harlem Unit. For example, Smith refused the white-authored dramas *Scarlet Sister Mary* and *When Jack Hollers*. While the first was dismissed as "unsuited for our audiences," the latter relied too heavily on "the sexual angle." As Smith explained, "the word angle wouldn't be liked here."[7] Although it was white administrators on the New York FTP Production Board who decided on the final production schedule, the black playreading committee made a "tentative selection, keeping in mind the Harlem audience and attempting to favour, wherever possible, Negro playwrights."[8]

After Houseman left in August 1936 to lead the FTP's Experimental Unit downtown, the black leadership of the Harlem Unit used the resources of the FTP to train black Americans in the theatre arts. As discussed in chapter 2, this included establishing the Negro Dramatists Laboratory, which offered a series of playwriting courses in 1936 and 1937. In spring 1937, the Harlem Negro Unit also established a studio workshop for actors and directors. Based at East 133rd Street, classes included topics such as the Stanislavsky method of stage direction and were taught by Negro Unit supervisor and director Bernard Kaplan, working alongside white instructors William Challee and Bobby Lewis. The latter two were members of the Group Theatre, and Challee would direct the Negro Unit in Eugene O'Neill's sea plays in October 1937. These programs, and the unit's strategy and planning documents, built on the legacy of Harlem's community theatres, as well as the recent history of collaboration between black and white theatre professionals on productions such as the Theatre Union's *Stevedore*.[9] Taken together, they provide an important context for understanding the Harlem Negro Unit as a community theatre interested in developing black theatre professionals and a black audience for new theatre, rather than simply as the producer of headline-grabbing hits such as *Macbeth*. Gus Smith was at pains to make this clear to his supervisors. Writing to New York City FTP director Philip W. Barber, Smith explained the significance of the training programs, commenting that "the demand of the actors to learn all they can is very great."[10]

If the records of the Harlem Negro Unit suggest a commitment to training and development, subsequent accounts have conjured a picture of the New York Units as exciting, chaotic spaces where life was lived on a knife edge and decisions made on the spur of the moment. Welles and Houseman's sensational *Macbeth* and their creative response to efforts to censor Marc Blitzstein's *The Cradle Will Rock* are important markers in such narratives. The race to find a vacant theatre and the cast's impromptu performances from the audience were vividly portrayed in Tim Robbins's 1999 film *Cradle Will Rock*. Such creative chaos, it seems, is the exclusive prerogative of the already privileged. For example, the FTP is often represented as opening new opportunities for high- status, unruly white men such as Welles and Houseman, both of whom were deemed willing and capable of, and even rewarded for, resisting Federal Theatre rules. By contrast, accounts of the Harlem Negro Unit often emphasize limit, restraint, and closed doors: white administrators are usually cast as the sole determinants of what plays were produced and the Negro Units as "always circumscribed by congressional cuts and theatrical prejudices, by racism, and by the politics of artistic choices."[11] That maverick director Orson Welles and established producer John Houseman were given breaks unavailable to black theatre professionals is hardly surprising. But it does not follow that African Americans were incapable of exerting pressure or using creative chaos to their own advantage. The black performance community in Harlem employed both strategies. A combination of sustained effort and high-profile, celebrity-endorsed campaigns placed FTP officials under considerable pressure, which sometimes led to change. Such activism was part of a much longer tradition of community theatre in Harlem, which mobilized broad constituencies to demand greater control over the roles available to black creatives on and off stage.[12]

One core and constant demand was that members of the Harlem Negro Unit be granted access to resources and training from theatre professionals across the program. Similarly, the demand for black autonomy, an issue McClendon had confronted at the outset, remained a constant source of pressure which shaped relations between the black performance community and both New York City and national FTP administrators. The black perfor-mance community in Harlem also exerted pressure on other Federal Theatre unit productions that featured representations of peoples of African descent. It would maintain this pressure throughout the life of the Harlem Negro Unit, and targeted campaigns would become increasingly regular following cuts to FTP budgets and jobs in summer 1937. From this point onward, charges of racial discrimination were brought by black FTP employees on a regular basis and were accompanied by demands that black Americans be given greater and more direct access to the increasingly scarce resources of the WPA Arts Projects. One of the most consistently articulated and in-creasingly urgent demands was that the Harlem Negro Unit gain autonomy over its choice of plays. This was seen a crucial step in allowing the unit to stage dramas that reflected contemporary black life from a black, rather than white, perspective. In this context, *Macbeth* was an important play for the Harlem Negro Unit, not because it attracted white critics and the attention of the theatrical world, but because it underscored the need for black audiences to experience black dramas about black life, rather than novelty versions of the classics that reflected white ideas of black life.

Macbeth: The First Hit

The Haitian-inspired *Macbeth* became the FTP's first "box-office" hit in 1936 in part because it reflected how white theatre audiences had been trained to imagine black Americans on the stage.[13] White critics attending the opening night on April 14 took pains to situate Welles's *Macbeth* on a continuum with Eugene O'Neill's still much performed *Emperor Jones*. First produced by the Provincetown Players in 1920, O'Neill's drama was also lo-cated on a tropical Caribbean island, "not yet self-determined by U.S. ma-rines," a clear reference to American occupation of Haiti, which was the first independent black republic. The play provided both entertainment and af-firmation of the black man's lack of self-mastery, and white audiences and critics would return again and again to see this "extraordinarily striking and dramatic study of panic fear." By the time the Harlem Unit staged *Macbeth* in 1936, the United States had withdrawn from a much weakened Haiti, O'Neill's place in American theatre was assured, and *Emperor Jones* had become the lens through which white Americans created and received serious dramatic representations of black manhood.[14] Burns Mantle drew on familiar imagery to interpret *Macbeth* for white New Yorkers: "It's a little as though O'Neill's Emperor Jones had re-established his kingdom in the South Sea Islands and staged a monster fete." Arthur Pollack declared "This *Macbeth* seems to have a cast full of Emperor Jones," while Brooks Atkinson saw "a voodoo show inspired by the Macbeth legend." He nevertheless praised those scenes that enabled black actors to showcase their "natural" talent: "when the play falls within their *Emperor Jones* caprice, they have the artists and actors who can translate supernaturalism into flaring excitement."[15] These and many other white critics applauded the color and excitement of *Macbeth* and warmly recommended the "experience" to their readers. As the *Vogue* critic explained, the production offered white Americans the opportunity to enjoy the warmth of a "simpler race," even as it affirmed white superiority: "the whites came in droves to spread their chilly fingers before the reviving fires of a warmer, happier, simpler race. . . . In watching them, we capture briefly what once we were, long centuries ago before our ancestors suffered the blights of thought, worry and the printed word."[16]

Critics connected the Harlem Negro Unit's *Macbeth* with *Emperor Jones*, not only on account of its tropical island setting but because the heroes of both dramas share the dismal fate of black men who aspire to self-determination. Macbeth, like Brutus Jones, is ultimately unmanned by a combination of voodoo and superstition. Transposed from Scotland to the sizzling forests of Haiti, whites saw in Welles's vision not the demise of a hero-villain whose wrong choices brought about a tragic ending, but rather a race of primitive beings whose destinies were not their own. Welles' script took lines uttered by ordinary mortals and put them into the mouths of supernatural figures. Placing the roles of the witches and Hecate (now a voodoo priest) at the center of the action, he cut those lines where mortal characters debate possible courses of action and make choices. Welles's Macbeth is driven not by his ambition, but by the will of the witches, ruled by voodoo priest Hecate. It is they who set in train a series of murderous acts that first elevate Macbeth to kingship but ultimately lead to his demise. Welles not only offered a stage peopled with so many Emperor Joneses, but the dark jungle scenery and constant voodoo drumming also evoked the earlier play. Indeed Welles's manuscript is replete with demands for a "voodoo effect," which was provided by the Sierra Leonean performer Asadata Dafora Hunton and his dance troupe, with "voodoo drumming" led by an "African witch doctor, known simply as Abdul." As Susan McCloskey argues, in Welles's hands, the drama of *Macbeth* was to be found in spectacle and melodrama, rather than the freedom to make the wrong choices that is usually associated with tragedy.[17]

Where white critics saw a stage full of Emperor Joneses, black critics saw a precious opportunity to create a serious black community theatre. Accordingly, they were keen to disassociate *Macbeth* from *Emperor Jones*. Writing in *New Theatre*, Roi Otley was particularly troubled by the *Emperor Jones* lens through which white critics viewed *Macbeth*, complaining of "the Broadway reviewers . . . [who] journeyed to Harlem with the idea of seeing a mixture of Emperor Jones and Stepin Fechit [Fetchit], with burlesque thrown in to season a palatable opinion many of their readers have of the Negro."[18] When the touring production reached Hartford, Connecticut, in July 1936, a reviewer for the *Hartford Courant* found *Macbeth* to be "flamboyant theater and rather less drama" and noted earlier criticisms about the production's racial twist: "there are some who say it is certainly not truly Negro, but rather the white man's idea of the Negro's idea of 'Macbeth.'"[19] These criticisms notwithstanding, many black newspapers appeared relieved that the Harlem Negro Unit had survived the ordeal without major injury. During the three long months of rehearsals, rumors had circulated that Welles and Houseman were preparing a Shakespearian burlesque intended to mock black aspirations to serious drama.[20] Keen to quash such speculation, black critics welcomed the production and urged their readers to spend an evening at the Lafayette. The *New York Age* gave an upbeat account of the play's reception: "the audience, white and Negro cheered itself hoarse," and declared it a major landmark in Harlem's theatre history: "this production proved to Harlem that it could create and support a Shakespearean play of its own." More than that, it "marked Harlem's cultural coming of age."[21] Ralph Matthews of the *Afro-American* suggested that *Macbeth* had answered the question, "'Can colored actors do Shakespeare?' . . . so completely that none but fools would venture such a query again."[22] Although black reviewers paid attention to many aspects of the production, they tended to emphasize the significance of Shakespeare being performed by black actors and watched by black audiences in Harlem. Adam Clayton Powell Jr. showered praised on the production, but lamented the closing of so many Harlem theatres in recent years. Stressing *Macbeth*'s important transitional role in Harlem's theatre history, he welcomed a production that might lead to the rebirth of serious black theatre: "Macbeth" he proclaimed, "has saved the day." But the production was only a first step; African Americans, he urged, must direct the theatre and its productions: "The Negro Theatre is not sufficient, it must be the Negro's."[23]

African American theatre critics and cultural commentators seized on *Macbeth* as proof that Harlem could sustain a black theatre. Its success was important because it demonstrated the need for, and viability of, a Negro Unit in Harlem and portended a future in which black Americans controlled black theatre. *Macbeth* played at the Lafayette for ten weeks, before moving downtown and then on to a nationwide tour of thirteen weeks, reaching an estimated 117,000 people.[24] Although *Macbeth* attracted large audiences, it was hardly the ideal vehicle for black community engagement: a weak black man, manipulated by a greedy wife and evil voodoo priest, is slain. What was needed was a play with the excitement and drama of "Voodoo *Macbeth*," but one that might also offer up an empowering image of black self-determination, a play, that was, in the Powell's judgment, "far superior to Macbeth."[25]

Haiti Comes to Harlem

After *Macbeth,* the Harlem Negro Unit was reorganized. Houseman and Welles left to set up the Experimental Unit, while the director Carlton Moss became managing project supervisor, Harry Edward was put in charge of administration, and actor, playwright, and director Gus Smith became managing producer.[26] Although the Negro Unit was now under black leadership, this did not mean that African Americans had control of programming. Smith and his team read and recommended plays, but the final authority rested with the New York City Planning Board. This citywide, all-white committee was led by George Kondulf, the conservative young producer who was moved from the Chicago project to take on the directorship of the New York Federal Theatre in summer 1937. In March of that year, the New York City Project was brought more firmly under the supervision of Hallie Flanagan and Federal Theatre headquarters was moved from Washington, D.C., to New York. At about the same time, Flanagan met with the black directors of the Negro Unit to agree on a strategy for choosing plays. In a memo to Ellen Woodward, she recorded her plan: "(1) of one series of revivals, such as The Show-Off, of sure fire entertainment previously done in the white theatre; and (2) one series of the best negro plays which they can find from their own dramatists; (3) an occasional big spectacle, to be directed by Houseman, or Walker Hart, or some white director whom they choose."[27] Since presenting *Macbeth,* the Negro Unit had staged just one black-authored play, *Turpentine*, which was co-authored by Gus Smith and the white writer Peter Morrell and was a moderate success. It was followed by a series of poorly attended white-authored plays, culminating in the spectacularly unsuccessful production of O'Neill's sea plays in autumn of 1937.[28] Having tried options one and two, perhaps the Production Board and Negro Unit directors decided it was time for a spectacle that might replicate the success of *Macbeth* but also reengage its Harlem constituency. The need to attract the Harlem community back to the theatre appears to have been a strong driving force behind the decision to stage *Haiti*. The playreaders' reports certainly speak to this agenda, recommending *Haiti* as "full of color and action," and envisaging "A roaring melodrama," with "background and material [which] will always have a strong appeal to Negro audiences."[29] However the making of *Haiti* into what the *Amsterdam News* styled "Harlem's type of play" would require considerable work.

It was not a foregone conclusion that *Haiti* could be made into Harlem's kind of play: it was another white-authored play and another white director had been brought in to direct. Maurice Clark "came into the Federal Theatre from every kind of theatre known to America." Starting off in "the typical old repertory company," he established a school of theatre at the University of Nebraska before going into stock companies and finally gaining experience on Broadway. Disillusioned with commercial theatre, he immersed himself in workers' theatre in the late 1930s and joined the Theatre Collective based in Washington Square. They played at the Provincetown Theatre but also on picket lines and in union halls. A strong union man, Clark became president of Local 100, the United Federal Workers of America, a group affiliated with the Congress of Industrial Organizations (CIO).[30] He came to the Harlem Unit from the FTP's New York Children's Theatre, where he had staged innovative productions of *Horse Play* with performers from vaudeville and the circus as well as Copenning's *Jack and the Beanstalk*. *Haiti* would be his directorial debut for the Harlem Negro Unit, but he would later be assigned to rehearse and direct Theodore Browne's new drama *Go Down Moses*.[31] In an interview many years later, Clark offered his version of how and why William Dubois's play was chosen. Describing Dubois as "a southerner, a real southern Cracker," who became passionately interested in miscegenation, Clark foregrounded his own role in transforming the script:

A play had been kicking around among the directors and no one wanted it. It was called Haiti. . . . Well it wasn't a good play, but the idea that such a theme was to go untouched I just couldn't take. So I called the playwright up to my apartment. I said, "Look, this play should be done in Harlem, but if it is done in Harlem, I can tell you one thing. They will come right over the footlights and tear us to pieces. But," I said, "We can make a play out of this that they will love." And so we went to work, and we rewrote this play from top to bottom. Each day he thought I had finished work, but each day he came by with a new version and I had another one for him. And on and on from top to bottom, this was practically a new play. It was about the victorious Haitian republic over the greatest army that had ever been in existence.[32]

In exchange for transforming Dubois's play, Clark admits to agreeing to Dubois's request that black and white actors would not touch each other on the stage, although he presented a mixed curtain call.[33] Clark's recollections have been used to explain the transformation of Dubois's play. But in relying only on Clark's testimony, we ignore the appetite for investing in theatre as a platform for social change that Harlem activists had developed over several decades and continued through the four years of the FTP. In spring 1938, the black performance community in Harlem labored to make this white-authored drama a commemoration of black resistance to white rule.[34] Understanding how this was brought about requires us to examine the different versions of the manuscript, the role of black critics in shaping the reception of the production, and the ways in which the broader black performance community engaged Haiti, not only as a drama, but also as a historical and contemporary concern.

Haiti had served as an important symbol of black agency ever since the successful slave revolution of 1791 and declaration of independence in 1804. In the nineteenth century, Gabriel Prosser and Denmark Vessey, leaders of slave rebellions in the United States, promised their followers that the Haitian republic would help them destroy white Americans. Black freedom fighters frequently evoked the Haitian revolution in ways that not only inspired their followers but also terrorized whites, drawing on their fears of potent black masculinity and powerful voodoo. In turn, white Americans summoned the specter of a Haitian bloodbath to justify severe punishment of slave insurrections.[35] The events of the Haitian revolution, and the meaning African Americans ascribed to them, continued to challenge white supremacy well into the twentieth century. In 1915, however, Haiti, as a political entity and as a symbol of black resistance, came under renewed attack. Following a military coup that ejected the incumbent president, the United States invaded and occupied the black republic on the pretext of rescuing it from anarchy and defending foreign interests.[36] During the nineteen-year occupation that ensued, Haitians lived under a puppet government held in place by U.S. forces. Facing press censorship, surveillance, and curfews, Haitian protest movements were brutally suppressed.[37] The occupation of the black republic by an increasingly dominant United States meant that tales of Christophe's fort, Toussaint's heroic leadership, and the defeat of Napoleon's army risked being supplanted by harrowing new accounts of twentieth-century colonial violence. In protesting U.S. occupation of an independent black state, African Americans resisted the emerging colonial narrative and called for the reinvigoration of Haiti as a place where peoples of African descent had not only successfully resisted white rule in the past, but must resist white rule in the future. As W. E. B. Du Bois explained in the November 1933 issue of *Crisis*, African Americans "must cease to think of Liberia and Haiti as failures in government. . . . these are the pictures of each other which white people have painted for us and which with engaging naïveté we accept, and then proceed to laugh at each other and criticize each other before we make any attempt to learn the truth."[38] By spring 1938, African Americans had learned one truth: U.S. occupation of Haiti had left in its place no model new democracy, but rather an authoritarian leader who presided over a state economically dependent on, and financially beneficial to, the United States.[39]

Harlem knew that Haitian heroes were coming to town in spring 1938. In the weeks leading up to opening night, which was scheduled for late February, black newspapers paid close attention to the progress of rehearsals, informing readers of casting decisions, revealing the secret marriage of its star, Rex Ingram, who would play the lead role of Christophe, and explaining why black Americans should be interested in contemporary political developments in Haiti.[40] It was also reported that cast members had been coached in the early history of Haiti by Arthur Schomburg, a collector, historian, and historiographer of black life, and that his lectures had emphasized the courage and heroism of Haiti's heroes Toussaint and Christophe.[41] While some black newspapers were still confused as to whether William Dubois was their very own W. E. B. Du Bois, the better informed *Amsterdam News* cast doubt on the capacity of a white playwright to render a drama of black resistance. Following a preview performance that took place on February 17, the *Amsterdam News* published a letter of complaint written by an audience member, Harold Williams. In his letter, which he had originally sent to the Federal Theatre's promotions department, Williams expressed his dismay at the portrayal of black manhood in *Haiti*. Claiming ownership of Haiti's history and culture for the black community, Williams explained: "Because of our knowledge of the Haitian Revolution my friends and

I believe the play did not correctly represent the spirit of Haiti. We think Mr. Dubois (of the New York Times Dramatic Department) is prejudiced in his outlook: in that he misrepresents the Blacks." Toussaint, he complained, was wrongly treated as a common soldier rather than as the Governor-General of Haiti: "the treatment given him in the play is a concoction typical of the American attitude toward Negroes." Moreover, Williams and his friends believed that Christophe was similarly represented through the sneering eyes of whites: "Christophe" he complained, "gives more the appearance of a well-bred house servant, than a mature, shrewd man capable of leading a people." He was also contemptuous of the errant story line that singled out Odette as being critical to the success of the Haitian revolution. A mixed-race French woman, Odette is unaware of her dual heritage but somehow feels compelled not to betray her knowledge of Haitian spies.[42]

The day following the preview the *New York Times* reported that *Haiti's* opening, scheduled for February 23, had been delayed, with no firm date set for the first night. In a press release covered by the *Amsterdam News* on February 26, the WPA Department of Information claimed the postponed opening was due to difficulties in procuring period furniture. However, a Federal Theatre memo dated January 24 suggests that delays in acquiring set materials were already accounted for and had pushed back the planned opening from the week of February 14 to February 23. Following the preview performance, opening night was postponed for a further week.[43] A writer for the *Afro-American* suspected something was up. When *Haiti* finally opened on March 2, the newspaper printed two articles that reported the widely held belief that the delay was a result of the unenthusiastic response of audiences to the preview performance: "Although no official statement has been given out, it is reported that adverse criticism given the play by a group of pre-viewers, is responsible. Critics objected to the characterization given Toussaint L'Ouverture by William Dubois, white, who authored the play. . . . It is being reported that the play is being mended and smoothed frantically during these days of waiting." The *Afro-American* repeated the charge in a follow-up article, explaining that Dubois's play "as first written" had not done justice to the bravery of Haitians and changes had to be made accordingly.[44] *Haiti* was hardly the first, nor would it be the last, Lafayette Federal Theatre offering to be delayed: *Macbeth* had opened behind schedule, while Harlemites had now been anticipating the opening of the musical *Sing for Your Supper* for more than eighteen months. *Amsterdam News* columnist Lou Layne joked that Harlemites had added a new simile to their vocabulary: "as indefinite as a Lafayette Theatre opening." Although there may have been a variety of reasons why a Federal Theatre opening might have been delayed, the *Afro-American*'s view that Haiti was "being mended" appears to be supported by textual evidence. In fact, Harold Williams's criticisms correspond very closely to a revised manuscript held in the Federal Theatre archive at George Mason University.[45]

The four versions of the manuscript contain subtle differences that appear to support the *Afro-American*'s claims of last-minute revisions. Two were published in 1938. The first, entitled "Publication 50-S," was published by the FTP in April 1938. A second version was published later that year by Random House as part of a collection entitled *Federal Theatre Plays*. In addition, the Performing Arts Library of the New York Public Library holds a manuscript version. It is smartly bound in navy blue leather and includes the author's name and the title "Complete Working Script" in gold lettering on the spine. Contained within this volume are photographs of the Lafayette production, stage designs, costume and property plots, and a light-hanging plot, as well as a frontispiece that includes the typewritten date of March 2, 1938, which was the opening night. The seeming completeness of this volume makes it tempting to see this as the working script used by the Harlem Negro Unit. In fact, this manuscript is very close to the two published manuscripts. By contrast, a fourth manuscript containing a greater number of significant variations is held in the FTP Archive at George Mason University. This unpublished and undated version is cataloged as "Revised Edition."[46]

In the absence of a director's report and production bulletin for *Haiti*, it is difficult to establish beyond doubt which if any of these was the version used for the seventeen-week run at the Lafayette. Each could be rendered sympathetic to the Haitian revolution in production, however, only the "Revised Edition" includes amendments that tie it to the criticisms reprinted in the *Amsterdam News* following the February preview. For much of the play the four manuscripts are identical. Set in Haiti in 1802 after the slaves have rebelled and killed their slave-masters, the island is governed by Toussaint L'Ouverture. The play opens with Toussaint and Henri Christophe contemplating the arrival of the French army. Led by Napoleon's brother-in-law General Leclerc, the French have come to reestablish French control over the island and reimpose slavery. Under Toussaint's direction, and with the reluctant compliance of his second-in-command, Christophe, the Haitians retreat to the hills, but they refuse to surrender. The French capture Toussaint through trickery but are finally forced to flee when Christophe, now the Haitian leader, leads a heroic expedition down from the hills that overwhelms the invaders. Important subplots include a romance, a father's search for his long-lost daughter, and a case of mistaken racial identity on the part of an apparently white French colonial woman named Odette. Married to a malevolent French colonel, Odette has an instinctive sympathy for the Haitians on account of her mixed-race heritage. She omits to tell her husband that Jacques and Christophe have been spying on the French headquarters, which is one of several factors leading to the Haitian victory. Although neither Odette nor her French compatriots know it, Odette is the product of a love affair between a Haitian slave, Jacques, and his slave-master's white wife. Harold Williams's complaint suggests that it was Odette's character that had originally been used by the playwright to illustrate the dangers of miscegenation.[47] If a production had presented Odette as the "tragic mulatta," is it easy to see how this play could have gone down the route of Griffith's *Birth of a Nation*: interracial sex leads to mixed-race progeny, mixed loyalties, and consequently, a short step toward black rule. However, the response of the black community to the play in spring 1938 suggests they saw a version where the heroism of Toussaint and Christophe took center stage.

All four manuscripts deliver a well-won Haitian independence. However, there are subtle variations between them that suggest that the "Revised Edition" was amended following the negative response to the preview performance. We can assume that the two published versions received the consent of the author, and in fact, these two versions are the most alike. The "Revised Edition," however, contains some variations in characterization that seem to support the *Afro-American*'s claims that *Haiti* needed to be fixed before it could open. Toussaint appears less naïve and Christophe steelier than in the Random House and FTP publications. For example, in all four versions, Toussaint is cautious and has patience enough to retreat to the hills to wait and see whether the French come in peace or, as his comrades suspect, to reimpose slavery and French control on the island. In both published scripts and in "Complete Working Script," Toussaint asks Christophe: "Did you think I'd give up all we won together? First I will taste General Leclerc's 'abundance-and-peace' from a safe distance." In the "Revised Edition," although Toussaint takes the same course, an additional phrase is inserted, in which Toussaint seems to explicitly reject charges of naïveté: "Did you think I'd give up all we won together—*like a trusting schoolboy?*" (revisions in italics).[48] In the "Revised Edition," Christophe is more bloodthirsty and merciless toward his enemy. Although there is no mention of it in the other scripts, in the "Revised Edition," Christophe nonchalantly recalls the mas-

FIGURE 16 Alvin Childress as Jacques, Louis Sharpe as Toussaint, and Rex Ingram as Henri Christophe in Act 1, Scene 1 of the Harlem Negro Unit's *Haiti*, 1938. Library of Congress, Music Division, Federal Theatre Project Collection, ML31.F44 Production Records, Photographic Prints File, Container 1177.

sacre of white slaveholders, observing that Odette's white mother left Haiti just in time: "We made a clean sweep of the Moreaus."[49] Later, in Act 2, Christophe's black nationalism is made more prominent. Informing Odette that he has killed her odious husband, Christophe declares: "There can be no truce between black blood and white." Christophe also introduces himself in the "Revised Edition" as the governor of Northern Haiti and "the first of the blacks."[50] These subtle changes may have been a response to Harold Williams's charge that Christophe appeared more as a "well-bred house servant, than a mature, shrewd man capable of leading a people."[51]

Further evidence to support the contention that the "Revised Edition" may have been the working script is found in the insertion of explanatory nouns, in place of technical terms, presumably to ensure the drama could be understood by the widest possible audience. For example, in all versions of the play, Christophe comments wryly on the luxuries that the French have brought with them to Haiti. But whereas in the two published scripts and

"Complete Working Script," Christophe dismisses French excess with the phrase: "a little Tuileries—on *our* island!," in the "Revised Edition," this reference to the French royal pleasure garden is explained with a preceding phrase. A reference to the Frenchmen's "Lace, Lackeys, gold chairs" clarifies and adds to the characterization of the French as arrogant, indulgent, and distracted by luxury even during wartime.[52]

The "Revised Edition" appears to be a response to the criticism of the preview performance on February 17; whether it was the version that opened at the Lafayette is difficulty to establish with absolute certainty. Two things, however, are clear: the manuscript was altered, following complaints from the audience published in the *Amsterdam News*; and the version of the drama that opened at the Lafayette on March 2, was one the black performance community could wholeheartedly embrace. *Haiti* was warmly received by black critics. Leading the praise, the *Amsterdam News* found it "Brilliantly staged, excellently acted and enthusiastically received." The newspaper's exuberant response to the first night was such that it declared itself prepared to overlook *Haiti*'s historical inaccuracies in favor of its inspirational tone: "That the play departs from the bounds of actual history is of little moment. The result is as stupendous as any production ground out by Hollywood cameras and upholds the WPA federal theatre tradition of prodigious accomplishment."[53] The *Atlanta Daily World* agreed, calling it "The finest play produced in New York City in recent years."[54] Black critics were satisfied that Lafayette audiences witnessed black male characters in positions of power, who did not succumb either to the powers of voodoo or self-doubt. Night after night, black audiences were able to watch some of their favorite black actors playing the role of restrained, authoritative, and successful heroes: Rex Ingram, in the role of Christophe, was a rugged and daring character who loses his shirt, but never his head; Louis Sharpe, as Toussaint, was wise, weary, and diplomatic; while Alvin Childress, who played Jacques, was singled out by critics for his controlled performance.[55] By contrast, the French soldiers are savage and unmanly: they send their inferiors into dangerous battles to settle grievances over women and swig cognac and rum to keep up their courage. The director, Clark, later recalled, "Haiti broke the pattern of unequal black and white parts and even made the black parts dominate. It dared to show that blacks could create a nation of their own with a superior culture and the courage to defend themselves."[56] The Negro Unit had turned *Haiti* into Harlem's kind of play, as Brooks Atkinson, theatre critic for the *New York Times*, acknowledged: "If it is a tale

FIGURE 17 Rex Ingram posing as Henri Christophe in the Harlem Negro Unit's *Haiti*, 1938. Library of Congress, Music Division, Federal Theatre Project Collection, ML31. F44 Production Records, Photographic Prints File, Container 1177.

that made the hair of the French army curl, it does the same for the toupee theatregoer. Not very many historical plays turn out so well for Harlem."[57]

"Heroes of Haiti Live Again": Bringing Black History to Life

Once *Haiti* opened, black commentators spent less time commenting on production details and dedicated their energies to determining and interpreting the meaning of *Haiti* for black Americans.[58] Black newspapers advertised and organized Haitian-themed events that drew on the interest generated by the production. For example, to coincide with the anticipated opening night, a special Haitian evening was held on February 23, which included talks by Arthur Schomburg, as well as cast members Ingram and Sharpe. Laura Bowman and her husband, Leroy Antoine, performed the Haitian music they had composed and arranged for the production.[59] Both individually, and as a group, the cast played an important role in translating past struggles into present-day concerns. The entire *Haiti* cast was presented at a benefit to raise money for black arts, hosted by the Negro People's Art Committee, whose board was comprised of Negro Unit members, including Rex Ingram as president and Add Bates as vice president.[60] The cast also frequently appeared at Schomburg's seminars and public lectures on Haiti between February and May 1938.[61] Schomburg curated a special exhibition of his collection at the 135th Street library, which featured a number of Haitian artifacts, including the signatures of Toussaint, Christophe, and Dessalines. Enthusing about the exhibition, the *Amsterdam News* proclaimed it even more exciting than the play.[62]

"Heroes of Haiti Live Again" and "Toussaint L'Ouverture Comes to Life," are typical of the headlines appearing in black newspapers in spring 1938. Black press coverage emphasized the contemporary relevance of Haiti's past to black Americans and included lengthy discussions on the history of the Haitian revolution and the key figures that readers would encounter in the play.[63] For example, the *Atlanta Daily World* lamented the fact that Toussaint L'Ouverture had for too long been "neglected by school books and heretofore ignored as material for the drama" but applauded the fact that "Now that he has been immortalized in the stirring drama by William Du Bois [sic], intelligent members of the Negro race everywhere are clamoring for more information about L'Ouverture."[64] Such knowledge would not be confined to the theatre or to those fortunate enough to secure seats for the sell-out show. Commencing on May 31st, "Haiti Week in Harlem" opened with a pageant to commemorate the coronation of "the liberator of Haiti." According to a WPA press release:

> The pageant will start as "royal procession" from the corner of 125th
> Street and Seventh Avenue, and will march to the accompaniment of
> Haitian ceremonial music to the Lafayette Theatre, with Rex Ingram
> and a guard of honor leading the parade. The procession will end on
> the stage of the Lafayette Theatre and, supplemented by a program of
> music and the presence of many Haitian and Harlem notables, the
> actual coronation scene will be enacted. Everyone is welcome to attend.
> Among the speakers will be Dr. Binga Dismond and Dr. Arthur A.
> Schomburg, well-known authorities on Haiti and its dramatic history.

During Haiti week, Haitian girls were to visit Mayor La Guardia to invite him to the coronation, while "Sound trucks will cruise the streets of Harlem" to announce "the coming coronation of Christophe, the man who ran Napoleon's armies off the islands and brought about the complete independence of Haiti." The week's festivities ended on June 5 with a celebration of the 135th anniversary of the birth of Toussaint L'Ouverture sponsored by the Federal Theatre and the National Negro Congress (NNC).[65] Described by the *Amsterdam News* as a "tremendous success," the closing ceremony, which was chaired by Max Yergan (vice president of the NNC), took place on the stage of the Lafayette, bringing the community back to the theatre. The stars of *Haiti* gave speeches, Richard B. Moore, the influential Barbadian communist, delivered an address, and Wendell Phillips's tribute to Toussaint was read. Attendees included representatives of the Haitian consulate, the American Friends of the Haitian People, the New York Association for the Study of Negro Life and History, the UNIA, the NAACP, the Brotherhood of Sleeping Car Porters, and local churches.[66] On these and other Haiti events they reported on, black columnists insisted that pan-African histories needed protecting from white-authored narratives out to steal the black past. The commemoration of the Haitian revolution served as bulwark in this endeavor; it reminded black Americans and Haitians in Harlem of their shared heritage and offered a correction to the dominant narrative that justified U.S. invasion and fostered white cultural exploitation of an independent black state.

Political leaders also found the production a valuable prop in connecting the Haitian past with the African American present. Adam Clayton Powell Jr. used his regular column in the *Amsterdam News* to urge Harlemites to see *Haiti* immediately. Black audiences, he said, would get "a strange thrill in that last act when the Haitian masses, led by Christophe, sweep down from the hills through the French line and establish their freedom."[67] Powell made a direct link between those black men and women who found strength and courage to resist the Napoleons of the past and those who would struggle against fascism and Hitler in the present: "In this hour, when the borders of liberty are becoming increasingly narrow and the frontiers of freedom are receding, it is inspiring to note that there were once raggedy fellow blacks who were able to rise up and crush Napoleon's best. As long as this spirit is free in the world, the Napoleons and Hitlers are not to be feared."[68] Powell went on to lament the paucity of men and women prepared to take risks to defend their freedom, reserving particular criticism for Austria's failure to stand up to Nazi Germany and the persecution of a local communist by the American Legion and the Catholic Church.[69] Linking the history of Haitian resistance, not only to contemporary black internationalist

FIGURE 18 Act 3, Final Scene of the Harlem Negro Unit's *Haiti*, 1938. Library of Congress, Music Division, Federal Theatre Project Collection, ML31.F44 Production Records, Photographic Prints File, Container 1177.

struggles, but also to the politics of the Harlem Negro Unit, Powell suggested black Americans had a duty to see the play and study the forces that led to self-emancipation.

Others used the production to focus special attention on Haiti's ongoing struggle to resist subordination both at the hands of the United States and also by the American-supported Rafael Trujillo, the authoritarian leader of the neighboring Dominican Republic. There had been extensive coverage in the black press of the Dominican Republican Army's massacre of Haitians in October 1937 as well as the negotiations that led to the payment by the Dominican Republic of a $750,000 indemnity.[70] Attention was also paid to groups beyond the United States and Haiti that were campaigning for black freedom on a global scale. For example, the *Chicago Defender* gave prominent coverage to the founding meeting of the International African Service Bureau in London. It quoted from its new manifesto, which affirmed the symbolic importance of Haiti and Liberia as "the only states where to be black is not a stigma . . . an example of the capacity of Africans and peoples of African descent to govern themselves."[71]

All this activity meant that when rumors circulated that *Haiti* was to be taken over by a commercial theatre company and moved to Broadway, it was not difficult to frame resistance to the takeover as part of the same struggle: just as Haitians had wrested their liberty from the French, then the Americans, and, more recently, the Dominican army, black Americans must resist white attempts to control Haiti's past. As part of that struggle, the black performance community would fight to keep *Haiti* in Harlem. Beginning in June 1938, Negro Unit workers, theatre unions, black newspapers, and political and civic organizations, orchestrated an intensive campaign to prevent *Haiti* from being moved downtown. On June 24, these diverse groups came together at a mass meeting at the Harlem YMCA to build a campaign to keep the Lafayette open and fight racial discrimination in the FTP. "Outstanding leaders" lending their support included Langston Hughes, playwright and actor Frank Wilson, Richard Moore and Adam Clayton Powell Jr. Leaders of the Negro Labor Committee, the NNC, and the Harlem YMCA all committed to using their resources to ensure that the theatre would not be closed down, even for the summer. Pickets were organized outside the Lafayette, with placards calling on Harlemites to "help us in our fight to save your community theatre," and promising, "your support will help us save your community theatre." Others declared "we protest the liquidation of the Negro theatre," and "our productions not only entertain but educate, see Haiti." The *Amsterdam News* was at the forefront of the campaign. *Haiti* was Harlem's play, and attracting Harlemites to the Lafayette Theatre was, the newspaper claimed, "the sole motivation behind the ultimate selection of "Haiti." Broadway was ignored. Every other demand, including the predilections of every group of theatrical force outside Harlem, was brushed aside to assure the production of "Harlem's type of play." Featuring the campaign on its pages throughout June, the newspaper suggested that higher black attendance (it estimated that fewer than 20,000 of the 74,000 theatregoers who attended *Haiti* were black) might help ensure the production stayed at the Lafayette. No official records were kept of the racial makeup of the audiences that saw *Haiti*, but its long run and well-documented popularity with black audiences suggest that it was likely seen by more black Americans than any other FTP show. Black newspapers reported repeat group bookings from a diverse range of black associations and organizations, while white critics, who attended early on in the

run, commented on the predominantly black audiences.[72] In its efforts to maintain black theatre audiences for the production, the *Amsterdam New* urged its readers to go and see the production in order to help ensure that "what is justly Harlem's own" remained in "its only rightful home in Harlem." It would be, the newspaper added, a source of great regret if those "actors, directors and technical experts, who have worked so hard to build a substantial Negro theatre in Harlem, must go outside Harlem for their reward."[73]

Behind the campaign was the fear that any decision to leave the Lafayette dark in summer 1938 might be a prelude to the permanent closure of the Harlem Unit. Such anxiety was not without substance: WPA budget cuts,

FIGURE 20 Poster advertising *Haiti* at the Copley Theatre, Boston. Library of Congress, Music Division, Federal Theatre Project Collection.

the rising cost of the Lafayette's rental charges, and the need to renegotiate the lease cast uncertainty over the Negro Unit's future.[74] Senior WPA administrators were quick to deny the charges, however. Flanagan insisted the decision to move *Haiti* from the Lafayette represented a temporary closure of the Harlem theatre on account of a desire to "draw in new audiences" for *Haiti* on Broadway. Certainly there was both ambition and precedent within the FTP for moving popular shows around the country to enable as many Americans as possible to see a successful production. To put it in perspective, *Macbeth* had played for ten weeks at the Lafayette before going downtown to the Adelphi and then on tour. *Haiti* ran uptown for just shy of seventeen weeks, the longest run in the Lafayette's twenty-five year history.[75]

Haiti ran for a record 103 performances at the Lafayette, where it was seen by an estimated 74,000 New Yorkers, before moving downtown to Daly's, where it opened on July 11. The black newspaper the *Atlanta Daily World* welcomed the opportunity afforded the Harlem Negro Unit to perform on the Great White Way and suggested it would encourage "Broadway [to] get over its scare-phobia as to how "NEGROPHOBES" might receive this mighty spectacle of . . . BLACK ISLAND DOMINANCE . . . and give "Milky Way" theatre-goers an opportunity to view some grand acting." Whites Americans, they suggested, might even benefit from seeing "plays where blacks gain dominance over whites . . . physically or mentally as the case may be."[76] In October, following the Broadway run, the troupe took the production to Boston for a short tour, playing at the same time as the Hartford Negro Unit, which was presenting its own four-night run of Dubois's drama at the Avery Memorial.[77] When *Haiti*'s run finally came to an end that autumn, black groups lamented its loss and questioned the motives for its discontinuance. The Colored Actors and Performers Association sent a strongly worded telegram to the WPA's national office: "We being necessarily interested in the advancement and development of Negro culture, see in the success of the Federal Theatre Production 'Haiti' the interpretative means towards realizing our objectives. Protesting therefore the unfair closing of Haiti we classify such tactics as rank discrimination and demand 'Haiti's' immediate reopening to continue this successful run."[78] They were informed by WPA administrator Ellen Woodward, that *Haiti*'s long run—in Harlem and on Broadway, followed by a two-week tour in Boston—had finally "exhausted" the audience for the show. Audience numbers had started to drop.[79] Shows such as *Haiti* were usually the most visible sites of negotiation between Harlem's performance community and senior Federal Theatre administrators. Individual productions often served as vehicles through which to channel underlying and structural issues about African American roles within the Federal Theatre. Behind the scenes, however, there was also a series of organizations, as well as loose-knit networks, which developed and evolved during the course of the Federal Theatre Project and influenced the programming and direction of the Harlem Negro Unit.

Protest, Pressure, and the Black Performance Community in Harlem

The public meeting at the Harlem YMCA in June 1938 to protest the moving of *Haiti* was the culmination of an interrelated series of campaigns, private lobbying, and public pressure which had shaped the unit since its inception. These campaigns would dominate the last year of the project. Demands for action took many forms and came from many quarters: delegations to WPA offices in Washington, D.C.; formal letters to WPA administrators; letters to newspapers; setting up of new networks and the organizing of public meetings. National organizations that lobbied and kept close watch on the New York FTP's handling of the Harlem Negro Unit included the NAACP, NUL, the NNC, and the Colored Actors and Performers Association. In addition, a variety of new organizations sprung up for the purpose of coordinating action between these groups and those working on the Federal Arts Projects including the Negro Arts Committee, which compiled a fifteen-page brief protesting racial discrimination in the FTP in spring 1939. The cuts to the Federal Theatre also inspired the formation of the Harlem Cultural Committee (HCC), which was sponsored by the NAACP, the Negro Actors Guild, NUL, and the NNC. In May, the HCC organized a two-day conference which considered the impact of the Federal Arts Programs and "specifically the extent to which Negroes have benefitted from the Federal Arts Projects both economically and culturally." The conference pledged to maintain pressure for the passage of legislation to establish a permanent Bureau of Fine Arts. When the FTP was closed down in June 1939, the HCC continued to meet regularly at the Lafayette Theatre to coordinate a campaign of redress. This included mobilizing its membership to pressure the Senate Subcommittee on Appropriations to restore funding to the Federal Theatre and attempting to get dismissed FTP workers assigned to other federal programs.[80]

The black performance community employed a variety of organizations and methods to change the Federal Theatre: advice, pressure, protest, and demands were communicated through prominent individuals and national and local civil rights organizations, as well as through alliances with other WPA workers and unions. Workers of all ethnicities from across the Arts Projects regularly protested job cuts and work conditions, as well as the type of work they were asked to carry out. In June 1937, Edna Thomas had been part of a seventy-five-strong delegation of Arts Projects workers from New York and Philadelphia who traveled to the WPA's administrative offices in Washington. The protestors refused to leave the WPA offices until they were granted a meeting with deputy WPA administrative assistant Aubrey Williams. In New York, pickets, strikes, and clashes with the police were not uncommon. According to the *New York Times*, six hundred artists were inspired to occupy the FTP's 42nd Street headquarters. Once inside, they held captive a WPA official as a bargaining tool to protest large-scale job cuts that hit the WPA in July 1937.[81] WPA officials, including FTP administrators, often found themselves on the receiving end of mass protests against budget cuts imposed by Congress, which they had been powerless to resist. As a jobs creation program, the greatest proportion of Federal Theatre expenditures was on salaries, and there was often little administrators felt they could do to offset the impact of widespread job losses. However, when it came to the complaints of African American project workers against racially discriminatory employment practices and programming, Federal Theatre administrators were responsible for, and vulnerable to, the charges leveled against them. On reading the correspondence of senior white administrators, you would be forgiven for thinking that they were impervious to criticism and unwilling to entertain any charges of racial discrimination. Yet this defensive posturing belied a real and, for some, growing awareness that the Federal Theatre was obligated to listen to, and engage with, the views of the community it purported to serve. The black performance community understood this from the start.

The Harlem Negro Unit's autonomy within the FTP depended on circumstances and changed over time. Often, but not always, it was directly shaped by the sustained pressure and campaigns organized by the black performance community. Action tended to revolve around a number of key issues: insufficient numbers of African Americans employed on the New York project in proportion to the black population of the city and the rate at which black employees were fired when the FTP faced budget cuts; the type of plays and roles available to black actors and theatre professionals within the FTP; discrimination on the project; and the demand for black autonomy and control of the Harlem Negro Unit. Although each of these issues surfaced throughout the four years in which the unit operated, the choice of plays and who did the choosing often served as a flashpoint for this broader array of concerns. Roy Wilkins, assistant secretary for the NAACP, put it bluntly in a letter to Lavery, written in April 1939: "Since the very beginning of the Federal Theatre Project, this association has made repeated objection to the plan and organization of the project which permitted certain persons not heretofore familiar with Negro life and thought to pass upon plays deemed to reflect accurately Negro life. . . . It seems to us too much to expect that white people, many of them without previous experience or knowledge of Negroes except the information they have received from newspaper headlines, should be set up as judges of plays of Negro life."[82] The NAACP was not the only national black rights organization to put pressure on Federal Theatre directors. The Urban League had pressured the Federal Theatre to appoint a black director of the Harlem Negro Unit in 1936, especially after Rose McClendon was forced to retire on account of ill health.[83]

During the first year of the Federal Theatre, the eleven, semiautonomous production units that made up the New York FTP were part of a decentralized system that allowed for a measure of control by individual units.[84] For the Negro Unit this meant a three-person team of Carlton Moss, Gus Smith, and Harry V. Edward, following the departure of John Houseman in summer 1936. This triumvirate of black directors had steered the unit, sometimes with competing visions and priorities through to April 1937 when Gus Smith was made the unit's managing producer, supported by four black supervisors.[85] The Negro Unit was also affected by changes further up the administrative chain. Following the reduction in personnel in the wake of WPA budget cuts in July 1937, all four Arts Projects were removed from the authority of the New York WPA administrator and reorganized into Federal Project No. 1 with Paul Edwards as administrator, reporting directly to Ellen Woodward, the head of the Women's and Professional Projects of the WPA in Washington D.C. George Kondulf became the director of the New York FTP, and under his leadership, the city's theatre project was centralized. Crucial to this was the establishment of a new "Production Board" with the authority to approve plays and appoint directors and producers. This posed a problem for the Harlem Negro Unit, for though the Production Board was comprised of unit producers, it did not include any representation from the Negro Unit. The same was true for the Board of Appeals. Set up to deal with instances of unfair dismissal, including allegations of discrimination, its all-white membership was a very public example of routine racial discrimination on the FTP.[86]

The continued lack of representation on the Production Board propelled many of the protests led by the black performance community in New York since only this body could approve new productions. Excluded from the new centralized bodies, members of the Harlem Negro Unit had few reasons to trust Kondulf. Gus Smith would later claim that Kondulf had little interest and less faith in "Negro culture" and that he had continually tried to get the Harlem Unit to perform the kind of "black drama favoured by whites, such as *The Emperor Jones* and *Mississippi Rainbow*."[87] At the same time, Smith and other black supervisors of the Harlem Negro Unit had to manage the expectations of the black performance community, whose members believed that the establishment of black leadership at the unit in 1936 would enable it to produce plays designed to appeal to the Harlem community. The gap between expectation and reality was a source of mounting tension between the Negro Unit and New York FTP's white administrators, which came to a head just as *Haiti* was playing at the Lafayette. In April 1938, following months of pressure, Paul Edwards set up a black advisory committee to meet with senior FTP officials, including Hallie Flanagan, for the express purpose of discussing "the type of shows to be produced" by the Harlem Negro Unit. The advisory committee was made up of Fredi Washington (stage and screen actress and a founder of the recently established Negro Actors Guild), Elmer Carter of *Opportunity*, Adam Clayton Powell Jr. and Walter White of the NAACP.[88] The aim of those who agreed to serve on the advisory board was to influence decision making on the development and production of black dramas, decisions currently made by the entirely white Production Board. Correspondence in the records of the NAACP, however, makes plain that the black advisory committee was hardly consulted. Just two months after the committee was formally established, White and Washington had come to the conclusion that the Production Board had used the advisory board as "window dressing."[89] The Negro Arts Committee went further, seeing the appointment of the committee as an attempt by Edwards to "virtually shut off further protest by organized workers on the WPA."[90]

Early in the summer of 1938, just as *Haiti* was being prepared for its transfer downtown, FTP administrators decided to move clerical staff and the workshop from the Lafayette Theatre to the 23rd Street FTP headquarters. Taken together, these decisions created what Walter White described in a letter to Paul Edwards as a "universal feeling that this is a step toward dissolution of the unit."[91] Meanwhile, black supervisors at the Harlem Negro Unit, including Thomas, Smith, Edward, Byron Webb, and Harmon Unthank met on June 9, 1938, to discuss the problems they faced. In a series of recommendations submitted to FTP managers and to Hallie Flanagan, they demanded a permanent Negro Theatre in Harlem to serve as "the chief operating centre for all Negro productions," and the appointment of a black supervisor of the Harlem Negro Unit who would have "executive authority" over all Negro Unit personnel. They also requested that the Board of Appeals include a "Negro" among its members. However chief among their demands was the insistence that an African American sit on the Production Board because it was regarded as the engine that drove programming and therefore shaped the range, number, and quality of roles available to African Americans. Such measures, they suggested "would go far in counteracting the subtle discrimination because of race or creed, that now exists."[92]

The Production Board never issued a formal reply to the demands of the Negro Unit supervisors, but it did meet with the black advisory committee soon after. In the wake of this meeting the WPA issued a press release announcing: "Federal Theatre Plans Varied and Extensive Program for Negro Actors." Emphasizing that *Haiti* was soon to be staged in the "Broadway area," with another "Negro production to be included on the next Caravan Theatre schedule," the June press release also took care to mention its recent conference with the black advisory board. The WPA's public statement suggests that the cumulative pressure had influenced programming. The autumn schedule would include two shows, both of which required sizeable black casts. Between *Sing for your Supper*, "the project's first big musical show" and a production of George Bernard Shaw's *Androcles and the Lion*, scheduled for September or October, over one hundred African Americans would be employed, a figure comparable to the numbers engaged in *Haiti*. Responding directly to the complaints leveled against the Production Board, the statement referred to the pleasing number of "worth-while Negro scripts" under consideration, the most promising of which was *Liberty Deferred*, Hill and Silvera's black Living Newspaper, which Maurice Clark and Gus Smith were apparently "whipping . . . into shape." As described in chapter 2, *Liberty Deferred* never made it to production. However, other manuscripts that had "captured the interest of project officials" and were "being given serious consideration as an integral part of the fall plans," included a "recently discovered script [that] concerns the intricacies of the underground railroad of the Civil War period," and Countee Cullen's *St. Louis Woman*. Promising an "uninterrupted program that will require large-scale employment of Negro artists through the summer and winter," Federal Theatre administrators suggested that "no previous program has compared with it."[93]

The promises made by the Production Board did little to relieve the pressure, and protests continued through summer 1938. Noting that they had received no formal reply to their joint letter, the Negro Unit supervisors again put forward their complaints, this time in a series of formal briefs presented by the Supervisors Chapter of local 100, a chapter of the United Federal Workers of America, a union set up to organize WPA workers and which was a member of the newly formed CIO. This time round the Negro

Unit supervisors enlisted statistical data to make the case that equality of opportunity had been denied to African American workers on the FTP. African Americans were not appointed to supervisory roles in numbers proportionate to the total number of workers on the project. With a total of 4,200 personnel on the project, of which 400 were African Americans, African American supervisors should occupy 10 percent, or 40 supervisory positions. As of August 1938, however, there were only 26 African American supervisors.[94]

Although the Harlem community struggled to get African Americans promoted to senior positions in numbers proportionate to their employment on the project, the number of black supervisors in the Federal Theatre was consistently and considerably higher than in any of the other Arts Projects.[95] The number of black directors and supervisors, moreover, is not the most reliable gauge of the extent to which black Federal Theatre employees and their supporters in the community were able to shape programming. Although it would be simplistic to view programming decisions across the Negro Units through a progressive frame—concessions were hard won and sometimes won on the back of previous intransigence—in the last year of the project, senior Federal Theatre administrators in New York City became more sensitive to, and even capitulated to black performance communities when it came to questions of programming. In January 1939, *Opportunity*, the journal of the Urban League, published a review of the Unit's current production, *Androcles and the Lion,* by Edward Lawson. Though he praised the acting, staging, and direction, he lamented that the Lafayette's latest show had played to largely white audiences and failed to "strike a responsive chord in the Negro community for which it was produced." Lawson called for the Federal Theatre to bring to Harlem: "a significant modern drama of Negro life that speaks its message directly to the masses and that entertains the Negro first, the white folks afterwards." This prompted Hallie Flanagan to write to the editor of *Opportunity* defending the FTP's record of production at the Lafayette and insisting that "We have always consulted with our Negro group as to choice of plays." Flanagan was right: the Federal Theatre had always attempted to "consult" black communities. It held, among its numerous research files, a "List of Representative Negro Citizens" who were asked for their opinions on the Negro Unit's repertoire in order to avoid "misunderstandings."[96] However the use of the possessive "our" by Flanagan is indicative of how nervous Federal Theatre administrators were of losing control of any consultation process. While Flanagan's sense of ownership strikes a troubling note, her desire, however motivated, to avoid "misunderstandings" was a view widely shared by Federal Theatre administrators unused to "dealing" directly with African Americans as equals or even as employees. By 1939, Flanagan's reiteration of the Federal Theatre's commitment to consulting communities was a defensive rather than a confident posture: the pressure from black performance communities over four years had pushed her, and other senior officials, to understand that consultation was not merely an exercise in public relations: the FTP had to first listen, and then act.

An example of how black community pressure worked, as well as the pushback from white FTP officials, is apparent in the debacle around the proposed scheduling of Octavus Roy Cohen's cliché-ridden racist drama *Come Seven* for the Negro Unit in Newark, New Jersey. White Federal Theatre administrators were adamant that black members of the Newark Negro Unit wanted to perform Cohen's dramatization of his "crap-shooting, chicken-stealing" stories, which had been serialized in the *Saturday Evening Post* over a decade earlier. First staged on Broadway in 1920, *Come Seven* had the dubious distinction of being the "first play on record with an entire white cast in black-face."[97] When the play was put into rehearsal at the Newark Negro Unit, members of the cast expressed their dissatisfaction to a range of groups including the Workers Alliance and the NAACP. When they, in turn, made representation to Emmet Lavery at the NSB, he and other FTP administrators repeatedly contested the notion that the black troupe was ill-disposed toward the Cohen play. Suggesting that black cast members had "insisted" the play be produced, Lavery deployed the argument that "Negro groups themselves have been pretty well divided on the question of what is and what is not a good Negro play."[98] While this is a fair characterization of debates within black theatre communities in general, there is no evidence to back Lavery's claim that Negro Unit cast members wanted to perform Cohen's drama. NAACP officials explained that complaints from Negro Units often came through them rather than directly to white FTP officials. Especially at a time of widespread job cuts, "The players cannot protest because of the fear of losing their jobs."[99] In an attempt to resolve the issue, Lavery called a conference in New York which included representatives from the Newark unit. Following the meeting the Cohen play was immediately withdrawn. In a letter explaining the outcome to the many organizations who had protested the choice of play, Lavery continued to defend the now aborted production on the somewhat irrelevant grounds that it had been assigned a prominent Broadway manager, Charles Hopkins.[100] Roy Wilkins was one of those who rejected wholesale Lavery's defense: African Americans, he conceded, might hold different views about what constituted good drama, but they were as one when it came to rejecting the "traditional stereotype treatment of the Negro" found in the work of Cohen. Moreover, Wilkins refuted the notion that being a Broadway producer offered any kind of re-assurance that a production would not cater to the lowest form of racial stereotyping: "The poorest recommendation a judge of Negro plays could have would be to say that he is a Broadway producer, because that means that he tends to judge Negro productions for their commercial rather than artistic value. The public, overwhelmingly white, will pay to see delineation of certain traditional roles and themes by or about the Negro, but will not support the portrayal of other themes even though the latter may be accurate, artistic, and expressive of true Negro life."[101]

When it came to questions of programming, a contested area that lay within their jurisdiction, Federal Theatre administrators were defensive of their record and keen to assert their commitment to promoting black theatre. Directly on the heels of the *Come Seven* debacle, *Opportunity*'s Edward Lawson wrote to FTP administrator J. Howard Miller, charging unfairness toward black employees on the project. In his response, Miller fell into hyperbole with the claim that "The Federal Theatre has done more for the cause of the Negro in the American Theatre than any organization in the past."[102] Finding themselves maneuvered into making exaggerated statements, white Federal Theatre officials had to find ways to live up to their own rhetoric and to resist the constant charges of racial discrimination. Frequently, this led white Federal Theatre administrators to backtrack and think again, to alter positions taken by senior white administrators, and to program the kind of dramas the black performance community was clamoring for. In June 1938, FTP administrators had bowed to pressure and issued a press release promising maximum employment for black actors in black dramas; when pressure mounted again in spring and summer 1939, some white FTP administrators stuck their necks out to get black dramas on stage.

African Slavery and the American Slave Trade on the Stage: *Panyared*

Black Federal Theatre workers and civil rights groups formed fluid black performance communities which shaped the dramas staged by Negro Units. The ability to effect change varied over time and place, and while there was no steady progressive march in the four years of the Federal Theatre, the cumulative effect of ongoing pressure can be seen in the functioning of both individual units and FTP departments such as the NSB. Official letters from the NAACP and strongly worded editorials in black newspapers demanded and usually received a direct response from white Federal Theatre officials. In turn, these forms of protest helped push the agendas of black Federal Theatre workers who organized in unions within the WPA and became part of flexible and temporary coalitions of cultural workers that sprang up to defend black Federal Arts Projects between 1935 and 1939. However, as described in chapter 2, sometimes this was not enough: even well-connected insiders such as Hill and Silvera, whose work was sponsored by the NSB, were unable to get their Living Newspaper staged. Nevertheless, black theatre manuscripts developed under the auspices of the FTP helped shape the landscape of what was imagined possible within the parameters of black Federal Theatre, even when they were not produced. In the case of the manuscript of *Liberty Deferred*, the contested revisions had a demonstrable impact on the ways in which white theatre practitioners within the FTP thought about the representation of black life on the American stage. This was particularly the case for the Director of the NSB, Emmet Lavery. In the wake of the failure to produce *Liberty Deferred*, Lavery went to great lengths to ensure that the next black manuscript to come his way did not meet the same fate.

Panyared, meaning "man seized" or "kidnapped," was the first installment of a trilogy of black histories by the Newark-based black playwright Hughes Allison. Allison was the author of the successful *The Trial of Dr. Beck*, which was first produced by the Negro Unit in New Jersey, and later by the Boston Negro Unit. The Federal Theatre also brought it to the Maxine Elliot Theatre for a run on Broadway in 1937. Allison's new drama begins in West Africa in 1800, and tells the story of the relationship between African intertribal warfare and the development of the international slave trade. It also portrays the horrors of the middle passage, Africans' resistance to enslavement, and the experiences of the enslaved on a plantation in South Carolina. Over three acts it follows the story of two West Africans, Bombo, a prince seized by American slavers as a result of a royal coup, and Zema, the mixed-race mistress of a white slaver on the West African coast. Both attempt to resist enslavement before, during, and after the Middle Passage. Allison uses white characters, including a priest, the ship's antislavery doctor, and a number of slavers, to consider the role of the church in supporting slavery as well as the devastating impact of the institution on both whites and blacks in America and Africa. White characters are not stock villains, and have a variety of motives for being involved in the slave trade. Africans are similarly motivated by diverse factors and are variously dignified, naïve, manipulative, altruistic, selfish, brave, and fearful. Their multiple roles, relationships with, and resistance to white slavers and plantation owners are interrogated through the course of the play. In its exploration of the intertwining of social, economic, and religious justifications of the slave trade, its depiction of the middle passage, and the complex relationships between slaves and slaveholders, *Panyared* met the FTP's mandate to produce original, well-developed drama that reflected the histories of the American people and nation.

Panyared also reflected debates taking place among African Americans about the merits of realism and the desire among some black theatre practitioners for a radical black realism. In the thirty-eight-page Foreword to his new trilogy, Allison argued that contemporary black theatre faced two hurdles: the neglect of African roots and a fear of realism. "Again and again the writer of Negro material has been warned that realistic Negro plays 'do not pay.' Why don't they pay? Because they offend."[103] Allison was not interested in debates about Brechtian alienation and catharsis. Rather, he was objecting to dramas such as Dorothy and DuBose Heyward's Broadway hit *Mamba's Daughters* (1939), that shielded theatre audiences from engaging with the realities of race in the United States by presenting African Americans in roles that were comical, musical, and entertaining. For men, this was usually the role of "Sambo" and for women, the role of the sexually available or at least conquerable black woman, such as *Mamba's Daughters'* "Lissa." Even *Stevedore* and Langston Hughes's 1935 drama *Mulatto*, he argued, deployed such stock characters. It was only in *Haiti*, a "blood and thunder melodrama" which made a "weak stab at history" that ""Sambo" and "Lissa" were given a much needed rest."[104] For Allison, the chance to develop a realistic black drama constituted a significant moment in the history of American theatre. By placing the histories of the slave trade and of slavery and its legacy on the stage, Allison believed Americans might get to know each other better. Indeed, he believed playwrights could serve as intermediaries, introducing Americans of different races to each other. Dedicating his playwriting talents to the cause of American democracy, Allison makes plain in the Foreword that *Panyared* is no tearing down of the American system. Rather, he is committed to pursuing what for many Americans was an equally radical proposition: "that the Negro is an integral part of America; that the Negro's destiny is now America's destiny."[105]

Emmet Lavery seemed to agree. Having failed to bring *Liberty Deferred* to production and in the face of growing protest from the black community in the spring of 1939, Lavery embraced this new black historical drama by a proven black author. In February, he began preparing publicity for *Panyared*. In a press statement issued on behalf of the NSB Lavery promised: "The first Negro trilogy ever attempted on the historical background of the American Negro is now in preparation for production by Federal Theatre." His reassurance that black drama was a priority went further: "It is the intention of Federal Theatre to present the first installment as soon as satisfactory arrangements for production can be made, following up the trilogy with later installments when ready."[106] Lavery sent the script out to local Federal Theatre units to drum up interest before passing it onto Hallie Flanagan in the hope of securing endorsement for a production at the highest level. Unfortunately Flanagan did not share Lavery's enthusiasm: it did not fit with her conception of race drama, and nor was it, in her view, authentic. Initially Flanagan couched her concerns in terms of how she imagined black Americans would respond, informing Lavery: "I do not wish this play released until it is very carefully checked by several very good Negroes. What would be the effect of such a production on our Negro companies?" Flanagan wanted *Panyared* checked by "very good Negroes," because the characterization, language, and story were at odds with how she thought Africans behaved. As she explained to Lavery: "The plot seems carefully worked out but I find the language of much of it impossible to swallow. Look at early scenes of *Bombo* and try to *imagine* a Negro saying: 'To find me uneasy about an enemy all of us have to face' etc." Flanagan's inability to imagine an African, even if he was a prince, speaking eloquently is suggestive of the broader limitations which shaped her approach to "the Negro" on the American stage. She was similarly dismissive of the African characters' names, which she found "dangerously comic."[107]

Although *Panyared* seemed to lack a certain realism, as Flanagan understood it, in other places it was all too realistic, particularly when it came to staging the violent capture and deportation of Africans. A scene wherein a feverish baby is separated from its mother before having its head smashed on a tree Flanagan pronounced "absolutely unproduceable." This was probably a fair assessment of this particular scene, but her peremptory conclusion that "By the end of the third scene it is apparent to me that a play dealing so violently with miscegenation is not possible for us; certainly not for any except a most gifted cast, director and designer," suggests that staged violence was the excuse rather than the reason to dismiss the play. In fact, the acts of staged violence were neither integral to, nor typical of, the play as a whole, which relied on threats of violence and on characters describing, rather than reenacting, the horrors of slavery. Allison was clearly aware that some white Americans might object to his representation (and perhaps any representation) of white violence, but in the Foreword to *Panyared* he insisted he had avoided sensationalism and in fact modified his depictions of racial violence "as much as any realist, with integrity, can modify them." Flanagan's conclusion that *"No one* could produce anything as horrible as this on *any* stage without being hauled off in a police wagon," suggested an unusual capitulation to the forces of conservatism for the Federal Theatre director who had supported plays on syphilis, slum housing, and attempted lynchings.[108]

Lavery composed his response to Flanagan's critique of *Panyared* just as he was weighing up how best to respond to accusations by the Negro Art Committee that he had deliberately obstructed production of the black Living Newspaper *Liberty Deferred*. In a frank, even impertinent letter to Flanagan, Lavery made an impassioned plea for *Panyared* and insisted she think again. Implying she had not read, or not properly read Act 3, Lavery notes: "you have no comments on Act III but it seems to me that the play cannot be understood without considering Act III in some detail." In her initial response to the play, Flanagan appeared to suggest that she had been reading an "African murder mysterie[s]". Frustrated by such an interpretation of *Panyared*, Lavery insisted: "It is not an African murder mystery . . . not a play about miscegenation, petty brutalities, or run-of-the-mill seductions. It is a play about slavery and how it really started, and I think you ought to re-read at once the very last page of the script." Lavery quoted at length from the final scene of the play in which Bombo, the enslaved African prince who has just received his freedom from the plantation owner, is asked what it feels like to be enslaved. Bombo replies: "It feels like de sky widout sun or moon or star; like de spring flowers buried under a deep winter snow; it's like de jungle widout a trail; it's a grave in de earth . . . wid you in it, alive."[109] Bombo's response, Lavery explained, was the 'key' to the play. Flanagan, he suggested, paid too much attention to the "inevitable crudities which would be eliminated in rehearsal, rather than to the imposing sweep of the story itself." Dismissing Flanagan's suggestion that to produce such a play would lead inevitably to censorship, Lavery insisted the play would develop understanding rather than arouse antagonism between the races.[110] Abram Hill, whom he asked to review the manuscript, agreed. Enthusiastically recommending production, he nevertheless shared Flanagan's reservations as to whether certain acts of violence could be staged, and suggested they take place off stage. Hill was presumably one of the "very good Negroes" whom Flanagan wanted to "check" the authenticity of Allison's play. Lavery took the trouble to send Hill's report to Flanagan, describing him as "one of our best playwrights here in the Bureau." Making *Panyared* a test case for black drama, Lavery put Flanagan under pressure, arguing that the decision came down to whether the Federal Theatre was about "encouraging or discouraging fine talent." Lavery was still urging the production of *Panyared* in April 1939, just months before the FTP was permanently closed.[111] Black dramas were finally getting the break they deserved. Had the project continued to operate through summer 1939, there is good reason to believe that with Lavery's backing, the Federal Theatre would have staged *Panyared*. While Lavery was advocating on behalf of Allison's play about slavery, the Harlem Negro Unit was busy rehearsing what would have been the Federal Theatre's first production of a black-authored drama about African Americans who fought and won freedom for themselves.

African American Agency and the U.S. Civil War in *Go Down Moses*

Browne wrote the drama of Harriet Tubman while he was still in Seattle, probably in early 1937. In early drafts it was a three-act playthat traced Tubman's experiences of slavery and her escape, as well as her many missions to rescue other enslaved women and men, and finally her experiences as a scout and nurse for the Union Army. Like all playwrights who wished to have their work performed by the Federal Theatre, Browne sent his manuscript to the NSB with a view to having it approved for production by a Federal Theatre unit. Although there is no extant manuscript of this version, we can piece together the plot from the playreaders' reports in July 1937. The early draft appears to have contained significant variation from the manuscript put into rehearsal by the Harlem Unit nearly two years later. For example, the 1937 version includes a melodramatic love story that begins on the Sedley plantation in Maryland, where Tubman grew up. When the man she loves escapes the plantation, Tubman is prompted to begin her own journey to freedom. John Silvera, who reviewed the manuscript for the Playreading Department, found it a "stirring and educational historical drama," and while he thought it appropriate for both black and white audiences, he suggested it was best suited for schools or "Negro Drama week." Although Silvera does not criticize the play, his hesitancy to recommend it for a Negro Unit production is noteworthy. Perhaps the criticism of other readers that it was melodramatic and wordy was one reason why. Fanny Malkin found the material interesting enough but felt it "poorly written and constructed," with too much "rambling and melodrama." Confident that this tried and tested author was capable of better, she recommended the script be revised. Another reader, Harold Callen, felt there was "too much exposition," resulting in a heavy, plodding plot.[112] Two years later, *Go Down Moses* had been trimmed to two acts. The manuscript devised in summer 1937, with its melodramatic and unwieldy plot, had become, by December 1938, a spare and unsentimental dramatization of how African Americans threw off American slavery.[113]

Browne left the Seattle Negro Unit in Spring 1938. In the winter of 1938–1939, he was employed as a playwright on the Boston Negro Unit. The move east was working well for him: both the Los Angeles and Harlem Units were considering staging a revised version of his latest drama. When in February 1939 the Federal Theatre's flagship Negro Unit in Harlem began casting for a major production of *Go Down Moses* Browne appeared to have taken the first step toward playwriting stardom.[114] Writing in anticipation of its opening in March 1939, Adam Clayton Powell Jr. used his "Soap Box" column in the *Amsterdam News* to pave the way for this "Gripping and thrilling," drama. Powell's comments suggest he had seen a manuscript considerably amended from the sentimental love story first presented to Federal Theatre play readers, for he noted, approvingly, that the "author keeps its feet flat on the ground."[115]

White Federal Theatre administrators on the New York project had long promised a program of black-authored dramas and this seemed like an ideal project to answer their critics. Yet the same administrators appear to have little concern for how it would impact other programs. The casting of Browne's drama became the source of new controversy on the New York project because of its indirect effect on the "Colored" Vaudeville Unit. Operating sporadically since summer 1937, members of the Vaudeville Unit were accustomed to fitting around other production units and schedules. But when, in early February 1939, its personnel were reassigned to audition for either *Go Down Moses* or *Sing for Your Supper,* actors and musicians in the Vaudeville Unit and the Negro Actors Guild of America protested the closure, arguing that it was yet one more instance of discrimination on the project.[116] Their protests fell on stony ground: white administrators dismissed the "validity" of their protest, since the majority of the vaudeville troupe was to be redeployed in a more serious drama.[117] George Kondulf, head of the New York FTP, felt entitled to "sacrifice other and perhaps lesser important activities," and insisted that Federal Theatre administrators need not consult individual units in order to make those decisions necessary for the "best possible functioning of the project."[118] Addressing the demand for serious "Negro drama" was one thing; respecting the work of black vaudevillians was quite another.

Go Down Moses presents a black hero not yet seen on the Federal Theatre stage: an armed, authoritative, and successful black woman, who leads the struggle against slavery and commands the respect of black and white men. In the revised manuscript, *Go Down Moses* opens with a brief prologue set in 1845 on the Sedley plantation in Maryland. Harriet and her mother Reba attempt to hide Harriet's brother, Jason, who has tried to escape the plantation to avoid being sold. Reba has been forced to bear multiple children, most of whom have been sold down the river. Fearing the unknown, Jason has given up on his journey to freedom and returned "home" to Harriet and Reba. Harriet attempts to hide him, risking her own and her mother's safety. When the overseer comes searching with a pack of dogs they soon uncover Jason's hiding place and take him off for a savage whipping. The juxtaposition of female and male characters in the prologue is striking: having witnessed her mother's agony in bearing children that will always be taken from her, Harriet discovers she has both the strength to resist and the authority to lead. However, unlike some of the men she encounters, her courage is rooted in and driven by the responsibility she feels for others. This theme is woven through Browne's two-act drama, for Harriet repeatedly challenges the gendered ideas of leadership and heroism held by many black as well as white Americans. Act 1 centers on Tubman's role in escorting slaves to freedom as a conductor on the Underground Railroad; Act 2 focuses on Tubman as a scout and nurse for the Union Army during the Civil War. In both roles she repeatedly encounters resistance from black and white men who question the legitimacy of black female leadership.

The characterization of women in *Go Down Moses* resists the stereotype of the strong black woman who emasculates black men. Both in the character of the Granny Sales, an elderly stationmaster on the railroad, and Harriet, the resolute leader of fugitives, women's leadership is rooted in their strong networks and relationships with each other, as well as their ability to work with and command the respect of black and white men working to end slavery. Such authority has been built through hard-fought battles

Auction Place for the sale of Slaves. See Model.

FIGURE 21 "Auction Place for the Sale of Slaves," set design for Theodore Browne's *Go Down Moses*. *Go Down Moses* Set Designs, Library of Congress, Music Division, Federal Theatre Project Collection. Set Designs File, Container 1127.

Log Cabin in Richmond Interior with Trap Door for hiding Slaves. See Model.

FIGURE 22 Granny's "Log Cabin with Trap Door for Hiding Slaves," set design for Theodore Browne's *Go Down Moses*. *Go Down Moses* Set Designs, Library of Congress, Music Division, Federal Theatre Project Collection. Set Designs File, Container 1127.

which have sometimes included confrontations with those who doubt women's capacity for leadership. But both women respect, and work alongside, men. For example, Granny and Harriet admire the passion for freedom evinced by the rebellious Cumbo, a mixed-race slave whom we meet on the auction block in Act 1, Scene 2. When the slave agent examines his teeth as if he were a horse, Cumbo knocks him unconscious. He steals the

The Recruiting Station in Boston.Color Suggestion. See Model.

FIGURE 23 Union "Recruiting Station in Boston," set design for Theodore Browne's *Go Down Moses*. *Go Down Moses* Set Designs, Library of Congress, Music Division, Federal Theatre Project Collection. Set Designs File, Container 1127.

white man's clothes to aid his getaway: "White man make me slave," he tells him, "White man gwine free me."[119]

Finding his way to the safe house of the pipe-smoking Granny Sales, Cumbo believes his rebellious spirit alone will set him free "Ah'm too much a man. Ah got sperrit! An' cain't nuffin kill dat sperrit."[120] Granny knows that spirit is not enough: knowledge, experience, and a reliable network are needed to prevent a freedom seeker from being torn limb from limb by the slave hunter's hounds. Nevertheless, she encourages Cumbo to tell his story of escape to help steady his resolve. But at the first sign of danger it is Granny's experience in handling white men in search of their "property" that saves Cumbo: she hides him from the slave hunters by performing the role of the frail, aging old woman that rendered elderly black women safe and dangerous at the same time. At Granny's mercy, Cumbo reluctantly follows her lead, but when Harriet arrives to lead him and a small group of fugitives on the treacherous journey north, he struggles to take orders from her. Cumbo's volatility poses a risk to the safety of the entire group, prompting Harriet to assert her authority in plain terms. Revealing her revolver, she lays out the rules of engagement: : "What Ah says is law an' gospel, you understand? What Ah tells yur ter do, Ah means fo' yuh ter do. Dat clar? No sass. No back talk. Ah won't stand fo' dat. Ah wonts de same respect you gib yo' mastuh. You ain't used ter takin' orduhs frum a nigguh. But membuh dis, a nigguh's takin' yuh ter freedom. She gwinter git yuh dar safe. Dar be hardships. But once you leabe dis room, dar ain't no turnin' back."[121] Harriet's efforts to wear the authority of the slave-master while sharing the faith of the freedom seeker are not enough, for she demands an absolute trust and a faith in another human being that enslavement has destroyed for Cumbo. When Harriet goes on ahead, to look out for slave patrollers, Cumbo is quick to question her authority: "Ah shouldna come wif dat 'oman," he tells the others.[122] Insisting that Harriet does not know her way to safety he sows seeds of division among the harried fugitives. Urging his companions to "free yosef," he turns on Jason, one of the men loyal to Harriet, who is traveling with his sick wife and baby. Harriet has given the infant a drink to keep him asleep and minimize the risk that the child might cry and expose their hiding place. Cumbo, however, insists that Harriet is using dark arts to maintain her influence over the group and has poisoned the child. Calling Jason a "weak, blind fool," he attacks his manhood: "What kince o'man is you? Wif yo' 'oman sick. . . . Won't do nuffin' fo' huh! Ef she was mine, Ah'd git huh outn dis place damn quick! Fo' she dies!"[123] Goaded into a fight, Jason is knocked down by Cumbo, just as Harriet returns. Pretending not to have seen the near mutiny, Harriet commands the fugitives to follow her into the creek to cover their tracks as the slave patrollers are in close pursuit. Desperately cold and tired, the rest of the group trusts her experience and enter the forbidding waters. But having lost face because the group has accepted the authority of a woman over his own, Cumbo cannot give way: "Ah'm thoo a-listnin' ter a nigguh actin' de white man ovuh me." From now on he will go it alone. Harriet is prepared to force him to follow them to freedom but Cumbo runs away. The risk that Cumbo is captured and forced to reveal their whereabouts is too great. Harriet shoots Cumbo dead, telling the escape party: "Daid nigguhs tell no tales."[124]

If the race and gender codes of the Underground Railroad are fluid, racial hierarchy remains firmly in place within abolitionist circles. In Act 1 we see Harriet interact with a number of men: the black preacher who exhorts his congregation to fund Harriet's trips to the slave South; Ralph Waldo Emerson, the poet and philosopher, who secures funding for Tubman from the wealthy abolitionists of Boston; the steady Quaker in Delaware who hides fugitives escaping to the North. The hierarchies within the abolitionist movement, however, are not glossed over: black men and women stand so white men can be seated; white men are called Mistuh and Suh, but address black Americans by their first names.

Within the formal arena of warfare, the figure of Tubman presented an even greater challenge to racial and gender conventions. Act 2 follows Tubman's employment as a Union Army scout and nurse. Browne's dramatization of the unconventional life of Tubman suggests a commitment to what would later be dubbed the self-emancipation thesis. White historians had long reconstructed the U.S. Civil War through the words and deeds of white politicians and generals. In such narratives, the noble desire to preserve either the Union, or the Confederacy, served as explanation for both cause and outcome of the conflict. The notion that the Civil War was a noble fight between a white North and white South and Reconstruction a terrible betrayal of the American ideal continued to shape both popular and academic histories of the conflict in the late 1930s. Responding to this deliberate whitewashing, first W. E. B. Du Bois, and then Herbert Apthecker found evidence for what many African Americans had always known: the Civil War was about slavery and the actions of the enslaved were crucial in making emancipation a central aim for the Union army.[125] Theodore Browne's Federal Theatre drama considers the self-emancipation thesis from the perspective of both black and white characters. In Act 2, Scene 2, Governor Andrew of Massachusetts and Colonel Robert Gould Shaw, who commanded the 54th Massachusetts Regiment (the first military unit of black soldiers in the North during the Civil War) discuss the meaning of the war to white northerners. For both men this is a war to free the slaves. But while it is a war white men will lead, the governor understands "It's their war," "Not ours." Shaw supports such a view: "They want a fight. Nobody's forcing them. They're forcing us."[126]

It is hard to overestimate the significance of a white actor playing the role of a famous white commander of a black military unit and declaring that African Americans had forced white politicians and generals to fight for their cause in the Civil War. Browne wrote his play, which includes a distressing scene set at a slave auction, at a time when the southern plantation myth was at the height of its popularity. The notion that slavery was a benign system of race relations where everyone knew their place and slaves were looked after was the centerpiece of Margaret Mitchell's bestselling 1936 novel *Gone with the Wind*. Made into a film in 1939, it broke box-office records. University history departments also played a crucial role in legitimizing and perpetuating the view that enslaved African Americans were inferior, passive, and ill-prepared for freedom. According to John Hope Franklin, Claude Bowers's, *The Tragic Era: The Revolution after Lincoln* (1929), was the most widely read account of the period, and one that provided the "intellectual foundation for the system of segregation and black disenfranchisement that followed Reconstruction."[127] By contrast, in *Go Down Moses* it is the actions of Harriet and other rebels that undermine slavery, both before and during the war. Browne's drama positions him firmly on the side of Du Bois, whose radical thesis on the role of African Americans in undermining slavery was published in 1935. In *Black Reconstruction in America,* Du Bois argued that the actions of slaves who ran away, fought in the Union Army, and sabotaged confederate production represented the largest general strike in history. He also lambasted Charles A. Dunning, John W. Burgess, and other professional historians who relied on exclusively white sources for promoting "the Propaganda of History."[128]

Du Bois and Browne's challenge to conventional narratives of African Americans' roles during the Civil War was part of a broader political and historical project that shaped Depression-era culture and that aimed at collecting and preserving, but also creating new sources to document the American past. One of the best known and most influential projects emerged from the Federal Writers Project (FWP), which conducted interviews with over 2,000 former slaves in seventeen states between 1936 and 1938. Officially titled "A Folk History of Slavery in the United States from Interviews with Former Slaves," the interviews were conducted predominantly by white FWP workers, though some African Americans were part of the interview team. Initially used by scholars of folklore, the WPA interviews remained marginal to historical accounts of slavery until the 1960s and 1970s, when the problems surrounding the reliability of the interviews (for example, in some cases, white descendants of slave owners asked former slaves what if felt like to be a slave) became the focus of scholarship. But as Stephanie Shaw reminds us, the interviews are also valuable sources documenting African American experience during the Depression.[129] The WPA slave interviews offer insight into how, and in what circumstances, white and black Americans were able to discuss slavery. Whether or not they offer reliable testimony for how former slaves experienced and remembered slavery, they are a reminder of just how uncommon it was for white Americans to hear, and for African Americans to tell whites about, black experiences of slavery.

The WPA interviews also remind us how long and how hard African Americans have been fighting to establish their roles in ridding the United States of its "original sin". Browne's harrowing picture of slavery, and affirmation of black Americans' vital role in fighting to end it, marked an important moment in American theatre history. At a time when popular culture and most academic histories were committed to whitewashing a defining moment in U.S. history, Browne and the Harlem Negro Unit could imagine an interracial cast, and an interracial audience, capable of something more. In Act 2, Browne dramatized not just the story of how African Americans fought for the right to fight, but how they had constantly to fight to recenter black freedom as the cause of the Civil War. In Massachusetts, two white men privately concede that the Civil War was a war for and about black Americans, yet when Harriet tries to enlist alongside black men in a regiment in New York State, she is told the war has nothing to do with her: "Den dey git tiahd o' seein' me all de time, so dey finely lowr' ter me dat dis war ain't got nuffin' ter do wif me—dat de white sojuhs ain't fightin' ter free de nigguhs nohow. Dey was fightin' ter save de Union! Whut Union?—Ah say, ef hit ain't de Union fo' freein' de slaves? An' dey hish up quick when Ah tells 'um dat!"[130] Harriet is eventually allowed to join the Union Army as a scout, and she plays a crucial role, first inspiring black soldiers in the field of battle and then tending to their wounds. Preparing for the battle to take Fort Wagner, Tubman reminds the black troops that their heroism will inspire other enslaved people to leave the plantation and join the Union Army. She also reminds them that the flag under which they fight is their flag, an American flag whose meaning is liberty for all Americans. White southerners, she says, have given up their right to the flag, and with it their right to define American liberty: "Unduh hit dey hab grind us up, an' put us in dar pockets fo' money. But de fust minute dey think dat old flag menas freedom fo' we culud people, dey pull hit down, an' dey run up a rag o'dar own."[131] The battle ends in military defeat: Fort Wagner was not taken by the 54th Massachusetts. But the participation of black soldiers has brought the freedom of African Americans one step closer. In the final scene, a group of liberated men, women, and children form a procession. As former slaves who have left their plantations to make their way to the Union Army, they are classified by federal policy as "contraband"; their liberty is the gift of the Union Amy. But the song they sing makes clear that African Americans own their freedom. Walking toward liberty and a "new life," they sing, "Free, Free—free at lass! Thank Gawd 'Amighty Ah'm free at lass!" While the chorus repeats the line "Thank Gawd 'Amighty Ah'm free at lass" their leader reminds us that though he had been held by Satan, "*Ah* broke de chains dat helt me fas'!"[132]

In the 1970s Browne was troubled by the new dramas of the Black Arts Movement. Amiri Baraka and Ed Bullins, he believed, made a fetish of insulting white audiences and forgot their predecessors too easily: "These people who have made it possible for us to have the things that we have now . . . the Walter Whites, Weldon Johnson and a Miss Bethune, . . . The kids don't realize what those people went through." Browne defended what he called "heroic" theatre. A theatre, he argued "should do something to uplift them, give them some hope."[133] Unlike *Natural Man*, Browne's earlier Federal Theatre drama, *Go Down Moses* is an uplifting and hopeful drama: it commemorates black heroes who resist, and, crucially, prevail, as well as the roles of white army commanders, Quakers, and abolitionists who worked alongside African Americans in the freedom struggle. Browne's Tubman drama did not seek to challenge white aesthetics or reject white involvement in the freedom struggle. In fact, the play celebrates the victories that interracial cooperation makes possible. While an older Browne sought to distance his work from that of Black Arts Movement dramatists, in fact both of his FTP dramas foreground what would become a central question for black dramatists seeking an independent and radical black theatre in the twentieth century: the relationship between heroism and liberty. This question shaped Browne's portraits of the defeated John Henry and the victorious Harriet Tubman, much as they would shape Richard Wright's Bigger Thomas, and subsequent black dramatic heroes. When, in 1941, Wright declared there could be no place for black heroes in America until the black man was free, he was echoing Browne's powerful study of black heroism in *Natural Man* and *Go Down Moses*.[134] In rooting his black heroes in the contested legacies of slavery, the Underground Railroad, and the U.S. Civil War, Browne's Federal Theatre dramas helped birth a black dramatic tradition that would endure, one in which black Americans could imagine being "Free at lass."

Conclusion
Making Space

· ·

Theodore Ward contended that the Federal Theatre Project had "extended to the Negro opportunities such as not even the boldest imagination dared dream previously."[1] The FTP did offer new opportunities to black theatre practitioners, but the creativity and ambition of black Americans also made certain things possible for the FTP. Black performance communities made space for daring dreaming within American theatre through their engagement with the FTP. Writing and developing *Liberty Deferred, Stars and Bars*, and *Go Down Moses*, and staging radical black dramas *Big White Fog* and *Natural Man* made the Federal Theatre bolder, compelling it to take leaps into the unknown. First and foremost, the history of black American engagement with the Federal Theatre Project is an important part of the history of American intellectual and creative life. It also offers an important intervention into the long-standing and ongoing debate about whether New Deal programs stimulated or co-opted worker agitation in the 1930s: African Americans were not waiting to be inspired or reined in by New Deal programs: they grasped the opportunities that were available, demanded more than was offered, and expanded the parameters of what was imagined possible for American theatre in the Federal Theatre Project.[2]

Before African Americans could create theatre manuscripts that could hold and nurture radical dreams, they had first to find ways to make space for black-authored drama. This was no easy task. That they were able to do so was the result of opportunities created by black performance communities. In such communities black Americans found ways to use the very dramatic conventions and theatrical forms that had helped to construct what it meant to be a black person in America, to first tear down, and then rebuild, those images. This meant getting at the root of racial inequality; it meant a reckoning with the dramatic forms, theories, traditions, and cannons that had long shaped American drama and theatre. In Living Newspapers, folk dramas, domestic tragedies, and adaptations of white dramas, African Americans examined the history of black performance and white spectatorship and its relationship to inequality in the United States past and present. African Americans created theatre manuscripts that reflected on and exposed the minstrel mask through which white Americans viewed their black brothers and sisters and through which black Americans peered back at white audiences. In placing black performance, and its role as an instrument of power within and beyond the theatre, at the center of black theatre manuscripts, African Americans developed a powerful tradition in black drama that would be continued through the twentieth and twenty-first centuries. From Alice Childress to George Wolfe and to Suzan-Lori Parks, African Americans have used theatre to explore the role of black performance in maintaining and resisting white supremacy.

In Federal Theatre manuscripts, black communities also created and debated roles that foregrounded black experiences, black history, and black heroes. If such heroes confounded whites, they also provoked debate and creative conflict within black communities. Some black Federal Theatre dramas took direct aim at the FTP and the New Deal; these were never staged. It is important to remember, however, that these dramas were paid for and developed by black and white dramatists and actors who were working for New Deal institutions. That this radical activity took place within the New Deal is significant, not least because it reminds us that radical potential is often "buried deep within the liberal mainstream."[3] Locating radical black theatre within the mainstream, rather than at the margins, requires that we attend to the parameters of what constitutes the mainstream. Published plays and playwrights whose work was staged often occupy the center ground of American theatre in historical narratives. Yet this rather elite category excludes many types of theatre, and is a particular obstacle for African American plays and playwrights. In the 1930s, however, participation in the Federal Theatre Project positioned African Americans at the forefront of innovative new theatre in the second half of the decade. Black Americans' participation as creative artists was frequently highlighted by critics and advocates alike. If white liberals trumpeted their progressive credentials by pointing to "our" Negro troupes, New Deal opponents in Congress were repeatedly drawn to black dramas and Negro Units to illustrate the dangerous radicals harbored by a state-sponsored theatre.[4]

Radical black theatre was not hidden from sight in the 1930s. There was, and still is, plenty of evidence to document its existence. Artifacts of a radical black Federal Theatre are everywhere: in newspapers, theatre journals, the records of black civil rights organizations, and the new theatres it inspired, such as the American Negro Theatre. Radical black theatre is also well documented in WPA archives and on the pages of black theatre manuscripts. The breadth and depth of the archive of radical black dramas developed on the Federal Theatre Project reminds us that it took energy and effort for the histories of the FTP and black writers and performance communities to be submerged. The neglect of FTP archives was no casual accident of the Cold War, but rather a central component of a system of racialized knowledge production in which what was kept, celebrated, and considered a valuable part of American history was directly connected to struggles for who would determine America's future in the second half of the twentieth century.

The marginalization of black culture within U.S. history and culture, and its isolation from broader radical black traditions of which it is a part, has long shaped knowledge production and the archival and academic institutions that support it. This helps explain why the early Black Arts Movement initially found little worthy of the name "radical" in the work of their predecessors. As the movement developed in the 1970s however, black theatre artists began to uncover and even cherish the work of early black theatre practitioners. It could be said that one of the Black Arts Movements central achievements was to inspire the recovery of that heritage. Commenting on the Federal Theatre in the late 1970s, Amiri Baraka acknowledged how crucial black theatre history was to the black theatre: "the collection at George Mason University is so important because you can go down there and consult a good body of what was actually taking place in the thirties. Generally, when you get to the thirties in this country, history—white and black—goes into a tunnel. You don't know what happens. That period just doesn't exist. To reconstruct that unknown history, it is necessary to preserve these things."[5] Understanding the impact of what Baraka calls "the tunnel" on black theatre history has been one of the aims of this book. The politics of anticommunism, the racial imperatives of the Federal Theatre and the knowledge hierarchies of the pre–Black Studies academy have long worked to obscure the significance of both black theatre manuscripts and the histories of the communities that developed them. Fortunately, many black Federal Theatre manuscripts and the archives of their production have survived, and even been replenished. Even so, the troubled history of the black Federal Theatre archive is not an episode that can serve as a reassuring reminder that the mistakes of the past are in the past. In fact, the painstaking and ongoing recovery of black Federal Theatre manuscripts reminds us of the continued precarity of the black archive and the painful consequences for black Americans in the late twentieth and twenty-first centuries that have been wrought by its neglect.

In 1974, eight years before his death, Ward saw one of his plays—*Big White Fog*—published for the first time. It was included in Hatch's landmark anthology, *Black Theater U.S.A.*, and Ward was appreciative of Hatch's efforts to promote his work. Nevertheless, publication marked a bittersweet moment for the dramatist: "It remains excruciating to me to realize that I have never received any compensation in my own right. It is as though I were a slave, so that even whatever I may think belongs to his Master."[6] Fortunately, between the publication of *Black Theater U.S.A.* in 1974 and Ward's death in 1982, this would change. This author of over twenty plays, including eight full-length dramas, would live to see renewed interest in his work. In the 1970s and 1980s, Ward's most popular drama, *Our Lan'*, was revived by community and college theatres and Ward was the recipient of numerous awards, fellowship, and commendations. In 1996, the Guthrie Theatre in Minneapolis staged a major new production of *Big White Fog*, and it had its European premier at the Almeida Theatre in London in 2007.

Ward had to wait too long for recognition, while other black Federal Theatre dramatists and the distinctive dramas developed by black performance communities in the 1930s remain on the margins of histories of American literature and theatre.[7] This book has examined how African American dramatists and theatre communities were at the center of American theatre in the 1930s and how they expanded the parameters of that mainstream through creating radical dramas. Being visible, documented within, and central to the story of American theatre, however, offers no guarantee that black stories survive. At a time when archivists and activists are exploring the role of new social media platforms in shaping "ArchivesForBlackLives," the history of the black Federal Theatre archive is a troubling reminder of how quickly and easily black history can be buried. At the same time, the use of social media platforms to challenge and hold to account "ArchivesSoWhite" reminds us that archives are living repositories shaped by new technologies and ongoing struggles for power which hold out the possibility for change. The history of the black Federal Theatre and its archive can also inspire: if black Federal Theatre manuscripts help us understand how black communities have used, and might still use, black dramas to imagine a better future, they also remind us that there is already a radical heritage on which those dreams can be built.

Appendix

Black Federal Theatre Manuscripts

Play: *Big White Fog*

Author: Theodore Ward

Date: 1937–1938

PUBLICATION

Hatch, ed., *Black Theater U.S.A.* (1974)

Hatch and Shine, eds., *Black Theatre U.S.A: Revised and Expanded, The Early Period, 1847–1938* (1996)

Hatch, James V. *Black Drama: African, African American, and Diaspora*, Third Edition.

Theodore Ward, *Big White Fog* (London: Nick Hern Books, 2007)

> The versions published in both Hatch anthologies and in *Black Drama* are based on the manuscript Ward gave to Hatch for the Hatch-Billops Collection. James V. Hatch, email to author, Jun. 17, 2012, in author's possession. In 2007 the Almeida Company produced its own version of the play, which it described as "an amalgamation of two original drafts of the play not enormously different from each other." See Nick Curtis, "Attenborough shaking up Almeida audience." *Evening Standard,* May 15, 2007 http://www.standard.co.uk/goingout/theatre/attenborough-shaking-up-almeida-audience-6582659.html

UNPUBLISHED MANUSCRIPTS

"Early Draft" (FTP-LOC, Playscripts File Box 597, Folder S166 [5])

> Held together by leather binding, "Early Draft" includes stage directions typed in red. It is considerably longer than the other manuscripts and contains material that does not appear in any other Federal Theatre manuscript. For example, it has a lengthy section at the opening of Act 2, Scene 1 that has been cut from other versions. It is likely that this means it is an early draft because it is missing crucial scenes that we know were performed by the Chicago Negro Unit in April 1938. In all the other Federal Theatre manuscripts, a group of Garveyites and Black Cross Nurses visit Vic in his home to present him with a service medal in Act 2, Scene 2. Photographs taken on the evening of the opening night suggest the medal ceremony was an important scene in the Chicago production.

"FTPa" and "FTPb" (FTP-LOC, Playscripts File, Box 597, Folder S166 [1] and S166 [2])

> These two manuscripts appear to be identical and are a revised version of "Early Draft."

"FTPc" (NA, RG69: Playscripts 1936–39, E914 Box 271)

This version was originally on file at the regional FTP bureau in Los Angeles. It is nearly the same as "FTPa" and "FTPb," but has been clearly been typed out anew. The occasional differences suggest copyist's errors rather than revision. All three manuscripts stem from, and appear to be revised versions of, "Early Draft."

"Last Version" (FTP-LOC, Playscripts File: Box 597, Folder S166 [4])

Photographs, cast lists, handwritten annotations, and typed amendments correspond closely to community criticism and complaints contained in Regional Office Chronological Correspondence File 1937–38, RG69, NA, E970, Box 618–621.

"Schomburg" (SCR: SC Rare 812-T)

The "Schomburg" version is very similar to "Last Version," with only minor differences. In the "Schomburg" version alone, Percy turns on the phonograph and plays the first few bars of Sousa's "Overthere" before quickly turning it off in disgust. In "Last Version," the record being played is "Jamaica Blues," a song about Marcus Garvey. The ending here is even more bleak than in "Last Version." Wanda is not written into the climactic scene and there is no reconciliation. The scene ends with the sound of the ambulance siren and the words, "desolation invests the scene."

"Guthrie" (NCOF+ 10-8327, Performing Arts Research Collection, NYPLPA)

With few variations, the "Guthrie" manuscript is very close to the version published in Hatch's *Black Theater U.S.A.* In the anthologized version, "Communists" no longer feature in the list of characters; rather, they are listed alongside other extras and described as "white and Negro workers." The Guthrie manuscript similarly omits any mention of communists. Les's friends are described simply as "workers," without regard to race. In both manuscripts the political affiliation of the workers in the final scene is evident.

PRODUCTIONS

Chicago: Chicago Negro Unit, Great Northern Theatre, April 7, 1938. Ran for thirty-seven performances before being transferred to the Chicago South Side.

New York City: Negro Playwrights Company, 135th Street Library, Harlem. *Big White Fog* was the only production of the NPC. It ran between October 22 and December 14, 1940.

Minneapolis, Penumbra, Guthrie Theatre, Dir. Lou Bellamy, Opened Sept. 22, 1995.

London: Almeida Theatre, Dir. Michael Attenborough, Opened May 11 2007

Play: *Go Down Moses: Based on the Life and Times of Harriet Tubman, A Play in Two Acts*

Alternative Title: *A Black Woman Called Moses*

Author: Theodore Browne

Date: December 9, 1938

PUBLICATION

Hatch, James V. *Black Drama: African, African American, and Diaspora,* Third Edition.

Identical copies of the two-act version rehearsed by the Harlem Negro Unit are held at the FTP-LOC (Box 657, Library Records) and in FTP-GMU (Box 161, Folder 2) and Emory University (Playscripts, Box 4, Camille Billops and James V. Hatch Archives).

In early 1938 Browne wrote a three-act manuscript of which there is no extant copy. See Reader's Reports on "Go Down Moses," by Harold Callen, July 10, 1937; Fanny Malkin, July 21, 1937; and John D. Silvera, July 25 1937; in WPA, Federal Theater Project, National Service Bureau, Negro Lists, *Black Freedom Struggle in the 20th Century: Federal Government Records.*

PRODUCTIONS

Cast and rehearsed by the Harlem Negro Unit in spring 1939 but never staged.

Play: *Haiti*

Author: William Dubois

Date: 1938

PUBLICATION

Publication Number 50-S (Federal Theatre Project, April 1938)

Multiple copies are available in FTP-GMU, Library Records, Box 167

Arent, Sundgaard, and de Rohan, eds., *Federal Theatre Plays,* (New York: Random House, 1938)

The Random House version was published later in 1938 alongside two other Federal Theatre dramas, E. P. Conkle's *Prologue to Glory* and the Living Newspaper, *One Third of a Nation.*

UNPUBLISHED MANUSCRIPTS

"Complete Working Script" (CWS) (Billy Rose Theatre Division, NYPLPA)

This version is bound in navy blue leather with the author's name and "Completing Working Script," written in gold lettering on the spine. It includes photographs of the production and stage designs, costumes and property plots, and a light-hanging plot, as well as a frontispiece that includes the typewritten date of opening night, March 2, 1938. This manuscript is very similar to the two published manuscripts, Publication "50-S" and "Random House."

"Revised Edition" (RE) (FTP-GMU, Library Records, Box 167)

This version has significant variation, which can be linked to community criticism of the preview performance published in the New York *Amsterdam News.* New lines are introduced that make Toussaint appear less trusting of the French and Christophe more resolute.

PRODUCTIONS

New York: Harlem Negro Unit, Lafayette Theatre, opened March 2, 1938 and ran for nearly seventeen weeks before being moved to a downtown theatre. Toured to Boston, in October 1938.

Hartford, Conn., Avery Memorial, October 26–29, 1938.

Play: *Hell's Half Acre*

Author: Abram Hill

Date: 1937

PUBLICATION
Hatch, James V. *Black Drama: African, African American, and Diaspora*, Third Edition.

UNPUBLISHED MANUSCRIPT
FTP-LOC, Playscripts Collection, Box 668

PRODUCTION
Staged by Unity Players of the Bronx in 1938. See Hill and Hatch, eds., *A History of African American Theatre,* 348.

Play: *Liberty Deferred*

Authors: Abram Hill and John Silvera

Date: 1937–1938

PUBLICATION
James V. Hatch and Ted Shine eds., *Black Theatre U.S.A.: Plays by African Americans: The Early Period, 1847–1938* (1996)
Hatch, James V. *Black Drama: African, African American, and Diaspora*, Third Edition.

> The first half of *Liberty Deferred* is published in both Hatch and Shine's *Black Theatre U.S.A.* and *Black Drama, Third Edition.* It is a heavily edited version that ends at the Civil War. First published in the 1974 version of the anthology with the permission of John Silvera, it is based on the Library of Congress Federal Theatre manuscripts.

Lorraine Brown, ed., *Liberty Deferred and Other Living Newspapers of the 1930s* (Fairfax, Va.: George Mason University Press, 1989)

> The version is strikingly different from all others: it has been extensively edited and new contexts added. For example, it opens with a televised minstrel show. It also has a new ending: President Roosevelt signs Executive Order 8802, which prohibited racial discrimination in government defense contracts and was a direct response to A. Philip Randolph's planned March on Washington in June 1941. This means it was amended and updated after the Federal Theatre Project closed in 1939. In the Preface to the published edition, Lorraine Brown acknowledges other extant versions of *Liberty Deferred,* but explains that "we have deliberately chosen versions of the [*sic*] included in the cache of materials packed up in 1939 and placed on permanent loan at George Mason University by the Library of Congress in 1974." See Brown, ed., *Liberty Deferred,* vii. In Brown's oral history interview with Abram Hill in 1978, Hill discusses the various endings, recalling one version that ended with a march on Washington during World War II and pointing out that "that had not occurred when this was written." See Abram Hill,

interviewed by Lorraine Brown and Swann, March 30, 1978, First tape, Side 2, 15A, OHC-GMU.

UNPUBLISHED MANUSCRIPTS

"Early Drafts" (FTP-LOC, Playscripts File, Box 694; FTP-GMU, Boxes 191 and 192)
    Two almost identical copies of the "Early Drafts" are held at the Library of Congress. Two further copies, and a third with an altered ending, are held at GMU.
"Liberty Deferred: a dramatic chronicle of the Negro," by John D. Silvera and Abram Hill, (NYPLPA, Call Number: NCOF+ (Silvera, J. D. Liberty deferred).
    This manuscript contains significant variation. It includes an FTP National Service Bureau frontispiece and a stamp reading, "Under supervision of the National Service Bureau Thru Ira Knaster," suggesting it was amended while the FTP was still in operation but later than October 1938, since Lavery was still complaining that the authors had not adopted his changes in early October. See Lavery to John Gibbs, Oct. 3, 1938, E879 Box 182, Folder: John Silvera, RG69, NA.

PRODUCTION
Not staged during the FTP.

Play: *Natural Man*

Author: Theodore Browne

Date: 1937–1941

PUBLICATION

Hatch, ed., *Black Theater U.S.A.: 45 Plays by Black Americans, 1847–1974* (1974)
Hatch and Shine, eds., *Black Theatre U.S.A: Revised and Expanded Edition, The Early Period, 1847–1938* (1996)
Hatch, James V. *Black Drama: African, African American, and Diaspora*, Third Edition.
    All three publications use the version revised for the ANT production which the playwright gave to James Hatch for the Hatch-Billops Collection.

UNPUBLISHED MANUSCRIPTS

"January Seattle" (FTP-LOC, Box 720)
    Eight episodes: this Federal Theatre manuscript was staged at the Seattle Metropolitan Theatre January 28–30, 1937. This is the only version of the manuscript that does not include the religious camp scene.
"February Seattle" (FTP-LOC Box 720)
    Nine episodes: this Federal Theatre manuscript has an additional scene. It was staged at the Seattle Metropolitan Theatre, February 18–20, 1938.
"ANT-GMU" (FTP-GMU, TBP, Box 2)
    Eight episodes: a version of this was manuscript was staged by the American Negro Theatre at the 135th Street Library on Wednesday, Friday, and Saturday nights through May and June 1941. Browne donated a copy to George Mason University in 1975 and authorized its publication in Hatch, ed., *Black Theater U.S.A.*,

in 1974. This is the version that most scholars use to analyze Browne's drama. It varies considerably from the version staged by the Federal Theatre Project in early 1937. Key variations include the removal of the northern labor scene, restructuring of the scene order, and a new, redemptive ending. John Henry's irresponsible behavior in a bar, rather than an interracial labor dispute, is the cause of his arrest and incarceration. New characters—the Creeper, the Jailer, and the Sheriff—are introduced. New music was commissioned and racial language was tempered in this version. The ANT program is an important source for determining that this was the version staged by the ANT.

"Schomburg" (SCR, SC Rare, 812 B)

Like "February Seattle," the "Schomburg" version has nine scenes, and like both Seattle manuscripts, it includes the northern labor scene and a final episode in which John Henry dies knowing he has not defeated the machine. The provenance of the "Schomburg" manuscript is unclear: the NYPL catalog entry describes the play as "The natural man (based on the legend of John Henry) a play in eight episodes." It offers a speculative date of 1936, which would line up with when Browne probably wrote the first version of the play in Seattle. However, the "Schomburg" is unlikely to date to 1936 because it clearly derives from the second Seattle production, which took place in February 1937. Some scholars have assumed the "Schomburg" is a version of the manuscript performed by the ANT. The playbill and reviews for the ANT production make clear this was not the manuscript used by the ANT.

"PAL" (NYPLPA, NCOF+ p.v. 82)

Seven episodes: this manuscript incorporates many of the key revisions made by the ANT including the redemptive ending, but retains more elements of the Seattle manuscripts, including its structure, than does "ANT-GMU." For example, in "PAL," the Beale Street bar scene has not yet been moved forward to Episode 3, as in "ANT-GMU", but it does contain the same alteration of the plot in that scene: John Henry is arrested after becoming drunk and the victim of black machination. As in "ANT-GMU," the labor scene is eliminated in "PAL." The character of the Creeper has been introduced, but he has a less developed role than in the ANT version held at GMU. For these reasons it is clear that the "PAL" version was not the one used by the ANT in production but rather an earlier draft.

PRODUCTION

Seattle: Seattle Negro Unit, Seattle Metropolitan Theatre, January 28–30, 1937. A second version opened three weeks later and ran for three nights between February 18 and February 20, 1937.

New York: American Negro Theatre, 135th Street Library, Harlem. A much revised version was staged by the ANT on Wednesday, Friday, and Saturday nights through May and June, 1941.

Shaw University, Raleigh, North Carolina, 1986. A videotape recording of the production is held in SCA-GMU.

Stanford University, Piggot Theatre, 2003, Dir. Harry Elam.

Play: *Panyared*

Author: Hughes Allison
Date: 1936–1939

PUBLICATION
Hatch, James V. *Black Drama: African, African American, and Diaspora*, Third Edition.

UNPUBLISHED MANUSCRIPT
A manuscript accompanied by a foreword from the author, dated 22 May 1939 is held in FTP-LOC, Box 734. A copy is also held in FTP-GMU, Box 223, Folder 1. This appears to be the source for the published version in *Black Drama*.

PRODUCTION
Not staged during the FTP.

Play: *Stars and Bars*

Alternative Title: *Bars and Stripes*
Authors: Ward Courtney and the Hartford Negro Unit
Date: 1937–1938

PUBLICATION
Not published.

UNPUBLISHED MANUSCRIPTS
The manuscript is available in RG69, NA. Copies of this manuscript are also held in the FTP-GMU, Box 6.

PRODUCTION
Not produced during the FTP. It was scheduled for production in the Eastern Region in Spring–Summer 1938. There is no record of why it was withdrawn from production.

Stars and Bars is frequently attributed to Ward Courtney alone. The Federal Theatre manuscript and records of collaboration between Courtney and members of the Negro Unit in Hartford detail the nature of the collaboration. In 2013 there was a public reading performed by the Working Actors Collective directed by CPTV's Ed Wierzbicki at the Mattatuck Museum in Waterbury, Conn. Presented in conjunction with the museum's exhibition, "Art for Everyone: The Federal Art Project in Connecticut." The Living Newspaper was credited to both Ward Courtney and the Negro Unit of the Connecticut Federal Theatre. See http://www.waterburyobserver .org/wod7/node/3559.

Notes

Abbreviations in the Notes

ANT	American Negro Theatre
FTP-GMU	Federal Theatre Project Collection, Special Collections and Archives, George Mason University Library
FTP-LOC	Federal Theatre Project Collection, Library of Congress
NA	National Archives
NDABA	*New Deal Agencies and Black America in the 1930s*
NYPL	New York Public Library
NYPLPA	New York Public Library for the Performing Arts
OHC-GMU	WPA Oral Histories Collection, George Mason University
PAL	Performing Arts Library
RG	Record Group at the National Archives
SCA-GMU	Special Collections and Archives, George Mason University Library
SCA-UWL	Special Collections and Archives, University of Washington Libraries
SCR	Schomburg Center for Research in Black Culture, New York Public Library
SRPL	Seattle Repertory Playhouse Log
SRPR	Seattle Repertory Playhouse Records
TBP	Theodore Browne Papers
TWP	Theodore Ward Papers
UWL	University of Washington Libraries

Introduction

1. Theodore Browne, *Go Down Moses: Based on the Life and Times of Harriet Tubman: A Play in Two Acts*, Dec. 9, 1938, 2-4-2; Library Records, Box 657, FTP-LOC.

2. In the theatre, African Americans had long resisted the use of the term "nigger" by white dramatists. Charles Gilpin enraged Eugene O'Neill by changing the disparaging epithet when he performed the eponymous role in the white dramatist's *Emperor Jones* in the early 1920s. See Krasner, "Whose Role Is It Anyway?," 484.

3. Joseph Staton, interviewed by John O'Connor, Jan. 7, 1976, Box 10, Folder, 6: 23, OHC-GMU.

4. "Release to Hartford Times," in "WPA Federal Theater Project Activities in Hartford, Connecticut," WPA RG69, Federal Theater Project, Connecticut, "A–L," in *Black Freedom Struggle in the 20th Century: Federal Government Records*.

5. Melosh, *Engendering Culture*, esp. chapter 4.

6. Federal Works Agency, *Final Report on the WPA Program, 1935–43*, 101.

7. Hallie Flanagan, "Report of the Director," *New York Times*, May 17, 1937, X2.

8. Federal Works Agency, *Final Report on the WPA Program, 1935–43*, 3.

9. Roses, *Black Bostonians*, 156.

10. Sitkoff, *A New Deal for Blacks*, 48–49, 70–71. For the relationship between the New Deal and the struggle for racial equality in the South, also see Sullivan, *Days of Hope*.

11. Sitkoff, *A New Deal for Blacks*, 70.

12. Flanagan, *Arena*, 20.

13. Flanagan, *Arena*, 20.

14. Flanagan, *Arena*, 45–46

15. Flanagan, *Arena*, 28.

16. Flanagan, "Prologue to a Season," *New York Times*, Sept. 12, 1937, X1.

17. Flanagan, *Arena*, 23.

18. Boston and Los Angeles are both significant Negro Units in their own right, but neither was an incubator for radical black theatre manuscripts. In Boston, Ralf Coleman was the only black director to run a Negro Unit for the entirety of the project. The Boston Negro Unit staged a number of original black folk dramas by H. Jack Bates, as well as black-authored dramas also staged by the Harlem Negro Unit including *Brother Mose* by Frank Wilson and *The Trial of Dr. Beck* by Hughes Allison. They also put on the classics, including a version of *Macbeth*, six months before the Harlem Negro Unit. See Roses, *Black Bostonians,* esp. chapter 7. The Los Angeles Negro Unit put on the standard white-authored repertoire for Negro Units, including *Androcles and the Lion, Black Empire, John Henry, Macbeth,* and *Noah.* Its most significance production was *Run Little Chillun,* the religious musical extravaganza directed by Clarence Muse, an acclaimed black actor on stage, screen, and radio, and the talented composer and musical director Hall Johnson. It featured numerous singers, actors, and dancers from New York and also drew on musicians from the Federal Music Project. It has been the subject of a number of studies, including Weisenfeld, "'The Secret at the Root,'" and Wittmer, "Performing Negro Folk Culture, Performing America." Determining the number of Negro Units established under the FTP depends on how you calculate them. For example, New York City had several Negro Units in addition to the drama unit based at the Lafayette, including the Negro Youth Theatre, Dance Unit, and Vaudeville Unit. "Negro" dramas were regularly staged outside of Negro Units or in short-lived Negro Units. For example, Philadelphia and Newark put on three and two "Negro" dramas, respectively, while on the West Coast, Oakland and San Francisco staged a couple of dramas each. In the South, predominantly white-authored "Negro" dramas were staged in Atlanta, Jacksonville, Florida, New Orleans, and Washington, D.C. Federal Theatre records list seventeen Negro Units in October 1936; see "Federal Theatre Projects, Negro Units, 22 Oct. 1936," in *NDABA*, Reel 24. Two months before the FTP was closed FTP administrator J. Howard Miller conducted a survey of black employment on the FTP and found that by April 1939, few units employed black federal theatre workers outside the seven core units. See J. Howard Miller to Edward Lawson, Apr. 13, 1939, in *NDABA*, Reel 25. For further information on the number of units,

see Brown et al., "Cultural Diversity in the Federal Theatre Project 1935–1939." Hill and Hatch reflect on the issue of how to calculate the number of Negro Units in *A History of African American Theatre,* 315.

19. "Theatre Project Faces an Inquiry," *New York Times,* Jul. 27, 1938, 19.

20. See, for example, Zanthe Taylor, "Singing for Their Supper"; Redd, "Staging Race"; West, "Others, Adults, Censored"; Fraden, *Blueprints for a Black Federal Theatre.*

21. Jones, "Slavery and the Design of African American Theatre," 20.

22. Hartman, *Scenes of Subjection,* 54, 56.

23. Lott, *Love and Theft,* 8.

24. Jones, "Slavery and the Design of African American Theatre," 21.

25. Jones, "Slavery and the Design of African American Theatre," 24.

26. Nathans, "Slave Rebellions on the National Stage," 51.

27. Hiram Motherwell memo, Jun. 4, 1936, in "Negro Drama Corr.," Nov. 1935 to Apr.1939, in *NDABA.* There has been little study of minstrel troupes in the Federal Theatre Project. There is a chapter in Kreizenbeck, "The Theatre Nobody Knows."

28. Eugene Gordon, "From Uncle Tom's Cabin' to 'Stevedore,'" *New Theatre,* 2:7 (July 1935): 22. Langston Hughes and Du Bois were also critical. See Fraden, *Blueprints for a Black Federal Theatre,* 101.For a positive view of Paul Green, see Locke and Gregory, eds., *Plays of Negro Life,* esp. the Introduction, "The Drama of Negro Life."

29. *The Federal Theatre Project: A Catalog-Calendar of Productions,* 251.

30. Hartman argues that minstrelsy and melodrama in the nineteenth century had much in common when it came to the "uses made of the black body." See Hartman, *Scenes of Subjection,* 26.

31. For the importance of "making noise" as a form of community building and political action, see Corbould, "Streets, Sounds and Identity in Interwar Harlem."

32. Bryant, *Victims and Heroes,* 3; Bernier, *Characters of Blood,* 6; Cora Kaplan, "Black Heroes/White Writers."

33. Christopher Bigsby discusses the instability of dramatic texts, shaped by "unacknowledged collaborators" in Bigsby, "A View from East Anglia," 132.

34. Barr, *Rooms with a View,* 11.

35. Richards, "Writing the Absent Potential," 65, 72–73.

36. See chapter 3. See also "John Henry," Production Bulletin, Production Records, Box 1026, FTP-LOC.

37. Barr, *Rooms with a View,* 22.

38. See chapter 5.

39. See chapter 4.

40. Barr, *Rooms with a View,* 18–19.

41. "Refusal to Say Yes Sir, Boss, Gave Rex Ingram Start," *Afro American,* Feb. 16, 1935, 9.

42. William Pickens, "Stevedore: A New Play on Negro Life," for the Associated Negro Press, *Amsterdam News,* May 5, 1934, 8; *Afro American,* May 4, 1934, 14; *Atlanta Daily World,* May 9, 1934, 2.

43. Kelley, "Black Study, Black Struggle Forum."

44. Hatch, "Here Comes Everybody."

45. Bigsby, "A View from East Anglia," 132.

46. For a recent and important intervention on how scholars select black dramas for study, see Mitchell, *Living with Lynching*, esp. the Introduction.

47. For a brief account of the recovery of the Federal Theatre archive, see O'Connor and Brown, Introduction, in *The Federal Theatre Project*, vii–viii. The history of the recovery of the FTP archive is told in *Federal One*, the newsletter published by the Research Center for Federal Theatre at GMU between 1975 and 1994 and available in SCA, GMU. The account published in the publication *Performing Arts Resources* offers detail on the many different parts of the Federal Theatre archive, but tends to trumpet the role of the Library of Congress. See Henderson, "Federal Theatre Project Records at George Mason University." Oral histories of FTP participants are catalogued under the WPA Oral Histories Collection, 1961–1984, OHC-GMU.

48. Neal, "The Black Arts Movement." Black Arts manifestos of the 1960s suggest their authors believed themselves to be the first generation to attempt revolutionary black theatre. By the late 1970s and early 1980s, both they and the emerging scholarship on Black Arts Movement theatre sought to position the movement within a longer tradition of revolutionary black dramatic literature that extended back to slavery. Among these, the most remarkable is Amiri Baraka's 1979 essay, "The Revolutionary Tradition in Afro American Literature," which was first published in a selection of his prose and dramas, and subsequently in *Black American Literature Forum*. Starting with the slave narrative and encompassing the "pre Civil War nationalists," the Harlem Renaissance, the Black Arts Movement, and beyond, Baraka singled out Theodore Ward's *Big White Fog* as "one of the finest plays written in this country" and acknowledged the "obscurity" that had been "heaped" on this often neglected playwright. See Baraka, "Afro American Literature and Class Struggle," *Black American Literature Forum*, 14:1 (Spring 1980), 9; Clark, "Restaging Langston Hughes' Scottsboro Limited," 165. See also Hill, "The Revolutionary Tradition in Black Drama."

49. See, for example, King and Milner, eds., *Black Drama Anthology*. Alongside other early 1970s anthologies, King and Milner's collection included a Langston Hughes drama. See, too, Brasmer and Consolo, eds., *Black Drama*. One of the first anthologies to include a number of earlier playwrights was Darwin T. Turner, *Black Drama in America*, in 1971. It made available a number of black dramas created in the early to mid-twentieth century, including Richardson's *The Chip Woman's Fortune*, and Hughes's *Emperor of Haiti*. It also included *Our Lan'*, the 1946 drama by federal theatre playwright Theodore Ward. The work of Langston Hughes, Arna Bontemps, and Countee Cullen was anthologized alongside later works in Patterson, *Black Theater*.

50. Hatch, ed., Foreword, in *Black Theater U.S.A.*, ix.

51. In the revised and expanded two-volume edition of *Black Theatre U.S.A.*, black federal theatre manuscripts were placed in the first volume (whose date span ended in 1938) rather than the second volume (dated from 1935 onward). The decision to place black federal theatre manuscripts alongside nineteenth- and early twentieth-

century dramas is significant, for it separates them from the social protest dramas of Langston Hughes and Richard Wright and the 1960s dramas anthologized in the second volume. See Hatch and Shine, eds., *Black Theatre U.S.A.: Plays by African Americans: The Early Period 1847–1938, Revised and Expanded Edition*; Hatch and Shine, eds., *Black Theatre U.S.A.: Plays by African Americans, The Recent Period 1935–Today, Revised and Expanded Edition*.

52. *Big White Fog* was revived by the Guthrie Theatre in Minneapolis in 1995 and had its UK premiere at the Almeida Theatre in London in 2007, where it was directed by Michael Attenborough. According to Attenborough, Ward's play was "discovered" by the Almeida's artistic director in *Black Theatre U.S.A.* See Attenborough, "My Search for the Lost Voice of Black America," *Guardian*, May 10, 2007, 28.

53. *Uncle Tom's Cabin*, *Green Pastures*, and *Porgy* were included in Gassner and Barnes, *Fifty Best Plays of the American Theater*.

54. Abramson considered Langston Hughes the only black dramatist capable of writing dramas of "universal" interest. Her judgment on Hill and Silvera's *Liberty Deferred* is one of many based on limited or no textual evidence. For her discussion of other black dramas, Abramson relies on manuscripts developed after the Federal Theatre Project though this is not made clear in the text. For example her discussion of both Ward and Browne's federal theatre dramas is based on later versions of the manuscripts used by the Negro Playwrights Company (1940) and America Negro Theatre (1941), respectively, rather than the federal theatre manuscripts. Abramson also analyzes two dramas by Frank Wilson without reference to any manuscript. See Abramson, *Negro Playwrights*, 45, 47, 49, 55, 59, 61, 67, 87; Gordon, "Book Review." 4, 36.

55. Henry Miller relies on Abramson's information about, and reading of, manuscripts in *Theorizing Black Theatre*, as does Elam in "The Politics of Black Masculinity," esp. 133; Abramson is frequently cited in Barnard Peterson, *Early Black American Playwrights*.

56. Online at https://alexanderstreet.com/products/black-drama-third-edition.

57. Colson, "Wrestling with the Left," 162–63.

58. The *Big White Fog* manuscript published in *Black Theater U.S.A.* is a version Ward gave to Hatch for the Hatch-Billops Collection. James V. Hatch, email to author, Jun. 17, 2012, in author's possession. Email exchanges with Alexander Street Press in 2014 and 2017 state that manuscripts were drawn from the following archives: Hatch-Billops Archives, New York Public Library and Schomburg Center for Research in Black Culture, Library of Congress, and George Mason University. In the case of Theodore Ward's dramas, the press also used copies from the literary estate managed by Ward's daughter Eloise Ward. The process that informed the manuscript selection process is not publicly documented on the website. Manuscripts published for the first time in *Black Drama* have their manuscript location included. However, some of the collections hold multiple variant manuscripts, and it is not clear which version was selected for inclusion or why. In the case of previously published manuscripts, such as Ward's *Big White Fog*, the version published in *Black Drama* is the same as that included in *Black Theater U.S.A.* Will Whalen of

Alexanderstreet.com, emails to author, Jan. 8, 2014, and Mar. 7, 2017, in the author's possession.

59. This tone was set by Flanagan herself in her 1940 account *Arena* and echoed by Edith Isaac, the longtime editor of *Theatre Arts*. In her 1947 study, Isaac declared: "No part of the Federal Theatre brought more ample returns to the project itself, than did the Negro units." See Isaacs, *The Negro in the American Theatre*, 106. For an early account that pays little attention to African Americans in the FTP, see Mathews, *The Federal Theatre, 1935–1939*. Emerging in the 1970s, the first studies to focus on the Negro Units relied on accounts by white federal theatre administrators and were more attentive to the administrative apparatus than the theatre they were purposed with producing. For example, in 1974 Ronald Ross was able to conclude that the federal theatre's "actual operation was as democratic as its rhetoric," and that African Americans were "involved at all levels in the planning of this new theatre venture." See Ross, "The Role of Blacks in the Federal Theatre."41.

60. Fraden, *Blueprints for a Black Federal Theatre*, xiv, 10.

61. The absence of black theatre manuscripts from discussions of the Negro Unit productions they generated is accounted for by a variety of factors, including the availability of manuscripts and the state of the federal theatre archive. In some cases there have been multiple manuscripts available, but scholars have not been interested in manuscripts and have instead used the version that appears in the 1974 anthology. When scholars have used black theatre manuscripts from the federal theatre archive, it is not clear which version was selected and why. While a number of studies cite federal theatre manuscripts (usually those held at the Library of Congress or George Mason University), there is as yet no study that offers a methodology for how to approach the study of federal theatre manuscripts in their variation and multiplicity. Osborne's study considers multiple manuscripts, but her focus is on white, rather than black, federal theatre manuscripts. See Osborne, *Staging the People*, 23–24, 193n25. Craig was one of the first to look at black federal theatre manuscripts at GMU in the 1970s. Her 1980 study uses a combination of FTP-GMU manuscripts and versions published in *Black Theater U.S.A.: Forty-five Plays by Black Americans, 1847–1974*, edited by James Hatch. See Craig, *Black Drama of the Federal Theatre Era*. Fraden used FTP manuscripts for her discussion of some unstaged plays, including Hughes Allison's *Panyared* and Hill and Silvera's *Liberty Deferred*. However, her detailed analysis of Ted Ward's important play *Big White Fog* uses the edition published in *Black Theater U.S.A.: Forty-Five Plays by Black Americans, 1847–1974*, edited by James Hatch. See Fraden, "The Cloudy History of Big White Fog," 26n19, and Fraden, *Blueprints for a Black Federal Theatre*, 228n57. John Poole's fascinating study of Morrison Wood's *Great Day*, which was developed but never staged by the Birmingham, Alabama, Negro Unit, uses FTP readers' reports, correspondence, and newspaper coverage to reconstruct this little-known play, but no manuscript seems to be available in the federal theatre archive, which is unusual. See Poole, "Making a Tree from Thirst." Evamarri Alexandria Johnson's 1981 PhD thesis uses a version of Theodore Browne's federal theatre manuscript for both *Lysistrata* and *Natural Man*, both of which are held at GMU, but it is unclear which version was selected. See Johnson, "A Production History of the Seattle Federal The-

atre Project." Similarly, Zanthe Taylor references FTP manuscripts held at GMU in her article, but it is unclear which version was used. See Zanthe Taylor, "Singing for Their Supper," 43–59. Barry Witham's fascinating case study of the Seattle Federal Theatre Project does not use black federal theatre manuscripts for his discussion of the Negro Unit. See Witham, *The Federal Theatre Project*. Tina Redd uses the text published by Civici-Friede in 1934 for her analysis of the Seattle Negro Unit's *Stevedore*. See Redd, "Staging Race," 83n61. Ron West's analysis of the Seattle Negro Unit production of *Lysistrata* draws on published editions available in the University of Washington Library rather than the "African" version adapted by Theodore Browne, which is available in the GMU Federal Theatre Play Script Collection. See West, "Others, Adults, Censored," esp. 110n15. Vanita Marian Vactor's PhD thesis on the history of the Chicago Negro Unit uses the version of *Big White Fog* published in volume 1 of the revised and expanded anthology, *Black Theatre U.S.A: The Early Period, 1847–1938*, edited by James V. Hatch and Ted Shine. See Vactor, "A History of the Chicago Federal Theatre Project Negro Unit."

62. See, for example, Zanthe Taylor, "Singing for Their Supper."

63. Sklaroff, *Black Culture in the New Deal*, 12, 263n131, 137; see also Macki Braconi, *Harlem's Theaters*, 19. Sklaroff cites a *Mikado* script held at the National Archives but does not discuss manuscripts other than to affirm that there were "few variations in the script." Instead, she sees black agency in the revised setting and costuming contained in the production archive and the three songs that were sung. See 65–71. Macki Braconi likewise remains silent on the question of how she chose which white-authored manuscripts to use. Macki Braconi tells us that for *The Show-Off*, "the text of the HNU's adaptation remains" and references a copy held in FTP-LOC. She similarly references the FTP-LOC collection as holding a "version" designated as the production manuscript. However, there are four versions of *The Show Off* at the Library of Congress and a further three at GMU. See Macki Braconi, *Harlem's Theaters*, 23, 221n10. Since certain plays were performed by more than one unit, the federal theatre collections at LOC and GMU often have multiple versions of a manuscript. Sometimes it is indicated on the manuscript which unit used a particular text, but oftentimes there are multiple versions of each unit's particular manuscript. Federal theatre manuscripts at both the LOC and GMU sometimes have handwritten comments such as "Last Version" or "Revised Edition," which can be useful but also misleading. For the need to research the provenance and chronology of manuscripts beyond designations made by unknown hands or catalogers, see Gray, "'Mara,' Angelina Grimké's Other Play and the Problems of Recovering Texts."

64. Unlike Osborne, I focus specifically on manuscripts developed by and for the Negro Units, and while, like Macki Braconi and Sklaroff, I examine a number of Negro Unit adaptations of white productions, my primary focus is on black theatre manuscripts. See Osborne, *Staging the People*, 23–24, 193n25.

65. Gates and Smith, eds., *Norton Anthology of African American Literature*; the Chicago Negro Unit and *Big White Fog* are mentioned in *A Companion to African American Literature,* see Gordon, "Chicago Renaissance," 274, 281–82.

66. Richards, "Writing the Absent Potential," 65.

67. Errol Hill and Hatch, *A History of African American Theatre*; Wilmeth and Bigsby, eds., *Cambridge History of American Theatre*, 21, 119, 328; Shandell, "The Negro Little Theatre Movement," 114–15; Perkins, "African American Drama, 1910–45"; Witham, "The Federal Theatre Project."

68. "Turpentine Rated Significant Drama," *New York Amsterdam News*, July 4, 1936, 8.

69. Manning, *Modern Dance, Negro Dance*, 83–93.

70. Most studies of Theodore Ward's *Big White Fog* and Theodore Browne's *Natural Man* use the anthologized version published in either of *Black Theater U.S.A.: Forty-five Plays by Black Americans, 1847 to 1974* edited by James Hatch or in Volume 1 of the revised and expanded edition, *Black Theatre U.S.A.* For *Big White Fog*, see Miller, *Theorizing Black Theatre*; Fraden, *Blueprints for a Black Federal Theatre*; Michelle Gordon, "The Chicago Renaissance": Michelle Gordon, "Black Literature of Revolutionary Protest from Chicago's South Side"; Hill and Hatch, eds., *A History of African American Theatre*; Rachel Peterson, "Adapting Left Culture to the Cold War." For *Natural Man*, see Craig, *Black Drama of the Federal Theatre Era*, 47–50; Johnson, "A Production History of the Seattle Federal Theatre Project," 111n38; Hill and Hatch, eds., *A History of African American Theatre*, 328; Shandell, "Looking beyond *Lucasta*"; Miller, *Theorizing Black Theatre*, 311–12; Elam, "The Politics of Black Masculinity."

71. Foley, *Wrestling with the Left*, 5–6.

72. See, for example, Fraden, *Blueprints for a Black Theatre*, 107–8; Browder, *Rousing the Nation*, 153; Cosgrove, "The Living Newspaper," 139. Foley makes a similar argument regarding writers and radicalism in the early 1950s. See Foley, *Wrestling with the Left*, 21.

73. Flanagan, *Arena*; "Vassar Granted Special Fund by Rockefeller Foundation," *Vassar College News*, Nov. 4, 1939, 1.

74. See, for example, Leuchtenburg, *Franklin D. Roosevelt*; Degler, *Out of Our Past*; Bernstein, "The New Deal."

75. For the idea that artists' radical visions were quashed by the demand that they be "responsible," see Pells, *Radical Visions and American Dreams*. A good summary of leftist critique in the late 1960s and early 1970s is Kidd's "Redefining the New Deal," esp. 414. For an analysis of historiography on the WPA arts projects, see Hirsh, "Culture on Relief," 270. See also Susman, "The Thirties."

76. Foley, *Radical Representations*, 58, 56, 54.

77. For the recovery of the Federal Writers Project archive, see Douglas Brinkley, "A Depression Project That Gave Rise to a Generation of Novelists," *New York Times*, Aug. 2, 2003, B7, B9; Denning, *The Cultural Front*. For the significance of Denning's work, see Glickman, "The Laboring of History and Culture," 321.

78. Dolinar, *The Black Cultural Front*; Mullen, *Popular Fronts*. Mullen has also disrupted both the timeframes and binaries ascribed to Richard Wright, and in particular the prewar communist, postwar anticommunist crusader framing. He highlights the diversity and rich archive of black cultural workers in 1930s and 1940s Chicago, including those who, like Ward and Margaret Walker, worked for the Federal Arts Projects in the Windy City.

79. Foley, *Radical Representations*; Mullen, *Popular Fronts*; Singh, "Retracing the Black-Red Thread"; Maxwell, *New Negro, Old Left*, 12; Wald, *Writing from the Left*.

80. Singh, "Retracing the Black-Red Thread," 835–36.

81. Singh, "Retracing the Black-Red Thread," 836.

82. Singh, "Retracing the Black-Red Thread," 835–36.

83. Only eight of the fifty subject files on William J. Maxwell's FB Eyes Digital Archive website, which were obtained under the U.S. Freedom of Information Act, are for women. See http://digital.wustl.edu/fbeyes/. For a counter to the "leading man" narrative that has neglected women's importance as radical activists and thinkers, see Gore, Theoharis and Woodard eds., *Want to Start a Revolution?*

84. Aschenbrenner, *Katherine Dunham*, 113–18; Shirley Graham Du Bois, interviewed by James V. Hatch and Camille Billops, May 28, 1975, Tape 1, Side 1, 15, in Hatch-Billops Collection. See also *Little Black Sambo*, Production Notebook, Production Records, Box 1032, FTP-LOC.

85. Adams and Keene, *Women, Art, and the New Deal*, 41–42. Also see FTP-LOC Online Finding Aid, http://rs5.loc.gov/service/music/eadxmlmusic/eadpdfmusic/1995/mu995001.pdf.

86. David Scott, "On the Very Idea of a Black Radical Tradition," 3.

87. Hill, in Cunningham, "A Queer Pier," 87.

88. Cunningham, "A Queer Pier."

89. Italics in original. Singh, in Cunningham, "A Queer Pier," 89. For other useful discussions of the black radical tradition, see Edwards, "The 'Autonomy' of Black Radicalism."

90. Greenspan, *William Wells Brown*, 356.

91. Sterling A. Brown, *Negro Poetry and Drama*, 109; Mitchell, *Black Drama*, 34.

92. Mitchell, *Living with Lynching*, 199.

93. Morris Watson, "The Living Newspaper" *New Theatre*, June 1936, 8.

Chapter One

1. William Pickens, "Stevedore: A New Play on Negro Life," *Amsterdam News*, May 5, 1934, 8.

2. Peters and Sklar, *Stevedore: A Play in Three Acts* 3:2:24. FTP Playscripts 1936–1939, Box 327, RG69, NA. This is the script held by the Regional Service Bureau for the Western Region in Los Angeles, which supplied scripts to the Seattle Units.

3. "A Play to Expose the Exploitation of Negroes," *Amsterdam News*, Jan. 17, 1934, 7.

4. J. A. Rogers, "Ruminations," *Amsterdam News*, May 26, 1934, 8.

5. Earl J. Morris, "'Stevedore' Is Burning Problem Drama,' Says Courier Staff Critic," *Pittsburgh Courier*, Nov. 10, 1934, A9. In Boston and Cleveland the authorities attempted to ban *Stevedore*.

6. "Broadway at Dixie," *Norfolk Journal and Guide*, Jun. 23, 1934, 8.

7. Brooks Atkinson, "Rioting on the Water Front," *New York Times*, Apr. 29, 1934, X1; "A Playreader on Playwrights," *New Theatre*, Oct. 1, 1934, 10–11, cited in Weisstuch, "The Theatre Union, 1933–1937," 260.

8. "The Theatre: New Play in Manhattan," *Time*, Apr. 30, 1934. See also Joseph Wood Krutch, *The Nation*, May 2, 1934, 516, cited in Goldstein, *The Political Stage*, 68. Goldstein reads *Stevedore* through the lens of 1930s white leftists, as an interracial labor union play.

9. Weisstuch, "The Theatre Union, 1933–1937," 189.

10. Goldstein, *The Political Stage*, 67.

11. Although there does not appear to be an extant manuscript of the earlier play, scenes from it were published in *New Masses* in November 1929 and April 1930 under the titles *"Wharf Nigger"* and *"On the Wharf."* See *New Masses*, Nov. 1929, 6. Other notable differences include Yallah Thompson's interaction with whites. The class angle in *Wharf Nigger* is notably absent, and in the earlier play, Thompson commits a cold, calculated act of murder, fueled by racial hostility.

12. The aborted production was not prepared by the Provincetown Players, but rather by an independent group of producers. See Weisstuch, "The Theatre Union, 1933–1937," 196; *New York Times*, Aug. 13, 1931, 24; "Theatrical Notes," *New York Times*, Sept. 11, 1931, 24.

13. Atkinson, "Rioting on the Water Front," X, X1.

14. John Anderson, "Tense and Exciting Drama of New Orleans Waterfront Draws Loud Cheers," *New York Evening Journal*, Apr. 14, 1934, 24.

15. Robert Garland, "'Stevedore' Exciting, Full of Violent Vitality," *New York Telegram*, Apr. 23, 1934, 12.

16. Naison, *Communists in Harlem during the Depression*, 19.

17. *Stevedore*, 2:2:18,

18. *Stevedore*, 3:1:9.

19. *Stevedore*, 3:1:11.

20. *Stevedore*, 3:1:14.

21. *Stevedore*, 3:2:23.

22. *Stevedore*, 3:2:24.

23. John Anderson, "'Stevedore' vs. 'Wharf Nigger': Collaborators Act on Theory That Problem in South Is Economic Not Racial," *New York Evening Journal*, Apr. 28, 1934, 10.

24. Anderson, "'Stevedore' vs. 'Wharf Nigger.'"

25. Weisstuch, "The Theatre Union, 1933–1937," 277.

26. "'Stevedore,' New Theatre Union Play Is Cheered by Workers at Its Preview," *Daily Worker*, Apr. 16, 1934, 5. See also Harold Edgar, "Play of New Orleans Negro Longshoremen Seethes with Struggle" *Daily Worker*, Apr. 20, 1934, 5.

27. Michael Gold, "Stevedore," *New Masses*, May 1, 1934, 28.

28. Ira Levine, *Left-Wing Dramatic Theory in the American Theatre*, 30.

29. Michael Gold, "Towards Proletarian Art," *Liberator*, Feb. 1921. For an in-depth discussion of 1920s leftist experimentation in New York theatre, see Ira Levine, *Left-Wing Dramatic Theory in the American Theatre*, especially chapter 2. See also Goldstein, *The Political Stage*.

30. Levine, *Left-Wing Dramatic Theory in the American Theatre*, 92.

31. Hallie Flanagan, "A Theatre Is Born," *Theatre Arts Monthly*, 15:1 (1931): 908.

32. Conrad Seiler, "Workers Theatre: A Criticism," *New Theatre*, Jun. 1934, 17, cited in Levine, *Left-Wing Dramatic Theory in the American Theatre*, 103.

33. For the difference between social realism and socialist realism, see David Shapiro, who defines social realism as the desire of artists to use their art to "communicate social values" that might transform society. See Shapiro, "Social Realism Reconsidered," 28. Social realism was meant to appeal to the working classes and bring about change by revealing the truth of capitalist exploitation. Socialist realism, on the other hand was more focused on the positive outcomes of a socialist state and/or life under the Soviet Union. As Mark Fearnow points out, socialist realism was hardly "realism" at all since it was less a "revelation of truth" and more a "Marxist vision of a world to come." See Fearnow, "A New Realism," 176; Levine, *Left-Wing Dramatic Theory in the American Theatre*, 108–9; Goldstein, *The Political Stage*, 158. Ilka Saal argues that this return to realism marked a shift of emphasis rather than a radical departure. See Saal, *New Deal Theater*, 60.

34. Levine, *Left-Wing Dramatic Theory in the American Theatre*, 102–4.

35. Levine, *Left-Wing Dramatic Theory in the American Theatre*, 110; Gus Smith to Philip Barber, Apr. 26, 1937, Corr. of the New York City Office, E915, Box 498, RG69, NA; Wendy Smith, *Real Life Drama;* Clurman, *The Fervent Years.*

36. Saal, *New Deal Theater*, 9–24

37. Saal, *New Deal Theater*, 36–45.

38. Saal, *New Deal Theater*, 57–58.

39. "Stevedore," *Afro American*, Jul. 21, 1934, 6.

40. "Ethel Walters Thinks 'Stevedore' Is Fine Play," *Chicago Defender*, Dec. 15, 1934, 8; See also "Bill Robinson Forgets All to Join 'Stevedore,'" *Chicago Defender*, Jul. 7, 1934, 7.

41. "Ethel Walters Thinks 'Stevedore' Is Fine Play."

42. Bessye Bearden, "Critics Says Stevedore Is Play for Race," *Chicago Defender*, Apr. 28, 1934, 8.

43. Richard Lockridge, *New York Sun*, Apr. 19, 1934; Percy Hammond, *New York Herald Tribune*, Apr. 19, 1934, both in Theatre Union Scrapbooks cited in Hyman, *Staging Strikes*, 56.

44. Quoted in Weisstuch, "The Theatre Union, 1933–1937," 273.

45. Brooks Atkinson, "The Play," *New York Times*, Apr. 19, 1934, 33.

46. "Stevedore," *Christian Science Monitor*, Apr. 28, 1934, 6.

47. Burns Mantle, "New Species of Negro Play Pops Up in New York," *Chicago Daily Tribune*, Apr. 28, 1934, D3.

48. John Mason Brown, "The Theatre Union Takes to the Soap Box Once More—Stevedore and the Race Problem in America," *New York Evening Post*, Apr. 21, 1934, cited in Michael Gold, "'Stevedore,' the Play," *Chicago Defender*, May 5, 1934, 8.

49. Gold, "Stevedore,' the Play."

50. See Lawson's 1936 book, *Theory and Technique of Playwriting.*

51. *New Theatre*, June, July–August, and November 1934 issues, esp. July–August 1934.

52. John Howard Lawson, "Straight from the Shoulder," *New Theatre*, Nov. 1934, 11–12.

53. Lawson, "Straight from the Shoulder."

54. Michael Blankfort, "Facing the New Audience," *New Theatre*, Nov. 1934, 25.

55. Levine, *Left-Wing Dramatic Theory in the American Theatre*, 111–12.

56. Blankfort, "Facing the New Audience," 25.

57. Blankfort, "Facing the New Audience," 25.

58. Weisstuch, "The Theatre Union, 1933–1937," 221.

59. "Jack Carter: The Man Who Came Back," *Afro American*, Aug. 4, 1934, 9; "Refusal to Say Yes Sir, Boss, Gave Rex Ingram Start," *Afro American*, Feb. 16, 1935, 9; "In the New Drama," *Amsterdam News*, Apr. 21, 1934, 1; "Given Top Mention in 'Stevedore,'" *Norfolk Journal and Guide*, Jun. 16, 1934, 13.

60. "Refusal to Say Yes Sir, Boss, Gave Rex Ingram Start."

61. "New Faces for Stevedore in its N.Y Revival," *Afro American*, Week of Sept. 29, 1934, 7.

62. "Trace Contribution of Race in Radio Skit," *Afro American*, Oct. 27, 1934, 6.

63. Henry Lee Moon, "Horrors Bared by Stevedore," *Amsterdam News*, Apr. 21, 1934, 7.

64. "Jobless Motor Here for Play," *Amsterdam News*, May 19, 1934, 6.

65. "Jobless Motor Here for Play." Sklar supports this assertion. See George Sklar, "Negro Actors Playing in Drama, 'Stevedore,'" *Amsterdam News*, May 5, 1934, 7.

66. Margaret Larkin, "On Propaganda," *New York Times*, Mar. 18, 1934, X2.

67. "'Stevedore,' New Theatre Union Play Is Cheered by Workers at Its Preview," *Daily Worker*, Apr. 16, 1934, 5. See also "Entertain "Stevedore" Cast", *Afro American,* Apr. 7 1934, 8 and "Stevedore Members Tendered Reception," *Amsterdam News,* Apr. 14, 1934, 7. Weisstuch, "The Theatre Union, 1933–1937," 228. The League of Struggle for Negro Rights was established by the Communist Party in Harlem in 1931 as an anti-lynching vehicle. But support for cultural endeavors had shaped it from the start, when it had succeeded in attracting Langston Hughes to act as its first president. It would also play a prominent role in challenging race discrimination in New Deal agencies including the Civil Works Administration. See Naison, *Communists in Harlem*, 42, 105–6.

68. "Herb with Theatre Union," *Amsterdam News*, May 19, 1934, 7; "Jobless Motor Here for Play," *Amsterdam News*, May 19, 1934, 6. For additional praise of the Theatre Union, see Vere E. Jones, "Stevedore," *New York Age*, Apr. 21, 1934, 4.

69. George Sklar, "Negro Actors Playing in Drama, 'Stevedore,'" *Amsterdam News*, May 5, 1934, 7.

70. Malcolm B. Fulcher, "Believe Me," *Afro American*, Dec. 1, 1934, 12; Goldstein, *The Political Stage*, 66.

71. "Scottsboro Mothers to see "Stevedore," *Afro American*, May 12, 1934, 13; "Stevedore Crowd Lauds Scottsboro Mothers," *Afro American*, Week of May 19, 1934, 8; "Scottsboro Mothers Have Day in East," *Chicago Defender*, May 19, 1934, 9.

72. Stephen Breszka, "Chicago Critics Knock Stevedore Groggy," *Pittsburgh Courier*, Jan. 5, 1935, A9.

73. Rob Roy, "'Stevedore' Is 'Theatre' Not Propaganda," *Chicago Defender*, Jan. 5, 1935, 8; James Woodlea, "Stevedore: Finest Play on American Stage," *Chicago Defender*, Jan. 19, 1935, 11.

74. "The Embassy Theatre," *Times*, May 7, 1935, 14; "The Week's Theatres," *Observer*, May 12, 1935, 17. For an overview of the critical reception of *Stevedore* in London, see Boyle and Bunie, *Paul Robeson*, 329–32.

75. Nancy Cunard, "Stevedore in London," *Crisis*, 42:8 (August 1935): 238. Nancy Cunard, "Many Types Seen in London Cast of Stevedore," *Afro American*, Jun. 15, 1935, 8.

76. Marcus Garvey, "Smiles for the Thoughtful," reprinted in Robert A. Hill, ed., *Marcus Garvey Life and Lessons*, 170–71. See also Garvey, "Paul Robeson and His Mission [Editorial]," *Black Man*, Jan. 1937, reprinted in Robert A. Hill, ed., *The Marcus Garvey and Universal Negro Improvement Association Papers*, 7:728–29.

77. Roi Ottley, "Hectic Harlem," *Amsterdam News*, Apr. 20, 1935, 9.

78. *Stevedore* was produced by Cleveland's Karamu House Theatre, a troupe of black amateurs directed by white husband-and-wife team Russell and Rowena Jelliffe in spring 1935. The production attracted considerable criticism from a group of black Baptist ministers as well as the proprietor of the *Cleveland Gazette*, Harry C. Smith, ostensibly on grounds of the language used in the play but also because the Karamu attracted mainly white audiences. Other black newspapers in Cleveland defended both the play and the Karamu House Theatre. See Harry C. Smith to Atty. Perry B. Jackson, Feb. 26, 1935, Karamu House Records, Western Reserve Historical Society, Sub-Series J: Box 12. See also "Ministers' Fight to Stop 'Stevedore' Fails as Play Continues with Crowds," Cleveland *Call and Post*, Mar. 16, 1935, 8; "Stevedore Hailed by Public as Great Play, Fought by Clergymen," Cleveland *Call and Post*, Mar. 9, 1935, 1; C. Ellsworth Lee, "Harlem Briefs," Cleveland *Call and Post*, Mar. 9, 1935, 6; "Cleveland Ministers Fail to Stop Play; Crowded Each Night," *Pittsburgh Courier*, Apr. 6, 1935, B10; "Stevedore under Fire," *Afro American*, Week of May 4, 1935, 9; Karamu House, "Revised Release," March 7, 1935, Karamu House Records, Box 12; "Down the Big Road: W.O.W," Cleveland *Call and Post*, Mar. 16, 1935, 6; Silver, "A History of the Karamu Theatre," 216, 289–94.

79. See, for example, the debate concerning the publication of Carl Van Vechten's *Nigger Heaven* (1926) and Claude McKay's *Home to Harlem* (1928). Artistic portrayals of "low life" prompted Du Bois to conduct a survey of leading commentators and artists on "The Negro in Art: How Shall He Be Portrayed." Responses from a variety of black and white commentators were published in the *Crisis* between March and November 1926.

80. George Streator, "The Nigger Did It," *Crisis*, 41:7 (July 1934): 216–17.

81. Albert Ottenheimer, interviewed by John O'Connor, Jan. 10, 1978, First tape, Side 1, 2, Box 8, OHC-GMU; Florence James, "Fists upon A Star" Draft manuscript, 1, Box 2, Folder 11, SCA-UWL; Elizabeth Corbett, "Uncle Tom Is Dead," *Theatre Guild Magazine*, Jan. 1931. See also "Last Days for 'Uncle Tom,'" *New York Times Magazine*, Jul. 12, 1931; R. Burton Rose, "The Death of Uncle Tom's Cabin," *Overland Monthly and Out West Magazine*, December 1931, online at http://utc.iath.virginia .edu/onstage/revus/osarhp.html.

82. James, "Fists upon A Star," 1; Albert Ottenheimer, SRPL, 26 Apr, 1936, Box 32, Folder 7, (SRPR) SCA-UWL.

83. James, "Fists upon A Star," 4–5.

84. Ottenheimer, SRPL, Jan. 9, 1933, Jan. 11, 1933.

85. Johnson, "A Production History of the Seattle Federal Theatre Project," 24; Quintard Taylor, *The Forging of a Black Community*, 51.

86. See, for example, West, "Left Out: The Seattle Repertory Playhouse," 205n52; Redd, "Staging Race," 71. Witham offers a more nuanced account in *The Federal Theatre Project*, 61–77.

87. Ottenheimer, SRPL, Apr. 26, 1936.

88. Sara Oliver, who would play many female leads for the Seattle Negro Unit, remembered the idea of the Negro Unit as coming from the black community. In an oral history interview, Oliver remembered the theatre as being started by Joe Steeton (presumably a mistyping of "Joe Staton," the name of the leading black actor) and "a friend of his, Frank Garvey," presumably Frederick Darby. These two men, she recalled, "went out and contacted Mrs. Burton James." Sara O. Jackson (nee Oliver), interviewed by Leona Pollack on Mar. 3, 1981; transcript, excerpts, and clippings in Sara O. Jackson Papers, SCA-UWL.

89. Sara Jackson interview, 7; Mumford, ed., *Seven Stars and Orion*, 70.

90. Ottenheimer, SRPL, Dec. 13, 1935.

91. The Seattle Negro Unit was eventually granted an exceptional allocation of 20 percent nonrelief employees. See Witham, *The Federal Theatre Project*, 66–67.

92. Ottenheimer SRPL, Nov. 1, 1935.

93. Ottenheimer SRPL, Jan. 31, 1936. In fact, the Negro Unit prepared two plays to open around the same time. Sharing much of the cast of *Stevedore*, Andre Obey's *Noah* had opened a few weeks earlier, in April. See SRPL, Apr. 26, 1936; May 22, 1936.

94. "Social Notes," *Northwest Enterprise*, May 8, 1936; "Federal Theater Troupe Pleases in 'Stevedore,'" *Seattle Post Intelligencer*, May 15, 1936.

95. Taylor, *The Forging of a Black Community*, 51–52.

96. Taylor, *The Forging of a Black Community*, 52.

97. Horace Cayton Jr. cited in Taylor, *The Forging of a Black Community*, 54.

98. Taylor, *The Forging of a Black Community*, 70.

99. Vokler, "The Power of Art and the Fear of Labor," online at http://depts .washington.edu/depress/seattle_waiting_for_lefty.shtml.

100. Vokler, "The Power of Art and the Fear of Labor."

101. James, "Fists upon a Star," and Playhouse logs, 256, both cited in Vokler, "The Power of Art and the Fear of Labor."

102. *Stevedore* Playbill, Jan.–Mar. 1937, in Western Regional Office Publicity Reports 1937, E120, Box 654, RG69, NA.

103. Ellen McGrath, "The Stage," *Argus,* May 15, 1936, in GMU Newspaper Review Clippings; "Albert M. Ottenheimer" GMU Newspaper Review Clippings; "Federal Theater Troupe Pleases in 'Stevedore,'" *Seattle Post Intelligencer*, May 15, 1936, GMU Newspaper Review Clippings.

104. See "Federal Theater Troupe Pleases in 'Stevedore'"; Hugh Thompson, "Curtain and Catcalls," *University of Washington Daily*, June 1936, in *Stevedore* Production Bulletin, Box 1073, FTP-LOC; Bill Holloman, "Stevedore Wins Praise," *Seattle Star*, GMU Newspaper Review Clippings; Ellen McGrath "The Stage," *Argus*, May 15,

1936, in GMU Newspaper Review Clippings; Review from the *University District Herald*, Stevedore Production Bulletin, Box 1073, FTP-LOC.

105. June Carlson, "'Stevedore' Depicts Negro's Fight against Whites in the South," n.d., GMU Newspaper Review Clippings.

106. Hugh Thompson, "Curtain and Catcalls," *University of Washington Daily*, June 1936, Stevedore Production Bulletin, Box 1073, FTP-LOC.

107. Bill Holloman, "Stevedore Wins Praise," *Seattle Star*; McGrath, "The Stage."

108. McGrath, "The Stage"; Joseph Staton, interviewed by John O'Connor, Jan. 7, 1976, Seattle, Washington, First Tape, Side 1, 1, OHC-GMU.

109. Neither the LOC nor GMU Federal Theatre collections contain manuscripts for *Stevedore*. The National Archives has a copy of a script that was held by the Los Angeles Regional Bureau of the FTP, Box 327, RG69, NA. The L.A. bureau usually issued scripts to the Seattle Negro Unit. However, this unmarked script at the NA is very close to the published version and therefore offers few clues; the Seattle Unit working script would have been marked up.

110. Synopsis, Stevedore Production Bulletin, Box 1073, FTP-LOC.

111. George Sklar, interviewed by John O'Connor, Jan. 2, 1976, L.A., California, Box 9, OHC-GMU, First Tape, Side 1, 6.

112. Sklar interview, First Tape, Side 1, 6.

113. Weisstuch, interview with Paul Peters, Jun. 17, 1978, and Aug. 20, 1978, cited in Weisstuch, "The Theatre Union, 1933–1937," 204.

114. Sklar interview, First Tape, Side 1, 8.

115. Press Release from Department of Information, FTP, Negro Unit, New York City, for the *Afro American*, Dec. 22, 1937, 2, *NDABA*, Reel 24.

116. Dick Campbell was an actor and former vaudeville star who went on to become an important director, manager, and producer in the 1930s. He founded the Rose McClendon Players as a tribute to the deceased actress in 1936. See Peterson, *The African American Theatre Directory, 1816–1960*, 148–49. In his dictionary of the Harlem Renaissance, Kellner suggests that the NPT was incorporated into the Harlem Negro Unit. See Kellner, *Harlem Renaissance*, 229.

117. Negro Peoples Theatre, Circular letter from Negro Peoples Theatre, Jun. 19, 1935, W. E. B. Du Bois Papers, MS 312.

118. Joe Foster, "Negro People's Theatre," *Daily Worker*, May 28, 1935, 2.

119. "The Show Must Go On! One Group Failed But Another One Will Make Bow Tonight: Negro Peoples Theatre Will Give 'Waiting for Lefty' at Rockland Palace," *Amsterdam News*, Jun. 1, 1935, 3.

120. Allen Chumley, "Negro Peoples Theatre," *New Masses*, Jun. 11, 1935, 27.

121. Joe Foster, "Negro People's Theatre," *Daily Worker*, May 28, 1935, 2.

122. Rose McClendon, "As to a Negro Stage," *New York Times*, Jun. 30, 1935, X1.

123. McClendon, "As to a Negro Stage"; "News of the Stage," *New York Times*, Jun. 29, 1935, 16.

124. The *New York Times* obituary for McClendon suggests the importance of the Negro People's Theatre to the Harlem Negro Unit. Jay Plum's account of McClendon's contribution to the Negro Units details how her central role is often excluded

from official records. For example, the Federal Theatre's own account of how the Negro Units were formed credits Welles and Houseman with "guiding the destinations of the Negro Theatre at its inception." See Plum, "Rose McClendon and the Black Units of the Federal Theatre Project," 144. Flanagan acknowledges McClendon's influence in the forming of the Harlem Negro Unit in her 1940 account. However, she claims that her own proposal, to have Negro Units led by African Americans from the outset, was resisted by McClendon, who felt "they would prefer to start under more experienced direction." See Flanagan, *Arena,* 63. Most accounts of the founding of the Harlem Negro Unit pay little attention to interracial and leftist groups like the Theatre Union and Group Theatre, focusing instead on Welles and Houseman. See, for example, Wendy Smith's essay, "The Play That Electrified Harlem" (*Civilization*, Jan.–Feb. 1996), which has been reproduced on the Library of Congress's American Memory website at https://www.loc.gov/collections/federal-theatre-project-1935-to-1939/articles-and-essays/play-that-electrified-harlem/.

125. Naison, *Communists in Harlem during the Depression*, 154.

126. Stevedore playbill, Oct. 1934, Canada Lee Papers, Box 5, SCR.

127. Staton interview, First Tape, Side 1, 1.

128. Theodore Browne, interviewed by Lorraine Brown, Oct. 22, 1975, Roxbury, Mass., First tape, Side 2, 19, Box 2, OHC-GMU; Monroe interview, First tape, Side 1, 15.

129. Charles Monroe, Interviewed by Lorraine Brown, Nov. 9, 1978; First tape, Side 2, 33, Box 7, OHC-GMU.

130. Redd, "Staging Race," 68, 71, 78–79.

131. Monroe interview, First tape, Side 1, 36.

Chapter Two

1. Joseph Staton, interviewed by John O'Connor, Jan. 7, 1976, Seattle, Washington, First Tape, Side 1, 1, Box 10, OHC-GMU.

2. A new Agricultural Act was passed in 1938 to get round the Supreme Court's ruling that the federal government had invaded the rights of states. See Badger, *The New Deal*, 160–61.

3. Cosgrove, "The Living Newspaper," 58, 111.

4. "Investigation of Un-American Propaganda Activities in the United States," *Hearings on House Resolution 282, Before the Special Committee on Un-American Activities*, 2862, 2878. For an account of the Dies Committee investigation of the FTP and its focus on Living Newspapers, see Dossett, "Gender and the Dies Committee Hearings on the Federal Theatre Project," 993–1017.

5. Flanagan, *Arena*, 64–65. Flanagan has often been viewed as critical to the development of the Living Newspaper. For example, Jane DeHart Matthews suggests that Flanagan's play *Can You Hear Their Voices?* served as an important model for the Living Newspaper in utilizing the device of the Loudspeaker and drawing heavily on factual material. See Matthews, *The Federal Theatre, 1935–39*, 62. In an interview given just before his death, Elmer Rice offered a rather different account, describing the development of the Living Newspaper as the product of his relationship with Morris Watson of the Newspaper Guild. See Isaac, "Ethiopia: The First Living Newspaper,"

16. Certainly some newspaper coverage seems to support this view, for example, "WPA Will Stage War New Events in Two-Week Run," *Brooklyn Eagle*, Jan. 19, 1936, Box 1006, FTP-LOC.

6. Flanagan, *Arena*, 70. While insisting on the Americanness of Living Newspapers, Flanagan acknowledged the "occasional reference" to the Blue Blouses and to the Volksbuhne (People's Theatre in Berlin), as well as to Meierhold, Eisenstein, and Bragaglia. See Cosgrove, "The Living Newspaper," 193, vii. Arthur Arent also insisted he knew of no influence on the Living Newspaper that was not entirely American. See Arent, "The Technique of the Living Newspaper," 820; Flanagan, *Shifting Scenes of the Modern European Theatre*.

7. Goldman, "Life and Death of a Living Newspaper Unit," esp. 69–70; McDermott, "The Living Newspaper as a Dramatic Form," 82–84; Cosgrove, "Introduction"; Cobb, "'Injunction Granted' in Its Times"; Laura Browder argues that the Living Newspaper delivered what radical novelists of the 1930s had struggled to achieve, namely, to "offer radical culture in a collective setting," and bring modernism to the masses. See Browder, *Rousing the Nation*, 117, 121–124. For the continued appeal and recent revival of *One Third of a Nation* see Ken Jaworoswki's review, "A Depression-Era Protest Ripped From the Headlines," *New York Times*, May 2, 2011, C3.

8. Ira Levine, *Left-Wing Dramatic Theory in the American Theatre*, 150.

9. Cosgrove, "The Living Newspaper," 194.

10. Saal, *New Deal Theater*, 130.

11. Goldman, "Life and Death of a Living Newspaper Unit," 83n44; Norford and Gandard's "Negro Script" was probably the Newark Living Newspaper on the history of the "Negro" that was mentioned by Flanagan in her Introduction to the Random House publication of three white Living Newspapers in May 1938. See Flanagan, "Introduction," in De Rohan, Arent, and Sundgaard, eds., *Federal Theatre Plays*, xii. Norford submitted a number of plays to the FTP, but none were produced. He went on to become one of the founders of the Negro Playwrights Company in Harlem after the demise of the FTP. See George Norford, interviewed by Lorraine Brown, Oct. 25, 1976, New York, N.Y., Box 8, abstract of untaped interview, OHC-GMU. Cosgrove suggests that the New York Living Newspaper Unit had three black-authored Living Newspapers manuscripts. See Cosgrove, "The Living Newspaper," 139.

12. Paul Nadler attributes *Stars and Bars* to Courtney. See Nadler, "Liberty Censored," 616.

13. Retman, *Real Folk*, 5, 20.

14. Brooks, *Bodies in Dissent*, 5.

15. Stott, *Documentary Expression and Thirties America*, xi.

16. Denning, *The Cultural Front*, 122–23.

17. Brooks, *Bodies in Dissent*, 5–6.

18. Historians who have considered the black Living Newspaper include Nadler, "Liberty Censored," 619, 621; Cosgrove, "The Living Newspaper," 86; 102, 139; and Craig, *Black Drama of the Federal Theatre Era*, 62–70. They are mentioned in passing in Fraden, *Blueprints for a Black Federal Theatre*, 107, and in Browder, *Rousing the Nation*, 153. For published versions of *Liberty Deferred*, see Brown, ed., *Liberty Deferred and Other Living Newspapers of the 1930s*. The first half of *Liberty Deferred*

is published in Hatch and Shine, eds., *Black Theatre U.S.A: Plays by African Americans, The Recent Period, 1935–Today, Revised and Expanded Edition*. A discussion of the different manuscripts of *Liberty Deferred* can be found in notes 71–73.

19. Flanagan, *Arena*, 217, 222; *The Federal Theatre Project: A Catalog-Calendar of Productions*, 117–18; Cosgrove, "Introduction," xvi–xvii; Browder, *Rousing the Nation*, 157.

20. In their accounts of the FTP's Living Newspaper, Saal and Levine base their analysis exclusively on *One Third*. See Saal, *New Deal Theater*, 123–36; Ira Levine, *Left-Wing Dramatic Theory in the American Theatre*, 155–66. Flanagan, *Arena*, devotes a chapter of her account of the Federal Theatre to *One Third*. See 207–22.

21. Cosgrove, "The Living Newspaper," 86, 102.

22. Cosgrove, "Introduction," xvi n14; Pierre de Rohan, "First Federal Summer Theatre: A Report," 12, n.d., Box 25, Folder 8F, in Shirley Graham Du Bois Papers, Arthur and Elizabeth Schlesinger Library, Radcliffe Institute.

23. Online at http://historymatters.gmu.edu/d/5105/; see also Browder, *Rousing the Nation*, 158.

24. Regional versions of *One Third of a Nation*, which were rolled out to ten cities, were sometimes more experimental in terms of their stagecraft. For example, Seattle had a projection slideshow of local slum conditions. See Cosgrove, "Introduction," xvi, xvii.

25. *One Third of a Nation: A Living Newspaper about Housing by Arthur Arent*, April 1938, FTP-GMU. Browder compares the Living Newspaper *One Third of a Nation* with the Hollywood movie version of 1939. In such a comparison, the stage version emerges as "coolly Brechtian rather than warmly sentimental." See Browder, *Rousing the Nation*, 160. However, when compared to other Living Newspapers, and especially the black Living Newspapers, the judgment does not hold up.

26. *One Third of a Nation*, 2:5:9.

27. "Techniques Available to the Living Newspaper Dramatist," 237–38.

28. Anne Mercer, "WPA Negro Theatre News," Jul. 8, 1937, in Negro Unit, New York City, Report/Narrative of NYC Negro Unit, RG69, NA; de Rohan, "First Federal Summer Theatre."

29. Flier for "New Summer Session of the Negro Dramatists Laboratory," *NDABA*, Reel 24.

30. "Meet New Leaders of Negro Theatre," *Amsterdam News*, Aug. 22, 1936, 8; "The Negro Theatre: Its Plans and Policies for the Development of a Negro Theatre," 3, in Corr. of the New York City FTP Office E 915, B98; RG69, NA; "Schedule, Lectures and Classes of the Negro Dramatist Laboratory," in WPA FTP Corr. Folder, Aug 1, 1936–May 31, 1937, *Black Freedom Struggle in the 20th Century: Federal Government Records*.

31. George Zorn, "Report of the Activities and Accomplishments of Negro Dramatists Laboratory," Apr. 1, 1937, in Corr. of the New York City Office, E915, Box 498. RG69, NA.

32. Flier for "New Summer Session of the Negro Dramatists Laboratory," *NDABA*, Reel 24.

33. Hill to Flanagan, Sept. 23, 1938, Series E839, Box 19, RG69, NA.

34. De Rohan, "First Federal Summer Theatre," 8.

35. "The Sincere Testimony to Anxiety, Labor, Patience, Time and Cordial, Constructive Criticism and to Memories Turbulent or Tender of Conn. Federal Theater October 1936 to May 6, 1939," in Gwen Reed Collection.

36. "Negroes on W.P.A Projects," in Connecticut Federal Theatre, E839, Box 32, Folder Negro, No. 3, 4, RG69, NA.

37. "Negroes on W.P.A Projects," 2; Gertrude Don Dero to William M. Stahl, Dec. 7, 1936, Production Records, New Haven, Connecticut, Box 1068, FTP-LOC; "Negro Drama Players Now Part of WPA," *Hartford Courant*, Sept. 11, 1936, 20.

38. "Conn. WPA Players Enjoy Popularity," *Amsterdam News*, Jun. 19, 1937, 20; W. Earle Smith, "The Charles Gilpin Players," Dec. 7, 1936, in Production Bulletin, *Sabine Women*, Box 1068, FTP-LOC.

39. "Negroes on W.P.A Projects," 9.

40. V. J. Sullivan to E. E. McCleish, May 11, 1937; Press Releases in "Hartford Negro Unit," WPA, FTP activities in Hartford, Connecticut, *Black Freedom Struggle in the 20th Century: Federal Government Records*.

41. Smith, "The Charles Gilpin Players."

42. "Federal Theatre to Give Haiti at Avery Memorial," *Hartford Courant*, Oct. 19, 1938; "Federal Theatre Combined Units Appear in Haiti," *Hartford Courant*, Oct. 28, 1938, in Vassar College Press Clippings on Plays, Press cuttings, Haiti Folder 1, Box 129, RG69, NA.

43. "The Sincere Testimony to Anxiety, Labor, Patience, Time and Cordial, Constructive Criticism and to Memories Turbulent or Tender of Conn. Federal Theater October 1936 to May 6, 1939," in Gwen Reed Collection; "WPA Production Will Return Here by Public Demand," *Hartford Courant*, Jan. 29, 1939, A4.

44. The latest dated references to Hartford newspapers and medical reports is January 1938, the same month *One Third* opened in New York City. See *Stars and Bars* manuscript.

45. Lavery's approval is cited in a colleague's letter. See Harold Koppleman to Blanding Sloan, Apr. 25, 1937, Series E878, Box 162. RG69, NA. There is no direct record of Lavery's views or those of other senior FTP administrators on *Stars and Bars*, nor a record indicating the latest version of the script he approved. At the time of Lavery's recorded approval, the Living Newspaper was still called *Bars and Stripes*. It was scheduled for production in the Eastern Region Schedule for May 12, 1938. See Lavery, Jun. 13, 1938, Series E878, Box 162. RG69, NA. Anthony D. Hill suggests it was produced around 1939 by the Hartford Negro Unit but there is no Federal Theatre record or other evidence to support this. See Hill and Barnett, *Historical Dictionary of African American Theater*, 120. In his article on black Living Newspapers, Nadler concurs that there is no record of any performance. See Nadler, "Liberty Censored," 618.

46. In November 1938, an article published in the *Hartford Courant* noted the forthcoming production of *One Third of a Nation* scheduled to open in the new year and asked what had become of the Hartford Living Newspaper, which had been approved for production the previous summer. See "The People's Forum," *Hartford Courant*, Nov. 9, 1938, 14.

47. "The Sincere Testimony to Anxiety, Labor, Patience, Time and Cordial, Constructive Criticism and to Memories Turbulent or Tender of Conn. Federal Theater October 1936 to May 6, 1939," in Gwen Reed Collection. See also Baker, "From Fields to Footlights," 319. FTP records indicate that this drama was later renamed *Mango* and was a collaborative piece developed with Hartford FTP colleague Russell Beckworth, who was listed as co-author. See Robert Russell to John McGee, 20 Apr. 20, 1938, E878, Box 162, RG69, NA; Charles E. Niles on *Trilogy in Black, Hartford Times*, Jun. 19, 1937, in E839, Box 5, RG69, NA; "'Trilogy in Black' is Presented by Federal Negro Unit," *Hartford Courant*, Jun. 19, 1937, 9; "Negro Theater in Performance of Danish Play," *Hartford Courant*, Jun. 20, 1938, 16.

48. Irwin A. Rubinstein to F. S. Belcher, Mar. 4, 1938, in FTP correspondence, Dec. 1, 1937–Dec. 31, 1938, in WPA, RG69, FTP, National Office, Subject File "N," in *Black Freedom Struggle in the 20th Century: Federal Government Records*. Rubinstein's confusion has been replicated in some historical accounts. Bernard L. Peterson identified Courtney as African American in his biographical directory of early black American playwrights. Nadler, however, correctly identifies Courtney as a young white playwright from Vermont. See Bernard L. Peterson, *Early Black American Playwrights*, 17; Nadler, "Liberty Censored," 616.

49. Ward Courtney, Preface to *Trilogy in Black*, Production Records, Box 1083, FTP-LOC.

50. Cosgrove, "The Living Newspaper," 179n7; Rampersad, *The Life of Langston Hughes*, 311–17.

51. "Release to Hartford Times, Noah," 1–2; "Release to Hartford Courant," WPA, FTP activities in Hartford, Connecticut, WPA, RG69, in *Black Freedom Struggle in the 20th Century: Federal Government Records*.

52. "Release to Hartford Times, Noah," 1–2.

53. Ward Courtney and Hartford Negro Unit, *Stars and Bars*, 1:1:1, Federal Theatre Project Play Script and Radio Script Collection, Box 6, SCA-GMU.

54. *Stars and Bars*, 1:1:1.

55. *Stars and Bars*, 1:1:2.

56. *Stars and Bars*, 1:4:5.

57. *Stars and Bars*, 1:4:3.

58. *Stars and Bars*, 1:4:7.

59. Brooks, *Bodies in Dissent*, 3, 12.

60. *Stars and Bars*, 1:4:7; 1:4:9.

61. *Stars and Bars*, 1:4:11; 1:5:1.

62. Brooks Atkinson, "Sage of the Slums: The Openings," *New York Times*, Jan. 30, 1938, 151; Cosgrove, "The Living Newspaper," 121, 130.

63. *Stars and Bars*, 2:4:5.

64. Glenn, "Taking Burlesque Seriously," 93, cited in Retman, *Real Folks*, 20.

65. *Stars and Bars*, 2:5:6; Brooks, *Bodies in Dissent*, 3.

66. *Stars and Bars*, 2:3:9–10.

67. *Stars and Bars*, 1:5:14, 1:5:15; "Gwen Reed: A Guide to the Collection at the Hartford History Center," accessed Aug. 13, 2013, http://hhc2.hplct.org/reed_pdf.pdf.

68. Alver Napper, "Aims, Values and Possibilities," in National Office, Subject File "N" RG 69, WPA, *NDABA*, Reel 25.

69. Retman, *Real Folks*, 239.

70. Abramson, *Negro Playwrights in the American Theatre*, 67. Abramson also compared Hill unfavorably to Theodore Ward and Richard Wright, describing him as a playwright who had "little to say and little will to discipline what talent he possessed," 156.

71. In her 1975 interview with Theodore Browne, Lorraine Brown suggested that Abramson had written to the FTP Collection at George Mason asking for copies of theatre manuscripts and suggesting "she was just going on what other people had said about it rather than the actual playscripts themselves." Theodore Browne, interviewed by Lorraine Brown, Oct. 22, 1975, First Tape, Side 1, 1, Box 2, OHC-GMU.

72. The two almost identical early drafts of *Liberty Deferred* upon which I base my analysis are held in the Playscripts File, Box 694, FTP-LOC. Three very similar photocopied versions are also available in Boxes 191 and 192 at the FTP-GMU.

73. The Billy Rose Theatre Division of the New York Public Library for the Performing Arts, (NYPLPA) holds the sixth, much altered version. It includes an FTP National Service Bureau frontispiece and a stamp reading, "Under supervision of the National Service Bureau Thru Ira Knaster," suggesting it was amended while the FTP was still in operation but after October 1938, when we know Lavery was still complaining that the authors had not adopted his changes. See "Liberty Deferred: A Dramatic Chronicle of the Negro," by John D. Silvera and Abram Hill, Performing Arts Research Collections, NYPLPA. For the dating of the manuscript, see Lavery to John Gibbs, Oct. 3, 1938, E879, Box 182, Folder: John Silvera RG69, NA.

Two versions of *Liberty Deferred* have been published. The first half of *Liberty Deferred* was included in the expanded and revised edition of Hatch and Shine's *Black Theatre U.S.A.*, published in 1996 with the permission of Silvera. This version contains only the first half of the play, ending at the Civil War. Although heavily edited, it appears to be based on the Library of Congress Federal Theatre manuscripts, which were the basis for this chapter, and indeed the editors describe it as an "early draft." See Hatch and Shine, *Black Theatre U.S.A.: Plays by African Americans: The Recent Period, 1935–Today, Revised and Expanded Edition*, 385. A much revised, additional manuscript was published as part of a collection of Federal Theatre Living Newspapers edited by Lorraine Brown: *Liberty Deferred and Other Living Newspapers of the 1930s*. Its conclusion has President Roosevelt signing Executive Order 8802, which prohibited racial discrimination in government defense contracts and was a direct response to A. Philip Randolph's planned March on Washington in June 1941. Since these events took place two years after the closure of the Federal Theatre, it is reasonable to surmise that this was a version amended and updated after the closure of the FTP. I have not been able to trace a copy of this manuscript even in the George Mason University collections. In her Preface to the published edition, Brown acknowledges other extant versions of *Liberty Deferred,* but explains that "we have deliberately chosen versions of the [*sic*] included in the cache of materials packed up in 1939 and placed on permanent loan at George Mason University by the Library of Congress in 1974." See Brown, ed., *Liberty Deferred and Other Living Newspapers of the 1930s*, vii. With an ending that references events that took place in 1941, this version clearly was not the one written before the Federal Theatre closed, but rather was revised after 1941. In Lorraine Brown's oral history interview with Abram Hill in 1978, Hill discusses the various endings, recalling one version that ended with a march on Washington during World War II and pointing out that "that had not occurred when this was written." See Abram Hill, interviewed by Lorraine Brown and Swann, March 30, 1978, First Tape, Side 2, 15A, Box 5, OHC-GMU (hereafter Hill interview, 1978). The version edited by Brown has a number of other differences from the early versions; most significantly, it has been extensively edited and new contexts added. For example, the emphasis on blackness being performed for the entertainment of whites is there, but in different forms. The Brown version also has other fascinating differences: it opens with a televised minstrel show, engaging with this increasingly popular form of entertainment and exploring the possibilities of televised entertainment shows for perpetuating racial stereotypes of minstrelsy.

74. Abram Hill, interviewed by Lorraine Brown, Feb. 27, 1977, First Tape, Side 1, 2–3, Box 5, OHC-GMU (hereafter Hill interview, 1977).

75. Lavery, himself a Catholic, took on the Catholic Church and the League of Decency when they leveled charges of communism against the FTP. See Barry Witham, "Censorship in the Federal Theatre," 12.

76. Hill interview, 1977, First Tape, Side 1, 1; John Silvera interviewed by Lorraine Brown, July 11, 1977, First Tape, Side 1, 2, 4–10; Box 9, OHC-GMU (hereafter Silvera interview, 1977). Hill had already written a full-length play, *Hell's Half Acre* (1936). Carlton Moss, one of the three directors of the Harlem Negro Unit and a longtime associate of Silvera later speculated that the Living Newspaper project must have belonged to Hill since Silvera's skills lay as a promoter rather than a writer. See Carlton Moss, interviewed by Lorraine Brown, Aug. 6, 1976, Hollywood, California, Second Tape, Side 3, 32, OHC-GMU.

77. Hill also recalled that those plays that did make it into production appeared to come out of nowhere. See Hill interview, 1977, 2–3; Silvera interview, 1977, 2; Abram Hill, interviewed by Cliff Mason, in *Breaking the Barriers*, Part 1.

78. *Liberty Deferred*, Playscripts File, Box 694, FTP-LOC, 3.

79. *Liberty Deferred*, 4

80. *Liberty Deferred*, 5.

81. *Liberty Deferred*, 5–6.

82. *Liberty Deferred*, 7.

83. *Liberty Deferred*, 29.

84. Cruse, *The Crisis of the Negro Intellectual*, 171–80.

85. *Liberty Deferred*, 136.

86. *Liberty Deferred*, 122–42.

87. *Liberty Deferred*, 141–42.

88. See for example Fraden, *Blueprints for a Black Federal Theatre*, 107–8; Browder and Cosgrove both mention the anti-lynching scene and the need to avoid offending

southern senators on the Dies Committee. See Browder, *Rousing the Nation*, 153; Cosgrove, "The Living Newspaper," 139; Walker, "The American Negro Theatre," 248; Lavery himself later denied that the Federal Theatre's production decisions were influenced by pressures from members of Congress. See Emmet Lavery interviewed by Mae Mallory Krulak and John O'Connor, Encino, California, Jan. 5, 1976, 62, Box 20, OHC-GMU.

89. Arent, "The Technique of the Living Newspaper," 822; Matthews, *The Federal Theatre*, 62–70. See also Diane Bowers, "Ethiopia—The First Living Newspaper." A draft script is available in Arent, "Ethiopia, the First 'Living Newspaper.'" The storyboards and Hjalmar Hermanson's *Ethiopia* set design sketches are available in the FTP-GMU.

90. Irwin Rhodes, general counsel for the FTP, cited in O'Connor and Brown, eds., *The Federal Theatre Project*, 169.

91. Browder, *Rousing the Nation*, 154.

92. Hill recalled hoping that *Liberty Deferred* would be staged downtown, "because it was not a black play though it was about black people." See Hill interview, 1977, First Tape, Side 1, 7, 3.

93. Dan Burley, "Liberty Deferred: Living Newspaper," *Amsterdam News*, Dec. 10, 1938, 20.

94. Lavery to Silvera, Dec. 21, 1937, Series E879, Box 182, RG69, NA; Lavery to Knaster, Dec. 21, 1937, E879, Box 182, RG69, NA.

95. *Stars and Bars*, 1:4:9.

96. Lavery to Silvera and Knaster, Dec. 22, 1937, E879, Box 182, RG69, NA.

97. *Liberty Deferred*, Playscripts File, Box 694, FTP-LOC, 29.

98. Lavery to Silvera and Knaster, Apr. 15, 1938, Series E879, Box 182, RG69, NA.

99. Retman, *Real Folk*, 21.

100. The original editor was to be fired "half way along the journey." It is difficult to be certain whether this was Lavery's idea or a positive response to a suggestion from the authors. The correspondence suggests it came from the authors, as does the desire on the part of Silvera and Hill to keep changing the perspective from which we view the events of the newspaper. *Stars and Bars* has a very similar scene, and we know that Lavery read that script. See Lavery to Silvera and Knaster, Apr. 15, 1938, E879, Box 182, RG69, NA; Harold Koppleman to Blanding Sloan, Apr. 25, 1937, E878, Box 162, RG69, NA.

101. Lavery to Silvera, and Knaster, Apr. 15, 1938, E879, Box 182, RG69, NA.

102. Nadler, "Liberty Censored," 617.

103. McDermott, "The Living Newspaper as a Dramatic Form," 90.

104. Lavery to Silvera, Jul. 6, 1938, E879, Box 182, RG69, NA.

105. *Liberty Deferred*, Playscripts File, Box 694, FTP-LOC, 111-13.

106. At ten pages long, Lynchotopia is one of the more extensive "contemporary" scenes in *Liberty Deferred*. See Playscripts File, Box 694, FTP-LOC, 110–20. On the infamous lynching of Claude Neal, see McGovern, *Anatomy of a Lynching*. On lynching as spectacle, see Wood, *Lynching and Spectacle*.

107. *Liberty Deferred*, Playscripts File, Box 694, FTP-LOC, 117; The Costigan-Wagner anti-lynching bill, which was introduced in the Senate in 1934 was defeated

by the filibustering of southern senators. The NAACP issued a pamphlet about the lynching of Claude Neal to raise publicity in support of the bill.

108. Clarke, "'Without Fear or Shame,'" 271, 274.

109. Mitchell, "Black-Authored Lynching Drama's Challenge to Theater History," 91–92.

110. Hill interview, 1978, First Tape, Side 1, 15–15A.

111. Abram Hill, *Hell's Half Acre*, Library Records, Playscripts Collection, Box 668, FTP-LOC.

112. John D. Silvera, Reader's Review, on Abram Hill, *Hell's Half Acre*, Aug. 5, 1937, Series 2, Box 45, FTP-GMU. The play was produced by Unity Players of the Bronx in 1938. See Hill and Hatch, *A History of African American Theatre*, 348.

113. Oral history interviews with Carton Moss (a close friend of Silvera for many years) as well as Silvera's own interviews suggest that Hill was the driving force in terms of dramatization. In her interview with Silvera, Lorraine Brown puts it to him that Lynchotopia was Silvera's brainchild, an assertion Silvera appears to confirm in discussing his inspiration for the scene. See Silvera interview, 1977, 11.

114. Silvera interview, 1977, 11.

115. *Liberty Deferred*, Playscripts File, Box 694, FTP-LOC, 70–71. Gilmore, *Defying Dixie*, 161.

116. Hine, *Black Victory*, 171.

117. *Liberty Deferred*, Playscripts File, Box 694, FTP-LOC, 74–75.

118. "Federal Theatre to Aid Program of Rededication," *Hartford Courant*, Jun. 14, 1938, 18; Lavery to Sloan, Jun. 6, 1938, E878, Box 162, RG69, NA.

119. "Federal Theatre to Aid Program of Rededication," *Hartford Courant*, Jun. 14, 1938, 18; "Harlem WPA Theatre Maps Out Ambitious Fall Programme," *Philadelphia Tribune*, Jul. 7, 1938, 15; "The News and Gossip of Broadway," *New York Times*, May 8, 1938, 157.

120. Lavery to Silvera, Jul. 6, 1938, E879, Box 182, RG69 NA.

121. Lavery to Kondulf, Jul. 13, 1938, E879, Box 182, RG69, NA.

122. Hill and Silvera to Lavery Jul. 27, 1938, E879, Box 182, RG69, NA.

123. Lavery to Kondulf, Sept. 9, 1938, E879, Box 182, RG69, NA.

124. Lavery to Gibbs, Oct. 3, 1938, E879, Box 182, RG69, NA.

125. Lavery to Knaster, Nov. 10, 1938, E879, Box 182, RG69, NA.

126. Hill to Flanagan, Sept. 23, 1938, E839, Box 19, RG69, NA.

127. Hill to Flanagan, Dec. 11, 1938; Flanagan to Hill, Dec. 19, 1938 in *NDABA*, Reel 24.

128. Kondulf to Edgar Brooks, Dec. 19, 1938, E878, Box 167, RG69, NA; Russak to Lavery, Jan. 11, 1939, Federal Theatre Project Correspondence—1938–1939, online at http://memory.loc.gov/cgi-bin/ampage?collId=ftscript&fileName=fpraf/09640038/ftscript.db&recNum=7; Dan Burley, "Liberty Deferred: Living Newspaper," *Amsterdam News*, Dec. 10, 1938, 20; William E. Clark of the *New York Age* to Colonel Harrington, May 4, 1939, E839, Box 16, RG69, NA. For further details see chapter 5, on Haiti.

129. "Negro Arts Committee Federal Arts Council Brief," 1939, E839, Box 16, RG69, NA. The NACFC represented, among others, the NAACP, Brotherhood of

Sleeping Car Porters, Southern Negro Youth Congress, NNC, Urban League, International Workers Order, and the Association for the Study of Negro Life and History. It is difficult to date the brief exactly, but it clearly arrived at the NSB sometime between mid-January and the end of March 1939. It cites dismissal figures for black FTP staff from Jan. 16, 1939, and someone has handwritten the date "3/27" at the top of the brief, suggesting this may be the date the NSB office received or actioned the letter. This would make sense, as Lavery responded just a few days later, on March 31.

130. Lavery to Negro Arts Committee Federal Arts Council c/o John Rimassa, Mar. 31, 1939, E878, Box 166, RG69, NA.

131. Lavery to Negro Arts Committee, Mar. 31, 1939.

132. Lavery interview, Jan. 5, 1976, 62.

133. See note 73.

134. Synopsis to *Liberty Deferred*, Billy Rose Theatre Division, NYPLPA.

135. *Liberty Deferred*, Playscripts File, Box 694, FTP-LOC, 4, 8.

136. Dunbar, "We Wear the Mask," in Braxton, ed., *The Collected Poetry of Paul Laurence Dunbar*, 71.

137. *Liberty Deferred*, Playscripts File, Box 694, FTP-LOC, 5.

Chapter Three

1. Lawrence Levine, *Black Culture and Black Consciousness*, 425. For a study of John Henry as legend and historical figure see Nelson, *Steel Drivin' Man*.

2. Foley, *Wrestling with the Left*, 81.

3. Hartman, *Scenes of Subjection*.

4. Linda Williams draws the term "moral legibility" from Peter Brooks, *The Melodramatic Imagination*. See Williams, *Playing the Race Card*, xiii.

5. Linda Williams, *Playing the Race Card*, 19.

6. Peter Brooks, *The Melodramatic Imagination*; Linda Williams, *Playing the Race Card*, esp. xiii–xiv.

7. Ann Wilson, "Negro's Own Play Proves Interesting," *Seattle Star*, Jan. 29, 1937, 6.

8. *Seattle Argus*, Feb. 9, 1937, press clippings in *Natural Man* Production Notebook, Box 1046, FTP-LOC. For further reviews, see "WPA Repertory Play Strikingly Staged at Met," *Seattle Post Intelligencer*, Jan. 29, 1937, 6; "WPA Federal Theatre," n.d., *Natural Man* Clippings File, SCA-GMU.

9. Taylor, *The Forging of a Black Community*, 92. The National Movement for a Forty-Ninth State was pioneered by Chicago lawyer and later NAACP branch president Oscar C. Brown. See Reed, *The Chicago NAACP*, 115.

10. "Natural Man Plays Again Feb. 18, 19 and 20," *Northwest Enterprise*, Feb. 12, 1937.

11. Frederick Darby, "Letter to the Editor," *Northwest Enterprise*, Feb. 5. 1937, 2.

12. According to Foley, "Narodnost signified both the distinctness of Russian folk culture and the responsibility of the artist to represent folk interests." See Foley, *Wrestling with the Left*, 81.

13. John Mason Brown, *New York Post*, quoted in ANT, *Natural Man* Program, Box 1, Folder 3, ANT Records, SCR; see also "Natural Man, without People's Choice, Fails to Ring Bell," *Afro American*, May 17, 1941, 14.

14. Hatch, ed., *Black Theater U.S.A.: Forty-Five Plays by Black Americans, 1847–1974*; Hatch and Shine, eds., *Black Theatre U.S.A.: Plays by African Americans: The Early Period, 1847–1938*. Those who base their analysis on the published version include Craig, *Black Drama of the Federal Theatre Era*, 47–50; Johnson, "A Production History of the Seattle Federal Theatre Project," 111n38; Hill and Hatch, *A History of African American Theatre*, 328; Shandell, "Looking beyond *Lucasta*"; Miller, *Theorizing Black Theatre*, 311–12. Elam, "The Politics of Black Masculinity in Theodore Browne's *Natural Man*," in Black and Shandell, eds., *Experiments in Democracy*, 126–46. The exception is Doris Abramson, who uses the Schomburg version. Abramson's study was conducted before the publication of the first *Black Theater U.S.A.* anthology and before Browne donated the ANT version to SCA-GMU. See Abramson, *Negro Playwrights in the American Theatre*, 307. Shaw University in Raleigh staged a production and workshop on *Natural Man* in 1986. A videotape recording of the production is held in SCA-GMU. Another version was staged in 2003 at Stanford University. Both productions used the ANT manuscript published in the Hatch anthology. For variant manuscripts, see the discussion later in this chapter.

15. Elam, "The Politics of Black Masculinity," 130; Shandell, "Looking beyond *Lucasta*," 540; Miller, *Theorizing Black Theatre*, 133.

16. "January Seattle," Episode 8, 67.

17. Rowley, "Backstage and Onstage," 236.

18. Linda Williams argues that a central feature of melodrama is the drive to "reconcile the irreconcilable." This means finding solutions through individual heroic acts, rather than challenging or changing systems. See Linda Williams, *Playing the Race Card*, 35–36.

19. Theodore Browne, interviewed by Lorraine Brown, Oct. 22, 1975, Box 2, Folder 11, First tape, Side 1, 4, 19, 6, OHC-GMU.

20. Charles Monroe, interviewed by Lorraine Brown, Nov. 9, 1978, Box 7 Folder 25, First tape, Side 1, 33, OHC-GMU.

21. Joseph Staton, interviewed by John O'Connor, Jan. 7, 1976, Box 10, Folder 6, First Tape, Side 1, 23, OHC-GMU. Sara Oliver (later Jackson) also remembered the ways in which the black troupe shaped the unit and its repertoire. See Sara O. Jackson, interviewed by Leona Pollack, Mar. 3, 1981, esp. Side 1,6 and 8, in Sara O. Jackson Papers, SCA-UWL.

22. Flanagan to Porter, Nov. 4, 1937, and Nov. 6, 1937, E839, Box 9, RG69, NA.

23. Esther Porter Lane, interviewed by John O'Connor and Karen Wicker, Jul. 11, 1977, Box 6, Folder 16, First Tape, Side 2, 23, OHC-GMU.

24. Esther Porter Lane, interviewed by Mae Mallory Krulak, Sept. 7, 1976, revised by interviewee, Feb. 1979, Box 6, Folder 16, Second Tape, Side 3, 37, OHC-GMU.

25. Witham, *The Federal Theatre Project*, 62.

26. Staton and Oliver interviews; Staton is variously listed as director or assistant director on the productions he staged. See Production Notebooks for *An Evening with Dunbar*, Box 1006, and *Taming of the Shrew*, Box 1079, FTP-LOC.

27. Miller to Flanagan, Sept. 26, 1936, 1–2, E839, Box 14, RG69, NA.

28. Robert St. Clair to Flanagan, Sept. 19, 1936, E839, Box 14, RG69, NA.

29. Monroe interview, First tape, Side 1, 14.

30. "Technical Report" and "Press Reports," in *It Can't Happen Here,* Production Notebook, Box 1025, FTP-LOC. For an overview of Seattle Negro Unit productions, see Johnson, "A Production History."

31. West, "Others, Adults, Censored," 110, 108. In his study of the Seattle Federal Theatre, Witham has complicated this picture and demonstrated how the balance of power between the black troupe of the Seattle Negro Unit and their white supervisors was dependent on the exigencies of local politics and regional and national WPA issues. See Witham, *The Federal Theatre Project,* 61–77.

32. Levine, *Black Culture and Black Consciousness,* 410, 420.

33. Tracy, *John Henry,* 145–51.

34. See, for example, Richard Watts Jr. "The Theaters," New York *Herald Tribune,* Jan. 11, 1940, in Paul Robeson Papers, Box 4, SCR. See also Tracy, *John Henry,* 33.

35. Zora Neale Hurston to Walter and Gladys White, July–August 1932, in Carla Kaplan, *Zora Neale Hurston,* 269.

36. Hiram Motherwell, "Play Reports: *John Henry,*" 3, in National Office, General Corr., E829, Box 229, RG69, NA.

37. *John Henry,* Playreaders Reports, Box 232, FTP-LOC.

38. "Press Notices" and "Director's Report" in *John Henry,* Production Bulletin, Production Records, Box 1026, FTP-LOC.

39. "'Music Drama' Shows Negro Life in Dixie," *Amsterdam News,* Oct. 6, 1937, 7; "Roll Sweet Chariot Lasts Only One Week on B'way," *Afro American,* Oct. 13, 1934, 6. Members of what would become the Boston Negro Unit, including its director, Ralf Coleman, and his brother, Warren Coleman, as well as Frank Wilson and Rose McClendon, were cast members in the production. See Ralf Coleman, interviewed by Paula Singer, Nov. 24, 1972, copy held in Box 3, OHC-GMU.

40. For a bibliography and discography of folk songs, plays, and novels about John Henry, see Tracy, *John Henry,* 36–51; Locke and Gregory, eds., *Plays of Negro Life,* esp. the Introduction, "The Drama of Negro Life," xiii–xviii.

41. The white critic was George Goldsmith for the *Herald Tribune,* quoted in Toohey, *A History of the Pulitzer Prize Plays,* 56. See also Eugene Gordon, "From 'Uncle Tom's Cabin' to 'Stevedore,'" *New Theatre,* 2:7 (July 1935): 22. Du Bois quoted in Fraden, *Blueprints for a Black Federal Theatre,* 101. On Hughes's *Mulatto* as a response to Green, see Hill and Hatch eds., *A History of African American Theatre,* 527n16.

42. Playreaders Reports "Roll Sweet Chariot," Box 297, FTP-LOC.

43. Playreaders Reports, "Roll Sweet Chariot"; Flanagan, *Arena,* 84–85.

44. *The Federal Theatre Project: A Catalog-Calendar of Productions,* 251.

45. Robert Johnson "Fists upon a Star" manuscript, July 15, 1952, Box 4, 11, Florence Bean James Papers, SCA-UWL.

46. Running over twenty performances from mid-January to March, *In Abraham's Bosom* attracted an average audience of 217, considerably higher than the Playhouse's

season average of 157. See Albert Ottenheimer, Seattle Repertory Playhouse Log (SRPL), Jan. 11, 1933; Mar. 11, 1933; May 2, 1936, Box 32, Folder 1, SRPR, SC-UWL.

47. There are five extant manuscripts of *Natural Man*. The ANT manuscripts are discussed later in this chapter and in notes 70, 71, and 144. For an overview of all manuscripts, see the Appendix. See "January Seattle" and "February Seattle," both in Play Scripts File, Box 720, FTP-LC; *Natural Man* Production Bulletin, Production Records, Box 1046, FTP-LOC; *Natural Man* Program, 28 Jan. 1937, Box 2, Folder 5, Theodore Browne Papers (hereafter TBP), SCA-GMU; "WPA Repertory Play Strikingly Staged at Met," *Seattle Post-Intelligencer*, Jan. 29, 1937, n.p., and "W.P.A. Federal Theatre," n.d., Box 2, Folder 4, TBP.

48. "January Seattle," Episode 6, 57.

49. "January Seattle," Episode 7, 62.

50. "January Seattle," Episode 7, 61, 62–63.

51. Hartman, *Scenes of Subjection*, 121, 134.

52. "January Seattle," Episode 7, 61.

53. "January Seattle," Episode 7, 64.

54. "January Seattle." Episode 7, 64.

55. "January Seattle," Episode 8, 67.

56. Synopsis in the Production Bulletin also supports this reading. See *Natural Man* Production Bulletin, Box 1046, FTP-LOC. For a discussion of the black heroic tradition in theatre, see Molette, "Black Heroes and Afrocentric Values in Theatre," 456–58.

57. For the additional scene, see Episode 4, "February Seattle." Also see Set Ground Plan in Production Bulletin, Production Records, Box 1046, FTP-LOC. For press coverage of the added scene, see "W.P.A. Federal Theatre," n.d., Box 2, Folder 4, TBP.

58. Frederick Darby, "Letter to the Editor," *Northwest Enterprise*, Feb. 5, 1937, 2.

59. Charles F. Maxwell, "Washington," *Chicago Defender*, Feb. 13, 1937, 18; Duffy, ed., *The Political Plays of Langston Hughes*, 163–64; Arlene M. Paiya, "Seattle Playwright Called to New York," *Pittsburgh Courier*, May 12, 1938, 21; John Silvera to Ben Russak, Apr. 26, 1938, "Federal Theatre Project Personal Papers, 1926–1991," Box 7, Folder 19, SCA-GMU.

60. *Go Down Moses*, Corr. and Set Designs in Production Records, Boxes 1012, 1127, FTP-LOC; see also "Plans for Brown's Play," *New York Times*, Apr. 12, 1939, in Vassar College Press Clippings on Plays, Box 129, RG69, NA; "Go Down Moses," General Corr. of the NSB, Talent Bureau, Box 213, RG69, NA; John Mack to J. Howard Miller, Mar. 1, 1939; "Negro Workers on Federal Theatre," *NDABA*, Reel 25; "Brown Wins $1000 reward," *Amsterdam Star News*, Apr. 12, 1941, 20. Theodore Browne interview, First Tape, Side 1, 8–10. Browne also continued to find employment as an actor. When ANT's *Natural Man* opened in Harlem in May 1941, Browne was performing as the doomed Brutus Jones in the New England Repertory Company's production of *Emperor Jones*.

61. "Points to Look for in an Analysis of Plays," Box 1, Folder 27, ANT Records.

62. Abram Hill, interviewed by Michelle Wallace, Jan. 19, 1974, cited in Shandell, "The American Negro Theatre," 96. For more on the NPC production of *Big White Fog*, see chapter 4.

63. Hill and Hatch, eds., *A History of African American Theatre*, 356; Shandell, "Looking beyond *Lucasta*." The ANT's programming and the extent to which *Lucasta*'s success distracted the ANT from its mission has been the focus of much of the scholarship on the ANT. Ethel Pitts Walker argued that it was the company's ambition to take a play to Broadway that led to their undoing, while Jonathan Shandell is interested in the dynamic between interracialism and ethnocentrism within African American culture. See Walker, "The American Negro Theatre," 257–59. Shandell, "The American Negro Theatre," vi, 3; Shandell, "Looking beyond *Lucasta*," 541. For the London tour of *Anna Lucasta* see Bourne, *War to Windrush: Black Women in Britain 1939 to 1948*, 164–69.

64. Shandell, "Looking beyond *Lucasta*," 534.

65. Shandell, "Looking beyond *Lucasta*," 535.

66. Shandell, "The American Negro Theatre," 126.

67. Theodore Browne interview, Tape 1, Side 1, 1. A photograph of Browne attending a performance of the ANT adaptation at the 135 Street Library in Harlem appears in "Star and Author Attend Show," *Amsterdam Star News*, Jun. 4, 1941, 20.

68. For this interpretation see Shandell, "Theodore Browne."

69. Browne Interview, Tape 1, Side 1, 8, 26.

70. The ANT manuscript donated by Browne to GMU can be found in Box 2, Folder 3, TBP. All extant manuscripts except "January Seattle" include the religious camp scene. The only scholar to base her reading of *Natural Man* on a text other than the ANT version published in Hatch and Shine is Doris Abramson. In her 1969 study, *Negro Playwrights*, Abramson based her analysis on a mimeographed version held at the Schomburg. Of the five existing manuscripts, the "Schomburg" is closest to the "February Seattle" manuscript. Like "February Seattle," the "Schomburg" has nine scenes, and like both Seattle manuscripts, it includes the northern labor scene and a final episode in which John Henry dies knowing he has not defeated the machine. The provenance of the "Schomburg" manuscript is unclear: the catalog entry at the "Schomburg" describes the play as *The natural man (based on the legend of John Henry): A play in eight episodes*. The catalog offers a speculative date of 1936, which would line up with the time when Browne probably wrote the first version of the play in Seattle. However, the "Schomburg" manuscript is unlikely to date to 1936 because it clearly derives from the second Seattle production, which took place in February 1937. Abramson assumes, wrongly, that the "Schomburg" was the version performed by the ANT, and she therefore reads it alongside critical reviews of the ANT production. For example, she offers a reading of the northern labor scene, yet this scene was not staged by the ANT. Abramson's misidentification of manuscripts is understandable, not least since it occurred prior to the recovery of the federal theatre archive of FTP manuscripts. However the blurring of different versions of *Natural Man* has caused considerable confusion for later scholars. Both Henry Miller, and more recently Harry Elam, who base their analysis on the version of the ANT manuscript published in *Black Theater U.S.A.*, defer to Abramson's reading of the "Schomburg" manuscript and follow her in misattributing the additional labor scene to the ANT production, rather than the Seattle production. In the *Cambridge History of African*

American Theatre, Hill and Hatch offer an account of the Seattle production, noting that Browne wrote *Natural Man* intending for Seattle Negro Unit actor Joe Staton to play John Henry. Their account of the play, however, relies on the ANT version, even though the citation is to "Theodore Browne, *Natural Man*, 1937." The problem here is that what they label "*Natural Man*, 1937" is not the play described in the *Cambridge History*; it is the ANT adaptation of *Natural Man* in 1941. See Hill and Hatch, *Cambridge History of African American Theatre*, 529n49. In a footnote Hill and Hatch note that the ANT's version did not use the music from the Seattle production, but there is no discussion of textual differences. See *Cambridge History of African American Theatre*, 529n50.

71. The ANT production ran at the 135th Street Library on Wednesday, Friday, and Saturday nights through May and June. See "New York 'Natural Man' in Premiere," *Amsterdam-Star News*, May 10, 1941, 17. The ANT program puts Episodes 7 (hobo camp) and Episode 8 (the final episode, at Big Bend Tunnel) into one episode (7), which is divided into Scene 1 and Scene 2. See ANT *Natural Man* program, Box 1, Folder 3, ANT Records and the GMU manuscript; Carl Carlford, "Natural Man Is New Negro Theater Play," *New Journal and Guide*, May 17, 1941, 15.

72. "Natural Man to Open Sans Author of Music," *Afro American*, Apr. 12, 1941, 13. In a 1986 recorded production by the Shaw Players of Shaw University, Raleigh, North Carolina, the Creeper was played for laughs, disrupting moments of dramatic tension. See *Natural man [videorecording]: Based on the legend of John Henry by Theodore Browne*, SCA-GMU.

73. The jailer hands John Henry over to the Sheriff, who thinks he can harness his "spirit" into productive hard labor, a plot device that gets John Henry sent back to the labor camp.

74. "January Seattle," Episode 7, 64; "February Seattle," Episode 8, 4; "ANT-GMU," Episode 4, 3. Frederick Darby, "Letter to the Editor," *Northwest Enterprise*, Feb. 5, 1937, 2.

75. "January Seattle," Episode 3, 25, 27, 29 and 33; "February Seattle," Episode 3, 2; "ANT-GMU," Episode 5, 2; Hatch anthology, Episode 5, 375; "ANT-GMU," Episode 4, 3. It is interesting that the *Afro American*, which printed a negative review of the ANT's *Natural Man*, complained about the use of the term "nigger" in the ANT production, which suggests either that even the sole use of the term was once too often, or that the actors had introduced it of their own volition. See "Natural Man, Without People's Choice, Fails to Ring Bell," *Afro American*, May 17, 1941, 14. Other black newspapers that might also have been expected to object, such as the *Amsterdam Star News*, do not mention the use of the term.

76. "ANT-GMU," Episode 8, 1.

77. For the precarious nature of empathy see Hartman, *Scenes of Subjection*, 4.

78. "ANT-GMU," Episode 8, 1–4.

79. Hartman, *Scenes of Subjection*, 125.

80. "ANT-GMU," Episode 8, 4.

81. Miller, *Theorizing Black Theatre*, 133; Elam, "The Politics of Black Masculinity," 143; Shandell, "Looking beyond *Lucasta*," 540; "January Seattle," Episode 8, 67.

82. Arthur Pollack, *Brooklyn Eagle*, quoted in ANT, *Natural Man* Program, included in "PAL" manuscript. See also Brooks Atkinson, "The Play," *New York Times*, May 8, 1941, 20.

83. Ralph Warnes, "A Stirring Revival of John Henry Legend," *Daily Worker*, in Box 2, TBP.

84. Marvel Cooke, "Natural Man, Fine Theatre," *Amsterdam Star News*, May 17, 1941, 16. "John Henry Legend Is Told in New Drama," *Atlanta Daily World*, May 19, 1941, 2; "Natural Man, without People's Choice, Fails to Ring Bell," *Afro American*, May 17, 1941, 14. For further black press coverage, see "Local Theatre One Year Old," *Amsterdam Star News*, May 31, 1941, 21, and Apr. 12, 1941, 20; "American Negro Theatre Sponsors Its First Forum Discussion," advertised in ANT *Natural Man* Program.

85. Arthur Pollack, *Brooklyn Daily Eagle*, May 8, 1941, 11.

86. "The American Negro Theatre: Behind the Scenes," 1, ANT Records; "American Negro Theatre Gives Natural Man," *Daily Worker*, Apr. 2, 1941, 7.

87. "New Theatre Group Work Wins Acclaim," *Amsterdam News*, Jan. 25, 1936, 12; Paul Green, "Hymn to the Rising Sun," *New Theatre*, Jan. 1936, 11–21.

88. Rowley, *Life and Times of Richard Wright*, 113–14, 538n24.

89. Avery, ed., *A Southern Life: Letters of Paul Green, 1916–1981* (hereafter *Letters of Paul Green*), 249–50n1.

90. Green, "Hymn to the Rising Sun," *New Theatre*, Jan. 1936, 11; Green, "Hymn to the Rising Sun," Playscripts File, Box 674, FTP-LOC; Green, *Hymn to the Rising Sun*, in Avery, *A Paul Green Reader*, 81; text first published in Gassner, ed., *Paul Green, Five Plays of the South*.

91. Hallie Flanagan recalled Green discussing with her how his ideas for the play shifted. Though he had "tried to write a play about those boys . . . it got all mixed up with the top sergeant who used to devil the life out of me in the war. Somehow before I knew it those boys were only one line in the play, but the sergeant was right there big as life." See Flanagan, *Arena*, 200.

92. Green, *Hymn to the Rising Sun*, 16, Playscripts, Box 674, FTP-LOC.

93. Green, *Hymn to the Rising Sun*, 17.

94. Green, *Hymn to the Rising Sun*, 4.

95. Percival Wilde to Green, Oct. 11, 1938, in Avery, ed., *Letters of Paul Green*, 249.

96. Wilde to Green, Oct. 11, 1938; Green to Wilde, Mid-October 1935, in Avery, ed., *Letters of Paul Green*, 249.

97. Green to Wilde, Mid-October 1935, in Avery, ed., *Letters of Paul Green*, 249.

98. Du Bois quoted in Fraden, *Blueprints for a Black Federal Theatre*, 101.

99. Wright, *Black Boy*, 364–65.

100. Hartman, *Scenes of Subjection*, esp. 20–21.

101. Fraden, *Blueprints for a Black Federal Theatre*, 101. See also Montgomery Gregory, "The No 'Count Boy," *Opportunity*, 3:28 (April 1925): 121; Eugene Gordon, "From 'Uncle Tom's Cabin' to 'Stevedore,'" *New Theatre*, 2:7 (July 1935): 22.

102. Blanding Sloan to Lavery, Apr. 25, 1938, Box 162, E878, RG69, NA; Thomas Wood Stevens to Flanagan, Jan. 31, 1936, Box 99, E856, RG69, NA.

103. Wright to Green, May 22, 1940, in Curtis R. Scott, "The Dramatization of Native Son," 8; Wright, *Black Boy*, 392.

104. Flanagan, *Arena*, 137.

105. Flanagan, *Arena*, 136.

106. Stevens to Flanagan, Jan. 31, 1936, Box 99, E856, RG69, NA.

107. *Chicago Tribune*, Oct. 10, 1936, 1; "Hymn to the Sun, Banned in Chicago," *Pittsburgh Courier*, Oct. 31, 1936, A9; Flanagan, *Arena*, 137.

108. The *Chicago Defender* admitted to dislike on the part of one or two members of the preview audiences, but suggested that these few had been "silenced, by a wave of favourable sentiment." See "First Loop Play of Race W.P.A Group Called Immoral," *Chicago Defender*, Oct. 24, 1936, 20. The more positive attitude toward Green's play following its cancellation was probably also fostered by growing concern about the "arbitrary banning" of plays in Chicago, especially when those plays were critical of the U.S. treatment of its citizens. A committee of leading black citizens formed to quiz Dunham on his decision. Led by A. C. MacNeal, president of the Chicago chapter of the NAACP, who would go on to play a leading role in trying to ban Theodore Ward's *Big White Fog* in spring 1938, the committee demanded to know on whose authority and with what justification Dunham had canceled the play. To aid their cause, the committee sponsored a reading of the play. Among those who signed a resolution offering endorsement of the play were representatives of the Chicago Urban League and the Public Library, as well as Lester Granger, national field secretary of the Worker's Bureau of the National Urban League in New York City. See "Citizens Fight Ban on Chain Gang Play," *Chicago Defender*, Oct. 24, 1936, 12.

109. *Chicago Tribune*, Oct. 10, 1936, 1; "Hymn to the Sun, Banned in Chicago," *Pittsburgh Courier*, Oct. 31, 1936, A9; Flanagan, *Arena*, 137. See also Witham, "Censorship in the Federal Theatre," 3–14.

110. Arthur Pollack, "Paul Green and Social Satire," *Christian Science Monitor*, May 11, 1937, 10.

111. Wright had received many offers to adapt his novel besides that from Green, including, according to Rowley, from his friend and rival Theodore Ward. Ward later adapted other elements of Wright's work, including "Bright and Morning Star," which he performed for the Harlem Suitcase Theatre. See Rowley, *The Life and Times of Richard Wright*, 115, 161, 174, 178.

112. Rowley, *The Life and Times of Richard Wright*, 191–92.

113. Wright to Green, May 22, 1940, in Avery, ed., *Letters of Paul Green*, 311.

114. For an account of Wright's time in Chapel Hill see Rowley, "Backstage and Onstage," 215–37.

115. Rowley, "Backstage and Onstage," 223, 226–27.

116. Pearce, "From Folklore to Mythology," 75–77; Malcolm Cowley, "The New Republic," Mar. 18, 1940 in Gates and Appiah, eds., *Richard Wright*, 11.

117. Hartman, *Scenes of Subjection*, 58, 56.

118. Rowley, "Backstage and Onstage," 221; Green to Doris Abramson, Sept. 29, 1965, in Abramson, *Negro Playwrights*, 138.

119. For example, Curtis Scott is scathing of Wright scholars who he believes lend too much credence to Houseman's account. Scott, however, is overly reliant on the

diaries and later reminisces of Green. See Curtis R. Scott, "The Dramatization of Native Son," 5–41. Wright scholars tend to be more critical of Green and his recollections of the collaboration, as recorded in oral history interviews in the 1970s. In one such interview, Green recalled that two conditions of his adapting the novel were that communism be "ridiculed" and taken less seriously than in the novel, and that Bigger Thomas take some moral responsibility for his actions. There is no evidence to support Green's contention that he made these demands beyond his own testimony. Wright scholars have argued that it is difficult to imagine Wright agreeing to such conditions. Moreover Green's recollections about the nature of the collaboration need to be placed alongside other uncorroborated Green claims. For example, Green recalled that he had generously allowed Wright to have his name on the script as co-author, yet the contract reveals it was always a joint project, with a majority (55 percent) of the share going to Wright and the remainder to Green. See Rowley "Backstage and Onstage," 217, 221–22. The editor of Green's published correspondence, Laurence Avery, reinforces the idea that Wright had agreed to Green's conditions, but his evidence similarly relies on Green's account of events in letters and later interviews. See Avery, ed., *Letters of Paul Green*, 323n2.

120. Rowley, "Backstage and Onstage," 236.

121. Green to W.A. Stanbury, Aug. 20, 1940, in Avery, ed., *Letters of Paul Green*, 318.

122. Richard Wright, "The Problem of the Hero," Draft Manuscript, Box 83, Richard Wright Papers.

123. Wright, "The Problem of the Hero,", Act I, 1

124. Wright, "The Problem of the Hero," Act II, 4.

125. Wright, "The Problem of the Hero," Act III, 5.

126. Wright, "The Problem of the Hero," Act III, 5.

127. Wright, "The Problem of the Hero," Act III, 5.

128. Wright, "The Problem of the Hero," Act IV, 6.

129. Wright to Green, Feb. 12, 1941, in Rowley, *The Life and Times of Richard Wright*, 228.

130. Wright, "The Problem of the Hero," Act IV, 7.

131. Wright to Green, Mar. 12, 1941, and Green to Wright, Mar. 12, 1941, in Rowley, "Backstage and Onstage," 232. Green later recalled Atkinson calling him up to tell him of Wright's proposed "attack on you," and responding that he was supportive of Wright's sketch being published. See Bauer, "'Call Me Paul,'" 534. This recollection is at odds with the advice Green gave Wright in his 1941 telegram. See Rowley, *Life and Times*, 244. In his review of the play, Brooks Atkinson recognized the very real differences between Wright, "the realist" and "Communist," and Green, "a man of religion and defender of democracy," but assiduously avoided any mention of disagreement in collaborating, instead concluding that "They are both interested in the welfare of the Negro race." See Brooks Atkinson, *New York Times*, Apr. 6, 1941, X1.

132. Green and Wright, *Native Son (the Biography of a Young American): A Play in Ten Scenes by Paul Green and Richard Wright*; Rowley, "Backstage and Onstage," 23.

133. Green and Wright, *Native Son*, 148; Rowley, "Backstage and Onstage," 55.

134. *Native Son: The Playbill for the St. James Theatre* (1941), 20; Mantle, *The Best Plays*, 41, 63.

135. Burns Mantle, "Native Son Is Praised by Drama Critic," *Chicago Daily Tribune*, Apr. 6, 1941.

136. *Native Son: The Playbill*; Green and Wright, *Native Son*.

137. The *Pittsburgh Courier, Amsterdam Star News*, and *New York Age* all covered the NAACP's sponsorship of the opening night of *Native Son*. See Kinnamon, ed., *The Richard Wright Bibliography*, 105. For examples of positive black press on Welles, see Marvel Cooke, "Orson Welles Conducts Native Son Rehearsal," and "New Play Revolutionary Theatrical Experience," both in *Amsterdam Star News*, Mar. 22, 1941, 20; "Canada Lee Will Play Role Of 'Bigger Thomas' in Stage Version Of Native Son," *Pittsburgh Courier*, Mar. 1, 1941, 20.

138. "What Canada Lee Thinks of Bigger Thomas," *Afro American*, Mar. 29, 1941, 14.

139. "Orson Welles Conducts Native Son Rehearsal" *Amsterdam Star News*, Mar. 21, 1941, 20; "Mercury's Native Son makes theatrical history," *Amsterdam Star News*, Mar. 29, 1941, 20. "'Native Son' as Drama is Real Broadway Theatre," *Chicago Defender*, Mar. 22, 1941, 11. "Lee Draws Praise as Bigger in Stage 'Native Son' Debut," *Atlanta Daily World*, Mar. 24, 1941, 2.

140. Du Bois described it as a "great piece of work" while Ellison applauded its "sheer emotional power." Lillian John was the first to express her doubts in public. See Rowley, *Life and Times*, 192–93. For further contemporary criticism see Kinnamon, ed., *The Richard Wright Bibliography*, and also Gates. and Appiah, eds., *Richard Wright*, 6–25.

141. Langston Hughes, "The Need for Heroes," 1941, 1, draft manuscript in Box 1, Langston Hughes Papers. For the published version, see *Crisis*, June 1941, 184–85.

142. *De Organizer* was another joint project with James P. Johnson, which was produced in New York in concert form at the International Ladies' Garment Workers' Union Convention. See Duffy ed., *The Political Plays of Langston Hughes*, 168–69. Hughes promoted *Natural Man* as the kind of play black amateur theatre groups should be producing. See *Chicago Defender*, May 8, 1943, 14.

143. "Slow Drag Blues—John Henry," in *De Organizer*. See Duffy, *The Political Plays of Langston Hughes*, 184–85.

144. Green and Wright, *Native Son*, 144, 148.

145. Billy Rose Theatre Division, NYPLPA. This manuscript incorporates many of the key revisions made by the ANT including the redemptive ending but retains more elements of the Seattle manuscripts, including in structure, than does "ANT-GMU." For example, in "PAL," the Beale Street bar scene has not yet been moved forward to Episode 3 as the ANT program indicates it was for the ANT production, but it does contain the same alteration of the plot in that scene: John Henry is arrested after becoming drunk and the victim of black machination. As in "ANT-GMU," the labor scene is eliminated in "PAL." The character of the Creeper is introduced, but he has a less developed role. For this reason it is clear that "PAL" was not the one used by the ANT in production but rather an earlier draft. For further discussion of manuscript variation, see the Appendix.

146. "PAL," Revised Final Episode, 1.

147. "PAL," Revised Final Episode, 5.

148. I draw here on Hartman's discussion of redress, as adapted from Victor Turner's notion of social drama. See Hartman, *Scenes of Subjection*, 77; Victor Turner, *Dramas, Fields, and Metaphors*, 41.

Chapter Four

1. Shirley Graham to Harry Minturn, Feb. 5, 1938, Regional Office, 1937–38, E970, Box 618–21, RG69, NA.

2. Graham to Minturn, Feb. 5, 1938.

3. Witham argues that the need to push back against charges of anti-Communism continues to "haunt" the FTP. See Witham, "The Federal Theatre Project," in Richards and Nathans, eds., *The Oxford Handbook of American Drama*, 297.

4. Michelle Gordon, "The Chicago Renaissance," 282; Wald, "Theodore Ward," 325, 329. In recent years a number of scholars of the Chicago Renaissance and leftist culture during the Cold War have attributed the controversies surrounding the play to its pro-communist politics. See Rachel Peterson, "Adapting Left Culture of the Cold Ward"; Michelle Gordon, "Black Literature of Revolutionary Protest."

5. Elam, "Post–World War II African American Theatre," 377.

6. Ward claimed that *Big White Fog* influenced his onetime FTP Chicago Unit collaborator Richard Wright. In particular Ward suggested his fog idea inspired Wright's mountain of hate in "Bright and Morning Star" and his novel *Native Son*. See Fabre, *The World of Richard Wright*, 19. For a discussion of black masculinity and gender conflict in Wilson's plays, see McDonough, *Staging Masculinity*, esp. chap. 6.

7. Denning, *The Cultural Front*, 136–51; Faue, *Community of Suffering*, 71; See also Melosh, *Engendering Culture*, 232. For a challenge to this dominant narrative, see Susan Manning's study of federal dance theatre: Manning, "Black Voices, White Bodies," 24–46.

8. For a brilliant study of how black nationalist women drove the global black freedom struggle in the mid-twentieth century, see Blain, *Set the World on Fire*.

9. Theodore Ward, interviewed by Lorraine Brown, Aug. 13, 1976, First Tape, Side 1, 11, Box 10, OHC-GMU.

10. Theodore Ward, "The Works of Theodore Ward: A Chronological Index and Descriptive Pattern of the Dramatic Contents," 1, Box 1, Folder 3, TWP.

11. Theodore Ward, interviewed by Camille Billops, Apr. 7, 1974, 82, Hatch-Billops Collection; Abramson, *Negro Playwrights in the American Theatre*.

12. On the "pro-Communist" drama and agenda, see Gordon, "The Chicago Renaissance," 282. "Ultimate victory" see Elam Jr. "Post-World War II African American Theatre," 377; Wald suggests that while such an "uplifting" ending "probably seemed plausible" in the context of the recent formation of the Congress of Industrial Organizations, by the time of the Cold War, the ending would have seemed "forced, contrived, anachronistic, and even somewhat perplexing." See Wald, "Theodore Ward," 329.

13. Fraden, *Blueprints for a Black Federal Theatre*, 118, and Hill and Hatch, eds., *A History of African American Theatre*, 323.

14. Earlier scholars detected ambivalence and pessimism in Ward's first full-length drama. Writing in 1980, Craig noted that "the socialist brotherhood brings only an aborted hope and a bullet for Les' father," and suggested the playwright had confirmed that this ambiguity was intentional. See Craig, *Black Theatre of the Federal Theatre Era*, 152–53.

15. The subtitle was dropped from the published versions. For reviews of the play as a tragedy, see, for example, Lloyd Lewis, "Pathos of Modern Negro Life Shown in Play a Negro Tragedy." See also *Daily News*, Apr. 8, 1938, and Paul T. Gilbert, "Race Problem Theme of Big White Fog," *Herald and Examiner*, Apr. 8, 1938, both in *Big White Fog* Production Notebook, Production Records, Box 983, FTP-LOC.

16. On the differences between socialist realism and classic realism, see Fearnow, "A New Realism," in Richards and Nathans, eds., *The Oxford Handbook of American Drama*, 176.

17. "Ward Play in Rehearsal," *Afro American*, Nov. 6, 1937, 11; Susan Glaspell to Emmet Lavery, Dec. 28, 1937, E878, Box 164, RG69, NA; Glaspell to Hallie Flanagan, Oct. 13, 1937, Box 1, TWP.

18. *Chicago Journal of Commerce and La Salle Street Journal*, Mar. 9, 1937, cited in Vactor, "A History of the Chicago Federal Theatre Project," 75, 76–78. See also *Chicago Herald and Examiner*, Mar. 8, 1937, in *Mississippi Rainbow* Production Notebook, Box 1041, FTP- LOC.

19. Enop P. Waters, "Federal Theatre Missing Opportunity for Service," *Chicago Defender*, May 30, 1936, 10.

20. Graham to Minturn, Feb. 5, 1938; Minturn to Flanagan, 5 Mar. 5, 1938, both in Regional Office Chronological Corr. File 1937–38, E970, Box 618–621, RG69, NA.

21. The idea that a black theatre must be situated in a black neighborhood, however, would later be challenged by groups like the Chicago NAACP, which felt that the FTP should take the flak for any controversy it provoked, as well as by the playwright, who wanted his play to command the attention and diverse audience that only an established theatre on the Chicago Loop could provide.

22. Gilmore, *Defying Dixie,* 123–27.

23. Graham to Minturn, Feb. 5, 1938; B. B. Church to Graham, Jan. 16, 1938; Shirley Graham, Memo to E. Kendall Davis, Jan. 24, 1938; and A. C. MacNeal to Shirley Graham, Jan. 22, 1938; all in Regional Office Chronological Corr. File 1937–38, E970, Box 618–621, RG69, NA. The South Side Boys Club was an organization for black youths that had inspired Richard Wright's creation of Bigger Thomas in *Native Son* when he worked there as a supervisor. According to Wright, the Boys Club was designed to distract wayward black youth with "ping-pong" and "checkers" so he might not "harm the valuable white property that adjoined the Black belt." See Richard Wright, "How Bigger Was Born," in *Native Son*, 22.

24. These racially abusive terms are in "Last Version," Act 1-2-13 and Act 1-2-5; see also Graham to Minturn, Feb. 5, 1938.

25. Graham to Minturn, Feb. 5, 1938.

26. Graham, Memo to Davis, Jan. 24, 1938.

27. Graham to Minturn, Feb. 5, 1938.

28. Graham to Minturn, Feb. 5, 1938.

29. Price to Minturn, Feb. 2, 1938; Graham, Memo to Davis, Jan. 24, 1938.

30. Minturn to Flanagan, Mar. 5, 1938.

31. Kay Ewing, Directors Report, 3, *Big White Fog Production* Notebook.

32. "Chi Ban on WPA's 'Fog' OK'd in Time for Preem; Race Prejudice Scored," Apr. 13, 1938, in Theodore Ward Clippings File, NYPLPA; "Ban Threatens Chicago Play on Negro Life," *New York Age*, Apr. 16, 1938, 7; Ward, interview by Brown, First Tape, Side 1, 7.

33. Most studies of *Big White Fog* use the anthologized version in *Black Theatre U.S.A.* See, for example, Miller, *Theorizing Black Theatre*; Fraden, *Blueprints for a Black Federal Theatre*; Gordon, "The Chicago Renaissance," and "Black Literature of Revolutionary Protest from Chicago's South Side"; Hill and Hatch, eds., *A History of African American Theatre*; Rachel Peterson, "Adapting Left Culture to the Cold War." Wald cites both the anthology and the Almeida version published with Nick Hern Books. See Wald, "Theodore Ward." Abramson uses the Schomburg version in *Negro Playwrights in American Theatre*. Craig is one of the few scholars to base her reading of black federal theatre drama on a federal theatre manuscript. She uses one of the earlier versions which was subsequently amended before the run at the Great Northern. Craig, *Black Theatre of the Federal Theatre Era*. The Performing Arts branch of the NYPL holds a copy of the Guthrie Theatre production manuscript. The Almeida version was published by Nick Hern Books in 2007.

34. "FTPa" and "FTPb" are both held in the Playscripts File of the FTP collection at the Library of Congress (Box 597, Folder S166[1] and S166[2], respectively) and appear to be identical. "FTPc" is held at the National Archives (Playscripts File, 1936–39, E914 Box 271, RG69) and was originally on file at the regional service bureau in Los Angeles. It is nearly the same as "FTPa" and "FTPb," but has been clearly been typed out anew. There are very occasional differences that suggest a copyist's error rather than revision. All three manuscripts stem from, and appear to be revised versions of, "Early Draft," which is also held at the Library of Congress (Playscripts File Box 597, Folder S166[5], FTP-LOC.) The revisions, for the most part, serve to cut out unnecessary explanatory dialogue, thus producing a leaner, more fluent manuscript. "Early Draft," is held in leather binding and has stage directions typed in red. It is considerably longer than the other manuscripts. Dialogue often serves to explain plot rather than develop characterization and characters frequently interpret events for an imagined audience rather than responding to each other or in character. "Early Draft" contains material that does not appear in any other federal theatre manuscript. For example. it has a lengthy section at the opening of Act 2, Scene 1, which was cut from other versions. It is likely that this makes it an early, rather than late, draft, because "Early Draft" is missing crucial scenes that we know were performed in Chicago. In all the other federal theatre manuscripts, a group of Garveyites and Black Cross Nurses visit Vic in his home to present him with a service medal in Act 2, Scene 2. Photographs taken on the evening of the opening night suggest that the medal ceremony was an important scene in the Chicago production.

35. "Last Version," (Box 597, Folder S166[4] FTP-LOC), unlike the other federal theatre manuscripts, includes Garveyite extras who we know appeared in the

Chicago production. Photographs taken of the preview performance on the stage of the Great Northern on April 6, 1938 support this, as do critics' comments about a crowded stage. See "Last Version," List of Characters; Program, in *Big White Fog* Production Notebook.

36. "Last Version," 3-3-7.

37. "Last Version," 2-3-7, 2-3-8, 2-3-9; "Early Draft," 2-3-75; "FTPa," 2-3-10, 2-3-11. Where "FTPa," "FTPb," and "FTPc" are the same, "FTPa" will be referenced. It is interesting that in the Hatch anthologized version, although Grandmother Brooks does not deploy the offensive term "nigger" herself, Vic uses the term sarcastically when challenging Brooks's description of him. See Hatch, ed., *Black Theater U.S.A.*, 305. "FTPa" and "Early Draft" have Ella challenging her husband more forcefully in some places. For example, in "Early Draft," Ella's mother attacks her husband for his dark skin and he responds by criticizing her pride in her white "raping ancestors." In "Early Draft," Ella retorts: "And you call yourself a man." See "Early Draft," 2-3-77. The theme of intrarace racism is also played up in "FTPa." For example, Vic refers to Brooks "and the rest of her kind." See "FTPa," 2-3-12.

38. See, for example, T. B. Poston, "Harlem Dislikes 'Nigger' in 'Emperor Jones' But Flocks to See Picture at Uptown House," *Amsterdam News*, Sept. 27, 1933, 9.

39. "Early Draft" and "FTPa," "FTPb," and "FTPc." See, for example, "FTPa," 3-3-119; "Last Version," 3-3-13.

40. Graham to Minturn, Feb. 5, 1938.

41. "Last Version" and Program in *Big White Fog* Production Notebook.

42. "Last Version," 3-3-13.

43. "Last Version," 1-1-13.

44. "Last Version," 1-1-14.

45. "Last Version," 1-2-12, 1-2-13, 1-2-14.

46. For a discussion of home as a site of African American resistance, see hooks, "Homeplace." For a discussion of the gender politics of Garveyism, see Summers, *Manliness and Its Discontents*. See also Blain, "We Want to Set the World on Fire," 194–212.

47. "Last Version," 3-1-7.

48. For an account of Garveyism that focuses on performance and mimicry, see Stephens, *Black Empire*, esp. chapter 3.

49. "Last Version," 1-1-2.

50. "Last Version," 1-2-7.

51. "Last Version," 1-2-8.

52. Summers, *Manliness and Its Discontents*, 68.

53. Mullen, *Popular Fronts*, 12.

54. Summers, *Manliness and Its Discontents*, 8; Mullen, *Popular Fronts*, 12.

55. *Negro World*, January 1, 1921, reprinted in the Baltimore *Afro-American*, and cited in Krasner, *A Beautiful Pageant*, 170.

56. "Last Version," 2-1-7; 2-1-2.

57. Meier and Rudwick, "The Origins of Non-Violent Direct Action in Afro American Protest."

58. "Last Version," 2-1-13.

59. "Last Version," 3-1-5.

60. The so-called black matriarch was most famously held responsible for endemic black poverty by Moynihan's 1965 report on the black family. See Daniel P. Moynihan, "The Negro Family: The Case for National Action," Office of Policy Planning and Research, U.S. Department of Labor, U.S. Government Printing Office, March 1965. For a critique of the mythical power of the black matriarch, see Wallace, *Black Macho and the Myth of the Black Superwoman*.

61. "Last Version," 3-1-8.

62. "Last Version," 3-1-9.

63. "Last Version," 3-1-12

64. "Last Version," 3-1-13.

65. Kelley, *Race Rebels*, 120.

66. Foner and Shapiro eds., American *Communism and Black Americans: A Documentary History, 1930–1934*, xi–xii.

67. Naison, *Communists in Harlem*, 35, 41.

68. Kelley, *Race Rebels*, 105.

69. Foley, *Radical Representations*, 219, 244–45. For further discussion of the woman question in Marxist ideology, see Vogel, *Marxism and the Oppression of Women*.

70. "Last Version," 3-3-3, 3-3-4.

71. "Last Version," 3-3-7, 3-3-8, 3-3-9.

72. "Last Version," 3-3-9.

73. "Last Version," 3-3-13

74. Fraden reads the play's ending as offering a hopeful, even "naïve," message of future interracial communist solidarity which will break through the fog. See *Blueprints for a Black Federal Theatre*, 118. Hill and Hatch read Ward's gathering of a mixed group of Communist allies on the stage as "making the curtain call a powerful emotional and political statement of populist unity in the face of capitalist racial oppression." See Hill and Hatch, eds., *A History of African American Theatre*, 323.

75. "Last Version," 3-3-13; Mr. Renfro and Miss Burns, Motion Picture South Side Club, quoted in Graham, Memo to Davis, Jan. 24, 1938; Regional Office, 1937–38, RG69, NA.

76. Charles Collins, "Drama Depicts Family Life of Chicago Negro," *Chicago Daily Tribune*, Apr. 8, 1938, 16.

77. Gail Borden, "Radical Plays Should Be Allowed," *Chicago Daily Times*; and Claudia Cassidy, "On the Aisle," *Journal of Commerce*, Apr .11, 1938; both in *Big White Fog*, Production Notebook. See also Lloyd Lewis, "Pathos of Modern Negro Life Shown in Play a Negro Tragedy," *Chicago Daily News*, Apr. 8, 1938.

78. "Chi Ban on WPA's 'Fog' OK'd in Time for Preem; Race Prejudice Scored," Apr. 13, 1938, in Ward Clippings File; Sterling Brown, "The Federal Theatre," 106.

79. Collins, "Drama Depicts Family Life of Chicago Negro," 16.

80. "WPA Play: Big White Fog," *Variety*, Apr. 2, 1938 in Ward Clippings File.

81. Ward, interview by Brown; Harry Minturn to John McGee, Feb. 14, 1930, and Susan Glaspell to Emmet Lavery, Dec. 28, 1937, both in, E876, Box 154, RG69, NA.

82. "Ban Threatens Chicago Play on Negro Life," *New York Age*, Apr. 16, 1938, 7.

83. Rampersad, *The Life of Langston Hughes, Volume 1: 1902–1941*, 356–358, 366.

84. "'Big White Fog' Reading Sunday," *New York Post*, May 13, 1938, in Ward Clippings files.

85. Rena Fraden concurs that the NPC production was "blasted by reviewers as anti-communist and un-American," but she cites the Ward interview rather than the reviews themselves. See Fraden, *Blueprints for a Black Federal Theatre*, 133. More noteworthy is Flanagan's hint in her 1940 account of the FTP that the Chicago production carried no "political definition," unlike the version produced by the NPC. Flanagan's book came out in 1940, so it is unlikely, but nonetheless possible, that she saw the NPC version, which opened in October 1940 before her book went to print. Whether or not Flanagan saw the NPC version of *Big White Fog*, her purpose in *Arena* was not really about interpreting Ward, *Big White Fog*, or black drama in general. *Arena* was Flanagan's nearly 500-page-long defense against the Dies Committee's insinuation that she and the project she directed were under the sway of communism. See Flanagan, *Arena*, 143.

86. It is hard to establish with any certainty which version of the manuscript was used for the NPC production. The manuscript held at the Schomburg has "New Theatre League" inscribed on the front page, suggesting it may have been connected to the public reading that took place two years previously. It is possible this version was used by the NPC at the Lincoln Theatre, but there is no evidence to connect it, or any other manuscript to the NPC production in 1940.

87. Theodore Ward, interviewed by Lorraine Brown, Aug. 13, 1976, First Tape, Side 1,11, OHC-GMU. See also Negro Playwrights Company, *Big White Fog* Playbill, Hatch-Billops Collection.

88. Ward, Interview by Brown, Aug. 13, 1976, First Tape, Side 1,12.

89. "Big White Fog Author is One of Country's Aces," *Amsterdam News*, Apr. 22, 1939.

90. "Ban Threatens Chicago Play on Negro Life," *New York Age*, Apr. 16, 1938, 7.

91. "Big White Fog, Triumph of Art, Faith, Sincerity," *Afro American*, Nov. 23, 1940, 13; "Big White Fog Play of the Year," *New Journal and Guide*, Nov. 2, 1940, 19; "Big White Fog Is Fine Drama of the Negro Problem," *New York Age*, Nov. 2, 1940, 4; Alain Locke, *Opportunity*, January 1941, reprinted in Gates and Appiah, eds., *Richard Wright*, 25.

92. Ralph Ellison, *New Masses*, November 12, 1940, 22, 23; Ellison to Wright, Aug. 5, 1945 Box 97, F131, Richard Wright Papers, cited in Foley, *Wrestling with the Left*, 364n8; Sterling Brown, "The Federal Theatre," 106.

93. Ralph Warner, "A Vital Drama of Negro Life," *Daily Worker*, Oct. 24, 1940, in Ward Clippings File.

94. Brooks Atkinson, "The Play," *New York Times*, Oct. 23, 1940, 26.

95. John Mason Brown, "'Big White Fog" Staged by Negro Playwrights," *New York Post*, Oct. 29, 1940; Burns Mantle, "'Big White Fog,' Is Opening Bill of Harlem Playwrights," Oct. 23, 1940; Richard Watts Jr. "The Theater: Harlem Has Its Day," n.d.; Arthur Pollack, "Two Plays Prove It's Not What You Do but the Way you Do It," n.d.; Louis Kronenberger, "New Negro Play Over-Ambitious," *PM Reviews*, Oct. 23, 1940; all in Ward Clippings File.

96. See, for example, Haynes, "The Cold War Debate Continues," and Ellen Schrecker's response at http://www.fas.harvard.edu/~hpcws/comment15.htm, accessed Aug. 6, 2014.

97. Biondi, *To Stand and Fight.*

98. Arnesen, "Civil Rights and the Cold War at Home," esp. 29.

99. Singh, "Retracing the Black Red Thread," 836.

100. Ward, interview by Brown, Aug. 13, 1976, First Tape, Side 2, 17. It is worth noting that in another interview, Ward also seems to blame international relations between Germany, the Soviet Union, and the United States for the "sabotage" of *Big White Fog* in Chicago. See Ward, interview by Billops, Apr. 7, 1974, 26.

101. Ward, interview by Brown, Aug. 13, 1976, First Tape, Side 1, 11–12.

102. For the view that the popular front was "destroyed" by the Nazi-Soviet pact. see Isserman, *Which Side Were You On?,* 37–38.

103. Abram Hill, interviewed by Lorraine Brown, Feb. 27, 1977, First Tape, Side 1, 13, OHC-GMU.

104. Bill Chase, "All Ears," *Amsterdam News,* Nov. 16, 1940, 13; Carl Lawrence, "Harlem Rounder," *Amsterdam News,* Nov. 16, 1940, 13; "Big White Fog Closes Dec. 14 with 64 Performances of Play," *Amsterdam News,* Dec. 14, 1940, 20; Bill Chase, "All Ears," *Amsterdam News,* Nov. 30, 1940, 13.

105. Bill Chase, "All Ears," *Amsterdam News,* Dec. 21, 1940, 13; "J. W. Krutch Heads the Drama Critics," *New York Times,* Oct. 22, 1940, 31.

106. Ward, interview by Brown, Aug. 13, 1976, First Tape, Side 2, 17.

107. Witham, "The Playhouse and the Committee," 147.

108. Hatch version, 1-1, 285, 3-3, 317, 3-1, 308; "Last Version," 1-1-11. Even the character of the used furniture salesman, an unsympathetic character in the play, was given the less suggestive name of Marks, rather than Marx.

109. Lou Bellamy, founder of the Twin Cities black theatre Penumbra, wanted "to remain faithful to the playwright's script" including the "1920s colloquialisms" and Ward's "unflinching treatment of issues" (Bellamy retained the use of the "n" word) which he predicted might trouble contemporary audiences just as they had those in the past. See Guthrie playbill, NYPLPA. Bellamy had been teaching *Big White Fog* in literature classes since he had first became aware of the play approximately twenty-five years earlier. This was the period when a number of neglected black dramas were made available for the first time in Hatch's *Black Theater U.S.A.* anthology. With a few variations, the Guthrie manuscript is very close to the version in that anthology. In the anthologized version, "Communists" no longer feature in the list of characters but rather are listed alongside other extras and described as "white and Negro workers." Similarly, the character list in the playbill for the Guthrie production omitted any mention of communists: Les's friends are described simply as "workers," without regard to race. As in the anthologized version, in the final scene of the Guthrie manuscript, the political affiliation of the workers in the final scene is evident. The Guthrie manuscript and playbill are both available at the Billy Rose Theatre Division, NYPLPA.

110. Theodore Ward, *Big White Fog,* xviii; Elise Ward, one of the playwright's two daughters, was initially involved in the production, but the two parties fell out. In

October 2007 she published a critical account in response to director Michael Attenborough's account of his discovery of the play and attempt to establish performance rights. See Elise Ward, "Big White Fog and the Almeida Theatre—A Study in Contradictions," 16 Oct. 16, 2007, http://africanamericanplaywrightsexchange .blogspot.co.uk/2007/10/elise-virginia-ward-responds-to.html; Michael Attenborough, "My Search for the Lost Voice of Black America," *Guardian*, May, 10, 2007, 28. Nick Curtis, "Attenborough Shaking Up Almeida Audience," *Evening Standard*, May 15, 2007. http://www.standard.co.uk/goingout/theatre/attenborough-shaking -up-almeida-audience-6582659.html.

111. Curtis, "Attenborough shaking up Almeida audience."

112. Curtis, "Attenborough shaking up Almeida audience"; Collins, "Drama Depicts Family Life of Chicago Negro," 16.

113. Foley, *Wrestling with the Left*, 5–6.

114. Clark, "Restaging Langston Hughes' Scottsboro Limited," 165.

Chapter Five

1. See, for example, Flanagan, *Arena*, and Houseman, *Run-Through*. The Harlem Unit's *Macbeth* also features prominently in the Library of Congress online digitization project, New Deal Stage. The project includes the digitization of sixty-one federal theatre scripts, including fourteen Shakespeare manuscripts and prompt books used in federal theatre productions. As of February 2019 it included no black-authored federal theatre manuscript. See https://memory.loc.gov/ammem/fedtp /fthome.html.

2. Flanagan, *Arena*, 134.

3. "The Negro Theatre: Its Plans and Policies for the Development of a Community Theatre," Corr. of the New York City Office, E915, Box 498, RG69, NA.

4. "The Negro Theatre: Its Plans and Policies."

5. McClendon is surprisingly absent from the federal theatre archive. McClendon's apparent approval of this arrangement rests on accounts by Flanagan, *Arena*, 63, and Houseman, *Run-Through*, 178. Jay Plum discusses McClendon's role and the establishment of the unit in "Rose McClendon and the Black Units of the Federal Theatre Project," 151. See also Carlton Moss's account in his interview with Lorraine Brown, Aug. 6, 1976, 11, Box 8, OHC-GMU.

6. Department of Information, "WPA Negro Theatre," Dec. 21, 1937, 4, in "Correspondence of Hallie Flanagan," E841, Box 41, RG69, NA.

7. Gus Smith to Philip Barber, Apr. 15, 1937, and Smith to Barber, Apr. 14, 1937, both in "Negro Theatre, Aug 1936 to May 1937," *NDABA*, Reel 24.

8. Department of Information, "WPA Negro Theatre," Dec. 21, 1937,4.

9. Smith to Barber, Apr. 26, 1937, Corr. of the New York City Office, E915, Box 498, RG69, NA. For a history of Harlem's community theatres, see Macki Braconi, *Harlem's Theaters*.

10. Smith to Barber, Apr. 26, 1937, Corr. of the New York City Office, E915, Box 498, RG69, NA.

11. Fraden, *Blueprints for a Black Federal Theatre*, 100; See also Taylor, "Singing for Their Supper," 46.

12. The NAACP's extensive files on film and drama attests to its long history of campaigning for better representation of African Americans on stage and screen. See especially NAACP Records, Administrative Files, Part 1. Manuscripts Division, Library of Congress.

13. Wilson's *Walk Together Chillun* and Fisher's *Conjure Man Dies* attracted audiences of 10,530 (5,057 of which were free tickets) and 83,588 (75,782 free tickets), respectively. This compares unfavorably with *Macbeth*'s figures of 117,244, of which only 21,647 seats were free. See "Negro Productions at the Lafayette Theatre" in "Press Releases of the Department of Information," Box 533, RG69, NA.

14. Alexander Woollcott, "Second Thoughts on First Nights," *New York Times*, Nov. 7, 1920, 88. For an analysis of how the Negro Unit production of *Macbeth* was haunted by *Emperor Jones*, see Dossett, "Commemorating Haiti on the Harlem Stage," esp. 89–92.

15. Burns Mantle, *New York Daily News*, Apr. 15, 1936. and Arthur Pollack, *Brooklyn Daily Eagle*, Apr. 16, 1936, both cited in France, "Introduction" to *Orson Welles on Shakespeare*, 15; Brooks Atkinson, "The Play," *New York Times*, Apr. 15, 1936, 25.

16. Robert Littell, "Macbeth in Chocolate," reprinted in *Reader's Digest*, Jan. 1937, 88–89, cited in O'Connor, "But Was It "Shakespeare?" 338.

17. France, *The Theatre of Orson Welles*, 65. For a discussion of scenery and costume, see Kliman, *Macbeth*, 115–18; McCloskey, "Shakespeare, Orson Welles and the 'Voodoo' Macbeth," 413–14.

18. Roi Ottley, "The Negro Theatre Macbeth," *New Theatre*, May 1936, 24.

19. T.H.P, "'Macbeth' Is Spectacle in Negro Hands," *Hartford Courant*, Jul. 29, 1936, 7.

20. "They Came to Scoff, But Left to Cheer Macbeth," *Afro-American*, Apr. 25, 1936, 10; "New York Macbeth Glamourous Presentation: Masses Turn Out to Jeer, Stay to Cheer, Applaud," *Pittsburgh Courier*, Apr. 25, 1936, A7; Houseman, *Run-Through*, 190–91; Estrin, *Orson Welles Interviews*, 154.

21. "Negroes Hail Real Theater as Macbeth Usurps Harlem," *New York Age*, Apr. 15, 1936, in Mona Z. Smith, *Becoming Something*, 57.

22. Ralph Matthews, *Afro-American*, Apr. 25, 1936, 10.

23. Adam Clayton Powell Jr. "Soapbox," *Amsterdam News*, May 9, 1936, 12.

24. "A Survey of the WPA Negro Theatre in New York City," in "Press Releases of the Department of Information," Box 533, RG69, NA.

25. Powell, "Soapbox," *Amsterdam News*, Mar. 19, 1938, 13.

26. Philip Barber to All Project Supervisors and Heads of Departments, Aug. 17, 1936, *NDABA*, Reel 25. For more information on Moss, Edward, and Smith, see Bernard L. Peterson, *Early Black Playwrights*.

27. Hallie Flanagan to Mrs. Woodward, Mar. 4, 1937, "General Correspondence of the National Office, 1935–39," E839, Box 32, RG69, NA.

28. Attendance figures for O'Neill's sea plays were 7,884, of which 5,802 were paid tickets. This low figure was surpassed only by *Horse Play*, which had figures of

5,355, over fewer performances. Since *Macbeth*, only George Kelly's *The Show Off* was a box office hit, with attendance figures of 96,048. Of these, 79,048 seats were free. *Turpentine* managed an audience of 23,791 over sixty-two performances, but no other play managed to attract more than 16,000 until *Haiti*. See "Negro Productions at the Lafayette Theatre," New York Project Corr., E915, Box 533, RG69, NA; Gus Smith, Report, Mar. 22, 1938, and I. Vinton's Report on Audience Reaction, both in "Corr. from the New York City Office," E915, Box 498, RG69, NA.

29. "Haiti," NSB Review, New Plays Survey, Box 26, FTP-LOC.

30. Maurice and Helen Fisher Clark, interviewed by John O'Connor, Aug. 7, 1976, Los Angeles, California, Revised by interviewee, January 1979, Tape 1, Side 1:1, 12, Box 3, OHC-GMU.

31. Maurice Clark to Louanne Wheeler, Nov. 12, 1976, Box 3, OHC-GMU.

32. Maurice and Helen Fisher Clark Interview, 1–2.

33. Additional statement by Maurice Clark, in letter dated Jan. 6, 1979, OHC-GMU.

34. Several accounts credit Maurice Clark with the transformation of *Haiti*, including O'Connor and Brown, eds., *The Federal Theatre Project*, 118–19, and Renda, *Taking Haiti*, 296. Sharon Rose Riley is especially critical of Brown and O'Connor for their reliance on Maurice Clark's description of the collaboration between himself and Dubois. Riley argues for the significance of the "interracial" collaboration between William Dubois and Maurice Clark, whom she mistakenly identifies as African American. Under this misapprehension, Riley refutes Clark's claims that Dubois was a southern white supremacist, on the grounds that he was prepared to come to the apartment of, and work with, the apparently black Maurice Clark. See Riley, "Mistaken Identities," 350; also 252–262. For a discussion of racial misidentification of dramatists and directors "presumed black," by contemporaries and scholars see chapter 2.

35. Jackson, "Friends of the Negro! Fly with Me," 61–66.

36. Plummer, *Haiti and the United States,* 90–91.

37. Plummer, *Haiti and the United States,* 102–3.

38. W. E. B. Du Bois, "Pan-Africa and New Racial Philosophy," *The Crisis,* 40 (Nov. 1933): 247, 262.

39. Plummer, *Haiti and the United States*, 139–44. For a discussion of the U.S. military occupation and subsequent withdrawal, see Renda, *Taking Haiti*.

40. "Haiti Cast Completed," *Pittsburgh Courier,* Feb. 12, 1938, 21; "Haiti Will Open Late in February," *Afro American,* Feb. 12, 1938, 11; "Rex Ingram Secretly Marries Franciene Everette," *Amsterdam News,* Feb. 19, 1938, 1; "Defender Sends Aid to Haiti," *Chicago Defender,* Feb. 5, 1938, 4.

41. Al Monroe, "Harlem WPA Players Hear Haiti's Early Tilt: Arthur Schomburg, Ace Curator, Ably Discusses Islanders," *Chicago Defender,* Feb. 5, 1938, 16; "Schomburg Addresses WPA Players on Haiti," *New Journal and Guide,* Feb. 5, 1938, 18.

42. "Technique of Play Flayed by Reader," *Amsterdam News,* Feb. 26, 1938, 19.

43. "Guild Undertakes Joint Production," *New York Times,* Feb. 18, 1938, 22; "Opening of 'Haiti' Play Postponed," *Amsterdam News,* Feb. 26, 1938, 16; James Ullman, "Haiti" Memo, Jan. 24, 1938, in General. Corr. of the NSB, Talent Bureau, 1937–1939, Box 213. RG69, NA.

44. "Opening of Haiti Postponed," *Afro-American*, Mar. 5, 1938, 11; "Rex Ingram Is Applauded for His Work in 'Haiti,'" *Afro American*, Mar. 12, 1938, 10.

45. "Macbeth Postponed," *Afro American*, Apr. 11, 1936, 10; "Supper Not Yet Done: On Way Eighteen Months," *Amsterdam News*, Dec. 3, 1938, 21; Lou Layne, "Moon over Harlem," *Amsterdam News,* Feb. 26, 1938, 16.

46. Random House edition (hereafter "RH"): Arent, Sundgaard, and de Ro-han, eds., *Federal Theatre Plays*; "Complete Working Script" (hereafter "CWS"): Billy Rose Theatre Collection, NYPLPA; Publication Number 50-S (hereafter "PS 50-S") and the Revised Edition (hereafter "RE"): Series 3, Library Records, Box 167, FTP-GMU.

47. "Technique of Play Flayed by Reader," *Amsterdam News,* Feb. 26, 1938, 19.

48. Act 1, Scene 1: "PS 50-S," 4; "RH," 7; "CWS," 5; "RE," 5.

49. Act 1, Scene 1: "RE," 9.

50. Act 2, Scene 2: "RE," 37; Act 1, Scene 2: "RE," 43.

51. Technique of Play Flayed by Reader."

52. Act 1, Scene 1: PS "50-S," 5; "RH," 8; "CWS," 4; "RE," 5.

53. "Brilliance Reigns at Haiti Opening," *Amsterdam News*, Mar. 12, 1938, 16.

54. Alvin Moses, "Footlight Flickers" *Atlanta Daily World*, Mar. 21, 1938, 2.

55. "Brilliance Reigns at Haiti Opening," *Amsterdam News*, Mar. 12, 1938, 16; "Role Lauded," *Pittsburgh Courier*, Jun. 11, 1938, 20.

56. Additional Statement by Maurice Clark, Jan. 6, 1979, OHC-GMU.

57. Brooks Atkinson, "The Play," *New York Times*, Mar. 3, 1938, 16.

58. "Technique of Play Flayed by Reader."

59. "Haiti Opens February 23," *Amsterdam News*, Feb. 19, 1938, 16.

60. "For Art's Sake," *Amsterdam News*, Mar. 19, 1938, 8.

61. Schomburg particularly stressed the "courage and heroism" of Toussaint and Christophe. See "Schomburg Addresses WPA Players on Haiti," *New Journal and Guide*, Feb. 5, 1938, 18.

62. "Library Exhibition on Haiti Matchless," *Amsterdam News*, May 7, 1938, 13.

63. "Heroes of Haiti Live Again in WPA Theatre Play 'Haiti,'" *New Journal and Guide*, Feb. 12, 1938, 16; "Toussaint L'Ouverture Comes to Life," *Afro American*, Mar. 12, 1938, 10.

64. "WPA's Haiti Recalls Famous Speech by Wendell Phillips," *Atlanta Daily World*, Jun. 6, 1938, 3.

65. Press Release, May 20, 1938, in "Vassar College Collections of Programs and Promotion Materials, 1935–1939," E877, Box 148, RG69, NA.

66. "L'Ouverture Memorial Attracts at Lafayette," *Amsterdam News*, Jun. 11, 1938, 9A. "Toussaint L'Ouverture Memorial Program," UNIA Papers Central Division, Box 11, Series 9, SCR; "Patriot to be Commemorated: Toussaint L'Ouverture Meeting, June 5," *Amsterdam News*, Jun. 4, 1938, 20.

67. Adam Clayton Powell Jr. "Soapbox," *Amsterdam News*, Mar. 19, 1938, 13.

68. Powell, "Soapbox."

69. Powell, "Soapbox."

70. "Haitians Killed by Dominicans," *Pittsburgh Courier*, Oct. 30, 1937, 24; "5000 Slaughtered in San Domingo," *Amsterdam News*, Nov. 13, 1937, 1; "Haiti Mobilizes

Troops along Frontier," *Chicago Defender*, Nov. 20, 1937, 24; "Dominican Republic Must Pay for Haitian Loss," *Philadelphia Tribune*, Feb. 3, 1938, 3.

71. "London Blacks in Appeal for Haiti, Liberia," *Chicago Defender*, May 21, 1938, 24.

72. "The Theatre," *Wall Street Journal*, Mar. 5, 1938, 2. "Haiti Passes Macbeth Record," *Amsterdam News*, Mar. 19, 1938, 19; "44,000 Have Seen Haiti: Advance Sale is 50,000," *Chicago Defender*, May 7, 1938, 5.

73. "Lafayette Incident Rebuke to Cultural Pride of Community," *Amsterdam News*, Jun. 4, 1938, 16; "Fight Moving of Lafayette," *Amsterdam News*, Jun. 25, 1938, 1, 11. See also "Harlem Will Get Work: WPA Theatre Promises," *Afro American*, Jul. 16, 1938, 10, which suggested that the play had been moved to Broadway because of greater chances of white patronage rather than black patronage.

74. "Haiti May Return to Lafayette," *Pittsburgh Courier*, Oct. 8, 1938, 20.

75. Hallie Flanagan, letter to Cecelia Cabaniss Saunders, Executive Secretary, 137th Street YWCA, Aug. 9, 1938, *NDABA*, Reel 24; Department of Information, "WPA Negro Theatre," Dec. 21, 1937, 4, in "Correspondence of Hallie Flanagan," E841, Box 41, RG69, NA; "'Haiti' Leaves Harlem and Is Now Being Seen on Broadway," *Chicago Defender*, Jul. 2, 1938, 18.

76. Alvin Moses, "Footlight Flickers," *Philadelphia Tribune*, Mar. 17, 1938, 14; Moses, "Footlight Flickers," *Atlanta Daily World*, Mar. 21, 1938, 2.

77. O'Connor and Brown, eds., *The Federal Theatre Project*, 118; "Final Performance of Haiti Tonight at Avery Memorial," *Hartford Courant*, Oct. 29, 1938, 5; "Two Plays Ending Runs Here Tonight," *New York Times*, Jul. 9, 1938, 10.

78. Colored Actors and Performers Association to Ellen Woodward, Nov. 15, 1938, *NDABA*, Reel 24.

79. Ellen Woodward to Colored Actors and Performer Association, Nov. 17, 1938, *NDABA*, Reel 24.

80. Marian Minus to Walter White, Mar. 14, 1939, NAACP Papers, Part 1, Administrative Files, C 298, Folder 10, LOC; "A Harlem Community Cultural Conference," Box 1, Richard B. Moore Papers, SCR; "Cultural Conference in Two Day Session," *Amsterdam News*, May 13, 1939, 24; "Cultural Conference to Sponsor Meeting," *Amsterdam News*, Jun. 3, 1939, 6.; "Protest WPA Cuts on Art Project Here," *Amsterdam News*, Jun. 24, 1939, 19; "Push Campaign on Art Firings," *Amsterdam News*, Aug. 5, 1939, 5.

81. Earl Brown, "Weekly Topics," *Amsterdam News*, Jul. 3, 1937, 14. "W.P.A. Official Held Captive In Strike: Arts Leader Imprisoned in Office," *New York Times*, Jun. 26, 1937, 1.

82. Roy Wilkins to Emmet Lavery, April 11, 1939, NAACP Papers, Part 1, Administrative Files, C: 298, Folder 10, LOC.

83. See, for example, James Hubert of the NUL to Phillip Barber, Aug. 3, 1936, and William Demont Evans to Phil W. Barbour, Aug. 10, 1938, Corr. of the New York City FTP Office, E915, Box 498, RG69, NA.

84. The eleven units were the Living Newspaper Unit, Children's Theatre, Negro Theatre, Experimental Theatre, Popular Price Theatre, Variety Theatre, Teaching of Theatre Technique, Radio Division, Puppet and Marionette Theatre, Municipal

Theatre (which included "special interest groups" such as the Jewish Theatre, German Theatre, Negro Youth Theatre, African Dance and Drama Unit, and Dance Group), and the Service Division which dealt with the making of scenery, costumes, transportation, stagehands, and so on. See "The Federal Theatre Project for New York vs. Harlem, Nation's largest Negro community," as told to Roy Wilkins Jun. 30, 1938, in Part 1: Administrative Files: I: C298, Folder 8, NAACP Papers, LOC.

85. Philip Barber Memo to Project Supervisors and Head of Departments, Aug. 14, 1936, *NDABA*, Reel 25; Flanagan to the Directors of the Negro Theatre, Corr. of the New York City Office, Apr. 13, 1937, E915, Box 498, RG69, NA.

86. "The Federal Theatre Project," Jun. 30, 1938, in NAACP Papers, Part 1: Administrative Files: Container I: C298, Folder 8, LOC.

87. "'I Was Fired,' Declares Gus Smith, Ex-FTP Head," *Amsterdam News*, Jun. 10, 1939, 17.

88. Paul Edwards to Walter White, Apr. 12, 1938, NAACP Papers, Part 1, Administrative Files, Container I: C298, LOC.

89. Walter White to Elmer A. Carter and Adam C. Powell Jr. Jun. 13, 1938, in NAACP Papers, Part 1, Administrative Files, Container I: C298, LOC.

90. Negro Arts Committee Federal Arts Council Brief, 1939, 6, E839, Box 16, RG69, NA.

91. Walter White to Paul Edwards, Jun. 17, 1938, NAACP Papers, Part 1, Administrative Files, Container I: C298, LOC.

92. "Meeting of Supervisors and Department Heads," Lafayette Theatre, Jun. 9, 1938, NAACP Papers, Part 1, Administrative Files, Container I: C298, LOC.

93. WPA Press Release, "Federal Theatre Plans Varied and Extensive Program for Negro Actors," Jun. 28, 1938, NAACP Papers, Part 1, Container I: C298, LOC.

94. "The Negro Theatre in New York City Federal Theatre Project," Brief prepared by the Adjustment Committee, Supervisors Chapter, Local 100, United Federal Workers of America, September 1938, in NAACP Papers, Part 1, Administrative Files, Container I: C298, LOC.

95. Negro Arts Committee Federal Arts Council Brief, 1939, 3, E839, Box 16, RG69, NA.

96. *Opportunity*, 17 (Jan. 1939), 15; Flanagan to Carter, 2 Jan. 27, 1939, Corr. from the New York City Office, E918, Box 498, RG69, NA. For further evidence of FTP officials' desire to consult the black community while controlling the frameworks and participants in that consultation, see the letter sent by the NSB to its "List of Representative Negro Citizens," n.d., Administrative Records, Box 114, FTP-LOC.

97. "The New Plays," *New York Times*, Jul. 18, 1920, 72.

98. William Morgan to Flanagan, Mar. 24, 1939, *NDABA*, Reel 24; Lavery to Flanagan, Mar. 28, 1939, E839, Box 16, RG69, NA.

99. George [unreadable last name] to E. Frederic Morrow, Mar. 6, 1939, NAACP Papers, Part 1, Administrative Files, C: 298, Folder 10, LOC.

100. Emmet Lavery to John Jones, NAACP, Newark Branch, Apr. 14, 1939, *NDABA*, Reel 24.

101. Wilkins to Lavery, Apr. 15, 1939, *NDABA*, Reel 24.

102. J. Howard Miller to Edward Lawson, May 15, 1939, E915, Box 498, RG69, NA.

103. Hughes Allison, "Foreword to *Panyared*," 22 May 1939, FTP-LOC, Box 734. 25, 27, 28.

104. Allison, "Foreword," 25. Allison was likely referring to Lissa, the daughter of Hagar in Dorothy and DuBose Heyward's *Mamba's Daughters* (1939). Played by Fredi Washington, Lissa escapes the hard life of her mother and grandmother in Charleston to become a celebrated singer but is also subject to sexual assault.

105. Allison, "Foreword," 1, 13.

106. Emmet Lavery to Thomas Maulsby, Feb. 9, 1939, NSB, Alphabetical Corr. File, E879, Box 174, RG69, NA.

107. See Flanagan's handwritten comments on Lavery to Flanagan, Interdepartmental Memorandum, Mar. 17, 1939. Flanagan's comments are typed up in a document dated Mar. 28, 1939. Both are in Corr. of Hallie Flanagan, June 1937–1939, E841, Box 43, RG69, NA.

108. Lavery to Flanagan, Interdepartmental Memorandum, Mar. 17, 1939. Hughes Allison supports his claims with a reference to a contemporary historical account by W. E. Woodward, *A New American History* (New York: Garden City Publishing Co., 1937), regarding the atrocities inflicted on African slaves in the United States. See Allison, "Foreword," 30.

109. Lavery to Flanagan, Interdepartmental Memorandum, Mar. 17, 1939, E879, Box 174, RG69, NA; Marion Brooks to Lavery, Mar. 28, 1939, E841, Box 43, RG69, NA; Lavery to Flanagan, Mar. 29, 1939, E841, Box 43, RG69, NA; Hughes Allison, *Panyared,* 3:3:9, Series 3. Library Records, 1885–1986, Box 233, FTP-GMU.

110. Lavery to Flanagan, Mar. 29, 1939, E841, Box 43, RG69, NA.

111. Abram Hill, Reader's Report on *Panyared*, Apr. 7, 1939, E879, Box 174, RG69, NA; Lavery Interdepartmental Memo to Flanagan, Apr. 11, 1939, E839, Box 19, RG69, NA; Lavery to Flanagan, Mar. 29, 1939, E841, Box 43, RG69, NA.

112. Reader's Reports on *Go Down Moses,* by Harold Callen, Jul. 10, 1937; Fanny Malkin, Jul. 21, 1937; and John D. Silvera, Jul. 25, 1937; in "W.P.A., FTP, NSB, Negro Lists," *Black Freedom Struggle in the 20th Century.*

113. Theodore Browne, *Go Down Moses: Based on the Life and Times of Harriet Tubman, A play in Two Acts*, Dec. 9, 1938, Library Records, Box 657, FTP-LOC.

114. "Sports, News, and World-Wide Events," *Negro Star*, Jan. 6, 1939, 3; "Negro Workers on Federal Theatre," circa Mar. 1, 1939, in correspondence between Jon Mack and J. Howard Miller, WPA, Federal Theater Project, National Office, Subject File "N," *Black Freedom Struggle in the 20th Century.*

115. Adam C. Powell Jr. "Soap Box," *Amsterdam News*, Mar. 18, 1939, 10.

116. Lou Layne to George Kondolf, Feb. 9, 1939, in Federal Theater Project, New York City, Alphabetical Subject File, M–P, *Black Freedom Struggle in the 20th Century.*

117. Florence Kerr to Blanche Younge, Feb. 11, 1939, Federal Theater Project, New York City, Alphabetical Subject File M–P, *Black Freedom Struggle in the 20th Century.*

118. George Kondulf to Lou Layne, Feb. 20, 1939, Federal Theater Project, New York City, Alphabetical Subject File M –P *Black Freedom Struggle in the 20th Century.*

119. Theodore Browne, *Go Down Moses,* 1-2-18.

120. Browne, *Go Down Moses,* 1-3-3.

121. Browne, *Go Down Moses,* 1-3-12.

122. Browne, *Go Down Moses,* 1-4-1.

123. Browne, *Go Down Moses,* 1-4-8.

124. Browne, *Go Down Moses,* 1-4-13.

125. W. E. B. Du Bois, *Black Reconstruction in America* (1935) ; Apthecker, "American Negro Slave Revolts"; For a more recent account see Williams, *I Freed Myself.*

126. Browne, *Go Down Moses,* 2-2-1.

127. Franklin, *Race and History,* 22. Eric Foner, "Why Reconstruction Matters," *New York Times,* Mar. 29, 2015, SR, 1. On early twentieth-century Reconstruction historiography, see Weisberger, "The Dark and Bloody Ground of Reconstruction Historiography." For a more recent assessment, see Parfait, "Reconstruction Reconsidered."

128. "The Propaganda of History" is the title of Chapter 17 in Du Bois, *Black Reconstruction in America.*

129. Botkin, ed., *Lay My Burden Down*; Saxon, Dreyer, and Tallant, eds., *Gumbo Ya-Ya*; Yetman, "The Background of the Slave Narrative Collection"; Vann Woodward, "History from Slave Sources," 470–81; Blassingame, "Using the Testimony of Ex-Slaves"; Shaw, "Using the WPA Ex-Slave Narratives to Study the Impact of the Great Depression." Shaw makes the case for the significance of the WPA interviews in documenting African American experiences of the Depression. For example, the propensity of some interviewees to offer up positive reflections on their time as a slave, especially in relation to memories of having enough to eat, tells us something about the desperate plight of many African Americans during the Depression.

130. Browne, *Go Down Moses,* 2-2-4.

131. Browne, *Go Down Moses,* 2-4-2, 2-4-3.

132. Browne, *Go Down Moses,* 2-4-6.

133. Theodore Browne, interviewed by Lorraine Brown, Oct. 22, 1975, Box 2, Folder 11, First tape, Side 1, 24, OHC-GMU.

134. Wright, "The Problems of the Hero," Act IV: 7, Draft Manuscript, Box 83, Richard Wright Papers.

Conclusion

1. Theodore Ward in Sterling A. Brown, "The Federal Theatre," 107.

2. Earlier debates in New Deal studies, which have been recently revived following the 2008 economic crisis, often revolved around whether the New Deal represented a reform of the current system or a more radical departure from American political traditions. Howard Zinn and Ronald Radosh argued that New Deal reforms helped stave off more radical reforms. See Zinn, ed., *New Deal Thought,* xv–xxxvi; Radosh, "The Myth of the New Deal." Tony Badger, however, has argued that New Deal programs tended to stimulate, rather than co-opt, worker agitation. See Badger, *The New Deal,* 303. For a more recent account of this debate, see Domhoff and Webber, *Class and Power in the New Deal.*

3. Oakes, "Radical Liberals, Liberal Radicals," 503.

4. Kate Dossett, "Gender and the Dies Committee Hearings on the Federal Theatre Project," 999.

5. Baraka, in Veve Clark, "Restaging Langston Hughes' Scottsboro Limited," 166.

6. Theodore Ward to James V. Hatch, Feb. 16, 1974, Box 2, Folder 5, TWP.

7. See the Introduction.

Bibliography

Manuscript Collections

Amherst, Massachusetts
    Special Collections and University Archives, University of Massachusetts
          Amherst Libraries
        W. E. B. Du Bois Papers
Atlanta, Georgia
    Emory University
        Stuart A. Rose Manuscript, Archives, and Rare Book Library
          Theodore Ward Papers
Cambridge, Massachusetts
    Schlesinger Library, Radcliffe Institute, Harvard University
        Shirley Graham Du Bois Papers
Cleveland, Ohio
    Western Reserve Historical Society
        Karamu House Records
College Park, Maryland
    National Archives
        RG 69 Records of the Work Progress Administration
Fairfax, Virginia
    George Mason University Special Collections and Archives
        Federal Theatre Project Collection
        Federal Theatre Project Personal Papers
        Federal Theatre Project Photograph Collection
        Natural Man [videorecording]: [based on the legend of John Henry] / by
          Theodore Browne
        Theodore Browne Papers
        Works Progress Administration Oral Histories Collection
Hartford, Connecticut
    Hartford History Center, Hartford Public Library
        Gwen Reed Collection
New York, New York
    Hatch Billops Collection
        Theodore Ward interview by Camille Billops, Apr. 7, 1974
    Schomburg Center for Research in Black Culture, Manuscripts and Archives
        (New York Public Library [NYPL])
        American Negro Theatre Records

Canada Lee Papers

Big White Fog manuscript, by Theodore Ward

Paul Robeson Papers

Richard B. Moore Papers

The Natural Man (based on the legend of John Henry), a play in eight
episodes, manuscript, by Theodore Browne

Universal Negro Improvement Association (UNIA) Papers Central Division

Performing Arts Library, Billie Rose Theatre Division (NYPL)

Big White Fog manuscript, by Theodore Ward

Haiti, "Complete Working Manuscript," by William Dubois

Hallie Flanagan Papers

Liberty Deferred: A Dramatic Chronicle of the Negro, by John D. Silvera and
Abram Hill

Natural Man, manuscript, by Theodore Browne

Theodore Ward Clippings File

New Haven, Connecticut

Yale University, Beinecke Library

Richard Wright Papers

San Marino, California

Huntington Library

Langston Hughes Papers

Seattle, Washington

University of Washington

Florence Bean James Papers

Sara O. Jackson Papers

Seattle Repertory Playhouse Collection

Washington, D.C.

Library of Congress

Manuscripts Division

Records of the Federal Theatre Project, Works Progress Administration

Papers of the National Association for the Advancement of Colored
People

Contemporary Journals and Periodicals

Crisis
Liberator
New Theatre
New Masses
Opportunity
Theatre Arts Monthly
Theatre Guild Magazine
Variety

Government Documents

Federal Works Agency. *Final Report on the WPA Program, 1935–43*. Washington, D.C.: U.S. Government Printing Office, 1946.

"Investigation of Un-American Propaganda Activities in the United States." *Hearings on House Resolution 282, Before the Special Committee on Un-American Activities*, 75th Cong., 3rd sess.–78th Cong., 2nd sess., Vol. 4, 1939.

Kirby, John B., Robert Lester, and Dale Reynolds. *New Deal Agencies and Black America in the 1930s*. Frederick, Md.: University Publications of America, 1983.

Moynihan, Daniel P. "The Negro Family: The Case for National Action." U.S. Government Printing Office: U.S. Department of Labor, Office of Policy Planning and Research, March 1965.

Newspapers

Atlanta Daily World	*New Journal and Guide*
Baltimore Afro-American	*New York Age*
Boston Chronicle	*New York Amsterdam News*
Brooklyn Daily Eagle	*New York Amsterdam Star News*
Chicago Defender	*New York Times*
Chicago Tribune	*Northwest Enterprise*
Christian Science Monitor	*Observer*
Cleveland Call and Post	*Philadelphia Tribune*
Daily Worker	*Pittsburgh Courier*
Hartford Courant	*Seattle Post-Intelligencer*
Hartford Times	*World Telegram*
London Times	

Books, Articles, Dissertations, and Unpublished Papers

Abramson, Doris. *Negro Playwrights in the American Theatre*. New York: Columbia University Press, 1969.

Adams, Katherine H., and Michael L. Keene. *Women, Art, and the New Deal*. Jefferson, N.C.: McFarland, 2016.

Hughes Allison, "Foreword to *Panyared*," 22 May 1939, FTP-LOC, Box 734.

Apthecker, Herbert. "American Negro Slave Revolts." PhD thesis, Columbia University, 1943.

Arent, Arthur. "Ethiopia, the First 'Living Newspaper.'" *Educational Theatre Journal*, 20:1 (Mar. 1968): 15–31.

———. "The Technique of the Living Newspaper." *Theatre Arts*, 22 (Nov. 1938): 820–25.

Arent, Arthur, Arnold Sundgaard, and Pierre de Rohan, eds. *Federal Theatre Plays*. New York: Random House, 1938. Reprint. Pierre de Rohan, Arthur Arent, and Arnold Sundgaard, eds. New York: Da Capo, 1973.

Arnesen, Eric. "Civil Rights and the Cold War at Home: Post-War Activism, Anticommunism, and the Decline of the Left." *American Communist History,* 11:1 (Apr. 2012): 5–44.

Aschenbrenner, Joyce. *Katherine Dunham: Dancing a Life.* Urbana: University of Illinois Press 2002.

Attenborough, Michael. "My Search for the Lost Voice of Black America." *Guardian,* May 10, 2007, 28.

Avery, Laurence G., ed. *A Paul Green Reader.* Chapel Hill: University of North Carolina Press, 1998.

———. *A Southern Life: Letters of Paul Green, 1916–1981.* Chapel Hill: University of North Carolina Press, 1994.

Badger, Anthony. *The New Deal: The Depression Years 1933–1940.* 1989. Reprint. Chicago: Ivan R. Dee, 2002.

Baker, Christopher. "From Fields to Footlights: Gwen Reed." In Elizabeth J. Normen, ed., *African American Connecticut Explored,* 315–21. Middletown, Conn.: Wesleyan University Press, 2013.

Baraka, Amiri. "Afro American Literature and Class Struggle." *Black American Literature Forum,* 14:1 (Spring 1980): 5–14.

Barr, Richard. *Rooms with a View: The Stages of Community in the Modern Theater.* Ann Arbor: University of Michigan Press, 1998.

Bauer, Margaret. "'Call Me Paul': The Long, Hot Summer of Paul Green and Richard Wright." *Mississippi Quarterly,* 64:4 (Fall 2008): 517–38.

Bernier, Celeste-Marie. *Characters of Blood: Black Heroism in the Transatlantic Imagination.* Charlottesville: University of Virginia Press, 2012.

Bernstein, Barton J. "The New Deal: The Conservative Achievements of Liberal Reform." In Barton J. Bernstein, ed., *Towards a New Past: Dissenting Essays in American History,* 263–88. London: Chatto and Windus, 1970.

Bigsby, C. E. "A View from East Anglia." *American Quarterly,* 41:1 (Mar. 1989): 128–32.

Biondi, Martha. *To Stand and Fight: The Struggle for Civil Rights in Post-War New York City.* Cambridge: Cambridge University Press, 2003.

Blain, Keisha. *Set the World on Fire: Black Nationalist Women and the Global Struggle for Freedom.* Philadelphia: University of Pennsylvania Press, 2018.

———. "'We Want to Set the World on Fire': Black Nationalist Women and Diasporic Politics in the *New Negro World,* 1940–1944." *Journal of Social History,* 49:1 (Fall 2015): 194–212.

Blassingame, John W. "Using the Testimony of Ex-Slaves: Approaches and Problems." *Journal of Southern History,* 41 (Nov. 1975): 473–92.

Botkin, B. A., ed. *Lay My Burden Down: A Folk History of Slavery.* Chicago, Ill: University of Chicago Press, 1945.

Bourne, Stephen, *War to Windrush: Black Women in Britain 1939 to 1948.* London: Jacaranda, 2018.

Bowers, Diane. "Ethiopia—The First Living Newspaper." *Phoebe,* 5:2 (1976): 6–15.

Boyle, Sheila Tully, and Andrew Bunie. *Paul Robeson: The Years of Promise and Achievement*. Amherst: University of Massachusetts Press, 2001.

Brasmer, William, and Dominick Consolo, eds. *Black Drama: An Anthology*. Columbus, Ohio: Merrill, 1970.

Braxton, Joanne M., ed. *The Collected Poetry of Paul Laurence Dunbar*. Charlottesville: University Press of Virginia, 1993.

Brinkley, Douglas. "A Depression Project That Gave Rise to a Generation of Novelists." *New York Times*, Aug. 2, 2003, B7, B9.

Brooks, Daphne. *Bodies in Dissent: Spectacular Performances of Race and Freedom, 1850–1910*. Durham, N.C.: Duke University Press, 2006.

Brooks, Peter. *The Melodramatic Imagination*. New Haven: Yale University Press. 1976. Reprint. 1995.

Browder, Laura. *Rousing the Nation: Radical Culture in Depression America*. Amherst: University of Massachusetts Press, 1998.

Brown, Lorraine, ed., *Liberty Deferred and Other Living Newspapers of the 1930s*. Fairfax, Va.: George Mason University Press, 1989.

Brown, Lorraine, et al. "Cultural Diversity in the Federal Theatre Project 1935–1939: Finding Aid of Ethnic Material." Library of Congress Federal Theatre Project Collection at George Mason University, n.d.

Brown, Sterling A. "The Federal Theatre." In Lindsay Patterson, ed., *Anthology of the American Negro in the Theatre: A Critical Approach*, 101–7. New York: Publishers Co., 1968.

——. *Negro Poetry and Drama: Revisiting the Voices of Early African American Figures*. 1937. Reprint. Washington, D.C.: Westphalia Press, 2014.

Bryant, Jerry. *Victims and Heroes: Racial Violence in the African American Novel*. Amherst: University of Massachusetts Press, 1997.

Clark, Veve. "Restaging Langston Hughes' Scottsboro Limited." *Black Scholar*, 10:10 (July–August 1979): 62–69. Reprinted in Charles Reilly, ed., *Conversations with Amiri Baraka*, 157–67. Jackson: University Press of Mississippi, 1994.

Clarke, James W. "'Without Fear or Shame': Lynching, Capital Punishment and the Subculture of Violence in the American South." *British Journal of Political Science*, 28:2 (April 1998): 269–89.

Clurman, Harold. *The Fervent Years: The Story of the Group Theatre and the Thirties*. New York: Harcourt Brace, 1945.

Cobb, Gerry. "'Injunction Granted' in Its Times: A Living Newspaper Reappraised." *New Theatre Quarterly*, 6 (1990): 279–96.

Colson, Dan. "Wrestling with the Left: The Making of Ralph Ellison's Invisible Man (review)." *Modern Fiction Studies*, 58:1 (2012): 162–63.

Corbould, Clare. "Streets, Sounds and Identity in Interwar Harlem." *Journal of Social History*, 40:4 (Summer 2007): 859–94.

Cosgrove, Stuart. "Introduction." In Lorraine Brown, ed., *Liberty Deferred and Other Living Newspapers of the 1930s*. Fairfax, VA: George Mason University Press, 1989.

——. "The Living Newspaper: History, Production and Form." PhD thesis, University of Hull, 1982.

Craig, E. Quita. *Black Drama of the Federal Theatre Era: Beyond the Formal Horizon.* Boston: University of Massachusetts Press, 1980.

Cruse, Harold. *The Crisis of the Negro Intellectual.* New York: New York Review of Books, 2005.

Cunningham, Nijah. "A Queer Pier: Roundtable on the Idea of a Black Radical Tradition." *Small Axe*, 17:1 (Mar. 2013): 86–95.

Davis-Craig, Andrea-La Toya. "Building Community: African Dancing and Drumming in the Little Village of Tallahassee, Florida." PhD thesis, Florida State University, 2009.

DeFrantz, Thomas F., and Anita Gonzalez, eds. *Black Performance Theory.* Durham, N.C.: Duke University Press, 2014.

Degler, Carl N. *Out of Our Past: The Forces That Shaped Modern America.* 2nd ed. New York: Harper and Row, 1970.

Denning, Michael. *The Cultural Front: The Laboring of American Culture in the Twentieth Century.* London: Verso, 1997.

Dolinar, Brian. *The Black Cultural Front: Black Writers and Artists of the Depression Generation.* Jackson: University Press of Mississippi, 2012.

Domhoff, G. William, and Michael J. Webber. *Class and Power in the New Deal: Corporate Moderates, Southern Democrats, and the Liberal-Labor Coalition.* Stanford, Calif.: Stanford University Press, 2011.

Dossett, Kate. "Commemorating Haiti on the Harlem Stage." *Journal of American Drama and Theatre*, 22:1 (Winter 2010): 83–119.

——. "Gender and the Dies Committee Hearings on the Federal Theatre Project." *Journal of American Studies*, 47:4 (Nov. 2013): 993–1017.

——. "Staging the Garveyite Home: Black Masculinity, Failure, and Redemption in Theodore Ward's Big White Fog." *African American Review*, 43.4 (Winter 2009): 557–76.

Du Bois, W. E. B. *Black Reconstruction in America: An Essay Toward a History of the Part Which Black Folk Played in the Attempt to Reconstruct Democracy in America, 1860–1880.* New York: Harcourt Brace, 1935.

——. "Pan-Africa and New Racial Philosophy." *Crisis*, 40 (Nov. 1933): 247, 262.

Duffy, Susan, ed. *The Political Plays of Langston Hughes.* Carbondale: Southern Illinois University Press, 2000.

Edwards, Brent Hayes. "The 'Autonomy' of Black Radicalism." *Social Text*, 67 (Summer 2001): 1–11.

Elam, Harry J., Jr. "The Politics of Black Masculinity in Theodore Browne's *Natural Man*, 1937." In Cheryl Black and Jonathan Shandell, eds., *Experiments in Democracy: Interracial and Cross-Cultural Exchange in American Theatre, 1912–1945*, 126–46. Carbondale: Southern Illinois University Press, 2016.

——. "Post–World War II African American Theatre." In Jeffrey H. Richards and Heather S. Nathans, eds., *The Oxford Handbook of American Drama*, 375–91. Oxford: Oxford University Press, 2014.

Estrin, Mark W. *Orson Welles Interviews.* Jackson: University Press of Mississippi, 2002.

Fabre, Michel. *The World of Richard Wright.* Jackson: University Press of Mississippi, 1985.

Faue, Elizabeth. *Community of Suffering: Women, Men, and the Labor Movement in Minneapolis, 1915–1945.* Chapel Hill: University of North Carolina Press, 1991.

Fearnow, Mark. "A New Realism." In *Oxford Handbook of American Drama,* 173–88. Oxford: Oxford University Press, 2014.

The Federal Theatre Project: A Catalog-Calendar of Productions. Westport, Conn.: Greenwood Press, 1986.

Flanagan, Hallie. *Arena.* New York: Duell, Sloan and Pearce, 1940.

———. "Introduction." In Arthur Arent, Arnold Sundgaard, and Pierre de Rohan, eds., *Federal Theatre Plays.* New York: Random House, 1938. Reprint. Pierre De Rohan, Arthur Arent, and Arnold Sundgaard, eds., *Federal Theatre Plays.* New York: Da Capo Press, 1973.

———. *Shifting Scenes of the Modern European Theatre.* New York: Coward McCann, 1928.

Foley, Barbara. *Radical Representations: Politics and Form in U.S. Proletarian Fiction, 1929–1941.* Durham, N.C.: Duke University Press, 1993.

———. *Wrestling with the Left: the Making of Ralph Ellison's Invisible Man.* Durham, N.C.: Duke University Press, 2010.

Foner, Philip S., and Herbert Shapiro. *American Communism and Black Americans: A Documentary History, 1930–1934.* Philadelphia: Temple University Press, 1991.

Fraden, Rena. *Blueprints for a Black Federal Theatre, 1935–1939.* Cambridge: Cambridge University Press, 1994.

———. "The Cloudy History of Big White Fog." *American Studies,* 29:1 (Spring 1988): 5–27.

France, Richard. "Introduction." In Richard France, ed., *Orson Welles on Shakespeare: The W.P.A and Mercury Theatre Playscripts,* 1–28. Westport, CT: Greenwood Press, 1990.

Franklin, John Hope. *Race and History: Selected Essays 1938–1988.* Baton Rouge: Louisiana State University Press, 1989.

Gassner, John, ed. *Paul Green, Five Plays of the South.* New York: Hill and Wang, 1963.

Gassner, John, and Clive Barnes. *Fifty Best Plays of the American Theater.* New York: Crown Publishers, 1969.

Gates, Henry Louis, Jr., and K. A. Appiah, eds. *Richard Wright: Critical Perspectives Past and Present.* New York: Amistad, 1993.

Gates, Henry Louis, Jr., and Nellie McKay, eds. *The Norton Anthology of African American Literature.* New York: W. W. Norton and Company, 2004.

Gates, Henry Louis, Jr., and Valerie A. Smith, eds. *The Norton Anthology of African American Literature.* New York: Norton, 2014.

Gilmore, Glenda. *Defying Dixie: The Radical Roots of Civil Rights, 1919–1950.* New York: W. W. Norton, 2008.

Glenn, Susan A. "Taking Burlesque Seriously." *Reviews in American History*, 21:1 (1993), 93–100.

Glickman, Lawrence B. "The Laboring of History and Culture." In "Michael Denning and the "Laboring" of American Culture: A Symposium." *Labor History*, 39:3 (Aug. 1998): 320–24.

Goldman, Arnold. "Life and Death of a Living Newspaper Unit." *Theatre Quarterly*, 3:9 (Jan. 1973): 69–89.

Goldstein, Malcolm. *The Political Stage: American Drama and Theater of the Great Depression*. New York: Oxford University Press, 1974.

Gordon, Charles. "Book Review: Negro Playwrights in America, 1925–1969, by Doris Abramson." *Black Theatre*, 4, 1969, 36. New York: New Lafayette Theatre.

Gordon, Michelle Yvonne. "Black Literature of Revolutionary Protest from Chicago's South Side: A Local Literary History, 1931–1959." PhD thesis, University of Madison-Wisconsin, 2008.

———. "The Chicago Renaissance." In Gene Andrew Jarrett, ed., *A Companion to African American Literature*, 271–85. Chichester, U.K.: Wiley-Blackwell, 2011.

Gore, Dayo F., Jeanne Theoharis, and Komozi Woodard, eds. *Want to Start a Revolution? Radical Women in the Black Freedom Struggle*. New York: NYU Press, 2009.

Gray, Christine R. "'Mara,' Angelina Grimké's Other Play and the Problems of Recovering Texts." In Carol P. Marsh-Lockett, ed., *Black Women Playwrights: Visions on the American Stage*, 69–88. New York: Garland, 1999.

Green, Paul, and Richard Wright. *Native Son (the Biography of a Young American): A Play in Ten Scenes by Paul Green and Richard Wright*. New York: Harper and Bros., 1941.

Greenspan, Ezra. *William Wells Brown: An African American Life*. W. W. Norton and Company, 2014.

Hartman, Saidiya V. *Scenes of Subjection: Terror, Slavery, and Self-Making in Nineteenth-Century America*. New York: Oxford University Press, 1997.

Hatch, James V., ed. *Black Theater U.S.A.: 45 Plays by Black Americans, 1847–1974*. New York: Free Press, 1974.

———. "Here Comes Everybody: Scholarship and Black Theatre History." In Thomas Postlewait and Bruce McConachie, eds., *Interpreting the Theatrical Past: Essays in the Historiography of Performance*, 148–65. Iowa City: University of Iowa Press, 1989.

Hatch, James V., and Ted Shine, eds. *Black Theatre U.S.A: Plays by African Americans: The Early Period, 1847–1938*. New York: Free Press, 1996.

Hatch, James V., and Ted Shine, eds. *Black Theatre U.S.A: Plays by African Americans: The Recent Period, 1935–Today, Revised and Expanded Edition*. New York: Free Press, 1996.

Haynes, John Earl. "The Cold War Debate Continues: A Traditionalist View of Historical Writing on Domestic Communism and Anti-Communism." *Journal of Cold War Studies*, 2:1 (Winter 2000): 76–115.

Henderson, Mary C., ed. "Federal Theatre Project Records at George Mason University." *Performing Arts Resources*, 6 (1980).

Hill, Anthony D., and Douglas Q. Barnett. *Historical Dictionary of African American Theater*. Lanham, Md.: Scarecrow Press, 2009.

Hill, Errol. "The Revolutionary Tradition in Black Drama." *Theatre Journal*, 38:4 (Dec. 1986): 408–26.

Hill, Errol G., and James V. Hatch. *A History of African American Theatre*. Cambridge: Cambridge University Press, 2003.

Hill, Robert A., ed. *The Marcus Garvey and Universal Negro Improvement Association Papers*, Vol. 7. Berkeley: University of California Press, 1990.

———. *Marcus Garvey Life and Lessons: A Centennial Companion to the Marcus Garvey and Universal Negro Improvement Association Papers*. Berkeley: University of California Press, 1987.

Hine, Darlene Clark. *Black Victory: The Rise and Fall of the White Primary in Texas*. Columbia: University of Missouri Press, 1979. Reprint. 2003.

Hirsh, Jerrold. "Culture on Relief: The New Deal and the Arts—A Review Essay." *Annals of Iowa*, 56 (1997): 267–78.

hooks, bell. "Homeplace: A Site of Resistance." In bell hooks, *Yearning, Race, Gender and Cultural Politics*, 41–49. London: Turnaround, 1991.

Houseman, John. *Run-Through*. New York: Simon and Schuster, 1980.

Hyman, Colette. *Staging Strikes: Workers' Theatre and the American Labor Movement*. Philadelphia: Temple University Press, 1997.

Isaac, Dan. "Ethiopia: The First Living Newspaper." *Educational Theatre Journal*, 20:1 (1968): 15–19.

Isaacs, Edith. *The Negro in the American Theatre*. New York: Theatre Arts, 1947.

Isserman, Maurice. *Which Side Were You On? The American Communist Party during the Second World War*. Urbana: University of Illinois Press, 1993.

Jackson, Maurice. "'Friends of the Negro! Fly with Me, The Path Is Open to the Sea': Remembering the Haitian Revolution in the History, Music, and Culture of the African American People." *Early American Studies: An Interdisciplinary Journal*, 6:1 (2008): 61–66.

Jarrett, Andrew Gene, ed. *A Companion to African American Literature*. Chichester, U.K.: Wiley-Blackwell, 2011.

Johnson, Evamarri Alexandria. "A Production History of the Seattle Federal Theatre Project, Negro Repertory Company, 1935–1939." PhD thesis, University of Washington, 1981.

Jones, Douglas A., Jr. "Slavery and the Design of African American Theatre." In Harvey Young, ed., *The Cambridge Companion to African American Theatre*, 15–33. Cambridge: Cambridge University Press, 2013.

Kaplan, Carla. *Zora Neale Hurston: A Life in Letters*. New York: Knopf Doubleday Publishing Group, 2007.

Kaplan, Cora. "Black Heroes/White Writers: Toussaint L'Ouverture and the Literary Imagination." *History Workshop Journal*, 46:33 (1998): 32–62.

Kelley, Robin D. G. *Race Rebels: Culture, Politics and the Black Working Class.* New York: Free Press, 1996.

Kellner, Bruce. *Harlem Renaissance: A Historical Dictionary for the Era.* Westport, Conn.: Greenwood Press, 1984.

Kidd, Stuart. "Redefining the New Deal: Some Thoughts on the Political and Cultural Perspectives of Revisionism." *Journal of American Studies*, 22:3 (Dec. 1988): 389–415.

King, Woodie, and Ron Milner, eds. *Black Drama Anthology.* New York: Columbia University Press, 1972.

Kinnamon, Kenneth, ed. *The Richard Wright Bibliography: 50 Years of Criticism and Commentary, 1932–1982.* Westport, Conn.: Greenwood Press, 1988.

Kliman, Bernice. *Macbeth.* 2nd ed. Manchester: Manchester University Press, 2004.

Krasner, David. *A Beautiful Pageant: African American Theatre, Drama, and Performance in the Harlem Renaissance, 1910–1927.* New York: Palgrave Macmillan, 2002.

——. "Whose Role Is It Anyway? Charles Gilpin and the Harlem Renaissance." *African American Review*, 29:3 (Autumn 1995): 483–96.

Kreizenbeck, Alan D. "The Theatre Nobody Knows: Forgotten Productions of the Federal Theatre Project, 1935–1939." PhD dissertation, New York University, 1979.

Lawson, John Howard, *Theory and Technique of Playwriting,* New York: G. P. Putnam, 1936.

Leuchtenburg, William E. *Franklin D. Roosevelt and the New Deal, 1932–1940.* New York: Harper and Row, 1963.

Levine, Ira. *Left-Wing Dramatic Theory in the American Theatre.* Ann Arbor, Mich.: UMI Research Press, 1985.

Levine, Lawrence. *Black Culture and Black Consciousness: Afro-American Folk Thought from Slavery to Freedom.* Thirtieth Anniversary Edition. Oxford: Oxford University Press, 2007.

Locke, Alain, and Montgomery Gregory, eds. *Plays of Negro Life: A Source-Book of Native American Drama.* 1927. Reprint. Westport, Conn.: Negro Universities Press, 1970.

Long, Richard A. *The Black Tradition in American Dance.* London: Prion, 1989.

Lott, Eric. *Love and Theft: Blackface Minstrelsy and the American Working Class.* New York: Oxford University Press, 1993.

Macki Braconi, Adrienne. *Harlem's Theaters: A Staging Ground for Community, Class, and Contradiction, 1923–1939.* Evanston, Ill.: Northwestern University Press, 2015.

Manning, Susan. "Black Voices, White Bodies: The Performance of Race and Gender in *How Long Brethren," American Quarterly*, 50:1 (Mar. 1998): 24–46.

——. *Modern Dance, Negro Dance: Race in Motion.* Minneapolis: University of Minnesota Press, 2004.

Mantle, Burns. *The Best Plays and the Year Book of the Drama in America, 1940–41.* New York: Dodd, Mead, 1941.

Mathews, Jane de Hart. *The Federal Theatre, 1935–1939: Plays, Relief, and Politics.* Princeton, N.J.: Princeton University Press, 1967.

Maxwell, William. *New Negro, Old Left: African American Writing and Communism between the Wars.* New York: Columbia University Press, 1999.

McCloskey, Susan. "Shakespeare, Orson Welles and the 'Voodoo' Macbeth." *Shakespeare Quarterly*, 36:4 (Winter 1985): 406–16.

McDermott, Douglas. "The Living Newspaper as a Dramatic Form." *Modern Drama*, 8:1 (May 1965): 82–94.

McDonough, Carla J. *Staging Masculinity: Male Identity in Contemporary American Drama.* Jefferson, N.C.: McFarland amd Co., 2006.

McGovern, J. R. *Anatomy of a Lynching: The Killing of Claude Neal.* Baton Rouge: Louisiana State University Press, 1982.

Meier, August, and Elliot Rudwick. "The Origins of Non-Violent Direct Action in Afro-American Protest." In August Meier and Elliot Rudwick, eds., *Along the Color Line: Explorations in the Black Experience*, 307–404. Urbana: University of Illinois Press, 2002.

Melosh, Barbara. *Engendering Culture Manhood and Womanhood in New Deal Public Art and Theater.* Washington, D.C.: Smithsonian Institution Press, 1991.

Miller, Henry. *Theorizing Black Theatre: Art versus Protest in Critical Writings, 1898–1965.* Jefferson, N.C.: McFarland, 2011.

Mitchell, Koritha. "Black-Authored Lynching Drama's Challenge to Theater History." In Thomas F. DeFrantz and Anita Gonzalez, eds., *Black Performance Theory*, 87–98. Durham, N.C.: Duke University Press, 2014.

——. *Living with Lynching: African American Lynching Plays, Performance, and Citizenship, 1890–1930.* Springfield: University of Illinois Press, 2011.

Mitchell, Loften. *Black Drama: The Story of the American Negro in the Theatre.* New York: Hawthorn Books, 1967.

Molette, Barbara. "Black Heroes and Afrocentric Values in Theatre." *Journal of Black Studies*, 15:4 (June 1985): 447–62.

Mullen, Bill. *Popular Fronts: Chicago and African-American Cultural Politics, 1935–46.* Urbana: University of Illinois Press, 1999.

Mumford, Esther Hall, ed. *Seven Stars and Orion: Reflections of the Past.* Seattle, Wash.: Ananse Press, 1980.

Nadler, Paul. "Liberty Censored: Black Living Newspapers of the Federal Theatre Project." *African American Review*, 29:4 (1995): 615–22.

Naison, Mark. *Communists in Harlem during the Depression.* Urbana: University of Illinois Press, 1983.

Nathans, Heather S. "Slave Rebellions on the National Stage." In Harvey Young, ed., *The Cambridge Companion to African American Theatre*, 34–58. Cambridge: Cambridge University Press, 2013.

Native Son: The Playbill for the St. James Theatre. New York: New York Theatre Program Corporation, 1941.

Neal, Larry. "The Black Arts Movement." In Ed Bullins, ed., "Black Theatre." Special issue, *The Drama Review*, 12:4 (Summer 1968): 28–39.

Nelson, Scott Reynolds. *Steel Drivin' Man: The Untold Story of an American Legend*. New York: Oxford University Press, 2006.

Oakes, James. "Radical Liberals, Liberal Radicals: The Dissenting Tradition in American Political Culture." *Reviews in American History*, 27:3 (Sept. 1999): 503–11.

O'Connor, John. "But Was It 'Shakespeare?': Welles's 'Macbeth' and 'Julius Caesar.'" *Theatre Journal*, 32:3 (Oct. 1980): 336–48.

O'Connor, John, and Lorraine Brown, eds. *The Federal Theatre Project: "Free, Adult, Uncensored."* London: Eyre Methuen, 1980.

Osborne, Elizabeth. *Staging the People: Community and Identity in the Federal Theatre Project*. New York: Palgrave Macmillan, 2011.

Parfait, Claire. "Reconstruction Reconsidered: A Historiography of Reconstruction, from the Late Nineteenth Century to the 1960s." *Études Anglaises*, 62:4 (Oct.–Nov.–Dec. 2009): 440–54.

Patterson, Lindsay. *Black Theater: A 20th Century Collection of the Work of Its Best Playwrights*. New York: Dodd Mead, 1971.

Pearce, Howard D. "From Folklore to Mythology: Paul Green's 'Roll Sweet Chariot.'" *Southern Literary Journal*, 3:2 (Spring 1971): 75–77.

Pells, Richard. *Radical Visions and American Dreams: Culture and Social Thought in the Depression Years*. New York: Harper and Row, 1973.

Perkins, Kathy. "African American Drama, 1910–45." In Jeffrey H. Richards and Heather S. Nathans, eds., *The Oxford Handbook of American Drama*, 307–21. Oxford: Oxford University Press, 2014.

Peters, Paul, and George Sklar. *Stevedore*. London: Jonathan Cape, 1935.

Peterson, Bernard L. *Early Black American Playwrights and Dramatic Writers: A Biographical Directory and Catalog of Plays, Films, and Broadcasting Scripts*. New York: Greenwood Press, 1990.

———. *The African American Theatre Directory, 1816–1960: a Comprehensive Guide to Early Black Theatre Organizations, Companies, Theatres, and Performing Groups*. Westport, Conn.: Greenwood Press 1997.

Peterson, Rachel. "Adapting Left Culture to the Cold War: Theodore Ward, Anne Petry and "Correspondence." PhD thesis, University of Michigan, 2008.

Plum, Jay. "Rose McClendon and the Black Units of the Federal Theatre Project: A Lost Contribution." *Theatre Survey*, 33 (Nov. 1992): 144–53.

Plummer, Brenda Gayle. *Haiti and the United States: The Psychological Moment*. Athens: University of Georgia Press, 1992.

Poole, John. "Making a Tree from Thirst: Acquiescence and Defiance in the Negro Federal Theatre Project in Birmingham, Alabama." *Theatre History Studies*, 21 (Jun. 2001): 27–42.

Radosh, Ronald. "The Myth of the New Deal." In Ronald Radosh and Murray Rothbard, eds., *A New History of Leviathan*. 146–87 . . . New York: Dutton, 1972

Rampersad, Arnold. *The Life of Langston Hughes, Volume 1: 1902–1941*. Oxford; New York: Oxford University Press, 1996.

Redd, Tina. "Staging Race: The Seattle Negro Unit Production of Stevedore." *Journal of American Drama and Theatre*, 7:2 (Spring 1995): 66–85.

Reed, Christopher Robert. *The Chicago NAACP and the Rise of Black Professional Leadership, 1910–1966*. Bloomington: Indiana University Press, 1997.

Renda, Mary. *Taking Haiti: Military Occupation and the Culture of U.S. Imperialism, 1915–1940*. Chapel Hill: University of North Carolina Press, 2001.

Retman, Sonnet H. *Real Folks: Race and Genre in the Great Depression*. Durham, N.C.: Duke University Press, 2011.

Richards, Jeffrey H., and Heather S. Nathans, eds. *The Oxford Handbook of American Drama*. Oxford: Oxford University Press, 2014.

Richards, Sandra. "Writing the Absent Potential: Drama, Performance, and the Canon of African-American Literature." In Andrew Parker and Eve Kosofsky Sedgwick, eds., *Performativity and Performance*, 64–88. New York: Routledge, 1995.

Riley, Shannon Rose. "Mistaken Identities, Miscegenation, and Missing Origins: The Curious Case of Haiti." *Performing Arts Resources*, 28 (2011): 252–62.

Roses, Lorraine Elena, *Black Bostonians and the Politics of Culture, 1920–1940*. Amherst, University of Massachusetts Press, 2017.

Ross, Ronald. "The Role of Blacks in the Federal Theatre, 1935–1939." *Journal of Negro History*, 59 (Jan. 1974): 38–50.

Rowley, Hazel. "Backstage and Onstage: The Drama of Native Son." *Mississippi Quarterly*, 52:2 (Spring 1999): 215–37.

——. *The Life and Times of Richard Wright*. New York: Henry Holt and Co, 2001.

Saal, Ilka. *New Deal Theater: The Vernacular Tradition in American Political Theater*. New York: Palgrave Macmillan, 2007.

Saxon, Lyle, Edward Dreyer, and Robert Tallant, eds. *Gumbo Ya-Ya: A Collection of Louisiana Folk Tales*. 1945. Reprint. New York: Bonanza Books, 1984.

Scott, Curtis R. "The Dramatization of Native Son: How 'Bigger' Was Reborn." *Journal of American Drama and Theatre*, 4:3 (1992): 5–41.

Scott, David. "On the Very Idea of a Black Radical Tradition." *Small Axe*, 17:1 (Mar. 2013): 1–6.

Scott, William. "Hubert F. Julian and the Italo-Ethiopian War: A Dark Episode in Pan-African Relations." *Umoja: A Scholarly Journal of Black Studies*, 2:2 (Apr. 1978): 77–93.

Shandell, Jonathan. "The American Negro Theatre: Staging Inter-Racialism in Harlem, 1940–49." PhD thesis, Yale University, 2006.

——. "Looking beyond *Lucasta*: The Black Dramas of the American Negro Theatre." *African American Review*, 42:3–4 (Fall 2008): 533–47.

——. "The Negro Little Theatre Movement." In Harvey Young, ed., *The Cambridge Companion to African American Theatre*, 103–17. Cambridge: Cambridge University Press, 2013.

——. "Theodore Browne." In Henry Louis Gates Jr. and Evelyn Brooks Higginbotham, eds., *African American National Biography*, 2: 21. Oxford: Oxford University Press, 2008.

Shapiro, David. "Social Realism Reconsidered." In David Shapiro, ed., *Social Realism: Art as a Weapon*, 3–35. New York: Frederick Ungar, 1973.

Shaw, Stephanie J. "Using the WPA Ex-Slave Narratives to Study the Impact of the Great Depression." *Journal of Southern History*, 63:9 (Aug. 2003): 623–58.

Silver, Reuben. "A History of the Karamu Theatre of Karamu House, 1915–1960." PhD thesis, Ohio State University, 1961.

Singh, Nikhil Pal. "Retracing the Black-Red Thread." *American Literary History*, 15:4 (Winter 2003): 830–40.

Sitkoff, Harvard. *A New Deal for Blacks: The Emergence of Civil Rights as a National Issue. Volume 1: The Depression Decade*. 1978. Reprint. New York: Oxford University Press, 1981.

Sklaroff, Lauren. *Black Culture in the New Deal: The Quest for Civil Rights in the Roosevelt Era*. Chapel Hill: University of North Carolina Press, 2009.

Smith, Mona Z. *Becoming Something: The Story of Canada Lee*. New York: Faber and Faber, 2004.

Smith, Wendy. *Real Life Drama: The Group Theatre and America, 1931–1940*. New York: Knopf, 1990.

Stephens, Michelle. *Black Empire: The Masculine Global Imaginary of Caribbean Intellectuals in the United States, 1914–1962*. Durham, N.C.: Duke University Press, 2005.

Stott, William. *Documentary Expression and Thirties America*. 1973. Reprint. Chicago: University of Chicago Press, 1986.

Sullivan, Patricia. *Days of Hope: Race and Democracy in the New Deal Era*. Chapel Hill: University of North Carolina Press, 1996.

Summers, Martin Anthony. *Manliness and Its Discontents: The Black Middle Class and the Transformation of Masculinity, 1900–1930*. Chapel Hill: University of North Carolina Press, 2004.

Susman, Warren I. "The Thirties." In Stanley Coben and Lorman Ratner, eds., *The Development of an American Culture*. Englewood Cliffs, N.J.: Prentice Hall, 1970.

Taylor, Quintard. *The Forging of a Black Community: Seattle's Central District from 1870 through the Civil Rights Era*. Seattle: University of Washington Press, 2004.

Taylor, Zanthe. "Singing for Their Supper: The Negro Units of the Federal Theater Project and Their Plays." *Theater*, 27:2–3 (1997): 43–59.

"Techniques Available to the Living Newspaper Dramatist Compiled by Members of the New York Living Newspaper Unit for Circulation to Students, Teachers and Theatre Practitioners." In Cosgrove, "The Living Newspaper: History, Production and Form," Appendix 1, 237–44.

Toohey, John H. *A History of the Pulitzer Prize Plays*. New York: Citadel Press, 1967.

Tracy, Steven C. *John Henry: Roark Bradford's Novel and Play*. Oxford: Oxford University Press, 2008.

Turner, Darwin T. *Black Drama in America: An Anthology*. Greenwich, Conn.: Fawcett Publications, 1971.

Turner, Victor, *Dramas, Fields, and Metaphors: Symbolic Action in Human Society*. Ithaca: Cornell University Press, 1974.

Vactor, Vanita Marian. "A History of the Chicago Federal Theatre Project Negro Unit, 1935–1939." PhD thesis, New York University, 1998.

Vann Woodward, C. "History from Slave Sources: A Review Article." *American Historical Review*, 79 (April 1974): 470–81.

Vogel, Lise. *Marxism and the Oppression of Women: Toward a Unitary Theory.* New Brunswick, N.J: Rutgers University Press, 1983.

Wald, Alan. "Theodore Ward." In Steven C. Tracey, ed., *Writers of the Black Chicago Renaissance*, 320–40. Urbana: University of Illinois Press, 2012.

——. *Writing from the Left: New Essays on Radical Culture and Politics.* London: Verso, 1994.

Walker, Ethel Pitts. "The American Negro Theatre." In Errol Hill, ed., *The Theater of Black Americans*, 257–59. New York: Applause, 1987.

Wallace, Michelle. *Black Macho and the Myth of the Black Superwoman.* New York: Dial, 1979.

Ward, Theodore. *Big White Fog.* London: Nick Hern Books, 2007.

Weisberger, Bernard A. "The Dark and Bloody Ground of Reconstruction Historiography." *Journal of Southern History*, 25:4 (Nov. 1959): 427–47.

Weisenfeld, Judith. "'The Secret at the Root': Performing African American Religious Modernity in Hall Johnson's *Run, Little Chillun*." *Religion and American Culture: A Journal of Interpretation*, 21:1 (Winter 2011): 39–80.

Weisstuch, Mark Wolf. "The Theatre Union, 1933–1937: A History." PhD thesis, University Microfilms International, Ann Arbor, Mich., 1982.

West, Ron. "Left Out: The Seattle Repertory Playhouse, Audience Inscription and the Problem of Leftist Theatre during the Depression Era." PhD dissertation, University of Washington, 1993.

——. "Others, Adults, Censored: The FTP's Black *Lysistrata* Cancellation." *Theatre Survey*, 37:2 (Nov. 1996): 93–11.

Williams, David. *I Freed Myself: African American Self-Emancipation in the Civil War Era.* New York: Cambridge University Press, 2014.

Williams, Linda. *Playing the Race Card: Melodramas of Black and White from Uncle Tom to O.J. Simpson.* Princeton, N.J.: Princeton University Press, 2002.

Wilmeth, Don B., and Christopher Bigsby, eds. *Cambridge History of American Theatre.* Cambridge: Cambridge University Press, 1999.

Witham, Barry. "Censorship in the Federal Theatre." *Theatre History Studies*, 17 (Jun. 1997): 3–14.

——. "The Federal Theatre Project." In Jeffrey H. Richards and Heather S. Nathans, eds., *The Oxford Handbook of American Drama*, 295–306. Oxford: Oxford University Press, 2014.

——. *The Federal Theatre Project: A Case Study.* Cambridge: Cambridge University Press, 2003.

——. "The Playhouse and the Committee." In Sue-Ellen Case and Janelle Reinhelt, eds., *The Performance of Power: Theatrical Discourse and Politics*, 146–62. Iowa City: University of Iowa Press, 1991.

Wittmer, Micah. "Performing Negro Folk Culture, Performing America: Hall Johnson's Choral and Dramatic Works (1925–1939)." PhD dissertation, Harvard University, 2016.

Wood, Amy Louise. *Lynching and Spectacle: Witnessing Racial Violence in America, 1890–1940.* Chapel Hill: University of North Carolina Press, 2009.

Wright, Richard. *Black Boy: American Hunger, a Record of Childhood and Youth.* New York: Harper Collins, 2005.

——. *Native Son.* London: Vintage, 2000.

Yetman, Norman R. "The Background of the Slave Narrative Collection." *American Quarterly,* 19 (Fall 1967): 534–53.

Young, Harvey, ed. *The Cambridge Companion to African American Theatre.* Cambridge. Cambridge University Press, 2013.

Zinn, Howard, ed., *New Deal Thought.* Indianapolis, Ind.: Bobbs-Merrill 1966.

Visual Material

Breaking the Barriers: Blacks of the Federal Theatre Project. Fairfax, Va.: George Mason University, Special Collections, Fenwick Library, 7 videocassettes (128 min.): sound, color; 3/4 in. 1978.

Online/Digital Sources

Black Freedom Struggle in the 20th Century: Federal Government Records. Proquest History Vault. https://proquest.libguides.com/historyvault/bfsfed

Curtis, Nick. "Attenborough Shaking up Almeida Audience." *Evening Standard,* May 15, 2007. http://www.standard.co.uk/goingout/theatre/attenborough -shaking-up-almeida-audience-6582659.html.

"Federal Theatre Project Collection." Library of Congress Online Finding Aid. http://rs5.loc.gov/service/music/eadxmlmusic/eadpdfmusic/1995/mu995001.pdf.

"The New Deal Stage." Library of Congress. https://www.loc.gov/teachers /classroommaterials/connections/new-deal-stage/index.html.

Hatch, James V. *Black Drama: African, African American, and Diaspora,* Third Edition.

Kelley, Robin D. G. "Black Study, Black Struggle Forum." *Boston Review,* Mar. 7, 2016. http://bostonreview.net/forum/robin-d-g-kelley-black-study-black -struggle.

Maxwell, William J. *FB Eyes Digital Archive.* http://digital.wustl.edu/fbeyes/. Accessed March 3, 2019.

Schrecker, Ellen. "Comments on John Earl Haynes', 'The Cold War Debate Continues: A Traditionalist View of Historical Writing on Domestic Communism and Anti-Communism,'" *Journal of Cold War Studies,* 2:1 (Winter 2000). Online at http://www.fas.harvard.edu/~hpcws/comment15.htm.

Smith, Wendy. "The Play That Electrified Harlem." *Civilization,* Jan.–Feb. 1996. Online at https://www.loc.gov/collections/federal-theatre-project-1935-to-1939 /articles-and-essays/play-that-electrified-harlem/

Voelker, Selena. "The Power of Art and the Fear of Labor: Seattle's Production of Waiting for Lefty in 1936." http://depts.washington.edu/depress/seattle _waiting_for_lefty.shtml

Ward, Elise Virginia. "Elise Virginia Ward Responds to Attenborough Production of *Big White Fog*." *African American Playwrights Exchange*, Oct. 16, 2007. http://africanamericanplaywrightsexchange.blogspot.co.uk/2007/10/elise -virginia-ward-responds-to.html.

Index

Panyared, 237, 239–41; and Roy
  Wilkins, 235–36; on *Stars and Bars*,
  281n45, 285n10
Lawson, John Howard, 55–56
League of Struggle for Negro Rights, 59,
  274n67
Lee, Canada, 18, 58, 74, 147, 160, 194, 199
Liberty Deferred, 19, 24, 35, 36, 78,
  80–84, 89, 101–21, 139, 140, 233, 237,
  239, 240, 251, 258–59, 267n54,
  268n61, 283–84n73, 279–80n18,
  283n72, 285n92, 285n106. *See also*
  Hill, Abram; Silvera, John
Lindsay, Powell, 139, 204
Living Newspapers, 24, 35–36, 78,
  84–87; black Living Newspapers,
  80–84, 87–121; See also *One Third of
  a Nation; Stars and Bars, Triple A
  Plowed Under* and *Liberty Deferred.*
Living Newspaper Unit, 35, 78–79, 85,
  87, 88, 106, 204
Locke, Alain, 132, 195
Lysistrata, 128–29.

Macbeth, Harlem Negro Unit production, 12, 38, 74, 90, 102, 160, 204,
  206–13, 216, 227, 304n1, 305n13m
  305n14; Boston Negro Unit production, 264; Los Angeles Negro Unit
  production, 264
McClendon, Rose, 30, 60, 73–74, 231,
  278n124, 289n39, 304n5. See also
  Rose McClendon Players
Miller, J. Howard, 116, 128, 236, 264n18
Minstrel tradition, 7–9, 76, 82–83, 139,
  252, 265n30; and the FTP, 265n27;
  and Wright, Richard, on Chicago
  Negro Unit preference for, 150–51;
  Liberty Deferred, on history of,
  284n73; black theatre manuscripts
  on, 250–51
Minturn, Harry, 164, 170–71, 173, 192
Mississippi Rainbow, 169–70, 231
Monroe, Charles, 75–76, 126, 128–29
Moore, Audley, 29

Moore, Richard, 18, 59, 223, 225
Moss, Carlton, 88, 128, 212, 231, 284n76,
  286n113

National Association for the Advancement of Colored People: 105, 183,
  204, 223, 305n12; and *Big White Fog*
  171, 176; and the black performance
  community, 14; and black self-
  determination, 45; and the Costigan-
  Wagner anti-lynching bill,
  285–86n107; and the CPUSA, 44,
  173; critical of the FTP, 229–31; 232,
  235, 237; and Napper, Alver, 91;
  sponsors of *Native Son,* 296; Seattle
  branch of, 123
National Council of Negro Women, 45
National Negro Congress, 105, 117, 223
National Urban League: and black
  performance communities, 14, 204;
  Seattle chapter on *Hymn to the Rising
  Son,* 294n108; and the Theatre Union,
  59; critical of FTP, 117, 229, 231, 234
Native Son. See Wright, Richard.
  See also Green, Paul; Welles, Orson;
  and Houseman, John
Natural Man. See Browne, Theodore
Napper, Alver, 35, 91, 98–100. See also
  Stars and Bars
Nazi-Soviet pact, 28, 195, 198
Negro Actors Guild, 14–15, 31, 229,
  232, 242
Negro Arts Committee, Federal Arts
  Council, 117–18, 229, 232
Negro Dramatists Laboratory (NDL),
  87–89, 207
Negro People's Theatre, 73–74
Negro Playwrights Company, 177,
  192–95, 199
Noah, 67, 90, 93–94, 127
Norford, George, 80, 279n11

Odets, Clifford, 69, 73, 148
Oliver, Sara, (also known as Sara
  Jackson), 3, 18, 66, 129, 288n21

Lightning Source UK Ltd.
Milton Keynes UK
UKHW011827231020
372122UK00002B/129